SILENT VILLAGE

Also by Robert Pike
Defying Vichy

SILENT VILLAGE

LIFE AND DEATH IN OCCUPIED FRANCE

ROBERT PIKE

First published 2021

The History Press
97 St George's Place, Cheltenham,
Gloucestershire, GL50 3QB
www.thehistorypress.co.uk

British Library Cataloguing in Publication Data.
A catalogue record for this book is available from the British Library.

ISBN 978 0 7509 9134 6

Typesetting and origination by The History Press
Printed and bound in Great Britain by TJ Books Limited, Padstow, Cornwall.

Trees for LYfe

For the people of Oradour-sur-Glane

A view of Oradour-sur-Glane's church of Saint-Martin.
(Collection Benoit Sadry)

Contents

Maps

Places of execution:
1. Bouchoule barn
2. Milord barn
3. Laudy-Mosnier barn
4. Desourteaux garage
5. Beaulieu storeroom
6. Denis wine cellar
7. The church

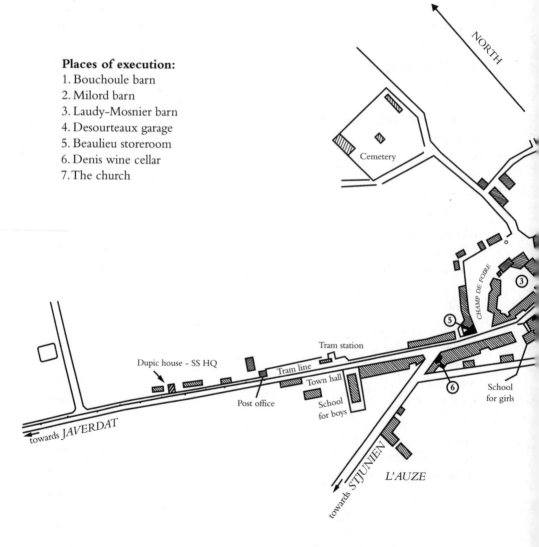

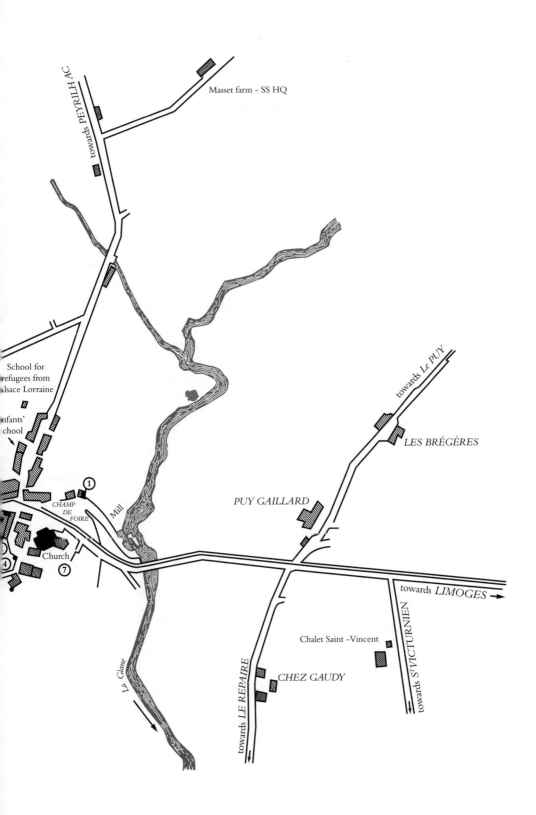

Masset farm – SS HQ

towards *PEYRILHAC*

School for refugees from Alsace Lorraine

Infants' School

towards *Le PUY*

LES BRÉGÈRES

① *CHAMP DE FOIRE*

Mill

PUY GAILLARD

Church

⑦

④

towards *LIMOGES*

La Glane

Chalet Saint -Vincent

towards *St VICTURNIEN*

towards *LE REPAIRE*

CHEZ GAUDY

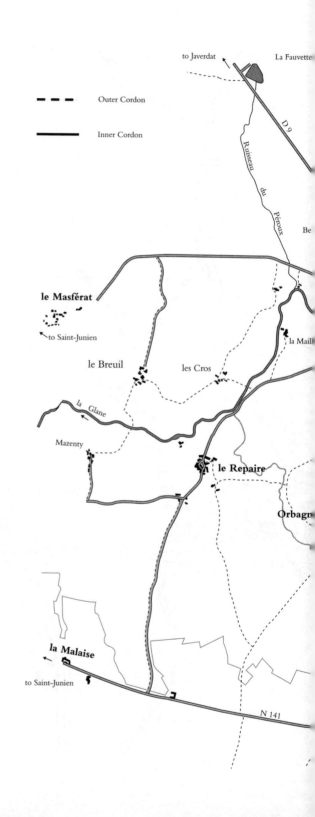

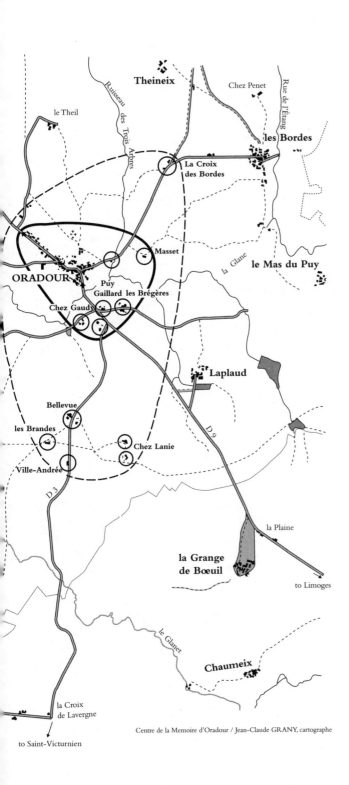

Centre de la Memoire d'Oradour / Jean-Claude GRANY, cartographe

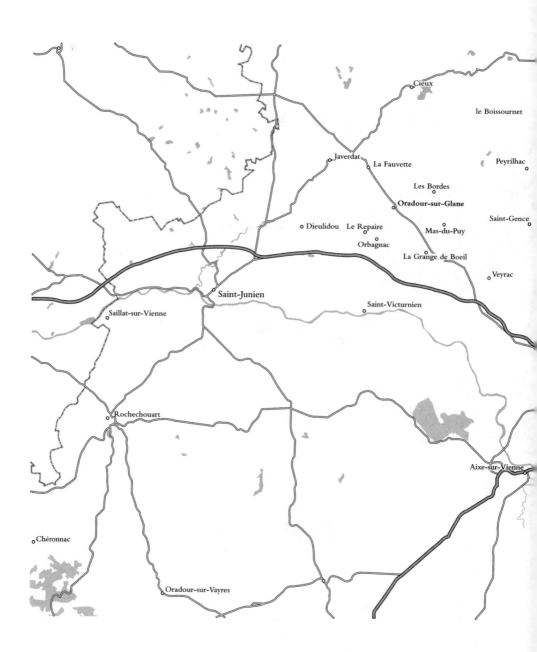

Cieux

le Boissournet

Javerdat   La Fauvette

Peyrilhac

Les Bordes

Oradour-sur-Glane

Saint-Gence

Dieulidou   Le Repaire   Mas-du-Puy

Orbagnac

La Grange de Boeil

Veyrac

Saint-Junien

Saint-Victurnien

Saillat-sur-Vienne

Rochechouart

Aixe-sur-Vienne

Chéronnac

Oradour-sur-Vayres

Timeline

1906

February Paul Desourteaux becomes mayor of Oradour-sur-Glane, taking over from his father Emile who dies in service.

1911

August The establishment of an electric tramway station in Oradour. *Président de la République* Raymond Poincaré visits.

1914–18

First World War Ninety-nine men from the *commune* are killed. With the mayor away serving in the army, socialist Joseph Beau acts as mayor. Many men return emotionally and physically scarred.

1919

December Joseph Beau is elected mayor of Oradour.

1938

10 April Edouard Daladier becomes head of government, ending the Popular Front (*Front Populaire*) which, for two years, had been a left-wing coalition under Léon Blum.

1939

January Mass arrival of Spanish refugees, fleeing Franco's regime, into southern France.

September Evacuees from Schiltigheim, Strasbourg, arrive in Oradour.

3 September Britain and France declare war on Germany.

26 September French Communist party outlawed.

1940

10 May German offensive in Belgium, Holland and Luxembourg.

May–June An estimated 8 million people flee south from northern France, Paris and the Low Countries in an unprecedented 'exodus'.

9 June French government quits Paris.

16 June Prime Minister Paul Reynaud resigns. Philippe Pétain takes over.

17 June Pétain broadcasts to the nation.

18 June De Gaulle issues his appeal from London.

22 June Franco-German armistice.

10 July National Assembly in Vichy votes full powers to Pétain.

27 September Jews in the southern zone are prohibited from returning to the occupied zone.

22–4 October Pierre Laval and then Pétain meet Adolf Hitler in Montoire.

1 November The German operation *Aktion D* begins in Alsace-Lorraine, leading to the arrival in Oradour-sur-Glane of refugees from the Moselle region.

1941

April Mayor Joseph Beau is caught up in a controversy regarding shoes for refugees. He is replaced by Paul Desourteaux.

Spring 643rd *Groupe de Travailleurs Étrangers* (GTE) is established just outside Oradour.

22 June Germany invades the USSR.

22 July Law on the aryanisation of Jewish property is passed.

October A Resistance group linked to *Libération-sud* is established in Limoges.

1942

27 March First French Jews sent to Auschwitz.

22 June Laval introduces *La Relève*, a programme that returns one prisoner of war held in Germany for every three volunteers sent to work in the Reich.

25 August Germans introduce conscription in Alsace-Lorraine.

26–8 August Round-ups of Jews in the non-occupied zone begin.

8 November Allied invasion of North Africa.

11 November Germany occupies the southern zone.

1943

26 January Creation of the *Mouvements Unis de la Résistance* (MUR), driven by Jean Moulin.

30 January The *Milice* is formed, headed by Joseph Darnand.

17 February The *Service du Travail Obligatoire* (STO) is brought into operation, replacing *La Relève*.

1944

Late March–April The Brehmer division terrorises the Limousin region.

6 June D-Day landings in Normandy.

7 June *Maquis* leader Georges Guingouin is urged by Communist party officials to liberate the city of Limoges. He refuses.

8 June Saint-Junien is occupied by the Wehrmacht after a soldier is shot by the *maquis*. Two days later, elements of the SS Panzer division *Das Reich* arrive.

9 June Tulle, briefly liberated by the *maquis*, is reclaimed by the Wehrmacht, aided by elements of *Das Reich*. Ninety-nine men are hanged from the town's lamp posts and a further 149 people are deported.

10 June The SS massacre in Oradour-sur-Glane.

21 June A service is held in Limoges Cathedral in memory of the victims, leading to tensions in the city centre.

25 August The Germans surrender in Paris.

1945

4 March General de Gaulle visits Oradour and promises to fund its conservation as a site of memory.
26 April Pétain gives himself up to the French authorities.
8 May Germany surrenders.
July Trial of Pétain in Paris.
October Trial and execution of Laval.

1953

12 February The *Procès de Bordeaux*, a military tribunal, opens and twenty-two men are tried for the events at Oradour.
19 February The French parliament votes an amnesty law, reducing the sentences passed in Bordeaux.
20 February The municipal council decides to return the *Croix de la Légion d'honneur* and the *Croix de Guerre* awarded to the village.

1983

May–June Heinz Barth becomes the most senior member of *Das Reich* to be put on trial in East Berlin. He is given a life sentence but is released in 1997.

Cast

Avril, Marie
Ran the *Hôtel Avril* after the death of her second husband. Her daughter, **Marguerite Laurence**, brought her husband **Henri** and their children to the village when Paris was occupied.

Avril, Michel
Wood merchant who also sold other fuels including petrol.

Bardet, Denise
Taught at the girls' school and lived with her mother, **Louise**, and brother, **Camille**, in a nearby hamlet.

Beau, Joseph
Socialist mayor of the village from 1914 to 1941.

Beaubreuil, Martial
An escaped prisoner of war; he hid in the grocery store.

Beaubreuil, Maurice
Evaded obligatory work service (STO) by hiding in the Mercier store with his older brother.

Bélivier, Marcel
Son of a farmer in the hamlet of Les Brégères.

Bergmann, Joseph
Barber in the *Café du Chêne*. German and Jewish by birth, though most believed him to be Austrian.

Besson, Robert
Young veteran of the 1940 war whose family ran a textile shop.

Bielsa, Millán
Former medic; refugee from Spain sent as an inmate to the 643rd *Groupe de Travailleurs Étrangers* (GTE).

Binet, Andrée
Head of the girls' school but absent in early 1944 due to a difficult pregnancy.

Biver, Gilberte
Refugee from Moselle; met **Jean Henry**, then a camp warden at the 643rd GTE, and moved with him to the Paris area.

Blum, Léon
Jewish politician; prime minister in the Popular Front (*Front Populaire*) government. Arrested by the Vichy authorities.

Bonnet, Madeleine	Ward of the state; worked as a live-in housemaid for Jeanne Mercier.
Borie, Mathieu	Builder from Limoges with a workshop in Oradour; part of a Resistance network.
Bouchoule, Léopold	One of the village's bakers.
Brandy, Eugénie	Owner of the *Café Central*. Of her three daughters, **Andrée** worked at the tram station and **Jeannine** worked as a hairdresser and was married to mechanic **Aimé Renaud**. Youngest daughter **Antoinette** worked alongside her mother in the café and, like her mother, also sewed gloves.
Brissaud, Martial	Wheelwright who worked with his father on the western edge of the village.
Chapelle, Jean-Baptiste	Oradour's long-serving priest.
Compain, Maurice	*Pâtissier* with a shop on the *Champ de foire*.
Coppenolle, Berthe and **Crombé, Jeanne**	Business partners from Roubaix who arrived as refugees with their families and moved into the La Lauze farm.
Coudert, Georges	Young police inspector based in Limoges.
Couty, Odette	Teacher brought in to replace Andrée Binet.
Couvidou, Germaine	Albert Valade's sister; young mother of four who lived at the Valade tenant farm.
Dagoury, Mélanie	Owner of *Le Restaurant de la Promenade* and her late husband's cement and masonry business.
Darnand, Joseph	Former soldier; created the *Milice* to combat the Resistance.
Darthout, Jean-Marcel	Part of the football team; aspired to be a teacher but had to find alternative work to avoid a call up to STO. His father, **François**, was a postal worker.
Denis, Léon	Wineseller, municipal councillor and leader of a musical society.
Desourteaux, André	Grandson of mayors Joseph Beau and Paul Desourteaux; son of grocers **Emile** and **Alice**.
Desourteaux, Hubert	Son of Paul; a mechanic with a garage on the main street.

Desourteaux, Paul Former mayor; political opponent of Joseph Beau. Head of the special delegation, mayor in all but name, in 1944.

Doutre, Paul Eldest of two brothers; hidden by his family when called up for STO in Germany.

Dupic, François and **Jean** Brothers who each ran their own textile shop.

Filliol, Jean *Directeur général* of the *Deuxième service*, the 'action and information' service – a kind of Gestapo of the French *Milice.*

Foussat, André Miller from a nearby hamlet; served on the municipal council and ran the amateur dramatic society.

Freund-Valade, Marc 'Prefect' of the Haute-Vienne from September 1943.

Gaudy, Yvonne Teenage girl who sewed gloves for the Saint-Junien factories.

de Gaulle, Charles Leader of the Free French who left for London in June 1940.

Godfrin, Roger Arrived with his family after the Moselle was cleared of Francophone elements; 7 years old in June 1944.

Gougeon, Fernand Teacher in Moselle; taught in the school for refugees.

Guingouin, Georges Former teacher and one of the first men to take to the *maquis.*

Hébras, Robert Son of **Jean**, a former employee of the tramway, and **Marie**, who sewed for extra money. Aspired to be a *pâtissier* but circumstances led to him becoming a mechanic in Limoges. He had three sisters, two older than him, one a decade his junior.

Henry, Jean Music teacher who became a guard at the Oradour camp. Met his wife, a refugee from Moselle, in Oradour.

Hyvernaud, Fernand Dealer in farm animals whose house and barns were next to the church. His daughter **Henriette Joyeux** had married and moved away but visited Oradour with husband **Marcel** and baby son **René**.

Jakobowicz, David Son of Jewish immigrants who became involved with the *maquis*.

Jakobowicz, Sarah Hidden by Martial Machefer when her brother David's clandestine activities placed the family in danger.

Kanzler, Joseph Jewish man who stayed in the village with his family when most of the Schiltigheim evacuees returned north to a nazified Strasbourg.

Lamaud, Marie and **Jean** Looked after various *pupilles de l'assistance publique* (wards of the state) at their Bellevue farm.

Lang, Jules and **Jeanne** Jewish couple who came to Oradour from Bordeaux.

Laval, Pierre Former lawyer who became head of the government under Pétain.

de Lavérine, Marie-Thérèse Owner of several properties in Oradour and the Chalet Saint-Vincent, where her son **Hubert** and his family lived after fleeing Paris.

Lesparat, Fernand Son of a wheelwright; first cousin of Resistance agent Albert Mirablon.

Lévignac, Alphonse Brought his sons **Serge** and **Charles** to the village to stay with families during the summer.

Lévy, Nathan Jewish dentist from Rennes who crossed the demarcation line when his business was expropriated.

Lorich, Jacques Curate for the village of Charly; arrived in Oradour with his fellow villagers and sister **Angélique**.

Machefer, Martial Married to Anna, with two young children. Let go from a paper mill because of his activism; set up as a cobbler but was still under surveillance for his past as a communist militant.

Maire, Gabriel Arrived with the refugees from Alsace-Lorraine and set up a butcher's shop.

Mercier, Jeanne Ran a café-bar and a grocery store in the lower village with son **René**.

Milord, Léon Restauranteur who ran the *Hôtel Milord* with his wife.

Morlieras, Lucien	Owner of a café-bar and barber shop, with attached hat shop, in the lower village. Married to **Catherine**, with a teenaged daughter called **Irène**.
Mosnier, Marie	Widowed owner of several properties and farms. Sheltered her nephew **Jacques Garaud**, who was avoiding STO.
Otto, José María	German with a Spanish background tasked with recruiting Spanish workers from the GTE camps, then put in charge of the Oradour camp.
Pascaud, Marcel	Young pharmacist who opened a business in the village in 1938.
Patry, Eugène	*Milicien* and interpreter for the Gestapo.
Penot, Robert	*Pupille de l'assistance publique* who was moved to the Bellevue farm.
Pétain, Philippe	Celebrated leader in the First World War; became prime minister under President Paul Reynaud before being awarded full powers as France's leader during the Vichy regime.
Picat, Maurice	*Regisseur* (land agent) and owner of La Lauze farm.
Pinède, Robert	Jewish leatherworker who brought his family to the village after his Bayonne business was appropriated.
Poutaraud, Pierre	Mechanic with a garage in the centre of the village; father to seven children.
Rastouil, Louis Paul	Bishop of Limoges.
Redon, Emile	Entrepreneur; ran a café-bar and grocer's on the *Champ de foire* with his daughter **Irène** and second wife. He also owned an apple press and sold building sand, which he dredged himself.
Redon, Hippolyte	Blacksmith farrrier who lived outside the village where his wife ran a lodging house.
Rouffanche, Marguerite	Tenant farmer (*métayer*) along with husband **Simon**. Moved from a farm in the centre to another in Puy-Gaillard, on the other side of the River Glane.

Roumy, Jean	Municipal councillor and head of the *Légion* (veteran's association); dealer in farming products. His son, **Albert**, was enrolled as part of the *operation Todt* in Bordeaux.
Rousseau, Léonard	Mayoral secretary; taught in the boys' school along with wife **Jeanne**.
Santrot, Jules and **Paul**	Father and son with a tailoring business.
Senon, Armand	Employed at the Bouchoule bakery; his father, **Jean**, rented and worked a farm on the *Champ de foire* with his brother-in-law. Broke his leg playing football the week before the SS came to Oradour.
Senon, Camille	Attended a professional training school in Limoges, returning to Oradour on the weekends; daughter of **Martial**, a roadworker, and **Catherine**.
Senon, Daniel	Escaped prisoner of war; postman.
Simon, Marguerite	Parisian girl sent by her single mother, **Amélie**, to live with her uncle, Hippolyte Redon.
Thomas, Marcellin	Baker with a shop near the lower village.
Tournier, Jean-Baptiste	Employee at the Limoges town hall; ran music lessons in Oradour and was head of the *l'Avenir Musical*.
Valade, Albert	Left school at 13 to work as a cattle herder on his father **Jean**'s tenant farm.
Valentin, Marie	Operated the town's weighing equipment opposite the *Champ de foire*; married to a barber, Jean.
de Vaugelas, Jean	*Directeur général du maintien de l'ordre* for the region of Haute-Vienne from spring 1944.
Verny, Françoise	Housemaid to wine merchant Léon Denis.
Villatte, Pierre	Retired soldier and farmworker who set up a *bureau-tabac* with his wife, **Mélanie**.
Villéger, Marguerite	Lived and worked at the Masset farm with husband **Jean** and their children.
Vincent, Raymonde	Teacher at the primary school; married, with a child.

Author's Note

Many of the sources used in the writing of this book were drawn directly from archives. One of the consequences of this is that use of language reflects contemporary understanding and beliefs. For this reason, it should be noted at the outset that the use of 'Germans' in relation to the Nazi SS troops who were at Oradour does not reflect the fact, only later known by the protagonists, that many of these soldiers were recruited from other countries, including France. These young men were often recruited forcibly. The use of the word 'Boche' in reference to Germans is outdated in France, as well as pejorative. These days it is rarely used and is only included here for historical accuracy.

Introduction

In the midst of a typically Limousin country scene where wide fields were dotted with woodland, and the stones of a stream filtered clear water through nooks and crannies that hid trout and crayfish, Oradour-sur-Glane stood.[1]

In January 2020, Spanish grandmother Ramona Domínguez Gil was pronounced by the Limoges High Court to be the 643rd victim of the massacre of the French village of Oradour-sur-Glane, which took place on 10 June 1944. She died alongside her daughter-in-law Marina, and her three grandchildren, 11-year-old Miquel, 7-year-old Harmonia, and 21-month-old Llibert. They were rounded up by the *Schutzstaffel* (SS) and locked in a church with hundreds of other women and children. The soldiers told them that their village was being searched while their husbands, fathers and sons were kept hostage. After a while the SS asphyxiated them with acrid black smoke, before riddling them with machine-gun bullets. Then the church was locked and set alight. Only one person, a grandmother herself, escaped.

Ramona Domínguez Gil, the 643rd Oradour victim. (Archives départementales de la Haute-Vienne, 985 W 1570)

Ramona's son, Juan Téllez Domínguez Almirall, met a similarly horrific fate. Like many of the village's men, he was locked in one of the nearby barns before being shot, covered with combustible materials and burned. The massacre took place four days after Allied soldiers landed in Normandy when, for the first time in four years, the people of southern France were feeling hopeful about the future. Word of the tragedy spread, albeit slowly, and when General de Gaulle went there to pay homage to its victims, he agreed that the ruins should be preserved as a monument to the martyrs of Oradour.

A list of 642 names of victims was assiduously put together over a number of years. The name of Ramona Domínguez Gil was not on it, despite the list appearing some time after a plaque to twenty Spanish victims was installed by the *Junta Española de Liberación* (JEL) between 1944 and 1945. By the time a later plaque was installed, based on the official list of 642 victims, two names had disappeared, including Ramona's. From that point on, the list was considered definitive and she was forgotten. Very few people remained from the village following the massacre, and they simply did not know the Spanish victims well enough. Most of the bodies in the church and the barns had been reduced to cinders and were unrecognisable.

In 2013, a plaque was placed in a hamlet called La Fauvette, a short stroll from the centre of the preserved village. Its purpose was to commemorate a site where Spanish exiles were 'interned' and thoroughly exploited for labour purposes between 1940 and 1942. This camp was the base of one of France's many *Groupes de Travailleurs Étrangers* (GTE). Coincidentally, the Oradour camp is listed as the 643rd GTE. The Spanish contingent in Oradour, and most throughout the rest of southern France, was fleeing the Franco regime. The men had fought the republican cause and brought their families with them, or some followed later, and most suffered awful conditions crossing the Pyrenees. When they arrived, they were interned by the French authorities before being redirected to GTE camps where, along with other undesirables such as Jews and communists, the men were made to work in menial jobs just to earn enough to keep their families alive. In late 1942 the camp was moved from Oradour to a different village nearby, but the families remained where they were. Some of the women had found jobs, and the children were enrolled in Oradour's schools. On Saturday 10 June 1944, most of the Spanish men were at assigned work. Hence, of the nineteen Spanish victims now known to have died in the flames of Oradour, six were women, eleven were children and only two were men, both of whom were extremely unlucky to be in the village at the moment the SS arrived.

Recent research has uncovered the story of the 643rd GTE Oradour and the people interned and assigned to work there.[2] The small Spanish contingent had become a footnote to a tragic event that led to the destruction of countless French families. But their presence is a significant detail in the story of France at the end of the Third Republic, the subsequent advent of an authoritarian and collaborationist regime known as Vichy France and the beginning of the period of full occupation by the Nazis. How the Spanish were treated, for example, tells us much about the various strata of society in a small community such as Oradour. How their individual stories have been established amongst 643 victims illustrates how important research of ordinary people is necessary, fascinating and impacts on the question of memorialisation.

Of Oradour's buildings, nothing was left standing. The Nazi aim had been to erase the community from the map. They very nearly succeeded. Three or four generations of families were murdered, and whole classes of schoolchildren were not spared. Those who lost their lives have always been referred to by the French as martyrs – a term assigned to them immediately after the war. But Oradour's people and their occupations, family ties and views on the world deserve to be better understood.

The village has been commemorated as idyllic – a mythical island in Vichy France. But the existence of the 643rd GTE was a part of its story that was almost lost in time, as was the interaction of its community with such outsiders. Oradour also played host to evacuees, refugees and expelled families from the north of France and further afield. In this respect, and many others, it was a typical village in the political cooking pot that was Vichy France. Jewish families hid there, as did evaders of forced work service and members of the illegal Communist party. Its local governance changed through scandal and the effects of national and international politics. The village was central to the lives of different sorts of people, including the peasant farmers of surrounding hamlets who did all they could to thrive under a new regime. The village's close links with bigger towns, including a tram link to the city of Limoges, gave it manifold benefits but also made it both susceptible and vulnerable to outsiders. The Vichy regime gave rise to resistance just as it did to people who chose to collaborate. This book is a case study of a small piece of Vichy France. The community before the massacre is placed under the microscope with a view to unravelling names from the collective martyrdom.

Why Oradour was chosen has emerged as a central question, giving rise to negationist history and even conspiracy theories. This book illustrates *how* the event came about. Some elements to certain questions are simply unanswerable. The context of the Oradour massacre was created entirely elsewhere, out of the hands of the village's inhabitants for whom the event was as unexpected as it was undeserved. It was simply an event that fitted into a much larger story.

This book is divided into three parts. The first part focuses on the town and people of Oradour in the years leading towards the fateful day in June 1944. The second part is an account of what happened, seen entirely through the eyes of those who were there, or nearby. The third part focuses on the context of events leading up to the massacre, and in the weeks that followed. Research is drawn largely from first-hand accounts given in the months after the massacre, or from oral accounts given in interviews with four survivors whose stories are central to the narrative. These same four people helped me enormously in the preparation of the first half of the book, as I was able to clarify details pertaining to their lives before and after the destruction of their home village.

Robert Hébras was one of only five men to escape the Laudy-Mosnier barn, itself one of five locations where the village's men were shot. His escape is a remarkable story, but he was also able to help me understand life for a young man in the village, as well as in nearby Limoges where he worked. Of his immediate family, he lost his mother and two sisters.

André Desourteaux, grandson of two of the town's mayors, was a 19-year-old witness to life in the village. The Desourteaux family was as much a part of Oradour as the main street which bore its name. André was working a shift at the postal office in Limoges when the SS arrived, and returned home to find his village destroyed and the soldiers still there. He had his key ready to open his front door, but there was no home left. He lost almost every member of his family.

Camille Senon lived and worked in Limoges and came back to her home village of Oradour to see her parents each Saturday evening. On 10 June 1944 she arrived by the evening tram to see her village in flames and was part of a group of passengers held by the SS for several hours, and taunted, before being dramatically released. She witnessed the ongoing destruction of the village and lost her father, grandfather, aunt and uncle, as well as a great number of other close family members.

Albert Valade lived on a farm in the nearby hamlet of Le Mas du Puy. He lost his older sister, who went to the village to collect two of her children from school. He witnessed the arrival of the soldiers and the anxious wait in the villages for the return of the schoolchildren. While watching from a field, a partially burned page, which he recognised as from a book of the catechism used at church, landed at his feet. He was able to help me understand life for Limousin farmers, the peasantry of the countryside.

PART ONE

THE LONG ROAD

Battles of a Priest

Over the course of decades, the sight of Oradour-sur-Glane's priest rushing to mass had become an integral feature of the village's landscape. Jean Baptiste Chapelle would 'pass right through the village, usually running late. His was a heavy silhouette, moving quickly, head down, greeting no-one, absorbed only in his thoughts.'[1] Occasionally, brave children would shout some quip at the sight of him, despite knowing that the old man disliked being made fun of. The following Sunday, he would not fail to make acid remarks about such behaviour in his sermon. Chapelle was 'a cold, serious man who always wore his round hat pulled tight to his skull, casting a shadow over a face chiselled by deep wrinkles. Large shoes, legendary in size, protruded from his long black cassock, further accentuating his stern appearance.'[2]

The man's commitment to his flock could not be disputed. Each Sunday morning, Chapelle embarked on a marathon of a routine. Following morning mass, sometimes taken alone, he would eat a hearty breakfast consisting of a bowl of *café au lait* topped with soaked bread. Then he walked to Javerdat, a large village some 5km north-west of Oradour, to where he had been expected to extend his ministry since the beginning of the First World War. After giving mass there he would walk back to Oradour to conduct yet another.

Born to the east of Limoges – a world away at the time – Chapelle had been Oradour's priest since 1911, the same year as the installation of a brand-new tram stop. This provided a direct and speedy link from the agricultural backwater that was Oradour-sur-Glane to the sprawling city of Limoges. During the decades preceding the dark years of German occupation, Chapelle faced his own battles. The first concerned the need to ensure that the size of his congregation did not shrink beyond respectability. In 1925 he indicated in a letter to the Archbishop of Limoges that only around 100 people were attending mass on a normal Sunday, which worked out at around 5 per cent of the population of the *commune*.[3] He also recorded his concerns regarding what he considered to be a struggle to maintain the Christian integrity of his parishioners. He did his best to bring them on board by organising retreats and even a diocesan pilgrimage to Lourdes. Special celebrations took place at Easter and on All Saints' Day, known in France as *Toussaint*, and these were generally well attended, as were baptisms, weddings and confirmations. He lamented that the church had become a place only for such occasions while numbers at Sunday worship continued to decline. During days set aside for worship, the younger generation, he reported, chose to engage in activities unbecoming to the Catholic faith. On 'Sundays, festival days and fairs', he claimed, 'young men and women, often encouraged by their mothers, indulge in voluptuous dances day and night until all hours'. This, he implied, was leading to a rise in 'relations forbidden by the law of God and honest people, sometimes result-ing in devastating scandals'.[4] He also bemoaned the regular consumption of too much alcohol, leading to drunkenness.

Chapelle relied heavily on early recruitment of parishioner children through an insistence on them attending a course of catechism. For the young baptised of Oradour, this meant an inescapable invitation to attend regular Bible studies on a Thursday morning, beginning at *Toussaint*. This was intended to prepare young-sters for the taking of communion, but it also helped Chapelle to limit falling attendance at mass. As Thursday was not a school day, parents were often happy for their children to receive religious instruction as a means of keeping them off the street, even if they themselves no longer regularly attended church, if indeed at all. The children were often less enthusiastic. Sessions were held in the morning for those who lived in the village, at midday for children from the surrounding villages and on Sunday for the children of a small school located in a hamlet called Deulidou. Chapelle would greet his students on the steps of the church before leading them to the two-storey sacristy at the building's rear where he would have already set out several rows of benches. Each new pupil would be given a well-used book of the catechism, to be paid for in a future session. The children were generally in awe of the man and listened intently to his deep, powerful voice.

For centuries, the Church had played a central role for the people of Oradour, but by the end of the 1920s even the rite of passage of catechism was less popular. Children of farming families were needed in the fields, and more and more children came from families with little or no connection to the Church. This situation would only worsen in the 1930s with the arrival of socialism, further extending the availability of secular education to all and dampening the flames of clerical authority.

In order to understand the village under the period of the Vichy regime and under the German occupation, it is important to consider how its community had been affected by the decades preceding it. The First World War had left a devastating effect on the country as a whole but the Limousin was spared the worst of its ravages. The fields of the Limousin were far from the blood-soaked trenches and flattened towns of the north, but the level of conscription meant that almost every household had been affected. The French as a whole had no wish to see a repeat of the conflict and the people of Oradour were no different. The *commune* had lost ninety-nine men. Others, such as wheelwright Martial Brissaud and textile merchant Jean Dupic, had returned with life-changing injuries. During the 1920s and 1930s, two associations, the *Mutilés du Limousin* and the *Combattants du Limousin,*[5] gave political voice to veterans, known as *poilus.* While such associations tended to reflect a right-wing worldview, pacifism reigned. So too did a certain apathy towards the political institutions that had taken France to war. In time, left-leaning politics would emerge from nearby industrial centres and agricultural unions to threaten the hegemony of the established leadership of clerics and right-leaning local politicians from established, wealthy families.

The influence of the Church may have been waning, but life within the village was still focused around its festivals. The *Radounauds,* as Oradour's villagers were known, were rightly proud of their ancient and sacred building. Nobody knows whether the *Église* Saint-Martin was the first church built in the village, but it is known that its central element, the choir, dates from the twelfth century. It was fortified during the religious wars as churches became central strongpoints. A visitor from Limoges, approaching the village from higher ground, would be struck by the square bell tower, which offered 'a very characteristic type of military architecture. The two corners of the western facade are supported by massive buttresses which meet at right angles and support turrets supported by corbels, veritable watch towers.'[6]

Though small, the Romanesque church had four altars, two on each side of the building, and a *maître-autel* (main altar) under three east-facing windows at the furthest end from the main entrance. Those windows gave over a small but steep bank that led down to the tracks of the tramway and the bridge over the River Glane. The main entrance was located underneath the ancient bell tower. There was one further exterior door, in the corner of the southern wall, where the Sainte-Anne chapel sat just metres from the edge of the rectory. A small window alongside that door was complemented by several other similarly sized windows in each of the other three small chapels, and the confessional box was tucked into the north-western corner of the nave, not visible from the main entrance. Due to a significant difference in the level of the ground, the radiating chapel was above cellars which served as storage areas. A further door could be found leading into one of these storage areas, latterly used as the lower level of the sacristy. And its upper level was accessed via a door to the left of the *maître-autel* in the south-eastern corner of the building. This was a room into which few villagers would have ventured except for catechism.

Despite the dwindling regular congregation, religious occasions dominated the rhythm of family life in Oradour. Baptism was followed by catechism, which led to communion and there was often later a wedding, and the cycle would begin again. Festivals, largely dictated by the Christian calendar and the agricultural year, dominated the social life of *Radounauds*. Throughout the countryside, festival dates were intended for the immediate community but, as word spread through newspaper announcements, people from all over would flock to any village known to put on a good show for major fairs. The biggest fixture in Oradour's diary was the annual *fête patronale*, known locally as the *Grande Frairie*. This usually began on the final Sunday of August and lasted until the end of the following day. It was a celebration of the end of the *gros travaux de l'été* (the major agricultural works of the summer), as well as *les moissons* (the harvest). Many of the attractions would arrive earlier in the week and the villagers were given the opportunity to preview what was to come before the crowds arrived, many of whom would be brought by the tramway.

At six o'clock on Sunday morning, festivities would begin with the fanfare (*reveil*) and with the firing of artillery. At nine o'clock, a fishing competition took place in the waters of the Glane – an extremely popular event with prizes to be won. A cycling race took place in the afternoon for which competitors had to sign up in advance either in Saint-Junien or Oradour by providing evidence that their cycle was licensed and paying the 3-franc entrance fee. Once the race was complete – for which a significant cash prize of over 100 francs could be won, as well as runners-up cash prizes – the evening festivities would begin. *L'Avenir Musical*, the village's own orchestra, gave a concert followed at nine o'clock by a firework display, and finally a music concert. An extra tram set off for Limoges at eleven thirty. The bars would be full throughout the day and the *pâtissier* would sell cheap cakes and bread rolls.

The following day's organised events began with a parade, showcasing music and traditional costumes of the villages, and Limousin dancing. In the early 1940s, a float – the disguised truck of garage owner Pierre Poutaraud – was followed by musicians and dancers as it made its way to the lower village before heading out to the surrounding countryside. André Foussat, a dignitary and director of the village's theatrical group, announced activities that were on offer that afternoon through a loudhailer. At four o'clock the games began, the most popular being the *mât de cocagne* (the greasy pole). This was held in the centre of the *Champ de foire* (fairground), Oradour's sizeable village green. Young people from all around would come and attempt to claim a prize from a bicycle wheel attached to the top of a well-soaped mast. As well as actual prizes attached to the wheel, there were also pieces of paper with prizes written on them – a leg of lamb, a ham, a turkey or (least desirable of all) a sausage. Before attempting the game in front of a baying crowd, competitors had to undergo an inspection of their shoes to check they were not cheating by adding grips. The game went on until all the prizes had gone.

There were sack races for the children, and the *jeu de la brouette*, the aim of which was to win a race while pushing a sideless wheelbarrow containing a hopping frog. The *jeu de la cruche* was for adults – a series of pitchers were suspended from a line at a height of around 2½ metres, most containing a piece of paper with a prize written on it, but one containing cold water. The participant was given a stick and then blindfolded and spun around. The object of the game was to hit a pitcher and receive either a prize or a soaking. Sweet stalls for children were accompanied by a barrel organ, target-shooting stands and any number of other attractions, such as lucky dips. Adults and children could ride on chairs suspended by chains that spun around, though the carousel with its wooden horses was specially reserved for little ones. The smell of sweet treats was everywhere and parents who brought their children from the farms would reward them more than they would on any other day of the year. Groups of children would run from stall to stall, warned not to stray further than the confines of the *place* (square). The villagers would head home as darkness descended, by which time the bars, cafés and restaurants would have done a good trade. On both days there would be a ball that would continue late into the night. Curious children might watch the dancers before finally giving in to tiredness and dreams of doing it all again the following year.

Before embarking on a period of Lent, which was generally respected by eating a less rich diet, *mardi gras* was celebrated with beef stew known as *pot-au-feu*. The children, given a day off school, dressed up as witches, burlesque ladies or mythical beings, and knocked on doors around the village, hoping for pieces of cake and other sweet treats. The *mi-carême*, or mid-lent, was celebrated with a masked ball in one of the village's hotels or cafés. After Lent came the *fête du bas du bourg*, a celebration held in the lower part of the village, around the covered market, overlooked by the church. Robert Hébras, a child during the late 1920s, described it as 'modest enough, it was little more than a small fairground ride, two or three cake and sweet stalls, a lucky dip stall and a shooting gallery. But our few pennies were used up after two goes on the roundabout, and a few sweets.'[7] While the adults went to the *Hôtel Milord* to dance, the children played hide and seek to the sound of an accordion playing until their parents put them to bed. The dance continued late into the night. Another day of simple pleasures, like the other festivals and celebrations that would only be missed when they disappeared from the lives of the *Radounauds*.

The Freedom Tree

In 1926, a journalist from Toulouse recalled an earlier visit to the peaceful, idyllic village:

> Oradour-sur-Glane! I remember it. You could get there on the mail cart. When you passed the bridge over the Glane, so lively and clear, you would see the village a slope before you, grey gables and red roofs in amongst the trees. The climb was steep as far as the church, humble on its little terrace, but contrasting with the sweeping frontage of the homes of the village squires. Further on was the *Champ de foire* and then, beyond the villas, the road to Javerdat stretched out into the sweet, deep chestnut groves. Somewhere nearby, behind the village centre, a pathway crossed a stream packed with enormous crayfish that we would catch and put into baskets made from bundles of thorn bushes. (*La Dépêche*, 23 February 1923)

The name Oradour, from the Latin *Oratio*, via its Occitan form of *Oradores* and Limousin patois *L'Ouradou*, means 'place of prayer'.[1] Another suggestion is that the name comes from *Oratorium* and indicates an old chapel, perhaps a chapel at a crossroads, which might have been preceded by a small pagan monument and could have had a role in the process of burying the dead.[2] Indeed, a further twelfth-century monument called the *lanterne des morts d'Oradour-sur-Glane* was erected in the middle of the cemetery. Recognised by ministerial decision as a precious monument in 1926, the stone structure was adorned with a covered top section in which candles were lit during times of mourning. It was originally located on the left bank of the Glane, near the church, but in 1773 the cemetery was relocated and the lantern dismantled and moved, stone by stone, to its current position in the cemetery. Just to the north of the tiny village of Oradour-Saint-Genest is a reminder of the commonality of the name in the Haute-Vienne. Due south, at a distance of some 30km or so, lies Oradour-sur-Vayres. Further east, on the other side of the nearby city of Limoges, the tiny hamlet of Oradour-les-Linards would eventually shelter a well-known Resistance chief.

For all its proximity to the city of Limoges, Oradour was a rural village, surrounded by agricultural land and forestry, both of which provided livelihoods for the *commune's* inhabitants. Quarries and marshes provided industry for tilemakers, and several sawmills scattered the area. The making of planks, the preparation of wood and charcoal, and the fabrication of paper were all important industries in the Haute-Vienne.

The monthly *foires* (fairs), were vital for Oradour-sur-Glane's local economy. Over the centuries, travelling merchants set up their own permanent shops in the village. Its micro-economy thrived as small businesses and tradesmen became central to the soul of the main village, or *bourg*. When, in 1789, it became the centre of the *commune* it boasted a baker, a wine seller, a carpenter, a butcher, two potters, a paper maker, a blacksmith farrier, two tailors, a miller and six textile workers. Over the coming decades it became a hub for the surrounding villages, with its businesses and all-important public services. New houses and villas were built, and the shops became more attractive to visit. Functionality led to expanded ranges advertised in local papers, quality items and even competition.

Even before electricity was supplied to the village, the construction of the electrified tram[3] boosted the local economy. Inaugurated in August 1911, the line from Limoges north-west to Bussière-Poitevine ran straight through the main street, the *rue Emile Desourteaux*. The narrow-gauge tracks became an integral part of the sloping street that brought together ancient rurality

The tram to Limoges alongside Oradour's station. The post office is visible on the left.
(Collection Benoit Sadry)

and forward-facing modernity. Every day the tram passed five times in each direction and for 1 franc and 35 centimes a passenger could take the one-and-a-quarter-hour journey to Limoges. In 1926 a separate post office was built to replace the rented building in which it had been previously located. This fine-looking detached building, complete with ornate decorative frontage, was located near the tram stop and the town hall.

In March 1848, after the proclamation of the Second Republic ushered in municipal elections, Jean Baptiste Desourteaux became the first elected mayor of Oradour. Previously the mayor and his deputy had been designated by the prefect, often for places that did not contain their own homes. The *chêne de la liberté* (freedom tree), planted near Desourteaux's home in his honour, was said to have bottles of wine among its roots.

The name of the well-to-do Desourteaux family became ingrained in the fabric of life and politics in Oradour-sur-Glane. Three generations would serve as mayor, as well as being the village's medical doctors. The Desourteaux mayors were right-wing republicans, and a well-established example of the landed gentry. The main street was named after Emile Desourteaux, the son of Jean-Baptiste, who was elected in May 1892 after twenty-two years on the municipal council. He died in service in February 1906 and was succeeded by his son Paul.

Having taken over the family's medical practice in the centre of Oradour, Paul married Marie from the Bourgogne. The couple had their first child, a daughter known as Alyette,[4] in 1903, a year after their wedding. At the age of 10 Alyette was given the honour of passing a bouquet of flowers to Raymond Poincaré, *Président de la République*, in front of the new tramway station. This simple ceremony marked a proud day for Paul Desourteaux.

Just eleven months later, the clouds of war descended over Europe. Paul was mobilised, serving as a medic until finally returning to Oradour in December 1919, by which time he had been awarded the title *Chevalier de la Légion d'honneur* by presidential decree.

While Paul was away, a replacement mayor was found in Joseph Beau, originally a *sabotier* (clog maker and seller) who had taken up the business of running a grocery store as well as printing and selling photographs of the town as postcards. Due to family responsibilities, Beau had not been mobilised and had been elected as a socialist councillor, on the opposition *Section française de l'Internationale ouvrière* (SFIO) list. As acting mayor he proved extremely popular. In the 1919 elections, Beau's socialist list overwhelmingly won the local elections taking all but one seat on the council – in which Paul Desourteaux would sit in opposition. Socialists winning seats on the municipal council was nothing new as they had made gains since winning their first in 1908, and theirs was a restrained socialism, one that fitted the moment and 'mixed pacifism, the defence of rural interests, secularism and anticlericalism'.[5] Desourteaux's republicanism – nationalist with a view to defending the status quo in society – felt outdated. The election of 1919 was, however, the first time the town had elected a socialist mayor with a majority.

Despite the political misalignments and clash in personalities between Joseph Beau and Paul Desourteaux, the men maintained a civil relationship while carrying out their municipal responsibilities, which were functional rather than overly political in nature. They did their work in much the same way as each other, displaying the utmost care for their community and attention to detail, though Beau would later prove to be more responsive to newcomers and refugees settling in the village. That the two men did not much like each other may have resulted from their differing backgrounds:[6] Beau was an artisan and keenly socialist, Desourteaux from a line of almost hereditary mayoral stock. It was only when a personal line was crossed that their relationship broke down further. In late 1924, Beau's 20-year-old daughter Alice announced that she was pregnant. The father of the child was the eldest of Paul Desourteaux's four sons, 20-year-old Emile. Up until that point the romance had been kept secret.[7]

Despite the couple's love for each other, Paul Desourteaux was unable to accept not only that his son had embarked on the affair, but that his political rival's daughter would be bearing his grandchild out of wedlock. The pair, it was decided, would have to marry as soon as Emile reached the age of 21, the age of majority. The baby boy, named André, was born in August 1925 and the pair married in Limoges in February 1926, less than a month after Emile turned 21. That the union of two of the most influential families in Oradour took place in Limoges, away from the eyes of the villagers, speaks volumes for how the Desourteaux parents felt. A Desourteaux wedding should have been an event for the whole village to enjoy but the union spelt shame. Emile was cut adrift from the family and he and Alice settled in Limoges, where they stayed until André was 7 and the first of his two sisters was born. As if to add insult to injury, in 1925, Desourteaux lost his seat on the municipal council. It would take four years for him to regain it.

The Glove-makers

In 1911, the supply of a station on the electric tram network that covered the Haute-Vienne provided the village of Oradour, the heart of the surrounding communities, with a vital artery. The city of Limoges lay just 20km further east. The *Radounauds* could live from the land without being isolated from the outside world. Oradour became a commuter village for workers in Limoges, and trams in both directions were routinely full. Many inhabitants of the bourg either worked in the city or went there to sell goods. At weekends, people came from Limoges to shop, relax or fish. Many came to dine in the *Hôtel Milord* where *tête de veau* (calf's head) was a speciality.

Jean Hébras was a former farm labourer who served in the First World War. After sustaining an injury in Champagne in September 1915, he was taken prisoner the following December. In August 1918, he finally returned to the farm and married Marie, his employer's daughter. The couple lived in the northern half of the Haute-Vienne before moving to Oradour in 1925. Jean, who had trained as an engineer, was offered a new job heading up a team looking after the upkeep of the electric tramway. The couple had two daughters, 6-year-old Odette and 3-year-old Georgette.

In the first instance, the family rented the same apartment that had been occupied by Marcelin Chalard, Jean's predecessor as *chef d'équipe*, who had been reassigned to Limoges. The apartment was just big enough for the family of four. The couple found it hard to settle in and make friends because of the significant variations in the local *patois*. Theirs derived from the old northern language, the *langue d'oïl*, while the dialect used in Oradour-sur-Glane, just 40km further south, had emerged from the *langue d'oc*, the language of the south from which the name of the Languedoc region derived. The family did all it could to establish itself in the *Radounaud* lifestyle. Marie was already pregnant with the couple's third child during the move to Oradour; baby Robert was born that June. Before long Jean and Marie decided that they had outgrown the apartment and moved into a rented house on the edge of the village, before finding a perfect little half-house on the main street of the village consisting of a dining room and kitchen, with two bedrooms upstairs. The Hébras family occupied the entire left side of the house, separated by a corridor from the right-hand side, which was divided into flats. Initially

Robert shared one of the bedrooms with his parents while the other was shared by the two girls. Only much later, when one of the two neighbours died, did Jean manage to rent an extra room for Robert.

The house was comfortable, and the family income was secure through Jean's employment. Their finances were, however, continually stretched, so Jean took on additional work delivering telegrams that arrived at the post office, which was a short walk away. These would have to be paid for by the recipient if they were delivered outside of the main village, but they were free to those who lived within. Jean had two bells wired up to the house. One was rung if there was a problem with the electricity along the 20km stretch of tram line for which he was responsible, the other if a telegram needed delivering. The extra income proved useful at the end of the month when funds were scarce and, during the summer when they were a little older, the girls cycled with the messages to their destinations. When the electricity on the tram failed, Jean would let his team know and investigate either on his bicycle or, when the weather was poor or when a team was needed on site quickly, he would call up the contracted designated transport. When Jean first took the job this task was fulfilled by a wineseller who owned a car, and later by a mechanic called Pierre Poutaraud who used his own Citroën truck. Both men benefitted from extra income when their transport services were called up.

Marie also helped to bring in additional funds by sewing. One of her employers was the well-known Dupic textile merchants – two brothers, François and Jean, who owned two shops in the village. After taking the children to school, Marie would sit at her sewing machine in the dining room, working on bed sheets, pillowcases and tea towels by the light from the bay window, which overlooked the main street. Many women in the village and surrounding hamlets also hand-sewed for the glove factories and tanneries, on which the economy of the nearest large town, Saint-Junien, was based. Local agents would distribute the work and collect the completed product, or some workers such as Marie would take the finished product, wrapped in a piece of black cloth known as a *cravate*, to their agents. They would be paid for work completed and, where possible, collect more gloves to sew. Marie's workroom had formerly been the front of a grocery store and the Hébras family had mounted a beautiful pendulum clock, the 'tic-toc' of which accompanied Marie as she sewed in the hours between looking after the rest of the family and cooking meals.

The only other downstairs room was the kitchen, the centerpiece of which was a large wood-burning stove on the same wall as a bricked-up former fireplace. In the winter the stove heated the house. There was a small stone

Women from the hamlet of Bellevue sewing for the glove factories of Saint-Junien.
(Collection Marcelle Lamaud)

sink, but water had to be retrieved from a pump in the garden. The only toilet was also outside. The kitchen had a wooden table and chairs and a sideboard, and the garden outside was big enough for the family to keep some chickens. Jean also rented some extra ground from his friend, the wheelwright Marcel Brissaud, who had lost a leg in the First World War. The plot was big enough to grow a modest amount of vegetables to feed the family. Jean was also friends with Jean Dupic, one of the tailor brothers for whom Marie worked. Like Hébras, Dupic was a veteran, returning to Oradour after having lost an eye. In the coming years, his son Pierre would attend school with Robert Hébras, young Martial Brissaud, son of the wheelwright, and André Desourteaux, grandson of both Paul Desourteaux and Joseph Beau.

Autarky

Despite the trials of growing up in a working-class family, Robert Hébras fondly remembers his childhood in the agricultural surrounds of a rural village in peace-time:

> I lived in Oradour for nineteen years. When I walk in the streets[1] I still hear the church bells and the anvil of the blacksmith shoeing cows and hobnailing our clogs [...] I still hear the wine merchant washing out his barrels with a chain: I used to live opposite his cellar and that sound used to wake me up in the morning. We used to walk the streets, and farmers used to cross the village with their carts pulled by cows.[2]

The Saint-Junien road joined *rue Emile Desourteaux*, Oradour's main street, at a junction very near the Hébras home, and opposite the main *Champ de foire*. On that junction was the *bascule*, a wooden platform for weighing animals or carts full of produce. About the size of two doors set into the road, it was operated from a corner property overlooking the junction. Just a few steps along was a farm, La Lauze, with a large courtyard and its own well and weighing scales, quite separate from the nearby municipal-owned equipment.[3] It was known locally as the Picat farm because it was owned by a former farmer called Maurice Picat who had become a broker of farming properties (*régisseur*). He arranged for the fulfilment of contracts for tenant farmers (*métayers*) and their families and, as such, was not always wholly popular. The Picat farm was a focal point for Robert Hébras when he was growing up. During Robert's formative years it was run by the Rouffanche family, and it was from this farm that many of the town's families bought their fresh milk, ladled into jugs by farmer Simon Rouffanche's wife, Marguerite.[4] As a boy, Robert only had to cross the street to go the farm where he would talk to the couple's two daughters, who were just a little older than he, while he waited. Robert also accompanied his mother to the *pêcherie derrière les Vies*, a wash house at the rear of the Picat farm to which his mother and he would push a wheelbarrow of laundry.

Oradour was a large village, some 13 hectares in size – large enough therefore to be considered a *bourg*, serving as a central hub and containing the town hall, schools and transport links. The wider municipality took in numerous hamlets and vast swathes of agricultural land worked by farming families who often rented their holdings on contracts of several years or less.

These people came to Oradour in order to procure certain supplies, but they were not dependent on it for survival. In the countryside, chickens were kept for eggs, and rabbits for meat and hides. The peasant farming families (*paysans*) were broadly self-sufficient, relying less on selling their products in the open marketplace than producing what they needed to consume and selling any surplus. Many *paysan* families baked their own bread, albeit sometimes only twice a month, traded amongst themselves, and many had cows for milk and cheese, also used alongside or instead of oxen as traction for transport and field work.

In the village itself, many families kept chickens and rabbits and produced their own vegetables in gardens. The monthly *foires* (trade fairs) brought the *paysan* families from the villages to a central spot where animal stock could be bought and sold, other purchases could be made, and small amounts of produce offered for sale. Fortunes would be discussed at one of the village's abundant watering holes.

There had always been *foires* in Oradour. A ruling by Charles IX in 1563 restricted them to four a year, although a market could be held every Monday. The royal decree set out where markets and fairs could be held in order to spread them out. A structure called *les halles*, a covered marketplace, was built close to the church so that trading could easily take place at the entrance to the village. Over the course of the year, merchants paid a proportion of their earnings into a fund run as part of the communal budget. Every hundred years the physical structure had to be renewed and, in 1903, 1,942 francs were paid for its reconstruction.

After 1808, trade fairs became monthly events, held on the fifteenth unless the date fell on a Sunday or public holiday, and the Oradour Monday markets were discontinued. On *foire* days the *paysans* would descend on the *bourg* in full force. One primary-school child, writing his response to the commonly set essay 'Describe a day at the Oradour fair', wrote:

> I went to the fair with my grandmother. There were lots of people and animals, calves mooing, horses neighing and pigs. A bit further on, I saw housewives buying butter, cheeses, rabbits, chickens and eggs. In one area some men were talking with each other, trying to sell their pigs.[5]

During the 1930s one of the popular eateries for farmers, particularly for those attending the monthly *foire*, was the restaurant run by Jean and Anna Desvignes. Men would gather around a single communal table to eat and drink: 'The mistress would serve a huge bowl of soup and bottles of red wine, and some men would do *chabrol*.' This meant eating the soaked bread first, then pouring the wine into the remaining soup in their dish. This was often followed by a cabbage salad, then by white beans, followed by a huge terrine of '*fromage blanc*'.[6] Anna died in 1936 and Jean, unable to continue in the hospitality business alone, turned the restaurant into a butcher's shop, subsequently taken over by his son Baptiste.

The animals were the focus of the *foire*. Early in the day farmers from neighbouring villages would descend on the town and compulsorily have their stock weighed on the village's *bascule*. From there, bovine stock would be taken to the green open expanse of the main *Champ de foire*, just a few steps away, while pigs and sheep were taken to the older marketplace and *les halles* in the lower village. It was there that the road from Limoges met another from the direction of Saint-Victurnien, an important neighbouring village of a similar size to Oradour, and the nearest railway link to Limoges and the industrial town of Saint-Junien.

Around both main areas of trading, bars and *débits* filled with locals who could enjoy a drink while comparing prices and cursing or praising their luck. In the lower village, set on a steep decline towards the water's edge and the old mill, visitors to the *foire* might buy and sell piglets under the shade of the open-walled *halles* and the ancient *chêne de la liberté*, whose leaves and branches gave respite from the baking summer sun. Visits to Oradour at other times would be primarily to access public or private services or occasionally to shop for clothes or hardware.

The self-sufficiency, bordering on autarky, by which most peasant farming families lived their lives would work well during the difficult times of occupation and restrictions that were to come. They were, however, built on already well-established rules of country living. Tenant farming families could rarely stay in one place for long. They went where there was work. The choice of farm was often put to them by the *régisseurs*, who often owned one or two farms themselves. Moves would take place around *Toussaint*, at the beginning of November, when the summer harvests had been completed and new crops planted. This period of *creux*, when farmers only had animals to take care of, was one of movement.

Paysan families also worked cooperatively, swapping tasks such as looking after a neighbour's herd of cattle in exchange for help when the major summer work season (*gros travaux d'été*) came around. Collecting potatoes in the fields and planting winter crops required extra hands. Such arrangements were not new but had proved particularly important when farms were short of men during wartime. French families were used to losing young men to national service but the First World War had provided a shortage of hitherto unknown proportions.

Farms dominated the countryside and its hamlets, but also dotted the edges of the *bourg* itself. As well as the Picat farm, several others were owned by a single landlord and rented out. One of these, located on the corner of the main *Champ de foire*, was run by two brothers-in-law – a common arrangement whereby labour was pooled, allowing women to run the household rather than having to work in the fields. In this case, Jean Senon's sister, Anne, was married to his own wife's brother, Jean Vergnaud. The previous generation was represented by Jean Senon's mother, Marguerite, whose husband, Léonard, had died in the early 1930s. In such cases two or even three generations of women could end up running the kitchen and household, allowing the men to work, and grandfathers could find themselves working in the fields with their sons or sons-in-law.

All this did not mean that the 1920s and early 1930s were idyllic for farmers in and around the region. Farms owned and run by families were suffering because an agricultural crisis had been born out of a lack of manpower. Machinery had been developed but most farm holdings in the Haute-Vienne were small and, since the soil of the region was not particularly fertile and cereal crops were never vast, the cost of equipment was too high given the meagreness of the return. What was grown made little money on the open market. Farms lacked capital to invest in machinery and short-term tenant farmers were certainly in no position to invest in improvements. The loss of a single hand on a farm would hurt a farming family's ability to earn and even, in the case of tenant farmers, to self-subsist. Market pressures were pressing farm-owning families who existed on a shoestring. In the Haute-Vienne it was not even the minimal amounts made by cereal crops that was hurting agriculture, but the severe dip in the price of animal stock for slaughter, especially given the price of rearing cows and pigs in the first place. This livestock, including the famous meat of Limousin cattle, was, for some larger farms, their main income source. Unemployment figures rose in the 1920s as the market for meat plunged and prices fell as a result. One socialist deputy called the situation '*la grande misère des campagnes*' ('the great misery of the countryside').[7]

A Well-to-do Village

In 1926, a journalist from Toulouse responded in his newspaper to a subscriber who lived in Oradour. The reader had sent in a tracing of a coin minted in 1909 in the image of Philippe, *Duc d'Orléans*, the exiled pretender to the French throne. La Flèche – the pen name of the Toulousain writer – gently mocks the reader's monarchism, aligning him with Charles Maurras, leader of Action française, the right-wing monarchist and anti-parliamentarism political movement. La Flèche clearly caricatures Oradour-sur-Glane as a well-to-do place where 'one can fish for crayfish in fresh, cool water or search for dark cep amongst the moss'.[1]

Before the First World War, Oradour had been a place of leisure and relative wealth, known for 'its pleasant countryside, its reputation for good dining and its proximity to Limoges'.[2] City dwellers with 'humble' tastes could arrive by tram and enjoy the quiet pleasure of Oradour's 'greenery and flowers' and 'meadows that fed reddish coloured cattle whose flesh was reputed', surrounded by bountiful orchards. There they might find the country folk 'proud to break up clumps of grateful earth, that dry spells had covered with moss'[3] and the rains with weeds, and for whom the numerous livestock that fed from the soil that they fertilised helped provide a '*joie de vivre*'. These people could 'enjoy in peace the profits of their labour'.[4] According to journalist Pierre Poitevin, 'before the war unhappiness was practically unheard of in Oradour. Each individual existed upon his work, and from the fruits of his labour. The trade fairs were large in size and played host to energetic buying and selling. There were few large fortunes, but affluence reigned in most homes.'[5]

First there was the right-wing idealism of the bourgeois class, the *châteliers*, owners of modest *châteaux*. These landed families were not rare in the area. Large houses and villas were dotted around the countryside, and certain surnames appear for centuries on municipal council lists. The Desourteaux family was one such family. The rather bourgeois Desourteaux home and medical surgery in which Paul lived with wife Marie was set back from the main road, opposite the village's tram stop. The couple employed domestic help – a capability that tended to mark out the middle classes in villages such as Oradour.

One of the two Dupic textile shops. During the monthly fair, shops displayed their range of products in the street. (Collection Benoit Sadry)

Some families, though not bourgeois, had built their land holdings over time using *régisseurs* (land agents), to help make money from the tenant system. Marriage between such families sometimes created considerable wealth. Marie Mosnier had been widowed since 1913 and, together with her daughter, owned a number of farm holdings in and around the *bourg*, as well as houses in the village itself. Not only did the farm on the *Champ de foire* on which the Senon family lived and worked belong to them, but they also owned the Masset or Villéger farm on the other side of the river. Marie's daughter, Marie-Louise, who had married a man named Louis Amédée Laudy, lived in Ajain, near Guéret. The couple, together with Marie, also owned a farm and barns near the *Champ de foire*, farmed by Jean Desbordes and known as *Chez Magnot*. One of its barns would become famous in the Oradour story as 'the Laudy barn'.

On the conglomeration's eastern side, agricultural holdings were separated from the village only by the Glane. From the tram stop at Puy-Gaillard, a number of small, family run-holdings were within a stone's throw. One of these – *Chez Gaudy*, owned by Guillaume Besson, of one of the village's textile merchant families – was rented out, as La Lauze was rented out by land agent Maurice Picat.

If Paul Desourteaux represented the right-wing, which included royalists and veterans, his greatest political opponent, Joseph Beau, represented a rising restrained socialism. The period was defined by a steady rise in the political power of the socialists, whose ideas sometimes rubbed off on peasant farmers. In the city of Limoges and the nearby industrial town of Saint-Junien, syndicalism had taken root at the beginning of the century. It developed rapidly during the 1920s and 1930s and seduced the workers of the countryside with talk of protection of the agricultural class at a time when they needed it. Socialism brought with it cooperative structures, at first welcomed by farmers who wished for some protection just as long as central government did not overplay its hand. In city suburbs, larger towns and villages, this also led to a pacifist outlook on the international front, as another war seemed almost unimaginable. At the end of the 1920s, a clear separation developed between the far- and centre-left. For communists, of whom there were a small but growing number in the countryside, the socialism of the SFIO represented the start of the right-wing. In the countryside, differences between the *petits* and the *gros*, 'those who worked and those who did not work such as curates, notables, landowners', asserted themselves at the ballot box. Joseph Beau was popular, and socialism continued to grow alongside anti-clericalism.

In the main, the farmers of the countryside around Oradour were only concerned by politics as far as its effects became apparent in their everyday lives. *L'abbé* Chapelle wrote in 1942 that, over the years, he had seen his parishioners 'remain indifferent in the face of events unless they directly affect them'.[6] But, as socialism became entrenched into the municipal council during the 1920s, the shoe was on the other foot. Not only had Chapelle been frustrated by the unwillingness of the socialist council to contribute to the upkeep and repair of the ancient church, but he had had to rely on 'the generosity of the Catholics and the resources of the local factories'.

The Way Home

Having served an exile imposed on him by his father, Emile Desourteaux brought his wife and their 7-year-old son André back to the family village in time for Alice to give birth to their second child, a daughter called Bernadette. In the early spring of 1932, they accepted the offer of Alice's father, socialist mayor Joseph Beau, to live at his home and run his grocery shop on Oradour's main street.

Joseph Beau had been widowed in 1910 when, at the age of 31, his wife Anne died giving birth to the couple's fifth child. The centrally placed grocer's shop and haberdashery was renamed the *Épicerie Desourteaux* by Joseph for his son-in-law. Emile and Alice's move back to Oradour was not without its difficulties, but the families coped well enough. Emile's brothers welcomed him and Alice back. André's two grandfathers were both important men in the community. Bitter rivals, they did not much like each other, but it was former shoemaker and grocer Beau who was politically more popular than the stern family doctor of the bourgeois right-wing, Paul Desourteaux. The breakdown of the 1935 election gives an indication of the relative popularity of the two men. Out of 552 *électeurs*, Joseph Beau won 351 votes, to 24 for Paul Desourteaux. A lifetime in municipal politics had, however, taught them diplomacy and compromise, and they never let their grandson sense their rancour.

Alice worked as the primary server in the shop and was a smiling, affable presence. Emile, meanwhile, looked after the not insignificant task of sales and deliveries in the surrounding hamlets. André, a small child for his age, helped out his mother in the shop, as did Bernadette once she was old enough. Another sister, Geneviève, was born in July 1936. The shop became a central meeting point and André soaked up all manner of conversation, be it scandal, rumour or local news, which he reported to his group of young friends that included Robert Hébras. The shop was situated next door to the girls' school, and André often peered over the windowsill into the playground.[1]

By the mid to late 1930s there were some twenty-two shops and twenty-six workshops of various descriptions which provided food and goods. It was enough that the villagers never had to travel to a bigger town, while also supporting the agricultural activity of the community at large. Textiles

Émile and Alice Desourteaux with their baby daughter, Bernadette, and young André. Once the second child was born, the family moved back to Oradour. (Collection André Desourteaux)

and dressmaking were particularly important. There were also several wheelwrights – vital because farmers relied almost exclusively on bovine traction. The community of Oradour was built on agriculture, and carts pulled by cows were still the most common way to transport goods. The business of the *charron* (wheelwright) was not only a skill passed from father to son across several generations but also essential to each community. In the early twentieth century one of Oradour's wheelwrights was former soldier Gilbert Chaleix who had set up his business after a long and distinguished military career. He died in 1914, just as the next conflict was beginning. His house and business bordered the road that began opposite the church and led north-east into the countryside towards the hamlet of Les Bordes, where his own father had run an inn. Gilbert had six daughters and no son to pass his skills on to. Anna, one of his younger daughters, was born in Oradour in March 1885. She began her working life as a schoolteacher but in 1906 she immigrated to the United States, taking with her 16-year-old Adèle, her youngest sister.

The girls joined their uncle, Pierre Chaleix. Since immigrating twenty-three years earlier, he had set up a charcuterie business among a community of European immigrants in New Jersey and married a German girl called Dora. It must have been an exciting adventure for 21-year-old Anna. The same year she arrived she married Ernest Mirablon, a Parisian fourteen years her senior and in the same business as her uncle. Three years later they had a baby boy, who they called Albert. Ernest and Anna ran a quality grocery store in the prosperous town of Paterson, which Albert would come to know as home. When, in 1917, Ernest went to France to fight for the land of his birth in the First World War, Anna accompanied her husband to Europe, taking their 8-year-old son with her. By the time Anna and 12-year-old Albert were listed on board *La Savoie* arriving back in New York on 16 May 1921, Anna was a widow.

Anna and Albert got back to Paterson in time for the wedding of her by then 21-year-old sister Adèle to Leo Pozzoni, who had lived with Pierre and Dora for at least a decade and was listed on the 1920 census as their grandson.[2] Adèle and Leo had two daughters before Adèle died in 1928. Anna and Albert, a bright young man who had completed his schooling in the United States, decided to return to France and set up home in Limoges in 1925, when Anna was 40 years old. In 1927 Albert was taken on by Crédit Lyonnais and in 1928 they travelled to the USA one more time to be at Adèle's side when she died. Albert did his military service and emerged as a *sous officier* in the reserve army. During this time he bought his first six-speed bicycle and became a dedicated cyclist while working at his other hobby, photography. Albert became fond of travel and an outdoor lifestyle while growing up in the United States, so he travelled Europe throughout the 1930s, taking many hundreds of pictures before he settled down, marrying Renée Foussat in 1938.

In the spring of 1944, Anna would move back to Oradour herself because she felt disturbed by Allied bombings in Limoges. There she would feel safe, being close to the cradle of her family. Her sister, Maria, still lived there, having decided not to travel to America with Anna and Adèle in 1906. Instead she had stayed and married Jean Lesparat who, after returning from the First World War, took over her father's wheelwright business. The couple had two children, a daughter, Renée, who married and moved away to Aixe-sur-Vienne, and a son, Fernand, born in 1906.

Fernand was a handsome young man and a good mechanic, but only too eager to be trained as a wheelwright by his father. After completing his military service, Fernand married 19-year-old Marcelle Grand in December 1931. Less than two years later they had a daughter, Monique, who grew to be a stunning girl with the glossy dark hair of both her parents. Fernand Lesparat and Albert Mirablon, first cousins, would remain close. Sometimes Albert would cycle to Oradour from Limoges to see his aunt and cousin.

As well as wheelwrights, most other businesses in Oradour were designed to support the agricultural community – blacksmiths, carpenters, joiners, stone masons, builders, well-diggers and dealers in grains and fertilisers. Some farmers had branched out in order to supplement their income. One of the general grocery stores as well as the firewood and charcoal merchant, Michel Avril, also sold petrol. One farmer, located just outside the village, had gone into the dealing of farming machinery while his wife brought in a little more money by fostering children.

The Entrepreneur

Each year, during the late summer days, just as school was beginning a new year, the village of Oradour would be overcome by the sweet aroma of warm apples. Wagons filled with the light green Limousin variety would pull into the village centre together with barrels made by coopers from Oradour or elsewhere. These peasant farmers had come to Oradour to get their fruit pulped.

Emile Redon was one of the village's entrepreneurs with an eye for money-making opportunities in every season. Sometimes he could be seen in a flat-bottomed barge on the Glane, extracting sand from the riverbank which he sold on to local builders. His first wife, a dressmaker named Marguerite, had died a month after giving birth to their daughter, Irène, in 1925. Emile, known as Milou, ran a grocery store and café alongside each other on the main *Champ de foire*. He was helped by his second wife Marie, who had been a conductor on the tramway before the death of her first husband, Jules Raynaud, in 1921. She had two sons, Pierre and Lucien, both of whom worked at the Thomas bakery. Teenager Irène lived with the couple and helped them in the *Café-épicerie*, in a barn next to which Emile had had the foresight to install a mechanical apple press.

After having their apples pulped and juiced, the farmers would lead their cow-drawn carts through the village and down to the bridge over the Glane where, twice a year for a period of about a fortnight, the patented distiller would be set up. Each farmer-customer would hand over enough wood to fire the gleaming copper machine as well as the necessary form from the Villatte *buraliste* (tobacconist shop), which also dealt with tickets and other such paperwork. With documents handed over, the apple pulp could be heated and distilled. As a measure of security and a guard against untaxed production of cider, the patented distiller – a Monsieur Roby from outside the village – would have to hand in the swan neck of the distillation machine when he was not on site. Cider was the drink of choice in the Haute-Vienne. Comparable with wine in its popularity, it was cheap to produce; Limousin orchards were plentiful and produced copious large, juicy, creamy-green fruit that lasted well.

Families had been forced to adapt during the manpower shortages of the First World War. Women and older children were forced to take on tasks on

Le Restaurant de la Promenade *owned by Mélanie Dagoury. The room she rented to* l'Avenir Musical *is above. (Collection Benoit Sadry)*

farms or in family businesses that otherwise would have been restricted to men. Additionally, economic circumstances required an element of diversification in order for family businesses to survive. On the western edge of the village, Mélanie Dagoury continued her husband's business as a supplier of cement and funereal monuments after his death in 1927. She also ran a café-restaurant known as *Le Restaurant de la Promenade,* and from 1933, rented out a large room above her workshop which served as a home for music lessons and performances by the local music group, *l'Avenir Musical.* Those attending concerts held under the auspices of the *Avenir,* including gala evenings, would traipse past the rather morbid gravestones, before being met by 'a vast stage towering over benches and chairs lined all along the white-washed walls. Several discoloured garlands tried their best to brighten up this festival room.'[1] Mélanie's daughters and son helped with her odd combination of businesses, and one of her daughters, Denise, also ran a dressmaking enterprise on the same patch of land.

Places to take a drink, sometimes referred to as *débits* or *éstaminets,* were plentiful in the village, but sometimes these small bars were add-ons to a main business. It was possible to get a drink at most grocery stores and, in some cases, women ran bars to supplement their husbands' work. Michel Avril's wife Adrienne looked after their café business while he primarily occupied himself selling wood and other fuels such as coal and petrol. His shop, with a fronting on to the main street, was located next to the Bouchole bakery and almost opposite the Thomas bakery – the perfect place for men to stop and have a chat over a drink. Not to be outdone, Maurice Compain's pâtisserie was also a café.

Diverse businesses might arise from the various interests of family members. Woodcutter François Brouillard ran a café and barber shop where his 67-year-old wife also made clothes. Lucien Morlieras owned and ran the *Café du Chêne* next to the church and *les halles*. It was one of the village's thriving meeting places, where the men played billiards or card games such as *belote*. It doubled as a barber shop and a hat shop, because Lucien's wife Catherine Morlieras was a *bonnetière*. As soon as she was old enough, daughter Irène looked after the café.

In Puy-Gaillard, on the eastern approach to the village from Limoges, widow Jeanne Mercier ran an *auberge* (hostel) where her daughter Marie, in her thirties, assisted while sewing gloves for the factories in Saint-Junien. Jeanne and her retired postman husband also ran a grocery store with their son, René. Retirement from a military career or a retreat from agriculture could lead to a less strenuous occupation in later life. Jean 'Torimo' Thomas and his second wife (sister of his first, for which the union required a presidential

The turning towards the cemetery. The Thomas bar, l'Éstaminet du centre, *is on the left, and the Villatte bureau de tabac is beyond.*

decree) was a retired farmer and veteran, and he ran a bar, *l'Éstaminet du centre*, on the main street, near the lower village.

No village was complete without its *recette buraliste*, a tobacconist with a sideline in tickets, stamps and stationery. In Oradour, the *buraliste* was called Pierre Villatte. He was no stranger to hard graft, having grown up working the fields with his father before completing his military service. With his wife, Mélanie, he had a daughter, Aimée, and a son, Amédée. During his time serving with the 107th *régimen d'infanterie* he badly injured his right leg and was finally sent home when it did not heal sufficiently. After returning to farm work, Pierre and his wife established their *bureau de tabac* in Oradour-sur-Glane in 1937.

A Future of Music

The *Radounauds* were rightly proud of *l'Avenir Musical* – the village's brass and wind orchestra. Inaugurated as a society in 1886 by some local musicians, it had grown gradually, becoming an official registered association fifteen years later. The society's events, always reported in local papers such as *Le Courrier du Centre*, dried up during the First World War, and struggled to get going again until the early 1920s. But throughout the 1930s the society thrived.

In 1933, concerts and practice were moved to the large *salle de musique* at the Dagoury residence. At this time, the association's president was the land agent Maurice Picat. Its musical director was Jean-Baptiste Tournier, a veteran of the Great War who lived in Limoges and worked at the town hall. Tournier came weekly to Oradour. He gave music lessons during the day and ran rehearsals for the society during the same evening. He would stay the

L'Avenir Musical. *Jean-Baptiste Tournier is in the centre, open-necked and wearing a dark cap. At his right shoulder is Maurice Picat and, alongside him, Paul Desourteaux.*
(Collection Marcel Thomas)

night at the Dagoury household and return to Limoges by the seven o'clock tram, ready to be back at work in the morning. Tournier had been an army musician and was a decorated veteran. He was extremely committed to music in Oradour and responsible for the growth of the orchestra into a respected entity. Portly, with white hair and a narrow moustache, he was well known among many youngsters to whom he delivered music lessons.

Jean Hébras played no instrument but rendered his services in whatever way he could, selling tickets on the day of events and performing other supportive tasks. He insisted that his son, Robert, show an interest in music and enrolled him in lessons with Tournier despite Robert's lack of interest and recent instatement in catechism classes. So, along with other boys and girls of the village, from whom Robert had heard nightmare stories about the complexities of music theory, Robert was sent to the *salle de musique* for lessons dryly known as *solfège*. These were held on Thursday, set aside by an 1882 law to allow for out-of-school religious instruction in a newly secular primary education system. Robert would have preferred to spend it playing marbles in the street. Instead he would climb the steps past the strange front courtyard shaded by lime trees, under which were stacked tombstones and crosses ready for the cemetery, to the *salle de musique*.

Like all students, Robert had to bide his time before touching any instruments. Early lessons were spent perched on chairs with their music theory books. If a child asked when they could try to play something, they were told by Tournier that, before playing, you had to know the theory. 'This', he insisted, 'would be like someone trying to read a book without knowing how to read.'[1]

The success of *l'Avenir Musical* stretched to travelling the country participating in and winning several competitions. The band consisted of thirty or so musicians and had outgrown other concert venues, such as the privately owned rooms that they had previously rented. A number of its players were not from Oradour or even the surrounding villages. To ensure an orchestra of the highest quality, Tournier brought in colleagues from Limoges. On the last Sunday of November each year, *l'Avenir Musical* organised a large celebration for the feast of St Cecilia, patron saint of musicians. As well as a concert, the event was followed by a shared meal and then a ball.

It was not the only musical society. The wine seller Léon Denis ran two others. The *Espérance d'Oradour-sur-Glane* was a youth band made up primarily of young women playing mandolins. Just as *avenir* means future, *espérance* means hope. It was inaugurated in November 1930 and, despite a rivalry between Denis, Tournier and Picat, the newer string group was intended to complement the much larger *Avenir Musical*. Administratively the *Espérance* fell under its banner. At the same time a smaller society called the *Rallye Mas Férat* formed, which consisted of a group of hunting horn players.

The village's theatrical society was attached to the musical association. Robert's two older sisters Odette and Georgette Hébras performed in short plays, along with other local girls including Lucien Morlieras's daughter Irène. During gala evenings, skits and short interpretations were followed by music by elements of *l'Avenir Musical*. For the young and inexperienced performers, nerves would build for weeks as the events got closer. The theatrical group was run by André Foussat, a well-respected miller who lived in the nearby hamlet of Les Bordes. He was thin with pronounced lips, bright eyes and protruding ears, and often took on the role of stand-up comedian under his pseudonym, Monsieur Dédée. Such gala evenings sometimes included touring guests such as circus acts, jazz bands, singers, vaudevillians and even magicians, but there was always a section of the evening reserved for *l'Avenir Musical* or its offshoots. Once the gala was over, a ball would take place, with music provided by a dozen or so musicians. The cost was included in the price of the ticket (between 3 and 5 francs), usually bought in advance from the tobacconist. Honorary members such as representatives of the *conseil municipal* got free entry.

Married women rarely attended bars or cafés, so all-consuming was their family role. For them, entertainment of any description outside of the home or homes of close friends was generally limited to formal occasions such as the village concerts and galas. Young women and men eagerly awaited the village *bals* (formal dances) that were held in the village from time to time. These were an extremely important element of their social existence. Younger women would usually be taken along by their mothers, and Marie Hébras took Odette and Georgette along herself. These events, accompanied by musicians drawn primarily from *l'Avenir*, would play for several hours straight. Venues had to be of a good size and were rotated between function rooms above *Hôtel Milord*, *Hôtel Avril* and, the Dagoury *salle de musique*. Dancers required stamina, with the events beginning around 3 p.m. and usually lasting late into the evening. Sometimes boys and girls not yet old enough to attend would do all they could to catch a glimpse of the young dancers, desperate for it to be their turn. Robert Hébras would stay at home with his father and little sister Denise, born in 1935. He recalled:

During the afternoon I sometimes sneaked up as far as the door at *Chez Avril* which, provided the weather was fine, would remain open. I would admire the dancing couples, looking forward to the day when it would be my turn to be able to go along.[2]

Printed flyers circulated and were displayed around the village when an event was going to take place, advertising a 'brilliant orchestra', with a prompt to 'tell your friends about it'.

'He Knows How to Teach'

Families in the surrounding hamlets depended on each other for material reasons such as the ability to get the foodstuffs they needed. Families of tenant farmers had to get on with each other because of the proximity of their homes, the need to take turns helping each other when harvest and planting season came, and also because of the transitory nature of the lifestyle. The children might gather to watch fields being harvested, or straw being cut. Each day, youngsters of a variety of ages who would play together in and around the dusty communal spaces often walked to school in small groups without adult accompaniment. In these tiny villages the same children would often be called on their return from school, or on their non-schooling days and holidays, to help their fathers and grandfathers in the fields.

An inspector to the classroom of the primary children in the early 1940s was scathing about the basic accommodation but noted 'with pleasure the cleanliness of the children who, for the most part, wear appropriate shoes, and whose physical state is good'.[1]

Most of Oradour's younger schoolchildren wore wooden *galoches* (clogs) typical of children in the region's countryside. Only a few would have moved on to boots. These clogs were made by the *sabotier* Jean Deglane, a tall man whose little workshop on Oradour's main street was visited by most local families. He was always seen in a leather apron, while his tools hung from a plank near his workstation. As well as *galoches* he made *sabots* – leather shoes with wooden soles. These were displayed on wires on the opposite wall and the floor was covered with sweet-smelling wood shavings. Once purchased, a child's *galoches* would need to be taken to a blacksmith such as Jean Baptiste Beaulieu, so that he could hobnail them in between shoeing cattle. The shoes would be left on a table in his forge on the corner of the *Champ de foire*, where they could be collected several days later ready to be worn to school.

No school existed in the village before 1830, at which point the municipal council took the decision to rent a small house near the church, paying 80 francs a year for its use. Unsurprisingly, attendance was low due to the monthly cost of 2 francs per pupil – a not insignificant sum in rural France at that time. In 1862, a house located in a more central position was purchased for 5,000 francs. Since numbers remained low, the single downstairs room was sufficient, while the upper floor served as the town hall.

Schooling in Oradour evolved rapidly when, in 1880, the Jules Ferry laws required all children to receive a basic education, free of charge. New properties had to be acquired or built so that every child could receive the same instruction. As a result of the removal of the monthly fee, even peasant families could send their children to school and were obliged to do so by law. Education had to be modernised, and localities had to be sufficiently spacious and equipped. The Limousin *patois* was outlawed and French had to be taught as part of a national curriculum. The municipal council had no option but to deal with the surge in numbers by constructing a new building in the upper village which was shared between the boys' school and the town hall. The house that had been bought in 1862 became the school for girls.

As the century turned, an infant school was established on a road opposite the church square that led towards the hamlet of Les Bordes. The building used had hitherto been the presbytery. During an inspection in the early 1940s the schoolroom was commented on as being 'too deep, dark with lighting on one side only [...] This room in the former presbytery', an inspector continued, 'should never have been accepted as a classroom.'[2]

One of the village's most experienced teachers, Léonard Rousseau, had begun his training in the midst of the First World War and was in his late forties by the years of occupation. During his military service he received the *Croix de Guerre* with a bronze star, having been shot in the chest while conducting a night-time operation in August 1915. He had also suffered an eye infection which impaired his vision, though it did not stop him completing his final year of teacher training once demobilised in 1919. He embarked on a series of placements east of Limoges, the area in which he had been raised with a twin brother, spending ten years at a school in Vaulry. Here he met his wife, Jeanne, and the pair had two children before he took up a position in Oradour as director of the boys' school, located opposite the town's tram stop.

A big, balding man with dark eyebrows, a strong face and a powerful voice, Rousseau was well respected in the village. As part of the conditions of his employment, he served as secretary to the mayor. He wore a tie without fail and an inspector commented, 'Monsieur Rousseau is a master at his work and fully informed. His years of experience permits him to lead his class with ease. He knows how to teach.' Jeanne taught the other boys' class and was also greatly experienced, though she struggled with her health. An inspector described her as a teacher who knew how to interest the children and get good results, but whose classroom was sometimes noisy.

As numbers grew to capacity in the 1920s and 1930s, the boys' school was improved. A covered yard was constructed to create space for classes, and a cinema projector purchased in an effort to modernise educational practice.

The municipality also decided that the time had come to expand its educational offerings. An area of land was bought behind the tram station, a stone's throw from the boys' school, where a new girls' school and infant school, a new town hall and four living quarters for teachers would be established, complete with central heating and an area of land for teaching agricultural skills. At a cost of 707,500 francs, the project was finally approved by the *conseil municipal* in October 1934, but was continually delayed as the economy suffered on a global scale. In 1936, future Resistance hero Jean Zay was Minister for Education in the left-wing *Front Populaire* and responsible for a new law that extended obligatory schooling from the age of 13 to 14. This had a susequent effect on pupil numbers. Plans for the new school, however, remained shelved and it would never see the light of day.

The housing of the pupils remained a frustration for teachers, municipal authorities and inspectors alike. The girls' school was cramped. The tiny playground shaded by two trees, into which André Desourteaux would peer from the grocery window next door, was pleasant enough. But inside, the space was insufficient for the two classes that were taught there. They were separated by a thin partition wall made of planks. The school was separated from the outside world by a large gate with pointed iron railings.

Andrée Binet taught the older class of girls preparing for their examinations. Originally from Nexon, she married Jean Binet in June 1936 before moving to Oradour to start her new job as deputy head of the girls' school that October. The job also included responsibility for the infant school. Andrée set about the task despite a pregnancy that would lead to the birth of her son Jean Pierre in April 1937.

Andrée began her teacher training in September 1932 at the age of 18. Her tutor commended her 'qualities of gentleness, kindness and education'. She was a 'well brought-up young girl, with a lovely personality 'who would 'make a conscientious teacher'. She embarked on a series of substitution posts before arriving in Oradour. An inspector commented in February 1937 that 'Madame Binet is an intelligent, gentle, hardworking schoolteacher with a desire to do well'.[3] A later report commented on her continued success: 'Preparations: regular and serious [...] Everything is planned, chosen, prepared in an intelligent way.'[4] In September 1939 an inspector commented that 'All in all, I am very satisfied with my visit to Madame Binet's class. She knows how to make all school subjects attractive. She is a good teacher who deserves our congratulations.' Andrée Binet would become headmistress in her own right in September 1941. She lived with Jean and their son in the village, in a four-room flat provided by the municipal council.

Just a Road Worker

Camille Senon began to appreciate her older brother far too late. However, by the time Raymond passed away on 26 June 1938, aged just 19, emaciated by tuberculosis, Camille had developed an extremely close bond with him. Born in May 1919, he was six years her elder and academically quite exceptional. He won a scholarship, keeping him away at school for long periods and depriving Camille of her brother's company. His next move was to be an *école normale*, teacher training college, and it was during the medical for entrance there that it was discovered he had contracted the devastating disease. This had happened whilst a boarder at the school for boys, preparing for the entrance examination. He would never recover, and his parents, Martial and Catherine, ploughed all the funds they could into his care. During his illness Raymond and Camille grew increasingly fond of each other. He helped her with her studies and was allowed to spend his final days in their home thanks to a local doctor who was a friend of the family. Camille helped her parents make Raymond's final days comfortable.

Camille and Raymond's father, Martial, was a war veteran who suffered from a chronic bronchial condition caused by a mustard gas attack in October 1918. His education had been limited by his family's need for him to work in the fields in the farm at which they were tenants near Oradour. Despite the Jules Ferry law which had made schooling obligatory, his was a not uncommon case of needs must. He only attended school during the winter months, when he was not needed for farm work. After doing his national service he was called up to the 63rd Infantry Regiment based in Limoges on 2 August 1914 and demobilised exactly five years later. His experience of war rendered him a pacifist for life. He had been appalled that soldiers were randomly chosen for execution following refusal of whole battalions to follow orders. In his own regiment a battalion had been made to watch as four soldiers were shot in Moselle in April 1915. The execution squad was chosen from new arrivals to the battalion. On 14 June 1917 he was one of a section of his regiment stationed in Mourmelon near Reims who refused to go back to the trenches. During this summer of 'mutinies', many of which were begun by left-wing militants in the ranks, more executions took place:

An image was carved into [my father's] memory; that of the commander of the 63rd who climbed down from the height of his horse to exhort them to take up combat again as part of the disciplinary procedures. He called them 'my children'. His face was sombre, his voice lightly trembling and sweat glistening on his cheeks.[1]

The only joy of his wartime experience came when he was granted special permission in October 1917 to return to Oradour and marry Catherine Chapelle from nearby Blond. He had been awarded the *Croix de Guerre* with bronze star for his bravery in helping to repel a German attack in August 1916, yet refused to recognise or even mention the medal for the rest of his life.

After demobilisation in August 1919, Martial returned to Oradour and struggled to find fulfilling work. For fifteen years he flitted between working as an agricultural hand, builder, worker in a paper mill and employee of the electric tramway company's expansion programme. In 1934 Martial sat an exam to become a road worker for the Haute-Vienne civil engineering service. During this time, the Senon family lived an itinerant life in the northern Haute-Vienne. They were rarely more than a few months in one place and Camille was sent to school in Le Dorat. Catherine helped with the farm work and sewed gloves, while Martial also received a small pension because of his injuries. They were a happy, loving family but life was not easy. Martial was desperate to return to Oradour, where his sister, Catherine, had married Lucien Morlieras. They had a daughter the same age as Camille and ran their café-cum-barber-shop-cum-hat-shop. Oradour-sur-Glane, was the 'cradle' of his family.

Camille was far less academic than Raymond but enjoyed her studies once her family had settled long enough in Le Dorat for her to concentrate. Her strengths were more practical than academic. However, Raymond's help had pushed her to perform better in her studies, and his death hit Camille very hard.

Martial's view of the world had rubbed off on both his children. He was a militant left-winger for the *Confédération générale du travail* (CGT) from 1934 to 1939 and a member of the *Section française de l'Internationale ouvrière* (SFIO) from 1913 to 1939. The events of the occupation years would move him closer to the underground Communist party. Raymond had been inspired to take up politics himself. Like their parents, both he and his sister had felt fulfilment through the success of the *Front Populaire* of 1936–38 – a left-wing coalition under the leadership of Léon Blum, who had briefly held governmental power. The likes of paid holidays, better levels of remuneration and solid unionisation had never before been seen. The Limousin was a region of strong leftist sympathies but, on a national level, the moderate SFIO had been

*Marie Marguerite 'Camille' Senon went on to
champion working rights, particularly for women.
(Collection Camille Senon)*

enjoying a surge replicated in larger Limousin towns with their own industries such as Limoges or Saint-Junien. In the countryside, agricultural workers
who had had to find winter work in the cities of the north had returned with
political talk from the factories and rail yards. This had fed into small towns
and villages such as Oradour, and socialist pacifist idealism had been the icing
on the cake. The breakdown of the 1935 list for Oradour-sur-Glane two years
before the *Front Populaire* came to power gives an indication. Joseph Beau had
wiped the floor with Paul Desourteaux.

In 1938, when France's economy stalled under pressure, the *Front Populaire*
and, very quickly, the Third Republic began to fall apart with international
politics a distraction. The right-wing 'establishment' had a ready-made scapegoat in communism and its leadership linked with Moscow and the Jewish
race. Anti-Semitism was already well ingrained into the French political class.
In September 1939, the country's president, Edouard Daladier, outlawed the
Communist party, driving them underground. Many communist militants
were rounded up and interned, sometimes under horrendous conditions.
Some who were known or suspected of militancy were kept under surveillance. In Oradour, Martial Machefer was fired from the very same paper
factory in which Martial Senon had temporarily worked, because he was
considered an agitator. He set up shop as a cobbler, and there were plenty of
others with whom he talked about his view of the world.

A Picture Postcard

As the 1930s were drawing to a close, the village was thriving. Card games, billiards or discussions on the issues of the day filled the smoky rooms and open terrace of the Morlieras-owned *Café du Chêne*, while Oradour's younger element tended to favour the *Café Central*, otherwise known as *Chez Brandy*. This was the family home of Eugénie Brandy, whose widowed father François Mercier lived with her brother Denis in Puy-Gaillard, just a stone's throw away on the other side of the River Glane. Eugénie's mother had previously run the café but had died at the age of just 27.

Chez Brandy, on a corner opposite *les halles* and the church, looked over the lower village. Eugénie's three daughters helped their mother in the café during their teenage years. Their war-veteran father, Amand, had been a carpenter but his health had been seriously affected by gas poisoning in combat. Briefly mobilised in 1939 to work in the construction of armaments in Châtellerault, he died in 1940 at the age of 43. Eldest daughter Andrée was employed to run the village tram stop, where she sold tickets and looked after the merchandise shed. Her youngest sister Antoinette helped her mother in the café and also sewed gloves for extra money, like almost all young women her age. Jeannine was the oldest of the Brandy girls, and she fell pregnant in the summer of 1939. She gave birth to her daughter Any in April 1940 and married the child's father, mechanic Aimé Renaud, a year later. Jeannine set up her own hairdressing business, *Chez Jeannine*, directly above the café, accessed from the road to Les Bordes. This gave Jeannine a degree of professional privacy while preserving the extended family unit so typical of the time. The Brandy girls were perhaps a reason why their mother's café was so successful and full of life.

One of the first buildings that passengers would see after disembarking the tram was the *Hôtel Avril*. Marie Avril, its owner and manager, had been widowed when she was 30 and had had three children by Joseph Lamige. Tragically, they had also lost two children under the age of 6. She married Pierre Avril at the age of 34 and for twenty-three years they ran the hotel together until his death. On summer weekends, pleasure seekers would come from the city and have a drink in one of the hotels, cafés or bars. They then might buy food from one of the grocers, especially that run by René Mercier and his mother in the lower village, before heading to the river or to the village's shops.[1] Some would rush to book a lunch table at the *Hôtel Milord* in the lower village. Léon Milord and his wife, Mélanie, were known not just for the quality of the food on offer, but also for their hospitality. The couple had two sons. The eldest, Théo, moved to Limoges where he worked on the railways. Younger brother Victor became a cook, but he also moved to Limoges where he and wife Mélanie started their own family after marrying in February 1939.

Those two main hotel-restaurants derived significant income between the wars as *hôtels de voyageurs* with a significant clientele of travelling salesmen who came to town to peddle their wares for a few days or so before moving on.[2] In Oradour so many women sewed gloves for the Saint-Junien factories or textile merchants that there was plenty of scope for travelling salesmen to sell items such as sewing machines and haberdashery supplies.

In February 1938, a newly married young pharmacist called Marcel Pascaud set up business in Oradour. The nearest dispensary was 8km away in Saint-Victurnien, with others further afield in Limoges or Saint-Junien. Pascaud's business filled a gap. Born in Charente in July 1912, Pascaud had studied in Limoges and then Toulouse, receiving his qualifications just one

The Champ de Foire *in the lower village. The* Hôtel Milord *was well known for its regional specialities. The handrails are in front of the café run by Eugénie Brandy and her daughters. (Collection Benoit Sadry)*

month before setting up his dispensary on the corner of the main street and the *Champ de foire*. The shop 'had a very nice appearance and was also very comfortable', while its handsome, dark-haired owner knew how to run a business with 'lots of competence and a great deal of availability'.[3] He was described by his professional association as a 'conscientious and honest pharmacist who has created a responsible and well-stocked business in an isolated part of the countryside'.

The pharmacy complemented the work of the village's two doctors, Paul and Jacques Desourteaux. The village's dental surgery was open just one day a week. It was run by Odette Regnier, who rented a two-storey property for the purpose. Described by a resident as a 'slender woman, in her radiant forties [...] she carried out her art with gentleness and patience, particularly with children'.[4]

Pierre Montazeaud, also a veteran of the First World War, was originally from Cieux in the Blond Hills. He had arrived in Oradour in 1924, three years after the birth of his daughter. He set up his solicitor business while his wife took on duties as postmistress. She retired in 1939. Her permanent replacement, Odette Boullière, appointed in November 1941, had grown up in Eymoutiers on the other side of Limoges. She was in her late thirties, childless, and saw the move as a fresh start. Her mother, Marie-Rose, came to join her and they lived above the post office, a smart standalone building next to the tram stop. Even then, travel around the *commune* was generally by foot or bicycle, though there were two mechanics' garages in the village. Carts drawn by cows and oxen were commonplace in the village as well as in the countryside. The people of Oradour knew that the electric tram was a blessing for their village, in some ways the lifeblood of their slightly inflated local economy and an unbreakable link to the outside world. Those with family members who worked on the trams could get free or reduced-price travel, so Oradour became a preferred destination along the five lines that left Limoges and covered the Haute-Vienne. People came to fish or bathe during the hot months amongst the flowing crystalline and well-stocked waters of the Glane.

City dwellers came to Oradour to relax, but some also came to shop. There were plenty of textile merchants and dressmakers. Léonie Dagoury made dresses next to her mother's café and cement business. In the lower village, the Alsace-born Albertine Ramnoux, née Zeller, kept a shop supplied with textiles from her father, a cloth merchant. In the heart of the village, near the boys' school and the *Champ de foire*, the war veteran Jean Dupic ran *Chez Dupic tissus et confection*, assisted with the accounts by his wife Marie. Inside 'was a large, well-lit room with a huge, light wooden counter that was used to display and cut fabrics. Behind that, all sorts of coloured fabrics were stacked on a high shelf. Suits, raincoats and velvet jackets hung from hangers, like disjointed puppets.'[5] Jean Dupic's father had been a tailor and cloth merchant and his brother François also had a business in Oradour near to the Dagoury café. François had returned from the First World War in 1915, having lost his right eye. He was awarded the *Croix de Guerre* and named *Chevalier de la Légion d'honneur* ten years after marrying Jeanne, who came from the Charente region.[6] Another family, headed by Guillaume Besson, ran a textile shop in the centre of the village while renting out their family farm to tenants.

Customers could buy wool from a well-known spinner called Jules Leblanc, whose wife Léontine was a seller of linen. There was a tailor shop run by father and son Jules and Paul Santrot, and a well-established cobbler in François Brissaud. Hats could be bought from Catherine Morlieras' *bonneterie* adjoined to the *Café du Chêne*, and shoes from Jean Deglane. There were barbers and hairdressers, grocers and wine sellers, a pâtisserie and several bakers, a butcher-charcuterie and a hardware store.

At the end of the 1930s there were a total of around 150 buildings in the village, including 'several modern shops, some stylish villas and also bourgeois houses'.[7] There were no factories but an array of artisans and traders worked in their own workshops or shops. Some lived elsewhere and came to Oradour to work. Builder Mathieu Borie, for example, travelled each day from Saint-Junien. The village of Oradour was home to only about a quarter of the inhabitants of the *commune*. There were opportunities to run businesses while living outside of the *bourg* itself. The Mercier family, who ran their grocery store in the lower village, lived over the river, a kilometre or so away, in a farmhouse where they also had a small café-bar. Other people made a living in whatever way they could. For example, with rabbits being kept by most farmers and some villagers for meat, one *commerçant* would go around the village and its surrounding hamlets collecting rabbit fur to sell on for use in the manufacture of clothing. Another knocked on the doors of houses selling salted fish from a basket.

Mobilisation

On Saturday 26 August 1939, a local weekly Rochechouart news-sheet called *L'Abeille de Saint-Junien* carried a small advertisement on its second page:

> We remind you that tomorrow is the grande Frairie d'Oradour-sur-Glane, for which we have already given you the programme.
> May we add that the prizes for the cycle race are as follows:
> 120, 80, 60,40 30, 20,15,15,10,10
> Entrance fee (3 frs and licence number) to the *Café de la Terrasse* in Saint Junien, and at M. Dupic, Oradour-sur-Glane.[1]

The programme published the previous week had promised the normal two days of events including fireworks, hot-air balloons and the traditional balls, lasting into the night. An extra tram for Limoges was advertised, laid on at 23.30. It warned: 'The committee does not take responsibility for accidents that might take place at the fair.' A great occasion was once again promised in Oradour.

The following day, the Sunday edition of the regional paper *Le Courrier du Centre* announced that the event would be organised for a later date. Many of the floats and stalls that had been set up in the lower village would remain in place and empty for months to come. *L'Avenir Musical* had given its final concert on 12 August on the *Place de l'église*. Music would have to pause in Oradour.

War against Nazi Germany was declared on 3 September, just over twenty years after peace had resumed. It was unthinkable. The news hit hard. Most of the musicians were of fighting age.

Robert Hébras was 14 when it happened: 'When the town crier beat his drum and announced that war had been declared, I witnessed grown men and women cry. My own mother was disconsolate because she knew that she had two brothers who would have to go.'[2] Jean Depierrefiche, a blacksmith who doubled as town crier, gathered the people to various crossroads in the town where he broke the news of the dreaded *mobilisation générale* (general draft). Posters had already appeared on the doors of the town hall and garages. Peasant farmers, tradesmen, shopkeepers, the haves and have-nots, knew that their lives would be changed yet again as 'Depierrefiche began his recital that plunged the *Radounauds* into despair'.[3] Hébras recalled a 'sadness in the town. Seeing men making their way to the little station on foot with their small suitcases to get onto the tram that would take them to Limoges.'[4] Word spread quickly and, over the coming days, each time an evening tram passed, the children of Oradour would watch the faces of called-up men as they trundled along the *rue Emile Desourteaux*, lethargic, sad and uprooted. For those left behind, who had spent twenty years wishing for anything but war, a feeling of fatalism set in.

Within weeks, rumours circulated that conditions on the front were nothing like two decades earlier. Instead of muddy, squalid, trenches filled with human debris and well-fed rats, word came back of the relative comfort of life on or behind the Maginot line. This fortified defensive wall in the north-east of France, supported by modernised underground caverns, was deemed unbreachable. If anything was to hurt the boys, the rumours and letters implied, it would be boredom as a protracted phony war played out. Oradour's wool merchant Jules Leblanc sold more of his wares than ever as women stocked up to knit pullovers and socks to send to their men at the front. The *Radounauds* were convinced that this was to be a quick war that would likely not last until the spring.

Just as before, wives, daughters and mothers stepped up and took on new work and familial roles. Gabrielle Bouchoule's baker husband, Léopold, was absent so she filled in the gaps in labour as best she could. This was excellent news for Robert Hébras. Having set his heart on becoming a *pâtissier*, he had secured an apprenticeship with the only one in town, Maurice Compain. But the opportunity disappeared when it became clear that bread would be in greater demand than cakes and restrictions were announced. Marie Hébras was offered the position at the Bouchoule bakery for her son and immediately accepted it for him.

Evacuees

By the summer of 1939, 2,257 Spanish republicans fleeing General Franco's new regime had come to the Haute-Vienne and been dispersed into communities open to the idea of welcoming these victims of fascism. Oradour and its surrounding villages had seen a few new arrivals including women working menial jobs in the village's hotels who were hardly noticed. But the advent of war would change Oradour forever, as it set in motion a well-planned operation in which large swathes of northern France – areas in which the French generals had calculated most fighting would take place – were evacuated. New waves of evacuees and refugees would stifle the breezy, laid-back lives of the *Radounauds* in myriad ways.

Articles had begun to appear in the local *L'Abeille de Saint-Junien*, taking up the space previously allotted to local events and fairs. One, in the 9 September edition, read:

Regarding refugees

A large number of refugees have just arrived in Saint-Junien, coming from Schiltigheim, near Strasbourg, and some of them speak only the Alsatian patois. It is to be remembered that these unfortunates are excellent French people; that they have a right to your respect and compassion; that they have had to abandon their belongings in circumstances made particularly painful due to the proximity of the fighting.

It would be very regrettable if our compatriots, at a time of great distress, feel further pushed away, accused or even bothered because they speak a dialect which resembles German. It is possible to speak German and be 100% French. This, let us not forget, is the case for our refugees.[1]

The inhabitants of Schiltigheim, a suburb of Strasbourg, had found themselves at Saint-Junien and its nearby *communes*. Schiltigheim's temporary town hall was set up at numbers 8 and 10 Place de la République, Saint-Junien. Officials drew up lists once whole families had been dispersed, squeezed into habitations of varying quality and comfort. Families could claim financial benefits based on whether members were living together or apart, and what their outgoing costs would be. Every affected *commune* had its list, including Oradour-sur-Glane which was chosen to accommodate 400 people from Schiltigheim. At the same time, functionaries called on businesses and farmers to bring 'offerings' to town halls – cattle, beans and pulses – to feed the French army in the war that was to come. Though payment would take some time, the government assured farmers that if this was done in the month of September of their own accord, their contributions would be recorded and assured of a fair price.

Madeleine Wolf travelled to Oradour from her home in Schiltigheim with her parents and sister, setting off on foot, luggage piled on to a cart. After a long voyage by truck and by train to Limoges, they arrived in Oradour via the tramway. They were not the first from their town to arrive and they were met by one Monsieur Georges who took them to their lodgings in a hamlet outside the main *bourg*. They were shocked by the standard of accommodation that awaited them: 'There was no heating in his home and that was a particularly tough winter. So Monsieur Depierrefiche, the ironmonger, with whom we became friendly, installed a wood burner.'[2] Over the coming months Madeleine's father took on work in the fields, under the employ of the David family, who lived nearby. Madeleine did some work with the pastor Charles Klein, who had also been evacuated to the area from Schiltigheim: 'I went around visiting people in the parish to see if there was anything that they needed.' Once a week she would walk to a farm near Orbagnac, 4km south of Oradour, to see a family named Boulestin and pick up butter, milk, eggs and other supplies.[3]

The Schiltigheim group included Emile Neumeyer, a 16-year-old boy who wanted to become a theology student and agreed to help *l'abbé* Chapelle in Oradour's *Église* Saint-Martin. Emile was the youngest of four children and arrived with his parents and two sisters, Odile, eleven years his senior, and Marie-Louise, who was approaching her eighteenth birthday. His 31-year-old brother, also a theology student, had not travelled with the family. Initially they were put up in a new building near the church and the adjoining presbytery. When other refugees came the following spring, most of the family was invited to move in with Chapelle. They had developed a close bond with the ageing priest, who lived alone. Emile and Odile stayed on before Emile departed for theology college. Odile took up a role as both a housekeeper and church warden.

The refugee situation led to shortages. Even as the northern evacuees arrived in the Haute-Vienne, local authorities reported having issues finding sufficient meat, coffee and sugar for them. In December 1939, the Third Republic government introduced additional restrictions to those introduced earlier. For example, on Fridays, the sale and consumption in restaurants of meat and charcuterie was prohibited. The men on the front, it was claimed, needed such produce more than the young, female or elderly population left behind. In March 1940, in the middle of the phony war when serious fighting was yet to break out, confectionary shops and *pâtisseries* were ordered to close three days in the week, while the sale of wine and other alcohol was capped to four days a week. Restaurants were to limit how much food they sold, and restrictions were placed on how much pastry, chocolate and bread could be produced. The following month a compulsory rationing scheme was announced. It became clear that most consumables, including clothes, would be rationed. The government announced through newspaper articles that the quantities allowed would be determined by age and occupation. Central heating was banned between April and October inclusive, and hot water was only to be used three days per week. The ability to source fuel such as wood, coal or even petrol would become vital during the winter months and this put the residents of Oradour at an advantage over the residents of cities such as Limoges or larger towns such as Rochechouart or Saint-Junien. Even so, the presence of the evacuees put an immense strain on the community.

Turmoil

France had been in a state of political turmoil prior to war with Germany. The 1920s had seen a succession of either failed coalition governments, or right-wing administrations. A shift to the left had culminated in the *Front Populaire*, a coalition led by Jewish politician Léon Blum that included the French Communist party, the socialist SFIO and the radical-socialists. Its election success reflected France's rejection of the European trend for fascism and promised social reforms on a hitherto unheard-of scale. That came crashing to an end in 1938 due to a resurgence of the right wing over affordability of work place reforms in the context of a European depression, the Spanish Civil War and France's refugee policies. In 1938 France's economy groaned under the strain of the forty-hour week and the senate rejected *Front Populaire* policies, regarded as socialist experiments. Edouard Daladier, leader of the Radical-Socialist party who had served as Blum's Minister of National Defence for two years, became head of government on 10 April. He changed direction, ending the *Front Populaire*. The weight of the senate had shifted right of centre and were attracted to Daladier who proposed to rule by decree and return to more nationalistic policies, greater productivity and increased rearmament. *Front Populaire* policies had, during the previous two years, been well received, but when the government crumbled in 1938, it was Blum, the left and communism who faced the blame.

The right wing also singled out Jews, pinpointing Blum for particular attention. Daladier introduced some repressive policies regarding immigration from Spain and the entrance into France of foreign Jews. On the international front, Blum's unwillingness to stand up to Franco or Hitler was repeated by Daladier, who was a signatory of the Munich Agreement in September 1938. But the following year he banned the Communist party, arresting militants. The right-wing press pushed the idea of a nation's integrity under threat from Jewish refugees coming from Germany and Eastern Europe. According to their narrative, the Spanish refugees were the tragic result of a civil war in which Blum had failed to intervene, whereas the arriving Jews were painted as self-appointed victims of a European war that they had themselves unleashed.

The communists were equally put forward as war mongers.[1] Daladier regarded the Soviets as a greater threat than Nazi Germany to France's future.

His government fell in March 1940, and his former Finance Minister Paul
Reynaud took over. Reynaud, whose position was untenable from the start
due to overwhelming pressure from the right, was no appeaser but the Battle
of France broke out just two months after his appointment.

In mid-May, German tanks breached the Meuse and wound through the
forest of the Ardennes, circumnavigating the concrete might of the Maginot
line. The world, and the French general, looked on amazed as the long
phony war became a nightmare for the French forces, as well as the British
Expeditionary Force, both of which were surrounded and pushed north. The
Dunkirk evacuation would lead to resentment from the British public who
felt that the French had failed militarily and given in to panic. The French felt
that Britain had acted valiantly only in the efficiency of their surrender. Not
without reason, the French army had believed itself to be one of the strongest
in the world – a belief shared even by Hitler. The courage of its soldiers could
not be doubted, nor the quality of its hardware. Its defeat came in part from
a refusal by its generals to modernise during the inter-war years. Its organisational structure and reliance on an army of reserves, combined with poor
military planning and communication, led to many breaches. It was too far
gone – punch-drunk and against the ropes – to resist.

Exodus

One month earlier a car had set off from *rue de Sébastopol*, Roubaix. It was filled to bursting with two brothers, Raymond and George Coppenolle, both in their late fifties, their 60-year-old sister Berthe, her business partner Jeanne Crombé and Jeanne's daughter Jeannette, who was engaged to be married to George's son, Raymond. Berthe and Jeanne were both widows. Berthe's husband Eugène had died in 1919 when just 39 years of age and Jeanne's husband Victor had fought in the First World War before being stationed in Casablanca. Young Raymond had been called up to fight and spent the next few years in a prisoner-of-war camp. Despite an age difference of nine years, the women were firm friends and had run a lingerie shop together in the city for a decade. The passengers were travelling light, unable to fit much luggage into and on top of the car. They had already decided to head west to Nantes.[1]

The four senior passengers had all lived through the occupation of Roubaix, a small city very close to the Belgian border, twenty years previously. During the long, cold winter of 1917 and 1918, the Roubaisiens had been forced to listen to the sound of guns firing on the front line, just 20 miles away. As Germany expanded its rail network, key to its war strategy, forced labour gangs had been rounded up from Roubaix, Lille and the nearby northern industrial towns. All youths of 16 years or more were sought by the feared green-uniformed *Feldgendarmerie*, who were always accompanied by Alsatian dogs. They went street by street searching for manpower to install railway lines, dig out trenches for telephone lines or barbed wire, or collect in crops from the southern Ardennes. In the city itself, families huddled in the cold, protected in the damaged buildings by whatever covers or coats they could gather. Nobody felt safe. Beds and furniture were burnt for firewood by the German army. In a city that had been renowned for its textiles during the nineteenth century, supplies had become rare. Families ate one meal a day, if at all. The Roubaisiens had known that to survive they should stay still. It had been a miserable existence.[2]

In May 1940, German troops had once again crossed into Belgium and France. This time, the Coppenolle siblings wanted to take their nearest and dearest as far from the danger zone as they could. The socialist mayor of Roubaix and MP Jean Baptiste Lebas was amongst those to recognise the desperate need to flee. This was a man who had been interned by the German authorities during the First World War. Heroically he had refused to hand over all 18-year-olds for forced labour. He would make his mark in the Second World War too, returning to Roubaix in a matter of months to play his part in the French Resistance.[3]

During the mass exodus south, French, Dutch, Belgian and Luxembourgish refugees did all they could to move slowly along blocked roads. Some northern cities such as Lille, whose population had reduced by 90 per cent, were quickly filled with refugees from Belgium who found that they could go no further and had to stay despite cut electricity and water lines.

The roads were packed with refugees and retreating soldiers but, after a few days, the Coppenolle family arrived in Nantes, their intended destination. Raymond was already feeling restless. He knew that the Germans would very shortly catch up as they looked to occupy the north and the French coast. As a group they decided that they had to head south.

They joined the many others on the roads. The journey was exhausting and uncomfortable, but at least they had transport, unlike most of the 8 million other refugees heading in the same direction. They arrived in Saint-Junien within a week of leaving Roubaix and liked its relative size and proximity to the city of Limoges. For several days they tried to settle in but could find nowhere permanent to stay. During their search another place was recommended to them – a place where one or two other families from their part of France had apparently already found homes. It was just 12km away and called Oradour-sur-Glane.

The Coppenolle car rolled into the centre of the quiet village and they sought out Mayor Joseph Beau, an SFIO man just like the mayor of Roubaix. Beau and others in the village were happy to help, despite the strain on the village's resources given the population displacement of the previous months. There was a lack of ready space but the Schiltigheim experience had prepared the town hall and villagers for the unfolding situation.

A few months later, Raymond and George Coppenolle drove their car back to Roubaix, but their sister Berthe and her friend and business partner Jeanne Crombé stayed behind. They had fallen in love with the beautiful Limousin countryside, its charming people and the slower pace of life. Jeanne's daughter, Jeannette, who had been a primary teacher in Roubaix, stayed too. The two widows and Jeannette decided that they would try the farming life, knowing that it would be hard, but it would also be peaceful and far from the horror of occupation, bombardment and forced labour. They would be away from their friends and family, but they would make new friends in Oradour. They had never felt more optimistic and safe.

The Road

During that exodus in the sweltering spring and early summer of 1940, swathes of southward-bound refugees clogged up the roads. French troops were also in retreat from the north, abandoning out-of-fuel military vehicles and leaving arms behind. Some of these arms were picked up by the likes of Marc Parrotin, a future Resistance leader in Creuse who stored them for future use. He described what he saw on 15 June 1940: 'Columns of vehicles of all types blocking up the highways, thereby paralysing the last remaining military units that were still combat-ready, but which had no more appetite for it.'[1] Parrotin and a friend collected little more than a few rifles, bullets and the odd rusty musket but he took pains to hide them in his vegetable garden.

Alfred Barthélémy, a southerner by birth, also arrived in Oradour during the *exode* of 1940. He brought with him his wife, Marcelle, his mother-in-law, Emilie, and son, Roger. Alfred was a painting contractor who also specialised in glazing and mirrors. He and Marcelle, the daughter of a musician in the orchestra of the *Opéra-Comique*, had run a business on the right bank of the Seine in the 1st *arrondissement* of Paris, some 4km from their home in the 18th. On the declaration of war, their employees were called up. Sensing what was to come, they shut up shop and spent the next ten months with Marcelle's parents just east of Tours in Montlouis-sur-Loire, during which time Marcelle's father passed away.

On Sunday 16 June 1940, six days after Roger's fifteenth birthday, and two days after the German army had rolled into the deserted streets of Paris, the family joined the mass of people heading south. Unlike the Coppenolles, they had the luxury of two motorcars – Alfred's and Emilie's. They decided to head for Libourne, near Bordeaux, but found the roads blocked at Saint-Germain-de-Confolens in Charente. They changed direction and finally ended up in Oradour-sur-Glane. While there they were greeted by the town's *tambour* who beat his drum to signal that everyone was to stop where they were and travel no more, as the French government had come to peace terms with Germany. The family were fortunate enough to find a home in the hamlet of Les Bordes and, despite a strong urge to get back to Montlouis-sur-Loire, they remained.

Throughout May and June, shortages in the towns became more acute. As well as wood and coal, a lack of petrol saw vehicles stranded on the roads.

The millions of newcomers put a massive strain on shopkeepers who could not get what they wanted along the supply chain. Prices rose significantly and, even in the agricultural south, wheat was in short supply. A new method of securing food became more prevalent for town and city dwellers. They went straight to suppliers, such as farmers or woodcutters, to get what was needed while cutting out the middleman of the shopkeeper or market trader.

The spring of 1940 brought refugees not just from northern France and the Low Countries, but also Parisiens such as the Barthélémy family, who were fleeing out of fear of bombing and what occupation by the Nazis might hold for them. Many more were Eastern Europeans fleeing the Nazis because, as was the case for Jewish families or other 'undesirables', they were trying to get to the so-called free zone and escape persecution. The final governments of the Third Republic had done all they could to lay blame for France's military disintegration on the left, on communists, Jews, Freemasons and any other scapegoats that could be found for what the right claimed to have been a morally bankrupt regime. They singularly failed to recognise the inadequate preparation of France's tactics nor its outdated modus operandi. Instead they were about to hand one of those same generals responsible for the outdated state of the French miiltary complete charge of France's dealings with its new occupier.

Reynaud's government had fled to Bordeaux via Tours when it was clear Paris could not be defended. Once there, he tried to persuade the Cabinet that France could continue. General Charles de Gaulle, who had been pro-moted to Under-Secretary for War and for whom Reynaud had great respect, went to Britain to negotiate a continuation of the fight with Churchill. Under the increasing weight of opinion of his senior ministers that an armistice was the only option, Reynaud offered his resignation to President Albert Lebrun on 16 June 1940 and power was handed to a group of military men headed by commander-in-chief Maxime Weygand and Philippe Pétain, who by then was 84 years old, one of Reynaud's senior ministers and a highly decorated and celebrated general of the First World War.

The following day Marshal Pétain made a speech to the nation using a mixture of religious phraseology and a trembling yet solemn voice in which he made a 'gift' of his person to guide the country. He announced that he intended to request an armistice and called on all French people to lay down their weapons. A cessation of violence was welcomed by a host of politi-cians and the vast majority of the French population. France's ignominious defeat was sealed when Hitler ordered the same railway carriage in which Germany's 1918 surrender was signed to be reused in the Compiègne Forest.

On 22 June 1940 generals signed the armistice agreement which imposed the terms of Germany's occupation on the French, which would come into effect three days later. France's army was to be restricted to 100,000 men and the zone that would be militarily occupied was larger than even Vichy's top politicians had expected, extending from the Spanish border along the western coast, widening further north and taking in the northern coast too. The Haute-Vienne fell on the other side of a heavily guarded border called the demarcation line. That zone would remain unoccupied and contained the spa town of Vichy, very near the city of Clermont-Ferrand in the Massif Central, where the French government would be based. A small French victory would arise from the negotiations. They had maintained the Mediterranean coastline and access to their overseas territories in Africa, in which Hitler showed little interest. On 10 July, France's *députés* and *senateurs* met at Vichy's casino and voted full powers to Pétain. France's defeat had led to the end of France's Third Republic and with it went parliamentary democracy, to be replaced by an authoritarian regime.

Pierre Laval, a former barrister from the Auvergne, had risen to the position of prime minister on two occasions in the first half of the 1930s. He began his career as a socialist before abandoning the party at the end of the First World War and becoming an independent socialist. An excellent negotiator, he was also keen on ensuring peace, but in doing so was happy to negotiate with Mussolini, Stalin, the British or whichever foreign power appeared to be France's best hope as a beneficial partner. Increasingly discouraged by parliamentary blocks on his policies and governments changing rapidly during the final years of the Third Republic, he became contemptuous of parliamentary democracy. The 1940 war resulted from a series of policies that he vehemently opposed, and subsequent defeat enabled him to claim a loud voice first at Bordeaux, then in Vichy. Pétain and Laval did not like each other much and clashed on an array of policies, but the older Pétain was, for Laval, a good fit for an autocratic ruler who would come across as a spiritual leader. Both men would come together over their view of what France should become and it was Laval who, behind the scenes, ensured that Pétain was voted full powers in July 1940.

When the war ended Robert Hébras, who was nearly 15, had no particular memories of it: 'It just happened, like that. The war was finished, and it was Pétain who was in power.'[2]

'A Surly Man of Great Pessimism'

Ordinary people saw little immediate change with the passing of power to Pétain. For them the procurement of food for the table or fuel for the winter was the main concern. Pétain did not barge his way to power, nor was he voted in, having been forthright with a promise of authoritarian rule. Having first served under Reynaud, the vote by parliamentarians to award him full powers was overwhelming. Newspapers ran campaigns under the slogan '*C'est Pétain qu'il faut*' (It's Pétain that we need) because his reputation preceded him. At the beginning of 1940, of the twenty-three elected *députés* and *senateurs* for the Limousin, taking in the Haute-Vienne, seventeen were of the left and had been sympathetic to the *Front Populaire*. When the opportunity came to vote on whether to pass full powers to Pétain on 10 July 1940, only three of these voted against, two from Creuse and one, Léon Roche, from the Haute-Vienne. Roche represented the *arrondissement* of Rochechouart under the banner of the socialist SFIO, and would become active with early Resistance in 1941.

The marshal was 84 years of age when the armistice was signed – just the beginning of the months-long process of preparing a lasting deal with Germany. He was widely adored. His image became a reassuring presence on everything from coins to school walls, mayoral offices to shops and restaurants. The majority of the public supported him, a true leader after France's years of chaotic democratic governance. Many were taken by his grandfatherly image, white moustache and piercing blue eyes. His voice may have been shaky, but people all over the country listened intently believing that he had their best interests at heart. How could he not? After all, this was the wartime hero of Verdun where, in 1916, his choice of conservative and defensive tactics had saved many lives.

Most veterans of the Great War had positive views on him: a compassionate leader whose ideas on rotating troops at the front had helped the French army continue to fight. Jean Hébras had fought in the Great War and his outlook was in line with many of his fellow veterans. 'People were not unhappy that the war was finished and that it was the Marshal who was in power because they had memories of him from the 1914–1918 conflict and they respected him,' said his son, Robert.[1] Some of those who had experience of working closer to the real man had a different view of him. This included Charles de Gaulle, who had been involved with him politically in the final days of the Third Republic, the two men having known each other for some time. De Gaulle knew that the French military strategy backed by Pétain in 1940 had been outdated and doomed to failure, but he knew Pétain as a surly man of great pessimism when it came to warfare. That pessimism and defeatism proved costly in June 1940, just as it had in 1918, and it was an attitude that spread like a virus.

Camille Senon had just turned 15 when the armistice was signed. Her father, Martial, still plagued by bronchial problems from mustard gas in the trenches, was apoplectic with rage. Despite being a confirmed pacifist, Martial was not so much angry at the armistice as the transfer of full powers to Pétain. Camille was shocked at her father's fury. Like de Gaulle, Martial Senon was concerned about Pétain's personality traits. Senon had lived through the 'mutinies' of 1917 which Pétain had later boasted of having subdued: 'My father had very bad memories of Marshal Pétain during the war […] because there were soldiers who refused to go to the front and Pétain had them shot as an example. My father was absolutely against Pétain.'[2] In June 1940, it was as if Pétain was now doing that for which former comrades had been sent to their deaths. The hatred was plain to see. Camille saw her father disturbed by events and his own memories, unable to sleep: 'He would call out Pétain's name in rage. "And the rats! And the lice! And the booze handed out before each assault. Us infantrymen were never any more than cannon fodder!"'[3]

The sentiments of de Gaulle, like those of the much less-celebrated tenant farmer Martial Senon, were not widespread. The situation in which France found itself was accepted in a manner reflective of the mood throughout the country as a whole. That mood dipped in the village of Oradour when news came via monthly lists that around twenty local men had been taken captive at the end of the hostilities. Germany had retained 1.8 million French prisoners of war. This, together with casualties of the conflict and the war of 1914–18, meant that there was a deficit of men. Families wanted their menfolk returned and Pétain promised this in good faith, having received reassurance from Hitler that this would be part of the agreement between the countries.

In August 1940, a gathering took place in the *Café de Bordeaux* in central Limoges. Led by Armand Dutreix, a local businessman, Freemason and veteran of the brief 1940 conflict, all participants had decided on action but were, at that moment, far from certain what they could do. Nobody really knew how to organise themselves into a coherent group, nor what their actual aims were. How that diverse group of people found each other is unclear. It would be mid-1941 before Dutreix developed links with a Resistance group called *Libération-sud* based in Lyon. The development of a clandestine press would prove to be key to the development of future Resistance networks. Albert Mirablon, the American-educated Frenchman whose family were from Oradour, was present at that meeting.

'Maréchal, Nous Voilà'

Pétain shook Adolf Hitler's hand at Montoire-sur-le-Loir on 24 October 1940, thereby beginning a period of cooperation with Nazi Germany. A propaganda push meant that a cult hero was elevated to an almost godlike status. Pétain appealed to everybody he needed on his side, beyond veterans who feted him. He was nominally Catholic, which played very well into the hands of the clerics, and regarded religion as a positive unifying force: no religions other than Judaism need feel threatened by Europe's latest authoritarian figure. He was a former soldier who had been Minister of War before being promoted first to deputy prime minister, then to prime minister during the chaotic week in mid-June 1940, until he became chief of the French state that July. He remained publicly subdued on matters of domestic politics, in which he had little interest. This impressed those of the centre left who saw him as a 'general for a republic' who would lead strongly and advocate a collaborative method of governance, though an authoritarian who relied heavily on the advice of others and delegated well. He was seen as a compassionate and very able leader which many people felt was just what France needed at that desperate moment. Importantly his humble origins in the rural northern Artois region, and a fabricated narrative around the idealism of a return to the countryside and basic family values, played well to the peasantry. Pétain knew that France would be reliant on farmers in the months and years to come. If the people of the countryside did not follow Pétain, France's productivity would suffer.

Through regular radio appearances, press reports and poster campaigns, the peasantry and the working class in the regions took in Pétain's promises of flowers in the garden and a thriving rural economy through bountiful harvests. That these harvests would be raided for export to the Reich was yet to be discovered. Pétain had no children of his own, but he had a genuine love for babies and the younger generation. Youth and renewal were central themes of his new French state. Children everywhere wrote to him telling him how much they loved and appreciated him, sometimes spontaneously, and most received a reply of sorts. Children sang the new chorus 'Maréchal, nous voilà' each day at school, and raised the flag alongside the image of the marshal. He embarked on long, exhausting tours of towns and villages within the southern zone, helping to create a connection to the people. The tours were hard for a man in his mid-eighties, but he was helped by shots of amphetamines. He was still some way from approaching senility, as some senior politicians thought he might be. He would prove neither easy to manipulate nor a mere figurehead. He was sharp and highly politically ambitious, not there to replace Marianne on bank notes and gold medals.

Much of his image was an illusion. His devotion to Catholicism was minimal, he was a serial womaniser and a great believer in an authoritarian republic run and guided by a single figure. However, even as the authority of the Vichy government began to wane, beginning as early as 1941, many people retained support of Pétain. They continued to trust in him as a figurehead, looking after the interests of the France he was sworn to protect.

By the time Pétain shook Hitler's hand, life in Oradour had changed. Some families – women and children in particular – had arrived from elsewhere in France. Some came from the Paris region, others from Avignon, Montpellier, Bordeaux, Nantes and elsewhere hoping to escape, among other things, the regular bombings. Some simply decided to uproot for the calm of the southern zone.

Marie Avril was delighted to welcome Marguerite, her daughter from her first marriage, back from Paris. Marguerite had, in 1933, married an army officer, already a *Croix de Guerre* with silver star, by the name of Henri Laurence. The couple had lived in Paris where Henri served as an instructor. They had two children, Bernard and Geneviève, and when Paris was occupied, they decided to come to live with Marie as she was alone. They lived in a house that adjoined the *Hôtel Avril* and Henri helped his mother-in-law run the business. They were happy in the knowledge that Oradour and its peaceful surroundings would offer security for their children. Marguerite took up employment with the postal service in Limoges, to which she travelled by tram each day.

Many of the village's men who had been called up the previous September had returned. This included Maurice Compain, which was good news for Robert Hébras, who had not taken to the night-time working patterns of a baker. Fifteen and no longer a schoolboy, he needed to settle into some sort of trade. Pierre Poutaraud was the mechanic who had, in the past, held a contract with the tramway company to drive Robert's father Jean and his team to faults in the tramline. Poutaraud, whose garage was in the village centre, had agreed to take on Robert as an apprentice. Dark haired and eternally youthful, Poutaraud had five children with his dressmaker wife Renée. The couple would go on to have another two children, one of whom would be

Friends coming of age. From left: Roger Barthélémy, André Desourteaux, Robert Hébras. (Collection Angèle Valladeau)

sent to live with a grandparent. Work, however, had already been affected by national events. Repair jobs for mechanics were beginning to dry up, and when restrictions were placed on petrol later that year, Poutaraud was unable to provide enough work in order for Robert to learn on the job. Instead he gave his apprentice duties as a childminder – a position from which Robert was keen to move on. Through his father's contacts, a job was found for him in a garage in Limoges to which Robert could afford to commute, benefitting from free travel as the son of a tram employee.

The Hébras family were not interested in spending their little disposable income on newspapers,[1] and Robert read little about current affairs. Like most *Radounauds*, however, he was up to date with the business of the people around him, and the village's wide variety of political beliefs was no closed book. According to contemporary journalist Pierre Poitevin, 'political battles were much less lively [in Oradour] than in many other areas of the department'.[2] Many families in the villages around were more concerned with everyday affairs than politics, however much the bigger picture ultimately affected their daily lives. Political discussions took place in the cafés, shops and the *bureau de tabac*, but they mostly tended to be about local issues.

By the end of August 1940, two-thirds of the evacuees from Alsace-Lorraine had returned home, many attracted by the implementation of Nazi authorities in the region. The availability of food and fuel improved but official rationing was brought in on 23 September 1940. Quantities would be determined by age, sex and occupation. This meant that every resident of the area was instructed to make a personal sacrifice that would be 'equally borne by all'.[3] As well as meat, milk, fat, bread, sugar, coffee and other food staples requiring coupons for purchase, other items such as soap were equally rationed. For the first time the French people were going without not for the troops on the front, nor for the very visible evacuees, but for a political reason – to help Pétain's 'National Revolution'.

The Mosellans

In November 1940, the people of Charly and Montoy-Flanville, two small villages in the north-eastern frontier region of Moselle, were given a matter of hours to prepare to leave their homes forever. They were not the first. From 20 July 1940 around a thousand inhabitants of Moselle had left the *département*. Then a major sweep began. In the first wave, between 16 August and 18 September, 23,000 people were targeted as known Francophiles or Germanophobes. It was not until the second wave that the two villages near Metz came under focus.

France's defeat in June 1940 led almost immediately to Germanisation of Alsace and Moselle. Though Alsace-Lorraine was never fully annexed, it was occupied as Berlin took control of it through a series of laws. Soldiers arrived to empty streets in Strasbourg and Metz, and Hitler made it a priority to refill the area with good Germans.

Firstly, the areas that had been evacuated prior to the war could be repopulated. This meant that the evacuees from Schiltigheim who had come to Saint-Junien and its surrounds, including Oradour, could return home. This did not include the 14,000 Jews who had been evacuated from Alsace-Lorraine. Strasbourg and Metz both had significant Jewish populations. The *Radounauds* were generally not sorry to see their lodgers leave. Schiltigheim was a well-to-do suburb of the city of Strasbourg. Those who had stayed in the agricultural surrounds of Oradour had been forthright with complaints about the difference in living standards in the Limousin compared to their more modern homes in the north. The return of most of these early evacuees, in the Limousin for temporary protection rather than expulsion, was welcomed by many with a sigh of relief.[1]

Some who were deemed unfit for the Reich stayed behind and it was these people who led the way in finding lodgings for the newcomers. For the most part, places were ready-made, having recently been vacated by the Schiltigheim departees, keen to get back to 'civilisation'.

In Moselle, which became part of the Rhineland-Palatinate, Hitler granted the local administration ten years to fully Germanise the area, but the process began with violent single-mindedness. Street names were changed, statues of French heroes were dismantled, and inhabitants deemed to be 'undesirable' were expelled, among them Jews, North Africans, French speakers, naturalised French citizens and those with an affinity for French culture. These people were felt to be impossible to Germanise.

By the time that Charly and Montoy-Flanville were dealt with, demobilised soldiers from the villages had begun to come home. The prune harvest, the second planting and the grape harvest were taking place. Potatoes were being pulled up. 'We were rushing to get in the beetroot so that, as per our custom, a good wheat could follow. Everyone was in the process of stocking up their homes.'[2] The German operation named *Aktion D* began on 1 November, when a major survey took place. The inhabitants were called to the town hall by the town drum and three members of the Gestapo, dressed in civilian clothes, explained that they were to be relocated in order to facilitate a 'calming of the borders'. They could opt for France or Poland. The problem with choosing Poland was that they would be put up in barracks due to a lack of space. Everybody signed up for France and heads of families filled in their details in the register. Before leaving the hall, they were told that each family would be allowed to bring 50kg of luggage and up to 100 marks (2,000 francs) with them. Goods left behind would be subject to an inventory and subsequent losses would be paid out by France in the coming years.

An extraordinary two-and-a-half-week period followed during which the affected inhabitants made sure that they left nothing behind that might help the German occupiers. They slaughtered livestock and ate choice cuts with their best bottles of wine and beer, and finest conserved foods normally preserved for special occasions. They dug holes and buried precious objects with packets of salt or hid their luxuries in the gutters of houses.

Farmers destroyed food products, sabotaged motors and machines, and cut chains that held farm stock. Work in the fields stopped abruptly and crops were left to spoil. Money and precious objects were hidden in wooden joints, under stairs and false floorboards. Anything of value which weighed heavily such as dinner sets, silverware and even curtains were concealed. Pin cushions, fur collars, shoulder pads, aspirin and jam pots were opened up to conceal money. Marie-Louise Pincemaille's father had already brought in a bailiff to make an inventory of their furniture because he fully expected them to be expelled. When the time came to leave, women and girls hid money in their corsets. Emile Gougeon, a farmer from Charly, thought of an ingenious way to ensure more cash could be carried: 'We made bread the night before our expulsion, so I tucked 2,000 francs inside a loaf before cooking it.'

The village of Charly saw 153 people expelled, around 90 per cent of its population. The Germans renamed the village Karlen. One hundred and four people were forced out of Montoy-Flanville, renamed Monten, which was 40 per cent of its population. Only qualifying factory and railway workers could remain. The trains carrying them arrived in Lyon on 16 November from where some were sent towards Corrèze, the rest towards Limoges. Thirty-nine people were directed towards Oradour-sur-Glane. These included the Gougeon family, who arrived on 17 November and were met by Joseph Beau. The majority of the evacuees from Schiltigheim had barely gone and had left behind a bitter taste. Suddenly the *Radounauds* had another wave of newcomers to deal with.

'Our welcome was pretty cold,' relates Georges Godfrin, 'the population having had a bad experience with the Alsatians. They took us to be just more of the same.'[3] However, the farming families of Oradour warmed to their new guests quickly when they saw that they were of similar background – farming peasantry – although goodwill was a little harder to find among rental agents and shopkeepers who had lost out due to unpaid bills. Nevertheless, the expelled status of the unfortunates from Moselle resonated with and garnered more support from the locals than had been the case with the evacuees.

The new arrivals were grateful for whatever accommodation they could get and fortunately the organisational structure for finding space remained in place following the recent departures. At first, most of them were lodged in the main village and were fed together in the village's restaurants. Arthur Godfrin's family of six were put in a single room. 'I can still see my parents' bed,' said Roger Godfrin later, 'my grand-father on a straw mattress and the four children on another, top-to-tail.'[4] Arthur Godfrin, a metal worker at the time of the family's expulsion, was quick to find work. He had to do so in order to support his ever-growing family, expanded when a fifth child, Josette, was born on 18 May 1941. He worked first as a woodcutter, before taking up a new job at the bakery belonging to Marcellin Thomas.

On the day of their arrival in the village, Marie-Louise Pincemaille was met off the tram at Laplaud, two stops before Oradour, where a small *château* still stands:

There were eight people in my family: my parents and six children aged from eleven to seventeen; I was fifteen at the time. We lived in a small house right next to the château. My father looked after a very large garden and the upkeep of several chickens, and my mother worked in the main house. My two brothers […] found a job in Limoges and my three sisters crocheted gloves for a regional factory in Saint-Junien. As for me, drawn in as I was by couture from a very young age, I […] started a dress-making apprenticeship in Limoges. Each morning I would take the tram there and return the same evening.

Later, when the German occupation began to sap France of its resources, electricity shortages prevented the tram from running every day, so with the agreement of the *Chambre de métiers de Limoges*, Marie-Louise obtained permission to pursue her contract elsewhere:

> A dressmaker in Oradour, Madame David, agreed to take me on in her workshop. She lived in La Métairie, just a few hundred metres to the northeast of the centre of Oradour. From then on, I went almost every day to the village for my work.[5]

Marie-Louise's three sisters, aged between 11 and 18 when they arrived, all sewed gloves for extra money. Their brother Alfred, a schoolboy, gained his *certificat d'études* during his stay and then worked at a grocery shop in Limoges. Everybody had to pay their way.

Some Moselle refugees shared accommodation that was insufficient in size, but for which they were so grateful that they never moved. One house, owned by the same widow who owned and ran the *Hôtel Avril*, was split into two. The Hébras family had one half and three refugee families squeezed into the other. The first of these, the Kanzler family, had been there some time. They had not returned to Schiltigheim because they were Jewish. Joseph Kanzler, who was born in Budapest in 1923, arrived with his wife Maria, originally from Warsaw. A hat-cutter by trade, Joseph had worked in Strasbourg and when the couple married in 1928, they moved to Schiltigheim. They had two daughters, 14-year-old Dora and 10-year-old Simone. The Kanzler family was quiet and withdrawn, and had settled into Limousin life without fully integrating.

With the new arrivals came two families who squeezed into the rest of the property. Auguste Pister, his wife Marie and their two children lived together with Auguste's sister, Marie, and her husband, Jules Haas. Haas was a baker and managed to find work for the tramway company in Limoges. They had a 2-year-old daughter when they arrived, but Marie Haas was heavily pregnant and gave birth to a daughter less than a month after arriving in the village. Their third child, a son, was born on 15 April 1944. Pister began by offering his services as a wheelwright in and around Oradour, but limited opportunities led to him also taking up employment with the regional tramways.

The *Mosellan* arrivals were largely well accepted in Oradour. Children began to play together. 'At the age of six,' Roger Godfrin recalled, 'I used to go fishing on the banks of the Glane, either all alone or sometimes with a friend, Marcel Poutaraud, the son of the of the garage owner. We would go swimming naked in the river.'[6] Adult friendships emerged out of mutual understanding and respect. Many refugees found work in the fields, where they filled the gaps left by absent prisoners of war.

Mosellan methods for routine tasks, such as cutting down trees and splitting logs for the winter, caused consternation among bosses and locals, but these petty differences were accepted in time. That the two communities were people of the earth proved to be revelatory. During the summer, when the major agricultural tasks had to be done, the Mosellans fully immersed with the locals, grateful for lasting work. Families got together to help with each other's harvests – as was traditional in the region. At threshing time, everybody helped out, including women. The season was long and plenty of work meant plenty of time for the people of the north to integrate with the people of the south. This too was the season of celebration, with much wine and cider shared at the end of long working days.

The differing farming methodologies mattered little, and the Mosellan farmers eventually took back with them plenty of knowledge about the rearing of good-quality cattle for meat. The Mosellans were happy to contribute to the success of their new friends and to the French economy in general. They also mostly stuck to the mantra '*c'nam po tojo*', 'it is not forever'.[7] Most hoped that one day they might be able to return home. Their arrival caused more shortages, but this was mainly in medium-sized and larger towns where shoppers were met with empty shelves in grocer's, butcher's and baker's shops. For this reason, trips to countryside villages and onward to farms became one of the only ways to supplement meagre rations. This helped supply the urban community with what they needed and had the added benefit of lining the pockets of the peasant class. Two significant societal shifts resulted, however. Firstly, the number of items sold at marketplaces and in shops reduced, and secondly, a black market formed, raising prices for all. An urban–rural animosity would arise as a result.

A Bigger Congregation

For *l'abbé* Chapelle, the newcomers were a breath of fresh air. While priests throughout the villages were sympathetic to the plight of these people, the population shifts presented unexpected benefits for clerics in villages where decades of dechristianisation had permeated amongst the *paysans*. Many newcomers were shocked at the lack of daily commitment to the Church. In questions of faith, the Limousin was almost a foreign land to the mostly devout Catholics who were not attuned to seeing empty pews in churches. *L'abbé* Chapelle would see congregations fill once more, and even the confessional booths were used again.

In Alsace-Lorraine the separation of State and Church had not happened to the same degree as elsewhere in France. The Jules Ferry laws of 1882 had made education secular in France, but after the return of Alsace and Moselle to France in 1919, four hours of religious instruction had been reinstated

A procession leaves the church, heading to the upper village. On the right is the open marketplace, les halles. (Collection Jean-Pierre Senon)

to public schools, to be taught by holy sisters. No such thing existed in the Limousin outside of private church schools. Furthermore, the Limousin was a region in which anticlericalism had taken root since the beginning of the twentieth century as part of the restrained socialism of the SFIO. The expelled Mosellans were proving to be much better guests than the Schiltigheim evacuees. As well as fitting in with the area's rural nature and a way of life to which they were well used, they added vibrancy to a congregation that had been meagre in number before. Better still, *l'abbé* Chapelle knew that there was little immediate hope of their return north.

The Church would also benefit from the support of Marshal Pétain. A large portion of blame for France's unreadiness for war was placed on the wastage and moral decadence of the Third Republic. France would have an opportunity to spiritually cleanse itself in a 'National Revolution'. The Catholic Church, which had suffered in the face of secularism, could now reclaim a central position with the support of Pétain, whose portrait found its way into churches. It did not much matter to the clerical population of Vichy France that the written principles of the 'Revolution' were deemed to be too restrictive of civil liberties by Pope Pius XII in Rome.

The burst of energy from the Church was not completely welcome in all quarters, and in Oradour the municipal council, still dominated by Joseph Beau and the SFIO, was forced to consider unexpected problems related to education. The Mosellan children were still entitled to receive religious education. The question of full integration was debated fiercely. Why, after all, should these youngsters follow a different school curriculum to that of the local children? Furthermore, the logistics of providing the instruction was difficult and doing so did not sit well with France's secular system.

Initially, the thirteen refugee children were incorporated into the three main village schools. Meanwhile, a case was put forward for a distinct establishment to be created for the Mosellan children. The man to lead that battle was Jacques Lorich, curate for the village of Charly, who had arrived with his fellow villagers and his sister Angélique. Jacques was 41 when he arrived, the eldest sibling in a large family, and Angélique 28. They had followed their parishioners to the Limousin and found themselves among sixty-four residents from Charly and fifteen from Montoy-Flanville, who arrived in Oradour on 17 November 1940. Lorich immediately set about trying to ensure the children continued to receive an education such as they were accustomed to. He met opposition to his idea of a new class. The minimum for a village school roll call was fifteen, and his group fell short. He came across political opposition too, because of the question of secularism. Finally, however, he succeeded. Writing in the newsletter of the bishop of Moselle, then based in Lyon,[1] in February 1941, he encouraged others in the same position to be resilient in the face of setbacks. He had overcome 'opposition from the socialist-minded municipal council' and insisted 'despite the discussions, the delays [...] the orders "in the name of the prefect" to send the children to the village schools'.

The municipality allocated funds for a separate building, albeit temporary, cheap and rather flimsy. A school for 'refugees' was established on the grounds of the infant school, not far from the doors of the church. Fernand Gougeon, the children's teacher in Charly, would teach the class, which incorporated students from the ages of 3 to 11. The Jewish Kanzler family from Schiltigheim, who had stayed on in Oradour, arranged for their two girls, Dora and Simone, to attend. They were listed as Protestant. This gave some protection to the two girls and their inclusion brought the numbers up to the required threshold of fifteen.

Curate Jacques Lorich assisted *l'abbé* Chapelle in whatever way he could, and Angélique lived with him, acting as his housekeeper. Once the school was established, he took on the religious instruction of the children and often preached sermons at the church.

One other child from Schiltigheim, Serge Bergmann, did not attend the refugee school. His mother, Maria, had worked as a domestic servant in and around Strasbourg as well as briefly trying her luck in Paris. She had fallen pregnant when she was 18 years old. By the time Serge was born, the father was absent. Maria then met Joseph Bergmann, a Jewish barber who had been born in the west German town of Ickern, where his father worked as a miner. The Bergmann family moved to Schiltigheim where relatives had already settled. Joseph was naturalised as French in November 1939 and the couple married the following April, having decided to settle in Oradour. Joseph became the adoptive father of Serge, who by that time was 5 years old and had known Joseph for most of his life.

Joseph found stable employment working as a barber for Lucien Morlieras in the *Café du Chêne* and became a popular member of the community, later playing for the village football team. The family became practising Catholics. Maria wrote to her brother, who had chosen to return to Schiltigheim, in 1943:

> Our Serge has grown taller, even we will not recognise him soon. He goes to school, and he is learning well. He also helps with mass at the church. I would not be surprised if one day he becomes a priest.[2]

The Camp

By the summer of 1939, 2,257 Spanish republicans had come to the Haute-Vienne and been dispersed into communities that would be open to welcoming these victims of fascism. The refugees almost unanimously refused to take the bait laid for them by Franco's new regime, which invited them to return to their homeland where they would, it was promised, be treated according to Christian values.

Men of a working age could stay in France only if they had the means to support themselves and their families. But the numbers crossing the border were such that holding camps were established by the French government. The first detention centre was opened in Rieucros, Lozère, in January 1939, under Daladier's premiership, and by the time of that month's mass ten-day exodus, France had put in place several more camps in which conditions were far from comfortable.

The advent of war in September 1939 had led to a worsening of conditions. The housing of Spanish refugees was pushed within the framework of a July 1938 law on 'the organisation of the nation in times of war'. This meant that the Spanish workforce could be used to plug the gaps opened up by the mobilisation of the French workforce. At the armistice, Vichy's politicians had to decide on a best course of action for a workforce that it wanted to retain, but it knew may be tricky due to considerable communist influence. The immigrants would be, after all, politically engaged, socialist or even anarchist. The government wanted the Spanish pushed from society, all the while retaining them as a potential workforce.

Its solution was a system of open retention: groups, rather than holding camps, that could keep men of the same nationality together and exploit them for the benefit of the economy. The *Groupes de Travailleurs Étrangers* (GTE) replaced an earlier scheme linking the workforce to the army. Instead, a network of camps was established, abundant in the Limousin region. The workers could be used in agriculture, industry, local businesses or, later, even sent to work for the Germans on the western coast, constructing defences for the occupiers under the *organisation Todt*. Some men, fearing deportation or retention in camps, fled into clandestinity, and a proportion of these would later join early Resistance groups.

Raimundo Tejedor Lluch was a boy of 8 when he arrived in France, having crossed the Pyrenees in a convoy of open trucks, exposed to the wind and attacks from planes flying above. He travelled with his sister, brother and parents, leaving behind a life of relative wealth. His father was an engineer and, back in Spain, the family had even employed a housekeeper who looked after the children. Upon arriving in southern France the family was split up. They finally reunited at the GTE camp in Oradour-sur-Glane. The change in circumstances could not have been more brutal. Raimundo's father had arrived before him and, along with others assigned to the company, had been told to build shelter for his family on a patch of land called La Fauvette, just north of the main village. No building materials were supplied so the workers had to use branches that they cut down themselves, meaning that the cabins provided little protection from the wind and rain.

Raimundo's father was assigned to work in a local quarry, where he broke rock and helped maintain the tools and rolling stock. 'Every morning the men would go to the village and salute the flag which obviously was red, white and blue.' The ceremony took place on the main *Champ de foire* in front of the pharmacy. 'After roll call, they lined up in four well-spaced rows and marched off at a rhythmic pace along the Saint-Junien road, a significant distance.' A hard day of labour awaited the men, and when winter descended

Spanish refugees of the 643rd GTE. They are raising the colours on the corner of the Champ de foire, *outside the Pascaud pharmacy, where the population would be gathered on 10 June 1944. (Collection Benoit Sadry)*

those used to a milder climate struggled with the intensity of the work, 'their poor bodies stripped bare and very badly nourished, gnawed away as they were by the memory of defeat in their homeland'.[1] Later the workers and their families were moved from the open camp in La Fauvette and squeezed into a defunct wool-carding building where, for young Raimundo, the enormous equipment 'looked to me like torture machines and to me were just the next part of the alliance between Spain and Germany which would return to Spain to finish its work of extermination. They scared me.'

The system aimed to exclude, repress and exploit the Spanish. Established in the spring of 1941, the Oradour camp's administrative centre was in the village centre. It was effectively an open camp and workers could come and go as they pleased, but the GTE camps were the only legal way for the refugees to exist in France. Of 220 or so registered members of Oradour's 643rd GTE, only around twenty worked in Oradour. Others were assigned to farms, while two whole sections were dispatched to work in forestry operations. Another was based around Saint-Junien. The camp could, in principle, welcome any undesirables into its ranks, and some Jews were registered, but it remained largely Spanish.

The government held all the cards. These men needed legal work as a means to support themselves and their families. As long as the workforce remained passive, docile even, then a large amount of unskilled hard work could be achieved for a minimum cost. Where else, for example, would sufficient bodies be found to break rocks in the quarries to quench the thirst of railway expansion in Eastern Europe? The contract between 'employer' and worker was heavily stacked in favour of the French industries or small businesses that might take the workers on. Agreed with the chief of each group, it:

> ensured the presence of a fixed employee perennially available, (only ten days off were allowed for in the contracts) and, better still, ensured an overall salary bill that was very small, less than that which would correspond to a 'normal' worker.[2]

Some of the workers were used to hard labour, but the back-breaking work was a shock to those who mended shoes or wrote contracts in their previous lives. Bullying and impossible production targets were commonplace. In one camp, workers were instructed to clear chestnut trees in a forest near Saint-Yrieix and an eyewitness remarked how 'real work requiring strength' was being 'done by workers who before the war were teachers, office workers and students'. They were forced to toil, 'torsos naked and shining with sweat, they puffed and panted under the burning sun. They were cut and scarred, and the chapping of their callused hands were bleeding despite the grease that they had covered them with.'[3]

Some worked as labourers on farms, in the quarries and cutting down trees. Others made charcoal for the many *gazogène*-driven trucks and cars. In towns, those deemed unfit for hard labour were taken on as assistants in small businesses such as butchers, cobblers and tailors. Some worked in the camp administration, others as secretaries and some drove carts.

The Shoes Scandal

The socialist mayor of Oradour, Joseph Beau, had worked hard not just to ensure Oradour's evacuees and refugees were dealt with, but to make newcomers feel welcome. The Pétain regime brought with it a wave of changes to local government. Mayors were replaced throughout the new Vichy France and socialist municipal councils were pressurised into dissolving themselves. In April 1941, Beau was caught up in a controversy that provided an ideal opportunity for his removal. The previous year, the municipality council had covered up the distribution of shoes to refugees. A source in the *Service de Réfugiés* had acquired them from military stocks partly to deprive the German army.[1] The situation was made worse because a nominal price had been charged (described later as 40 sous). The local government fell below the threshold to be dissolved entirely but a means had been found to replace Beau: the *conseil municipal* could be dissolved and a Vichy-style special delegation nominated to replace it. Its incoming head would be Paul Desourteaux[2] aided by wineseller Léon Denis and miller André Foussat, all three more sympathetic to Pétain than Beau and his committees. In the investigation that followed the shoe scandal, the link man who enabled the requisition of the stocks was acquitted of any responsibility, but Beau was made the scapegoat. Desourteaux was again mayor in all but name. He had never won an election and once again was unelected in the role. André Desourteaux, the grandson of both Paul Desourteaux and Joseph Beau, later described the action taken by Beau over the shoes for refugees as the first act of resistance in Oradour-sur-Glane.[3]

The changes in Oradour were sweetened for the Vichy authorities by the fact that Beau was not a military veteran. Family commitments had meant that he was not mobilised for the First World War. That his political line preached secularism and pacifism, and his local party used Freemasonry membership as a means of selection to electoral lists, added to the justification for his removal. Over the previous two decades, Beau had pursued policies that had clashed with the thinking of right-wingers. He had sought educational improvements under the banner of '*l'école de la République*', frustrated only by a lack of funds rather than ambition. He had pitched the *mairie* against the interests of the clergy. *L'abbé* Chapelle, hardly a young modern priest but rather

Joseph Beau, socialist mayor of Oradour from 1919
until his removal in 1941 over a scandal relating to the
supply of army surplus shoes to refugees. He was André
Desourteaux's maternal grandfather.
(Collection André Desourteaux)

ultra-conservative, saw Pétain and his National Revolution as a blessing for a
rural area for which the Christian faith had become unimportant.

The bishop of Limoges, Monseigneur Louis Paul Rastouil, set out to ensure
that the powerful influence of the Catholic Church in the region was seen to
be firmly in support of Pétain. The bishop was a committed member of the
Légion française des combattants et volontaires de la Révolution nationale, a Pétainst
organisation initially born of veterans of the First World War and created to
promote the National Revolution. It was formed on 29 August 1940, replacing
all other veteran organisations. Right wing in outlook, it was from the *Légion*
that the *Service d'ordre légionnaire* (SOL) would spring in December 1941, as
its militant arm under the direction of Joseph Darnand. In January 1943, the
SOL would become the dreaded *Milice* (militia).

The Oradour section of the *Légion* was small but in line with numerous others around the region. It took part in a number of key local events, including the visit of Marshal Pétain to Saint-Junien and Limoges on 19–20 June 1941. Its membership won some leadership influence when Beau was replaced. It was made up primarily of opponents of Beau, whose removal gave an excellent opportunity for these men to ensure Oradour's municipal governance treaded the Pétainist path.

According to a January 1942 report by agents of the BCRA, de Gaulle's information-gathering service, the *Légion* became 'vital for shopkeepers or businessmen who wish to succeed, or even to eke out a living. These days people are enrolling in the *Légion* because of the social placement gained by those that wear the insignia.'[4]

Available records name only five definite members of the Oradour-sur-Glane *Légion* in 1941, though there would certainly have been more.[5] Its president was Jean Roumy, who had a business in the village selling seeds and fertilisers. Roumy also owned a farm in nearby Les Brandes. Former postman Matthieu Mercier was treasurer. Some association with the *Légion* is unsurprising as most men over the age of 40 would have been veterans of the First World War, and the *Légion* provided support. Returning veterans from the 1940 conflict might equally join. Records list one much younger member, Robert Besson, the son of textile merchant Guillaume who was in his mid-twenties and a card-carrying member of the *Légion*. He had been called up in September 1939 and demobilised in June 1940. His older brother, Abel, was still a prisoner of war. Paul Desourteaux was, according to his grandson André, never a member, and the paperwork is inconclusive, though it has been claimed that he held a prominent position.[6] Even if he was not a member, Desourteaux was eagerly supported by the influential *Légion*. His special delegation was made up of 'prominent citizens, craftsmen and merchants' which 'corresponded to the leadership team of the local *Légion* section'.[7]

Vichy policies supported by the *Légion* in and around the Limousin included the removal of large numbers of Jews displaced by GTE camps, or because of the region's proximity to the demarcation line. The *Légion* supported the open expression of anti-Semitism. The region *sous-préfet* of Rochechouart mentioned Oradour in an August 1942 report in which he drew attention to places where contingents of Jews had become too large and were, he suggests, having a detrimental effect on prices due to their readiness to trade on the black market. Whether the Oradour section of the *Légion* supported this notion is unknown and there is little to suggest this kind of economic effect was ever felt in Oradour, where there was never a large number of Jews.

In January 1942, the *Légion* was described as 'strong in numbers, and numbers only. The number of those that are sincere about it is very small. The *Légion* is rather like a flock of sheep.' It would slowly decline in importance from mid-1942.

L'Avenir Musical had strong associations with the *Légion*. Roumy was on its board and Matthieu Mercier was its treasurer. André Foussat, in charge of the theatrical section and also on the municipal council, was the son of Louis Foussat, responsible for the families of the men who were still prisoners from the 1939–40 conflict. Some musicians who had returned from the war played at a ceremony at the raising of the French flag, and that of the *Légion*, on Sunday 15 June 1941. On 8 February 1942 it provided backing for the young people of Oradour to hold a get-together in the Poutaraud garage on the village's main street. The event was held as a benefit for the absent prisoners of war. This was the last time an official musical gathering would take place in Oradour: no more concerts or balls took place during the Vichy regime. Even the monthly *foires* came to a halt. As of June 1940, *l'Avenir Musical* and its other societies, such as the theatre group, ceased all activities. Jean Baptiste Tournier, however, was not finished. He was determined to ensure a musical future for the youngsters of the village. Despite the end of concerts, he announced that he would resume his music theory lessons, *le solfège*, on Saturdays. Those interested would need to sign up with René Mercier, at the grocery store opposite the church. This he would do every Saturday until June 1944.

The Camp Commander

During a sunny spring morning in 1941, Commander José María Otto came to the 643rd GTE in Oradour. He arrived with an assistant who, according to Millán Bielsa, who was there that day, 'resembled a gorilla'.[1] Otto did his best to win over the men by talking to them in calm tones, even introducing jokes and phrases in Catalan. The men had been called that day to the special obligatory meeting in a well-manicured field near their camp at La Fauvette. At first, they listened to the commander, who was dressed 'in a black suit on a rather chubby frame, with a round head, fat face and a small moustache'.[2] He praised the men's bravery during the Spanish conflict and 'stoicism in France'. He declared that Germany could and would not lose, acerbically taking a wrecking ball to France's treatment of the Spanish. He spoke in a polished flow, like a comedian repeating his phraseology in a measured, well-rehearsed style. But, when he told the gathered men to sign up, for the *organisation Todt*, set up to recruit a cheap workforce to build defences quickly on the nearby western coast, they refused. Otto, whose demeanour changed completely, responded furiously. He shouted and threatened, 'If you won't volunteer, you will go by force', but he would leave empty-handed. One local witness who lived near to the camp described how, during this – the only German visit to Oradour – the man who spoke did all he could to incite the Spanish men to work for the Germans by insisting that they were being badly treated by the French.[3]

Otto had been born in Barcelona to German parents but lived most of his life in Catalonia, where he had married. Starting the Spanish conflict in 1936 on the side of the Republic, he later fought with the *Brigade Internationale*, where he gained the grade 'major' before fleeing to France. While interned in a camp for Spanish refugees he was contacted by the occupation forces, his own countrymen, with whom he struck a deal. He would work for the Gestapo in exchange for his freedom. He covered swathes of western and central France visiting GTE camps with a mission: to enrol voluntarily as many able Spanish as he could to the construction of the German coastline defences. During his visits he preached the virtues of Nazi Germany and illustrated the sins of the French who he claimed were exploiting the Spanish refugees for all they were worth. Based in Niel, Bordeaux, he would return to barracks, often having failed miserably to attract the workforce and being faced with having to draw up plans to recruit the men forcefully. As well as supplying men to those same barracks at Niel, he was tasked with filling up the *Todt* centres in Lorient and Brest, where huge submarine bases were under construction.

The Spanish were enduring hardship, but they had fled to France to escape fascism. They recognised the agenda of Otto. According to Bielsa:

> We were mutually well adopted [in Oradour] and our life as refugees during which we earned an obligatory wage of 0,50 francs per hour, would have been worse had it not been for the warm and welcoming presence of the village population.[4]

Bielsa's memories of Oradour were of a 'peaceful and welcoming Limousin village'. His time there was 'the two most amazing years of my nine years of war'. Before the Spanish war, Bielsa had been a medical student. He had come to the 643rd GTE as a nurse so was given accommodation in the village. His job was to attend to injuries and complaints of the company's internees, in collaboration with the village's own medical staff. Bielsa, born in Aragon in 1915, had been an officer in the republican army before fleeing to France as Franco's forces approached. He had spent time in a refugee camp before working in an underground factory building aeroplanes. In 1940 he was included in a group sent to the Oradour camp.

Bielsa rapidly learned to speak fluent French, choosing to keep a personal diary in the language. His medical duties and linguistic ability helped him to integrate and he became close to the Brandy family. It was while sipping drinks at their café in the lower village that he met and fell in love with Andrée, one of the three sisters, who not only ran the café but also worked as Oradour's station master. The couple became inseparable and Andrée agreed to marry him. During their short time together, she even helped him to send letters to his mother in Spain by circumventing the official postal censorship system. It would not be long before events would pull them apart.

Talented musician Jean Henry had been assigned to the role of chief warden of the 643rd GTE the day after his thirty-first birthday. Born in Épinal in the Vosges, his family moved to Paris shortly after the First World War and settled in Sartrouville, where he began learning the violin. Soon thereafter he switched to the flute which became his passion. Mobilised in September 1940, he served in the infantry, based in Riom. While there he was demobilised in order to take up his new position.

Andrée Brandy with Millán Bielsa, a Spanish refugee at the 643rd GTE who would become her fiancé until the camp was moved to another village. (Collection Anne-Marie Rigon)

When he got to the Oradour GTE he served under Capitaine Dezzou and his deputy, Lieutenant Simonin. Henry was a gentle man with a generous nature, but as always, he did the job to which he had been assigned to the best of his ability. While living there he met a young woman with film-star blonde hair and wide dreamy eyes. Gilberte Biver had come to Oradour from Montoy-Flanville in Moselle when her family had been amongst those evicted in November 1940. Head of the family group with whom she had arrived was Louis Perette, her stepfather. She had lost her own father ten years previously. The family, like most from Moselle, had settled well into Limousin life.

As chief warden, Jean Henry was lodged in the village itself. The administrative section of the GTE was well integrated there, and the camp was not as detached from village life as it might have been. The camp's staff, such as Henry, and even some of the Spanish men, such as Bielsa, were able to mix with the *Radounauds*. Gilberte had been 18 years old at the time of her arrival in the countryside and would have sought out the limited opportunities for social interaction in Oradour. The couple fell in love and married just eight months after first meeting, on 29 August 1941.

A Return to Roots

Vichy restrictions had pushed Camille Senon's family to a financial edge. They had relocated once more and Camille's new school environment further disrupted her already chaotic upbringing. She enjoyed meeting Alsatian refugees there but struggled to make friends of her own age. She hated telling her father that each day she had to sing '*Maréchal nous voilà*' in front of an image of the old man. A new life of ration cards for food, textiles and tobacco further squeezed her parents' ability to provide for her. Allocations partially protected agricultural workers, but prices rose as goods were shipped to Germany and the black market emerged.

Camille had failed her *brevet élémentaire* in 1939 after a turbulent year of study during which she mourned the loss of her beloved brother. To resit the year, there would be an associated cost and her parents could hardly afford to pay. They had accrued significant debt with Raymond's medical fees. Camille's mother Catherine was, however, determined to prevent her daughter from being confined to a life at home as she had been. Despite some initial protestations from Martial, Catherine enrolled Camille at the Pigier school in Limoges for her to learn secretarial skills. The well-established but accessible private school further stretched the family's finances but Catherine and eventually Martial sacrificed all they could. In August 1941, Martial got his wish and managed to get a transfer to Oradour.

Martial was overjoyed at being able to 'rejoin his tribe'. His career in road maintenance was secure and the move offered normality and stability in their lives, and the support of nearby family. Camille's first cousin Irène, two years her junior at 14 years old, lived with Uncle and Aunt Lucien and Catherine Morlieras in the *Café du Chêne* on the church square, where the ancient oak, the *chêne de la liberté*, reached into the quiet country air. Irène had also been deeply affected by the death of her first cousin Raymond. Despite her young age when it had happened, she had never wanted to continue with her studies because it would mean living away from home, and she chose to remain close to her parents. She shared her grandfather François with Camille. He lived a stone's throw from the café with his second wife.

The lower village, the old *Champ de foire* and especially the *Café du Chêne* felt to Martial, and to Camille, like a spiritual home. It was always a hub of

Outside the Café du Chêne, *run by Lucien Morlieras. His wife, Catherine, also made and sold hats. (Collection Benoit Sadry)*

activity. Its covered marketplace, opposite the *Hôtel Milord*, faced the Mercier grocery store outside which the tram tracks of the eastern edge of the town sloped to the ancient bridge over the calm glassy waters of the Glane. In the autumn of 1941, however, Martial and Catherine found that no properties were available to rent in the village due to the recent influx of refugee families from Spain and Alsace-Lorraine. They were happy to set up in the hamlet of Le Repaire, 2km away, still within the *commune* of Oradour-sur-Glane and perfectly accessible by foot or bicycle:

> We found a house with a garden and a courtyard bordered by oak trees. Our life was greatly improved because of solidarity provided by our neighbours as well as our new-found ability to grow vegetables and bring up chickens and rabbits.[1]

Camille would attend the Pigier school in Limoges during the week and return 'home' only at weekends.

The Senon family found themselves amongst the peasantry of Oradour and the advent of the Vichy regime had changed the lives of the peasant class. The 'revolution' to which the new French state aspired made much of a return to the earth and to solidarity between families who would work together.

Pétain did not like the term 'revolution' because it reminded him of anarchy. He preferred 'renewal', which he used in his speeches. During the Third Republic, a time deemed to have been one of excesses and wastage, women had, according to Pétain, wasted time getting jobs. The Vichy narrative spoke of a France that had concentrated on the expansion of heavy industries. 'Renewal' meant that the country could go back in time. Traditional family roles could be resumed. Pétain recognised that the state would have to intervene to expedite this, so he created an organisation to try to add some structure to the agricultural world. This would enable it to contribute to the *Révolution nationale* by establishing a link between state and farmer. The resulting *Corporation paysanne*, formed in December 1940, enjoyed only limited success. Its overriding mission was to bring together pre-war agricultural structures, both those with their roots in unions and those of employers, together with banks and insurance companies working in the agricultural sector. A 'savings service for a return to the land' was inaugurated to help those families who bought into the ideals of the National Revolution and who went into agriculture. Help was also provided to former farming businesses wishing to re-establish themselves through a *Mission de restauration paysanne*. In 1941 a *Service civique rural* was created in order to make young people participate in the *grands travaux agricoles* and mitigate the missing workforce caused by both the continued absence of prisoners of war or, later, forced labour to Germany. Paul Veyriras had been a high-school student with Henri Bouchoule, the son of a baker family in Oradour and childhood friend of André Desourteaux:

> The school year had ended prematurely in May. We had sat the baccalaureate, reduced that year to written tests [...] I was participating in the *grands travaux*, both for family reasons and because young people were meant to accomplish a *service rural*, though it was not at all well monitored.[2]

The *Corporation paysanne* was similarly not much welcomed nor successful because many farmers felt that the government was trying to monitor closely their lives and businesses. It became increasingly difficult to escape Vichy's demands for the requisition of goods to Germany. Its propaganda claimed that a fair price had been impossible under the Third Republic because of the 'manoeuvres of political parties which acted to the detriment of the economy'. Instead, in partnership with the German economy it promised 'for the grower, a well-established price, and the certitude of selling'.[3] But the prices, the propaganda did not make clear, would be low and many of the sold goods would be routed straight to Germany.

Under Surveillance

Forced out of office in April 1941, former mayor Joseph Beau was included on a list of people of special interest in the village of Oradour-sur-Glane, who were under surveillance by Vichy authorities. The list included mainly Spanish inmates of the 643rd GTE, and former members of the local Communist party, of which many of its leaders had been either pursued by Vichy authorities or already interned or deported. In May 1941 the official *Parti Communist* (PCF), which had been driven underground with its leaders either hunted or already interned, created the *Front National* (FN). The new party, meant to be pluralist, was run by communists who occupied the main positions. In January 1942 the BCRA reported that 'the Communists, of which the exact strength is unknown (just that it is quite considerable) seems since the outbreak of the Germano-Russian war to have gained ground'.[1]

The Nazi invasion of the Soviet Union on 22 June 1941 had clarified the position for communists feeling torn, and criticism of the Vichy regime by the underground Communist party, which had centred on points such as prisoner-of-war release and food supplies, could now extend to Nazism and German foreign policy.

In November 1941 an anonymous letter was sent to Vichy denouncing activities by members of the now dissolved party in Oradour. A police investigation followed, but the men mentioned in the letter were, for the most part, already under surveillance by the Vichy representative in Limoges anyway, just like so many others around the Haute-Vienne. The list included father and son Jules and Paul Santrot, Oradour's tailors. Son Paul had, for some time, acted as the local agent for communist newspaper *L'Humanité*. Clog maker Aimé Faugeras lived in the nearby hamlet of Le Clos and had been the secretary of the local cell. He too remained of interest.[2]

Despite ongoing surveillance, little came of any enquiries and the list was later whittled down to five men who 'in any period of social tension must be immediately apprehended'.[3] This included Martial Machefer, 'an inhabitant of the town and notoriously a communist and leader of strike actions'. Machefer had been employed at a paper-making plant in nearby Saint-Brice but was fired for being an 'inciter of strikes'. He set up as a cobbler in the lower part of Oradour. Underneath his workshop, a cavernous cellar stretched to a length

of 30m, almost to the edge of the Glane. In 1596, during the reign of the
Bourbon King Henri IV, Oradour was razed to the ground and it is rumoured
that some of the village's inhabitants sought shelter in the cellar. A company
of soldiers stopped at the village on their way north to join the royal army
which was attempting to regain Calais from the Spanish. According to the
company commander, some of the locals fired on the soldiers, who proceeded
to close the villagers inside the church and several houses before pillaging the
village and setting fire to it. Several villagers were killed.[4]

Machefer, like the other men under surveillance following the letter of
November 1941 and the diligent investigation that followed, went about his
business. It was no secret to the village community that communists lived
amongst them. The presence of right wingers was more prevalent still, but
people were not that interested in the marginal political views of people who
were, first and foremost, *Radounauds*.[5]

The police investigators following up the letter in November 1941 were
met with a wall of silence from neighbours in the village because there was
a general distrust, hatred even, of the representatives of central power.[6] One
practical measure was taken as a result of the denunciation and investigation. Junien Leboutet, an employee of the tramway company (CDHV), had
his motorcycle taken away. He was suspected of using it for missions for
the Communist party that might lead to militancy. Leboutet and his wife,
Germanine, a dressmaker, both originated from the 'red' town of Saint-
Junien. They had been living in Limoges until their marriage in 1927, when
they moved to Oradour.

As a city in the 'free zone', Limoges fell under the jurisdiction of the Vichy
government. There were Germans in the city, but they were sure to be discreet. Vichy authorities had agreed to the establishment of German 'offices' in
Vichy in order to keep an eye on the running of the country. It was, however,
imperative that the French people did not feel that they were occupied in all
but name. When Germans in uniform came to Limoges as part of the *com-
mission d'armistice*, small spontaneous gatherings of locals took place, taking
on the form of small demonstrations. This was attention that the Germans
learned to avoid.

Germans living and working in France on behalf of the Nazis wore plain
clothes and their important job was primarily the gathering of information.
Firstly, they were to identify businesses and industries that would be useful
to the German economy, and work with Vichy in procuring what materials
they needed for the war effort. They established records of people too,
especially those who may need dealing with by Vichy, or by Germany when

the time came for full occupation. The Germans, with or without Vichy help depending on what they needed, ensured that they knew all about the Limousin and its people and profiled the country so that when the time for annexation of the 'free zone' came, the Wehrmacht could take up position in a terrain that was anything but foreign to them.

During this time, something resembling an idea of resistance was beginning to form. Léon Roche, the SFIO MP who represented the *arrondissement*, had voted against passing full powers to Pétain. Surveillance closed in on him, as it did many parliamentarians of the left, and he was forced to go into hiding before becoming active with early Resistance in 1941.[7]

Before structures developed that could be termed movements, individuals acting spontaneously and for their own ends were the sole forms of 'Resistance'. At first this 'primo resistance' was expressed through refusal or acts of protest against 'the unacceptable'.[8] While some protested about France's agreement with Germany, they would only do so openly in small numbers. Participants of any sort of action in the very early days tended to act individually. Political considerations were yet to emerge as relevant. Early propaganda primarily called out the German occupiers before some also began to include the Vichy regime and Pétain. Gatherings might take place without participants necessarily knowing what their true goals were. They might spring from pre-war political or social groupings. Sports clubs or socialist gatherings gave rise to meetings, as did youth movements. Work cooperatives, mutual benefit societies or semi-political discussion groups all hosted gatherings where discussions might give rise to the most fragile combinations solidifying into the beginnings of the network. In some instances, the structure of Freemasonry 'gave cement to the ensemble'.[9]

Albert Mirablon, with roots in Oradour and an American education, had been living in Limoges since 1938, where he had married his wife Renée. He was mobilised to the French army during the final days of August 1939 and a son, Claude, was born at the end of November. He returned to his family the following June having been awarded the *Croix de guerre*. The demobilised Albert rejoined Crédit Lyonnais and it was not long before he heard talk of resistance. Having travelled Europe extensively, he was ready to do what he could, however small, to help undermine the Vichy government and the occupier in the north. He attended early meetings in Limoges talking about activity in the occupied zone and was inspired to help.

When a Limoges Resistance group linked to *Libération-sud* sprang up in October 1941, Mirablon joined up almost at once.[10]

The earliest armed resistance groups, *maquis*, in the south of France were generally formed from decommissioned military men eager to do 'something' in preparation for being called on to act. A fighting *maquis* was not something to which General Charles de Gaulle initially gave any support. Having made his famous 18 June 1940 call from London, de Gaulle envisaged France liberating itself, but primarily by men gathered abroad, in France and North Africa. These would never be enough and he recognised the need for cooperation with other nations, but de Gaulle saw no real value of small internal armies of largely untrained and under-resourced men.

Sometimes celebrated as the very first *maquisard*, Georges Guingouin was a man of the Haute-Vienne. He initially envisaged his *maquis* of a handful of men not as a fighting army, but as a potentially invaluable disruptor of Hitler's attempts to use France for the Reich's own material means, through requisitions of crops, machinery and food. Guingouin had returned to his role as a primary-school teacher when demobilised and had to weigh up his belief in resisting German domination and the Communist party's stance, muddied because of Soviet–German non-aggression pacts. Guingouin had already decided to go it alone when the Nazis invaded the Soviet Union. He escaped arrest for circulating propaganda and literally went underground, digging out a shelter in woodland before just about anyone else 'had taken to the *maquis*'. He was particularly successful in organising raids that sent strong signals to Vichy authorities, just as much as the Germans, that the French of the countryside would keep control of their own lives. Most of Guingouin's operations were conducted in a relatively small area in the east of the Haute-Vienne, on the other side of Limoges from Oradour, but word spread and others followed in his wake.

A Restricted Life

L'abbé Jean Baptiste Chapelle was a staunch supporter of Pétain and had been only too pleased to see the dissolution of the socialist council in April 1941 and, with it, the elevation of Paul Desourteaux to head of the special delegation. Throughout 1941 to 1943, Chapelle maintained correspondence with a family who had come to Oradour as part of the 1940 exodus before returning to the Paris region later that year. He sent Madame Deleuze, of Juvisy-sur-Orge, parcels containing vegetables, and despite using his influence to acquire the very best packaging, he apologised on each occasion that the produce might be past its best by the time it arrived. On accompanying cards, he wrote about the difficulties of everyday life but maintained his trust in Pétain. On 26 March 1942, he told Madame Deleuze that more faith should be shown in the old war hero as further restrictions began to challenge the patience of people:

> I think and I very much hope that all of our health will continue despite the restrictions and that we will be able to see a time with fewer shortages. This is the focus of our hopes based on the words of the marshal in Châteauroux. He promised that the peace treaty would not be hard on France if all French people remain united to his person. It is theirs to see, because he represents France better than any other.[1]

The postage of family packages had become a popular way for the people in towns and cities to acquire goods from the countryside. Just like trips out to farmers, however, they also contributed to the unintended result of less produce sold at market and emptier shelves due to supply chain issues. Farmer's wife Marie Valade made her family some money to purchase essentials by taking additional vegetables or poultry to Limoges to sell. The earnings allowed her to make occasional visits to the butcher's, baker's or textile shops in Oradour. Any dairy products produced from the cows were for consumption at the farm, though they occasionally sold a little to people they knew well. 'It was just clothes that needed to be bought, and shoes.'[2] Going to the city carried with it costs such as travel fees and administrative charges.

L'abbé Jean Baptiste Chapelle, Oradour's long-serving curate, with Madame Deleuze, a refugee with whom he maintained a long correspondence, and her son. (Centre de la Mémoire, Oradour-sur-Glane)

Métayer (tenant) farms were family businesses that operated on practically no profit margin. Paperwork submitted by Marie's husband Jean in 1942 gives a clear outline of the farm's size and activity. It lists three people over the working age of 14, with one employee looking after the cows. The other two workers were Jean's father and brother-in-law. The women were not listed because they were not full-time farm workers, but they would have done their bit, especially at harvest and planting time. The farm had a total area of 32 hectares, one of which was non-agricultural and included the house. The rest was split between workable land, most of which was pasture, and a little that was not cultivated with a small amount of woodland. There were twenty-three cattle, of which eleven were listed as working cows or bullocks, and twelve were calves. Two non-working oxen were listed too. The farm also had a small flock of sheep: twelve ewes and one ram with five lambs. There was a sow and eight piglets, less than 6 months in age. In the farmyard, *le basse-cour*, the Valade family kept fifteen chickens, including a cockerel and ten laying hens. They also had a turkey and ten rabbits.

The workable land consisted of 7 hectares of wheat – the only cereal that they grew – and less substantial areas of not quite a hectare each for potatoes and Jerusalem artichokes. Smaller still was an area reserved for growing beans listed alongside produce such as lentils and peas as *légumes secs*. A similarly sized area was reserved for growing rape, while 1½ hectare was given over to growing red clover, produced for fodder because it helped improve the nitrous quality of the manure for fertiliser. Pockets of ground were reserved as temporary land for pasture, and intervals between crops.

Valade had been forced to take on the farm at Le Mas du Puy when the owner, a land agent himself, was unable to follow through with a promised move from one farm to another in nearby La Barre. It was a precarious existence, but such peasant families suffered less than most when restrictions were further stepped up. They did, however, have to adapt. On 5 August 1940, a Vichy law came into force that pronounced that bread must be one day old before being sold in an effort to slow down consumption of France's favourite staple. In March 1941 bread rations were reduced by 20 per cent. Rather than buying bread, peasant families made it instead. Unlike some families who made a large batch twice a month, therefore eating primarily stale bread, the Valade family made it a couple of times a week:

> There was an oven on the farm; in fact practically all farms had a bread oven. My mother and my brother-in-law ground the flour and made the dough, and then my father cooked it in the oven. And it really was good bread. I've never had such good bread since.[3]

'The Prestige of the Marshal Remains Intact'

Jean-Marcel Darthout had been born to a *paysan* family in 1924. He was bright, gained his *certificat d'études* in 1936 (second place in the whole parish) and received a bursary to study in Saint-Junien. As a young man he hoped and intended to become a primary-school teacher.

Darthout remembered life in and around the village as feeling detached from the war due to the way that families traded goods amongst themselves: 'You could eat well in the country. You could find whatever you wanted. You could easily get poultry.' But even within a village such as Oradour, where bakers had to be careful to follow the law, the purchase of bread was a problem. Some villagers asked friends with ovens to bake bread for them: 'If we bought bread it wasn't very good. But it you could find white flour, it could be alright.' Whereas city and town dwellers were actually going hungry, in Oradour, Darthout recalled 'a very agreeable life'.[1]

Camille Senon passed the week in Limoges and returned home each weekend. 'People suffered less from restrictions in Oradour,' she said. 'Of course there was the need for tickets for food, and also for textiles, clothes and shoes. But with regard to food, people were easily able to get by. They could buy milk from farms, they could grow products in their gardens and they could have chickens and rabbits. So all in all the restrictions on food were not all that hard.'[2] After each trip home Camille would return to the city with a box containing provisions such as conserves and eggs.

Robert Hébras' family lived right in the centre of the village. They were not from farming stock nor well off, but 'ate their fill'. Meat was easier to come by in the countryside because the butchers either owned livestock or purchased locally slaughtered beasts. Though not necessarily legal, it was in nobody's interests to inform; 'even the gendarmes knew about it'. As long as prices and exchange rates were reasonable, nobody intervened. Most families' diet consisted of a little meat consumed with plenty of vegetables and beans. The Hébras family were typical in that they also kept some rabbits and chickens, which provided additional meat and eggs.

Manual workers in towns such as Saint-Junien, and the middle classes in particular, were feeling the pinch of higher prices and scarcity of important foodstuffs. Fat products were hard to come by, as were eggs. The price of wine was inflated because of an obligation to buy a litre of *appellation contrôlé* for every allowed ration purchased. Local produce was insufficient to meet the needs of the population even when it could be imported from other areas of the country. The food-buying opportunities offered by the countryside and villages such as Oradour with its tram link was beneficial for the local economy, so Saturday was always a busy day there. The tram became ever more central to the life of the peasantry. People from towns and cities, where shop shelves were empty, would have to travel to the countryside for provisions. This was not just because it was easier for the producers and their families. Travel costs were reduced and they could avoid having to pay into the system. The tram stopped at an *octroi* (a station), where all goods had to be declared, and excise taxes paid. A very marked shift in societal relationships took place over the Vichy period as the rural community became the more comfortable members of society and masters of their own destinies.

Vichy's ever-growing rationing frameworks led to more people, who might otherwise have never dreamed of breaking the law, looking to manipulate or 'fudge' the system. A parallel economy emerged. The 'grey market', or the selling of goods to family, friends or regular contacts at a price slightly higher than that set by Vichy (which was often too low), became commonplace. This kind of transaction was usually carried out for the purposes of supplementing the ever-meaner rationing of key food products. But, according to Vichy, any 'transaction, action or economic exchange that constitutes an infraction against a state regulation' was punishable by law. Over time the grey market became so commonplace that the authorities chose not to follow up all denunciations for fear of being overwhelmed. However, black marketeers, those selling desired produce at a significantly inflated price to those who had the means to buy, was highly illegal and pursued by the authorities.

Most French people defaulted to the French '*système D*',³ a state of mind referring to getting by using whatever means necessary. Peasant farmers raised rabbits and chickens, sold eggs, cheese, butter and milk, and usually kept prices low so that their clients would return. The exchange of ration tickets did not need to take place. People with a bit of land could garden, producing ample vegetables for themselves and for those from the cities, to which fresh produce had ceased to be delivered. Bartering could take place in the countryside, which was impossible in stores where strict consumer laws had to be adhered to. All of this activity became entirely commonplace. In the countryside clandestine slaughtering of pigs led to the sharing of meat and conserves. Transactions took place on trams between the villages before any checks could be carried out at the edge of the city, and families 'made do' by regularly breaking the law. Guilt was non-existent because people needed to survive.

The authority of Pétain and the Vichy government was, however, breached almost from day one by masses of people on a daily basis. Even those who retained a sense of loyalty towards Pétain became used to breaking his increasingly complex rationing and requisitioning policies.[4] Vichy rules and regulations grew in response to profiteering from a system that was of its own creation. As well as buying and selling above the legal price, the rules looked to hamper those who used counterfeit rationing documents, avoided the exchange of ration tickets altogether, or hoarded goods. Few people never engaged in any of these minor infractions, particularly in towns where shelves were becoming increasingly empty. The procurement of milk, butter or vegetables from a farmer became part of life for many families, and the finding and retaining of contacts became extremely important. Saturday bicycle rides to the countryside were particularly useful because it was the only legal way of travelling solo other than by foot, and it was possible to avoid the checks along the way. The *paysans* in the hamlets dotted around Oradour were easily reachable by tram or bicycle.

The peasantry were not without their own complaints, such as low taxation on the price of requisitioned cattle, a reduced bread ration of 350g and a lack of shoes and clothing to be able to complete their heavy work. In early 1942 one of the main concerns for the people of the countryside was their claim for 'an additional ration of wine for the period of the major summer works'.

It was not just food that was in short supply. A shortage of fuel, bicycle tyres and items such as paper affected everyone, leading to changes in the way people lived their lives; it affected how they travelled and how they bought and sold.

In February 1942 a report noted a new reason for resentment towards the new structure of society in which the have-nots of the countryside were thriving:

> In Saint-Junien, the glove workers sector has been unhappy to see certain bosses trust work known as 'hand sewing' to some farmers, work which can then be completed at home, and which results in a partial lack of work for them.[5]

Marie Hébras was one of countless women in and around Oradour who were employed in this way. Further pennies were shifting towards the countryside where work could be carried out cheaply:

This means of recruitment [...] less expensive for the bosses, seems to be becoming more widespread. It would be wise to put an end to it so that the glove workers are not dispossessed of their work at the profit of the farmers who already are benefitting from the products that they grow.

Reports drawn up by Vichy authorities as a result of letter-opening and made by the *préfecture* to the Vichy police attest to a growing feeling of dissatisfaction towards France's place in the so-called partnership with Germany, as well as towards the National Revolution. 'The prestige of the marshal remains intact,' said one. But there was evidence of protest. Communists were preaching by way of clandestine materials printed using stencils. People were aggrieved not only by growing hunger due to German requisitions, but also by the ineffectual attempts of their own government's dealings with Germany. The benefits seemed to be one way.

Whereas Pétain had busied himself with national renewal, Prime Minister Pierre Laval was the main figure behind France's policy of collaboration with Germany. In July 1940, he was tasked with conducting negotiations with the German ambassador to Vichy, Otto Abentz, and he was insistent on France gaining an excellent position in Nazi Europe.

For Laval, Pétain was the figurehead he had needed to dismantle the vestiges of the Third Republic and implement an autocracy. However, Laval did not agree with a number of Pétain's many ideas regarding the National Revolution, and his machinations upset most other Vichy ministers. He was eventually replaced as head of the government by Admiral Darlan in December 1940, largely as a result of the pair's personal differences. The French public, who had been alarmed by the Pétain–Hitler handshake in October 1940, were largely pleased to see the back of Laval, but Darlan proved to be a far less effective negotiator, ceding too much to Germany. Pétain accepted that he needed Laval back and reappointed him as head of the government in April 1942. The two men, separated by a full twenty-five years in age and still unenamoured with each other, set about reshaping France. They were free of any parliamentary scrutiny and dealing with ever-growing German requests.

Laval was disliked by French ministers and German negotiators alike, largely due to his stubbornness and off-handishness. Even Pétain disliked him due to a tendency to blow smoke literally in the marshal's face. Nazi Minister for Labour Fritz Sauckel also had an ambivalent relationship with Laval. It was he who informed Laval in the spring of 1942 that Germany needed labour from France.

The departure of workers to Germany or to the construction of the Atlantic wall became the biggest cause of rancour for the French population in towns and villages alike. Laval negotiated and announced a scheme that he called *la Relève* (changeover). This was an exchange on a voluntary basis of one French prisoner of war for every three young volunteers sent to work in the Reich. His announcement speech for the scheme put an immediate dampener on it. Laval declared his wish for 'the victory of Germany' in order to ensure a defeat of Bolshevism in Europe. In terms of public opinion, this was a serious blow to the popularity and perceived trustworthiness of the Vichy regime, if not Pétain. If one policy of the Vichy regime served to politicise the young and their immediate families, it was *la Relève* which was to prove to be an abject failure, especially given the high numbers of young people requested by Germany. The scheme would be extended during the autumn of 1942 to include a mixture of voluntary and press-ganged labour.

In the Haute-Vienne, take-up numbers for *la Relève* or incorporation into the *organisation Todt* were initially pleasing despite unrealistically high expectations. The policies provoked anger throughout society but Laval's actions were, according to prefectorial reports, better understood in the better-informed middle classes where wide availability of a censured press allowed for Vichy propaganda to be dispersed effectively: 'Certain mayors in rural areas believe that propaganda amongst the peasant classes is insufficient.' It would be necessary, it continued, 'to enlighten them on the government's policies, particularly in relation to the politics of the exterior, which they either do not know about or do not know much about.'[6]

Bellevue

Madeleine Bonnet is remembered as a happy and smiling girl who was known to friends as 'Mado'. Brought up in Chamboret, north of Limoges, Madeleine had been abandoned on the day of her birth in August 1926, and the identity of her parents was never known to her. Official records of her life before she arrived in Oradour have disappeared.[1] Memories of her live on in André Desourteaux, with whom she became good friends. He describes her as a bright and funny girl, and the recollection of her name still brings a smile of fondness to his face. Very recently two photographs of her were discovered. A family in the countryside who had got to know her by inviting her to their home on certain Sundays had become equally fond of the captivating and cheeky young woman.

Madeleine was the only *pupille de l'assistance publique* (a ward of the state) placed in the village in 1944. One or two others had been registered as such when single parents found themselves overcome by circumstances. Madeleine lived with and worked as a maid for Jeanne Mercier, who ran the grocery store in the lower village alongside her son René. Madeleine helped in the shop too.

Fostering children came with state payments sizeable enough that some farming families, who largely produced their own food, could justify having one, or more, additional mouth to feed. They may, like Madeleine, prove economically useful to their placement family in other ways and could stay on sometimes. When the children became old enough to work, these payments would go towards a subsidised wage.

Seventeen-year-old Roger Gazan had endured a traumatic childhood. The year after his birth in Toulouse, his parents married and subsequently relocated to Limoges. Following complaints in October 1936, a police commissioner had visited the family home. There he had found 'four puny children shivering from cold in a room where disorder reigned, and the lack of cleanliness was repugnant'.[2] Two rudimentary beds were surrounded by dirty linen and 'debris of all sorts' on which lay the youngest child, 2-year-old Andrée-Yvette. The other children were 4, 6 and 9 years old. Their parents were sleeping. The mother, Andrée, was struggling with motherhood, trying to earn some money as a florist while suffering with alcoholism. Whenever her grip on running the household slipped, her husband absented himself from the home. Neighbours had often taken pity on the children, giving them something to eat or a few coins, though they suspected that these would make their way back to Andrée to be spent on drink. The report claimed that the father did his best not to bring money home in an attempt to keep it out of her hands. The children were taken into the care of the state, deemed under the law to have been 'morally abandoned' by both parents. Roger spent time in the town's hospice, finally ending up in Bellevue, a farm on the edge of Oradour, in August 1941. Once he had finished school he was integrated into his new family and worked the fields just like any other *Radounaud* son.

The Bellevue farm, run by Marie and Jean Lamaud, was on the road that led south into the Vienne valley, and was always full and bristling with life. As well as their son and daughter-in-law, their 4-year-old granddaughter, Marie-Thérèse, lived with them. Additionally, Marie's brother, François, something of a simpleton, worked the farm and called it his home, as did her 64-year-old mother Marthe. Jean ran his own business, dealing in threshing equipment and other farming machinery. This meant that help from his strong but vulnerable brother-in-law was welcome. So too was that of his own father, also called François, an energetic 71-year-old despite injuries sustained in the First World War. Despite a packed household, Marie and Jean also took on several *pupilles de l'assistance publique*.

In March 1942, Marie-Louise Penot, aged 20, left the farm run by the Lamaud family for good. She was no longer to be looked after by the state. Marie-Louise was to be married, and just a few months later she was living with her new husband 21km away in the village of Couzeix. Her place was immediately taken by a 16-year-old called Lucie Moreau.

Just weeks later, Marie-Louise wrote to the authorities asking them to allow her to take charge of her brother Robert, ten years her junior, hoping that she and her husband could raise him until the age of majority. Fosterer Marie Lamaud had to tell her young charge of his sister's approach. She explained that they would probably have to accept the circumstances. Marie-Louise had written of Robert as being her only family.[3] The heartbroken 12-year-old Robert wrote his own letter, in neat handwriting, to the director of the service:

Monsieur le directeur,
On Thursday Madame Lamaud told me that, according to you, my sister wants to take me to live with her. Why would this be? Things have been so good for me here with Monsieur Lamaud, who has promised that when I get my certificate[4] he will buy me a bicycle. Also this year I have gone up

into the first class. So why does she want me? It was she who, when she was here too, would always cause arguments with me. All too often she would hit me for no reason. When she went out she never wanted me to go with her. Also, and I have not mentioned this to anyone, she came to the village the other day and she did not even look at me. She had written a letter for Monsieur Lamaud, very ungrateful in tone. Madame Lamaud showed it to me and effectively she was just asking for my social security number. She did not so much as say hello to me. Now she says she wants to look after me when I was so happy here – the opposite to before she left. Luci [sic], who replaced her, is so friendly towards me and we get on so well. I would not want to leave but Madame Lamaud says that you have to take me, and that my brother-in-law and his parents are actually much nicer than her. But I want to let you know that if they make my life a misery, I will come back here to Bellevue. Monsieur Lamaud [...] told me that he will always be ready to have me back because I am not like her. Indeed I would like to come back to visit some Sundays.[5]

Robert had arrived in Bellevue in November 1938 after five years at the home of a widow north of Limoges. Robert never knew the identity of his father and had been taken from his mother, Marie-Élise, shortly after his birth because of her admission into a mental institution. Her daughter, Marie-Louise, had already been taken. She was a troubled woman with many years of mental difficulties behind her, but correspondence shows that she loved her children. Writing to the children's inspector in January 1933, she begged for news of baby Robert and proclaimed her love for both her children, asking that the inspector write to the mayor of Cromac to allow her to be reunited with them if she was released. The mayor's response was blunt. He telephoned to say that 'in the case that this person be released, her children should not be returned to her'. According to him, 'the young boy would be unhappy and the older girl would start to beg again.' This rather brutal assessment gives an insight into how mother and daughter had fared together. In June 1935 Marie-Élise wrote again to the inspector. In a few short but rambling paragraphs in which spelling, handwriting and clarity seem to have deserted her, she begged for news of her daughter who was soon, she says, to be 14. She claimed that the guardian of her daughter was being unreasonable in not letting the two correspond, saying that Marie-Louise would be old enough to make her own decisions, but the confused narrative of the letter is difficult to follow.

Marie-Louise, placed at the Bellevue, begged Marie and Jean Lamaud to allow her younger brother to join her. Eventually, in the early summer of

1938, Marie Lamaud, backed by the mayor of Oradour, had written a letter asking for an exchange of child. A 4-year-old boy was exchanged for Robert. It is impossible to say whether the Lamauds knew of the letter sent by Robert, but the Lamaud farm in Bellevue was a loving household, and for the first time in his life young Robert Penot felt safe and happy.

When his sister tried to claim him, two *gendarmes* visited Marie-Louise's new familial home and reported that the husband's family seemed well-off enough to take Robert, and that witnesses, including the mayor, attested to the good nature of the family, despite not knowing Marie-Louise herself particularly well. In August 1942 the move looked set to go ahead. The inspector, however, had reservations about the sister's motives. Robert Penot's letter had, perhaps, had the required effect. He decided to write to her one more time 'before making my final decision' and told her that 'the child knows of your desire and has formally demonstrated the intention to stay with his guardians where he is doing particularly well from all points of view'. He then added that, prior to making a decision in the best interests of the child, she should know that his services as well as the allowance paid for such *pupilles de l'assistance publique* would stop. No remunerations could be made thereafter. He asked that she think over this information before making her final decision. As a result, Robert Penot never left the Lamaud family.

Robert's sister had been replaced by Lucie Moreau. She had been born to a 23-year-old chambermaid called Léontine, originally from Rochechouart. Léontine had been trying to make a living in central Limoges when she had fallen pregnant. Just a month after being born without a named father, Lucie was given up for adoption and, after a childhood spent in and around Bellac and Limoges, she arrived at the Bellevue farm.

Having lived through some trauma or another, the state wards were dealt with sensitively by the inspectorate. Marie-Louise Labrousse, a relation of the Lamaud family who lived in nearby Le Repaire, had taken in a sensitive 11-year-old boy called Guy Canin in February 1942. He had been rescued from the streets of Saint-Junien and had two younger sisters. Their mother had died in February 1940 at the age of 28, leaving their father Joseph, who, like her, had worked in a local paper factory, to care for all three children. He did not cope well, and the two sisters had already been taken into care in November 1941. Just four days later a Saint-Junien resident took pity on Guy, finding him roaming the streets 'dying of hunger'.[6] She took him in, looked after him for several days and, when the authorities collected him, she reported that he was bedwetting every night. He was sent to Le Repaire and enrolled at school in Oradour, where he remained.

Robert Penot with Lucie Moreau, both fostered at Bellevue. Robert
was unhappy when his sister, whom he disliked, tried to adopt him.
This was partly because of the kindness shown by Marie and Jean
Lamaud and partly because he and Lucie were so close.
(Collection Benoit Sadry)

Some placements were less successful. One girl called Hélène Bossavie
was assigned to a family in the hamlet of Le Mas du Puy, the family being
described as 'not very loving [...] the mother [...] was more concerned with
looking after the cows'.[7] Hélène attended school in Oradour.

Another, Germaine Picat, given up just hours after she had been born,
had lived with an older woman in Saint-Victurnien for eleven years before
a family had come in to adopt her. They had unsurprisingly struggled with

a girl who wanted nothing more than to return to her previous home and they gave up on her when she refused to eat, went missing for hours at a time and even complained that the walls in their house were too dark. She wrote to her former host begging to return there, even supplying useful addresses in her letter, but her wishes could never be fulfilled. Instead she ended up in a home in Orbagnac, where one of the two sons was a prisoner of war.

Pierre Coudert had also been given up as a newborn. Between the ages of 2 and 4, he had been looked after by a widow in Droux who earned her living entirely from looking after children. In March 1942, an inspector was dispatched to the address following complaints about the behaviour and character of the widow. Following interviews with locals, including the mayor of the village, the regrettable decision was made to take the children away: 'I cannot leave the care of these children for whom I am responsible both morally and materially, in the hands of someone whose morality is, at best, doubtful.'

Occupation

It was while enrolled at the Pigier school in Limoges to learn secretarial skills that Camille Senon witnessed the arrival of the German army into the 'free zone' on 11 November 1942.

Until then, German soldiers had been predominantly unseen, even in Limoges. Allied forces had landed in North Africa three days earlier, cutting off Vichy from its overseas territories in North Africa, leaving the German High Command nervous of an invasion on the Mediterranean coast. Pétain had reluctantly agreed to the scuttling of the French naval fleet in Toulon in order to prevent that power passing into either Allied or German hands. The marshal's claim to have saved at least half of France from occupation was moribund.

In Limoges, uniformed German soldiers appeared in the street in significant numbers. The night before, German army vehicles had been driven through Oradour-sur-Glane – possibly the only time a German soldier set foot in the *bourg* throughout the occupation until June 1944. After November 1942 German soldiers were regularly seen in towns and cities, and they were generally well behaved and respectful. These Wehrmacht troops were older and less battle-hardened than some of the reinforcements and SS divisions that would arrive later having experienced the turbulence of the violent Eastern Front. Town and city locals became used to seeing troops in places where German battalions were established, and civilians did what they had to do to remain under the radar. People were on edge but did not yet feel threatened. In villages, throughout the whole occupation, German soldiers were rarely seen in any numbers. These places were the preserve of the *gendarmeries*, as well as the French police.

The Vichy authorities were often crueller towards civilians than the German occupiers. The establishment in November 1942 of a Gestapo headquarters in Limoges added a new level of fear.[1] The 'Villa Tivoli' was centrally located and became notorious as more and more French agents were brought on board to work in tandem with the Gestapo and, later, the *Milice*. Limoges was a city home to a wide variety of factory workers, as well as the centrepoint of a vast agricultural region. Gnome and Rhône, makers of aircraft engines, were of strategic importance to the war effort. As capital of the department of the Haute-Vienne, it was, as far as military planning was concerned, the heart of the Limousin region that also took in the departments of Indre, Creuse, Corrèze and Dordogne, as well as sections of Cher, Loir-et-Cher, Indre-et-Loire, Vienne and Charente, which straddled the demarcation line. After full occupation, the demarcation line remained as an important internal checkpoint. The Gestapo ensured that key strategic points were held securely, such as Limoges' main railway station and the radio transmitter in Nieul, just north of Oradour. The German occupiers ensured that the mine in Saint-Léonard-de-Noblat, which produced wolfram, a key ingredient in the making of explosives, was requisitioned and they set up a country field hospital in Magnac-Laval.[2] Meanwhile censorship and propaganda offices were set up in Limoges, along with two offices dedicated to workforce and two Gestapo offices, one of which, on the *rue de Tivoli*, would become notorious.

Camille Senon had moved into a Catholic boarding house called the *Protection de la Jeune Fille*, where half of the building had been requisitioned in order to house the German *Kommandantur*. The women rarely passed the soldiers going to and from the command centre, as the two parts of the building gave on to two perpendicular avenues. Camille was wary of the Germans, but unafraid. The manageress ran a strict establishment. She was a tall, thin woman nearing her seventies who always wore a black dress. She was staunchly Pétainist despite trust in the marshal falling away when the demarcation line was crossed. Illustrative of the sort of monarchist conservative background that still blamed the fall of France on the paid holidays introduced by the *Front Populaire*, she insisted on meals being taken together, accompanied by lodgers chosen to read enriching prose. Marshal Pétain was given an almost cult religious status: 'he who had given the gift of his person to France to hold off its misfortune just as Jesus had offered his life to humanity to wash away its original sins.'[3] The young ladies who lived there – nurses, secretaries, administrators – would secretly laugh at their lot and the anachronistic ways of their hostess. But it was not an environment in which Camille felt comfortable, speaking out about her belief that people ought to do something to resist the fate reserved for France.

Instead she settled into a regular pattern of life. At the end of each Saturday she took the six o'clock tram to Oradour via the winding streets of the city's western suburbs and out into the lush countryside. The journey lasted just over an hour and a quarter, and each time Camille joined the tram at its terminus at the *Gare de Charente*. Camille's weekly stay was brief, her arrival coinciding with the onset of evening before a good night's sleep and a long Sunday spent with her parents and then the return leg to the city in the evening.

There was little for a young woman of her age to do other than read, take bike rides or watch the young men of the village play football in the weekly matches, sometimes adding their own comedy commentaries. In 1941 several young men in Oradour had struck on the idea of re-forming the village football club. There had been a team in the 1920s, in which many of the village's more mature men had played or been actively involved. It had also lent itself to a healthy social life that included singing, acting, eating and drinking. Some of these men, such as Doctor Jacques Desourteaux and André Foussat, were only too happy to revive the team, and they established it officially as an association, *l'Union Sportive d'Oradour-sur-Glane*. Desourteaux took on the presidency, while Foussat was vice president and village grocer René Mercier was secretary. The club became so popular that it ran a second team. Just like its previous incarnation, it became a hub for social contact and gatherings. On match days, which took place at the Bellevue farm, locals both young and old, male and female, would gather to watch the young men who became a successful team. The club also helped to integrate those who may

The football team. Back row: René Mercier, Henri Bouchoule, Aimé Darthout, Robert Besson, Joseph Bergmann, Marcel Darthout, Henri Beaubreuil. Kneeling: Martial Brissaud, Jean Blancher, Martial Beaubreuil. Seated: Maurice Beaubreuil, Matou Rouchaud, Armand Senon. (Collection Maurice Beaubreuil)

otherwise have felt like outsiders. Jewish Barber Joseph Bergmann was an integral member of the team, as was Felix Aliotti, a pilot born in Tunisia of Corsican parents, demobilised in 1928 and stationed in Avignon. Hearing from a friend how the village was calm and far from trouble, Aliotti brought his wife Cléa and two infant daughters to Oradour in September 1942. Aliotti travelled to and from the village, always ensuring he was available for the football matches on a Sunday.

Public dances, the staple social occasion for young people in rural communities, were forbidden in the name of the period of mourning decreed by Pétain after the defeat. Camille did not attend the *bals clandestins*, which she considered to be risky events. Evenings were spent with neighbours and in houses with shutters down, listening to radio broadcasts from London or Moscow.

A Store Cupboard for the Reich

Robert Hébras also spent the weekdays in Limoges, where he worked at the garage after a job had been found for him following the failed placement at Poutaraud's business in Oradour. He commonly saw large numbers of German soldiers in Limoges during his time there.[1] One of the garage's main sources of work, especially since civilian vehicles had been largely prohibited, was the German army. As well as fitting *gazogène* engines on to locally sourced cars, the mechanics also had to service vehicles that had been requisitioned and deliver them back to an address, once they had been repainted white. Many garages were doing the same and owners were told that this had to take precedence over other work.

Prefects bemoaned the requisition of lorries which, they claimed, had begun to damage the local economy. Even vehicles that were not in working order were targeted and this meant that spare parts for repairs became increasingly hard to come by. There was a note of desperation in the prefect's plea when he said:

> it would be desirable that, in a region where everything necessary for the imposed contingencies by the German authorities is done, that they abstain from looking to requisition or even confiscating, vehicles outside of service, even when they are military in origin.[2]

The adult population of France had experienced rationing and restrictions during the latter part of the First World War. In 1917, measures had had to be taken to restrict the consumption of certain food products. Bread was not rationed until the last days of January 1918, resulting in shortages. People had, however, had to manage. The government at that moment retained widespread support when people were able to recognise that their sacrifices were directly benefitting their men, and that their difficulties in no way measured up to the hardships that the men in the trenches were forced to endure. The people felt a moral responsibility to suffer.[3]

There had been no such cause to work towards under the Vichy regime. Soon after the men were demobilised, Vichy's measures were imposed. The sacrifices that French people were being asked to make appeared to benefit only the German war effort or an abstract 'need of the nation', which was emotionally difficult for many to adopt. When the fighting had ended, internal politics relating to Vichy policies over prisoners of war, collaboration, requisition and restriction were openly discussed around the country. More and more people did not buy into the ideological narratives of the National Revolution, nor wished to support the German war effort. Shortages and requisitions produced problems that became political in nature. As transport around the country became patchy, crops that were meant for internal consumption suffered or rotted while awaiting transportation. Paperwork and heavily weighted ratios of goods to be transported out of the country resulted in people looking for loopholes to retain their goods.

Very few Frenchmen supported either collaboration with Germany or Laval's politics. A great many did, however, believe in Pétain as a figure-head beyond Vichy, and even as a man playing a game of double bluff with Germany in order to protect France's interests. The November 1942 occupation was a watershed moment and support for the marshal waned. Small numbers of people had decided to resist even within his own government due to his increasingly tenuous grip on France's destiny.

As for the general population, Pétain could not live up to the hopes that he had built for the nation, nor the promises he had made in June 1940 when he gave himself as a 'gift' for the French people. As time went on even those who supported him split into two groups – 'active Pétainists' of the type who wrote letters of denunciation and worked for the Vichy authorities or militia groups, and 'passive Pétainists' who retained the mental image of Pétain as a leader and continued to believe that he was holding back a 'trump' card.

In cities, life was becoming ever harder because of a lack of food on ever-lighter shelves. In the countryside, on the other hand, some farmers thrived. Those who lived north of the demarcation line were less enamoured by Pétain than those who had benefitted from two years of relative freedom. Many northern crops, resources such as coal and high-value produce such as milk and cheese were immediately plundered for the occupiers.

Pétain had, for many, successfully portrayed his 1940 relationship with Hitler as one of statesman-like equality – a kind of working partnership. He certainly never believed that Hitler would be as malevolent towards France as he turned out to be. The marshal was duped, and Hitler saw France as little more than a battleground and store cupboard for the Reich, to be emptied of food, material and men.

French people began to lose faith in Pétain as France's spiritual leader. He had promised that he would get the country's 1.6 million prisoners of war home, but very few arrived. Moments such as the 1940 handshake with Hitler at Montoire-sur-le-Loir were recalled. Increasingly collaborationist policies followed the reappointment of Pierre Laval to government, as the self-confessed Germanophile became ever more influential in dealings with senior Nazis. The full occupation of the country and the pressure to fill work quotas for Germany through *la Relève* disquieted Frenchmen and -women who had shown faith in Pétain's 'double game'.

Vichy's inhumane treatment of those deemed to be anti-French became important too. The persecuted included those with rejected political ideas, communists, Freemasons, foreigners and Jews. The notion of 'undesirables' became the subject of an increasingly brutal policy that clarified over time. Jews – initially foreign and later French-born – were first targeted for removal from any influential roles in society. Subsequently, they were stripped of property and during the summer of 1942 round-ups began that lasted until the summer of 1944. Many were deported after first being processed in holding camps, and many were sent to death camps such as Auschwitz. Gypsies and other 'undesirables', such as Spanish refugees and Freemasons, were equally maltreated.

The Tanner

Robert Pinède was a war veteran. He served in the final months of the 1914–18 conflict and was demobilised in March 1921, having achieved the rank of sergeant. He became a tanner, working in the preparation of leather,[1] dealing primarily in sheep and goat skins for the production of gloves, shoes and clothing. By the onset of the Second World War he was running his own business. He was also Sephardic Jewish[2] and he lived with his family in Bayonne, near the Spanish border.

In January 1925 he married Carmen, a young woman originally from the Spanish port of Bilbao. By the time the couple had had their three children, Robert was within a circle of the town's more influential businessmen and municipal politicians. 'Honourably known in Bayonne,' he was 'noted as a radical socialist with socialist tendencies'.[3] Through his contacts in the world of industry and the military, Robert became heavily involved with Freemasonry. It was almost inevitable, therefore, that he would be tracked by the Vichy authorities.

In 1941 the *Union générale des israélites de France* (UGIF) had been created as a means for Vichy to keep track of the many Jewish associations that were in existence, and its offices were in the same building as the Pinède family's Bayonne home. Much to the ignorance of the rest of his family, Robert got involved, particularly in relation to the management of benefits and looking after the interests of Jewish citizens of Bayonne and the surrounding area. He did all this without the knowledge of his by then teenage daughters.

Things changed for the Pinède family in July 1942 when, as a result of the Vichy spoliations laws, Robert's business was expropriated:

> One fine morning we found a rather grand poster attached to the door of the tannery that said simply 'Jewish property for sale' […] From that moment my father began to busy himself. Much of the [Jewish] community had already managed to get to the free zone by their own means. There only remained the poor, and my father took it upon himself to take care of them.[4]

Since the beginning of the occupation, Robert had worked to assure the authorities in Bayonne of his family's French lineage. One of his wife's ancestors had even been personal physician to Louis XV. However, this proved to be immaterial and after June 1942 the family, like all Jews, was forced to wear the yellow star of David. Robert and Carmen did their best to hide their disquiet. Nobody in the family openly complained about the need to wear the star, nor about the requirement to have all documents stamped with the word '*Juif*'. The family's daily life, however, became increasingly difficult. The children were pulled from school and taught at home. They could no longer go to Bayonne's fabulous beach, nor the cinema and other public places. Jews had to get on the last 'wagon' of the tramway and even shop during a one-hour period between three and four in the afternoon, when most goods had disappeared from the shelves. Up until 1942 the general feeling was one of frustration and anger between the older members of the family, but in the summer of 1942 that turned to fear. The Pinède family began to think of ways they too could get to the free zone, where Robert was determined to carry on his career as a tanner.

The Pinède family would make their way towards the Limousin in 1943, but they were by no means the first to do so. Aron Jakobowicz, his wife Golda and their two children, David and baby Sarah, left Poland in 1930 amid an economic crisis and a wave of anti-Semitism. They arrived in Paris hoping for a brighter future, but as non-French Jews their status turned them into a target for deportation. When the German invasion threatened Paris in May 1940, the family fled. They reached Limoges, which they thought would be far enough into the free zone for them to remain in relative safety. They were helped to find accommodation in a nearby hamlet. They were given an upstairs flat in a large house known as *Maison-Blanche* on the edge of forestry that stretched from a hamlet called La Malaise bordering the N141 downhill to the larger village of Saint-Victurnien.

When they arrived in 1941, daughter Sarah was 11 years of age and considered herself French. Her older brother David had applied for and been given French national status. He married a local girl from Saint-Victurnien, found work as a lumberjack and played football for the local team. The family existed quite happily in the area. The mayor of Saint-Victurnien, Antoine Bardet, busied himself with housing evacuees and refugees, as well as GTE workers, both Spanish and Jewish. Of the newly arrived Jewish families, one by the name of Stein hid in an attic provided to them by Bardet. The Polish-born father, Adam, had been a French citizen since the 1930s, having been medically trained in the country, but with the Vichy regime latterly targeting those Jews who had arrived since 1933, he brought his family to the Limousin in 1942. Adam and his wife would later help the *maquis* as medics and, when they were absent, other villagers looked after their children.

One of these children recalled years later that there were certainly other Jews in Saint-Victurnien. She recalled a couple with a baby who always seemed sad, like her parents.[5] Mayor Antoine Bardet's own daughter, who was in her twenties at the time, also recalled three Jewish families in Saint-Victurnien, and a rabbi who came every day to procure milk.[6] In nearby Oradour-sur-Glane, Joseph Bergmann, the popular barber who worked for Lucien Morlieras in the barber shop of the *Café du Chêne*, hid that he was born in Germany, most people assuming that he was Austrian by birth. But as to whether he was Jewish, the young men with whom he became friends and football teammates, and the many clients whose hair he cut, never even asked. The Kanzler family kept themselves to themselves and were even protected by those around them despite their very withdrawn nature. In April 1943 the prefect of the police wrote to Paul Desourteaux asking for information about the Kanzler family. The mayor's response confirmed that the couple's daughters, Dora and Simone, were French but that their parents, Joseph and Maria, were not fluent in the language. This allowed him to cloud over the questions of their religion. The Kanzler girls were part of the school for refugees and therefore subject to a Christian education. Desourteaux concluded that the linguistic difficulties and uncommunicative nature of their parents were such that it would be better if the police followed up on the case. The office of *renseignements généraux*, the French internal security service, in its report on the couple, was conclusive that the family were 'doubtless of the Jewish race' but that Joseph 'claimed to be of the protestant persuasion'. The family were not bothered after that and the report concluded that they had not been subject to any 'unfavourable notice' and saw 'very few people', but because they were foreigners, and most of all Jewish, 'they do not enjoy the sympathy of the population'.[7]

If the Kanzlers did not enjoy the confidence of the population it is unlikely that this would have been because they were Jewish, but rather because they were withdrawn in character and from Schiltigheim, from where the evacuees were not particularly fondly remembered.

The Kanzler family remained in Oradour and would be joined by the Pinède family. Neither tried to hide their Jewishness. These people were far removed from the Vichy caricatures of greedy Jewish businessmen or politicians intent on installing communism around the world. When they were in need of protection, the people of Oradour, like most in the extended region, obliged. There were no denunciations – and, in fact, very few throughout the wider region – based on Jewishness.

During the summer of 1942 the Vichy government pushed their anti-Semitic policies, and the mass round-ups that took place within the free zone brought public support noticeably towards the Jewish people. Whereas French anti-Semitism – even the governmentally led type up to that point – had aimed to exclude Jews from important jobs and decision-making activities. But the Nazi-type treatment of the Jews adopted by the collaborationist government was distasteful to most ordinary French people. In the Limousin countryside huge numbers of refugees had arrived in areas where Jews had rarely ever lived before. Mistrust was levelled at outsiders in general, with the exception of those who were known or perceived to have come from Germany.

As Marguerite Lederberg, daughter of Doctor Adam Stein, pointed out during their stay in Saint-Victurnien when she was a child, 'we may not have been accepted, we may not have been liked, but we were not turned in.'

The Return of Otto

When the Germans occupied the free zone, the management of GTE camps fell under German control. New regulations were put in place, denying members of the GTE the chance to socialise with the local population. Andrée Brandy could no longer see her fiancé Millán Bielsa. Soon afterwards, before the end of 1942, the camp was transferred to Aixe-sur-Vienne. The pair continued to write to each other until he was caught up in a disciplinary issue. He was sent to work at a peat bog in the Cher, and then found himself in the Vernet d'Ariège, where he would stay until 1944. He would have to wait to find his fiancée, who he called 'Dédée'.

The bringing of the camp under German control resulted in an unexpected twist. Commandant Otto, who on previous visits had been unable to recruit any inmates for work on the Atlantic coast, returned. This time he was to run the camp on behalf of his German masters. This resulted in new procedures and life becoming much harder. Several men were deported to Germany following reports that he made. Morning exercises and chores were introduced, together with physical inspections of the bedraggled men, who would be beaten on the backs of their legs if Otto was not satisfied. According to Raimundo Lluch, Otto used a horse whip or even his weapon to beat the men. He reigned through an application of terror unlike anything that had gone before. Lluch witnessed men being kicked from behind when they could not keep up with the pace of marching due to fatigue and hunger. Where others saw illness or physical injury, Otto saw disobedience or, worse, revolt. He would not tolerate even the faintest murmur as they marched. He wrongly insisted that the men were all 'reds'.

One day Otto's demeanour led to a violent outburst. Several men, in sight of Raimundo and his family, turned on Otto and pinned him to the ground. One of the men involved was Manuel Tejedor, Raimundo's father who was hardened by years of guerrilla warfare in Spain. As he got up to flee from the scene, Otto fired at him from the ground. The family, initially unsure of his fate, were encouraged by the lack of blood on the ground. Word soon arrived that he was in Creuse, where he had begun working on buses and machinery, all of which were for the benefit of local Resistance groups. It was the end of an unhappy period at Oradour for Raimundo and his family, in contrast to Millán Bielsa's experience. Whereas Bielsa's medical background had enabled him to integrate with the population, the Lluch family were in the majority: kept apart. Raimundo remembered being turned away from mass by the curate, probably *l'abbé* Chapelle, who told them that despite their Catholicism, they were simply not welcome.[1]

Réfractaires

Fernand Hyvernaud and his wife Marie gave the *Radounauds* an event to remember at the end of 1942, when their first-born daughter, Henriette, married a mechanic from Limoges called Marcel Joyeux. The wedding took place just five weeks after the 'free zone' had been fully occupied by the Germans. Henriette and her new husband posed for the traditional photograph outside the village church, surrounded by their friends and family, before walking in a procession through the village and on to a fine reception.

The bride's mother Marie had given birth to nine children: six boys and three girls. She had been pregnant on the outbreak of hostilities and this son, André, was born on November 1940. He was her tenth and final child. Originally one of five children herself, she was from a family of growers who had moved around the area before settling in nearby Peyrilhac. It was

The wedding of Henriette Hyvernaud to Marcel Joyeux. Her father, a cattle trader named Fernand, is at her shoulder, alongside her mother, Marie. During the massacre, Henriette tried to climb out of the church window but was shot, along with her baby René.
(Collection Famille Hyvernaud)

there she met Fernand Hyvernaud in 1920. Fernand, born and brought up in Limoges, was a veteran of the First World War. He served in the *Armée française de l'orient* before demobilisation in 1920 and a return to agricultural work. By November of the same year the couple were married.

At the time war was declared with Nazi Germany, the couple were living in the lower village, very near the church. Fernand was a buyer and seller of cattle, and owned a yard and several sheds just a few steps from the family home. They owned and worked a property in Saint-Gence, 12km east of Oradour, and their two oldest sons, Marcel and René, had begun working there, travelling by bicycle as and when they needed.

It was an uncomfortable time to be a young man in France. Sauckel had requested more and more labour for Germany but Laval's *Relève* was not bringing the numbers required, and prisoners of war who returned were often sick or incapacitated. Laval agreed to boost the scheme in September by expanding the qualification age and opening the scheme further to women. Results were poor and Laval's heel dragging was annoying the Germans.

In February, *la Relève* was replaced by the *Service du travail obligatoire* (STO). This was a significant turning point because it obliged rather than requested the majority of young men born between 1920 and 1922 – that is the majority of men aged 20–23 – to leave France and go elsewhere in the Reich, probably Germany, to work. Targets set by Sauckel and the Germans skyrocketed month on month, while Laval tried at first to protect agricultural workers, students and women. They were eventually called up but public opinion and protest from the Church meant that very few women actually departed. The remaining French army had been disbanded the previous November and compulsory work service had been prohibited under the terms of the armistice. With decency, a respect for authority, national pride and personal responsibility, key strands of the National Revolution's outline for youth, the scout-influenced *Chantiers de la jeunesse*, had been created as compulsory work camps. The 24,000 young men who were at a *chantier* were, therefore, fair game to be called up.

At the time of their marriage, Henriette's new husband, Marcel Joyeux, had opted not to depart for Germany and his job justified his resistance to it. His birthdate fell within the announced range and a call-up was inevitable. But as a mechanic in Limoges, probably servicing German military vehicles, he may have benefitted from a blind eye on the part of the authorities. Henriette's brother, also called Marcel and born a year later than her in 1922, was called up and sent to Germany as were several others from the immediate area, including Lucien Bélivier, son of a nearby farmer who lived just the other side of the River Glane. That February, public opinion turned further against Vichy collaborationism. The prefect reported a 'fatalism of the population' towards not just the work programme, but also shortages of food and very slow and difficult transport. More people had begun to listen to foreign radio, and Allied propaganda dropped by British planes was filling some of the gaps in knowledge of events for people in the countryside. On 13 March 1943, Georges Guingouin's *maquis* targeted the Bussy-Varache viaduct west of Limoges. By blowing up the first trainload of workers being sent to Germany, STO was prevented from setting off and delayed for several days.

The advent of STO meant that young men could either agree to do what their call-up letter instructed, or they could hide. Across France some 200,000 men chose the latter option. Of these, around a quarter would go into the Resistance. The rest would simply exist in a state of irregularity, having to remain in full sight with falsified papers if they could get them, or more commonly go into hiding. These young men were known as *réfractaires*.

Oradour was not unusual in having a number of *réfractaires*. Some chose to keep their presence a complete secret while others were more open about their *situation irrégulière*. Paul Doutre, a 20-year-old carpenter, had been called up to a *chantiers de jeunesse*.[1] When word arrived that he would soon be sent to Germany for obligatory work service, he fled the camp and lived under his parents roof. Even his next-door neighbours were unaware that his parents hid him there for three months. Maurice Beaubreuil had received the call up to STO so was given accommodation at the grocery shop belonging to his paternal aunt Jeanne Mercier in the lower village. Jacques Garaud, a 22-year-old mechanic in Vouziers in the Ardennes, came to Oradour to stay with his aunt Marie Mosnier, a widow who owned several of the farms in and around the village. His neighbour, Robert Besson, had returned from fighting in June 1940 only to be called up for STO, but he failed to show up as instructed on several occasions. Besson had a brother, Abel, who had been detained in Germany as a prisoner of war. That there were reportedly *réfractaires* hiding in the family home of Paul Doire, a baker who was absent at that time and probably serving a *maquis* unit further north, cannot have easily been kept quiet. Doire's home was on the main *Champ de foire*.

At his farm in Le Mas du Puy, Jean Valade's family hosted Marcel Barrière. Jean's son, Albert, did not know Marcel, his second cousin, well. He arrived with his father one Sunday morning and, at first, Albert thought that they were people from the city who had come to search for food to buy. Marcel, an engineer in Limoges, had been at a *chantier de jeunesse* when he had heard that he would soon be deported under STO. He had asked for a short leave of absence, and then failed to turn up at the barracks. For Albert, the young man who was 'older than me [...] was the ideal friend, a godsend. He was tall, strong and a trusted mate. I remember that the girls used to smile at him dreamily.' As an engineer, Marcel also had his uses around the farm: 'He had no equal for repairing bicycles, which was a precious quality at that time when people had no other way of getting around.' Like the Beaubreuil brothers, his presence was no secret: 'He had false papers, he was hiding, but he went out and about.'[2]

Maurice Beaubreuil's older brother Martial was also hiding out at the Mercier grocery store. He was a 31-year-old escaped prisoner of war. Daniel Senon, another escapee from German captivity who had managed to return home in 1941, found a job working as a postman and lived on a farm just across the Glane. It should be noted, therefore, that the *Légion* never had much of an influence in Oradour, especially after 1942 when the organisation had lost most of its influence anyway. Matthieu Mercier, listed as its treasurer in 1942, was, by 1944, providing a hiding place for the Beaubreuil brothers. STO evader Robert Besson had actually belonged to the *Légion* in 1942. Even its president, Jean Roumy, and his wife became friendly with the Jewish Pinède family who arrived in April 1943. The *Légion*, as much as it still existed in Oradour, by that time seems to have entirely turned its back on Vichy collaborative policies such as STO and anti-Semitic sentiments.

The *Petites Juives*

Robert Pinède brought his family to Oradour from Bayonne on the south-western tip of France in April 1943, by which time his eldest daughter Jacqueline was 18. Her sister Francine was 16, and their brother André, 8 years old, had special physical and mental needs.

The whole western coast of France had been occupied since the armistice of June 1940, and by the beginning of 1943 the German authorities had decided to rid the southern coastal regions of all Jews. As part of UGIF and a business owner, Robert Pinède played a key role in negotiating with the German authorities the conditions under which the remaining Jewish people of Bayonne could leave. With the chief rabbi arrested, it fell to Robert to work with the town hall and the local commander to ensure some quite unique terms – that remaining Jews could leave voluntarily, even if obligatorily. They were allowed to cross the demarcation line, by then a checkpoint, into what had been the free zone. France was fully occupied but central France offered some respite from German activity, and at least they were not immediately deported. This was a triumph, especially given that the terms also allowed for these Jewish people to take their property with them, which included personal objects and even furniture, provided they left before 29 May. As part of the agreement, all Jewish families, including Robert and Carmen Pinède, received a note from the *sous-préfet* of Bayonne which was written in French and German and acted as a '*laissez-passer*'. The family's business was already in the course of being sold.

Many of the remaining Jewish families were sent to the region of Pau but Robert wanted to find a way to work, a right of which many Jewish people had been deprived. Working for UGIF was permitted but Robert did not know how long he might be allowed to continue. He managed to obtain a truck to carry furniture and then had to make a decision as to where to head. His leatherworking contacts had proven useful in finding two possibilities. They could head to Millau, a small town nestled at the foot of a valley in Aveyron. However, his mother, who would accompany them, feared the oppressive heat there. Instead they opted for Saint-Junien, known for its tanning and glove-making businesses. Robert had even been promised a job there.

The Pinède family trundled into Saint-Junien with just about everything they owned to meet their contact, a Monsieur Pérucaud. Pétain had managed to negotiate that Jews in the Vichy zone need not wear stars, but the family arrived in the Limousin with papers that were in order and bearing the stamp that announced that they were Jewish.[1] They did not know what to expect but were pleasantly surprised. They sensed an atmosphere of peace. No accommodation could be found for them in Saint-Junien so they were taken instead to Oradour. The house that awaited them was basic. There was no sink and washing had to be done from a bowl. Toilet facilities, such as they were, were located at the bottom of the garden.

They were neighboured by the tramway station and the *Hôtel Avril*, and Carmen was delighted by the small garden and the setting behind the house which gave on to open fields. Carmen knew that the garden would help André settle into his new surroundings. Jacqueline and Francine, already extremely close, explored their new surroundings together.

They found that food was far easier to come by than had been the case in Bayonne. There was no need for them to wear their stars as nobody seemed to care that they were Jewish. During the summer of 1943 they made the most of the gatherings of youngsters in the fields and the occasional cinema screenings in the *Hôtel Avril*. They went on errands on their bicycles in the warm morning air to collect food from nearby farms. In the afternoons they bathed in the Glane.[2] They began to feel like complete young women again.

'Really everything was done for us to forget the humiliations of the occupation [...] We were never hungry and everybody helped each other out.'[3] They cultivated close relationships with some of the families from Moselle. Robert's mother Gabrielle, given a room in the *Hôtel Avril*, was a little irked by the lack of basic comforts in the countryside, but she grew accustomed. They were open about being Jewish André Desourteaux, Robert Hébras and other youngsters of the same age playfully called them *les petites juives*. Next door to them lived the Roumy family who had developed a reputation as loyal to Marshal Pétain. Nevertheless, all members of the Roumy household were 'charming' with them. Carmen even gave her jewellery to the Roumy family for safe keeping.

They remained concerned about their situation as Jews in a country known to be deporting more and more French Jews, but knew more than they let on to their daughters, who they allowed to get on with their young lives. They listened to the BBC every night, illegally. Let down by his contacts and unable to find work in the factories, Robert continued his work with UGIF without the knowledge of his daughters, both of whom assumed he had taken up

From left: Jacqueline, André and Francine Pinède. The Pinède family were open about their Jewish identity and settled into life in Oradour without issue. (Centre de la Mémoire, Oradour-sur-Glane)

employment in Saint-Junien. Instead he spent the working week in Limoges and Brive, working partly as an accountant, while providing relief to Jews who were either interned in camps or integrated into GTE camps.[4] When the leader of the Jewish community in Limoges was arrested Robert decided he needed to protect his family. Believing that he would be looked for by the authorities, he rented a smaller apartment opposite the family home. He moved the girls and André there in case the authorities came during the night.

Robert Pinède became very sensitive to any mention of round-ups but he continued his life, playing billiards in the *Hôtel Avril* with Henri Laurence, the owner's son-in-law who had arrived from Paris in 1942. With their father so often out of town, the girls and Carmen looked after André and his mother, and got to know their new community which had welcomed them with open arms.

The Sign of the Gamma

The paramilitary *Service d'ordre légionnaire* (SOL) had, in December 1941, emerged from the ranks of the veterans' *Légion* as a paramilitary organisation under the leadership of Joseph Darnand. It had a twenty-one-point manifesto 'Against Jewish leprosy. For French purity' and 'Against democracy, for authority'. From January 1943 a new organisation was launched which, Chief Darnand hoped, would stamp out opposition to the Vichy regime and promote a radical version of the National Revolution.[1] Its advent marked the start of a new period of active collaboration.

According to Camille Senon, 'the population was divided. There was a fringe of active collaborators and from the moment it was created there was a significant organisation around the *Milice*.' Travelling to and from Limoges on the tram, Robert Hébras began catching sight of a young man who he had known as a teenager on the tramway wearing a *Milice* uniform.[2] The boy would pretend that he had not seen Robert or his friends.

Oradour, according to verbal testimonies, hardly ever saw any uniformed *miliciens*. Robert Hébras never saw any such people. The *Milice* had no reason to come to Oradour. It was created as a 'paramilitary vanguard of the National Revolution, intensely loyal to the person of Marshal Pétain',[3] but, even by the time of its creation, its raison d'être was changing with the decline of Pétain's influence over events in France. It became a tool of Vichy-style fascism and very quickly its readiness to work with and for the Germans made it hated. It was made up of 'rootless'[4] young men who wanted to leap-frog rivals and gave them the weapons to do so.

Surveillance of the Limousin was essential to German commanders who recognised its central position on the edge of the Massif Central and in the way of smooth communications between Vichy and the Atlantic coast. Active Resistance there had potential to disrupt troop movements on either a north–south or west–east axis. The installation of a successful collection of organisations that could report on the level of support for Resistance activities was paramount in Limoges. The *Milice* was a key part of this. The 'Villa Tivoli', the Gestapo headquarters in Limoges, was centrally located and became notorious as more and more French agents were brought on board to work in tandem with the Gestapo and the *Milice*. Writing about the town

of Saint-Amour in the Jura in his contemporary diary, Jewish writer Léon
Werth illustrates how locals came to feel about those who collaborated in this
active manner. The experiences of that town and those of Oradour are strik-
ingly similar. They hardly saw a German soldier and those they did see were
in bigger towns and generally behaved entirely properly. The people who the
inhabitants of small towns came to despise were the young men who chose to
join the *Milice* and strutted around wearing the sign of the gamma. Oradour,
a village, never saw *miliciens*, unlike the town of Saint-Amour or indeed local
equivalents such as Rochechouart, Saint-Junien or Limoges. There were very
few open collaborators in Oradour and letters of denunciation were just
about unknown.

To Camille Senon, politically engaged and a resident of both Oradour and
Limoges, it seemed most people kept a middle ground: 'There were some
people who were absolutely for the Resistance. But the largest part of the
population were those people who remained spectators.'[5] For the majority
of people, what mattered most was putting food on the table and a trou-
ble-free existence for their family. In the hamlets around Oradour, members
of the peasantry watched, waited and did what was needed to get by. Most
people who struggled to make a living did not become accomplices in the
Vichy tragedy. The temptation to get ahead of business rivals who may have
been dipping into the grey market did not lead to letters of denunciation.
Neither did the relatively open existence of communists, Jews and *réfractaires*
in Oradour invite any such betrayals of community.

Watching in a Rigorous Silence

Jeanne Crombé had settled into country life on the farm of La Lauze having arrived from Roubaix with her friend Berthe Coppenolle. Her daughter Jeannette, who had been a primary-school teacher in Roubaix, had also decided to stay in the Limousin rather than return home. She had taken up work as a domestic servant in a nearby *château*. She had perhaps told her mother of other *châteaux* that had been visited, or raided, by *maquisards*. Jeanne wrote:

> We are seeing all sorts of criminal things during this war they are killing people like poultry. You would have thought perhaps that war killed enough anyway. This terrorist movement is hitting everywhere, and nobody is managing to defend themselves from it. The tobacconists, the farmers, the chateau owners, so numerous here, are often visited. Jeannette is luckily not fearful.[1]

Throughout the course of 1942 and into 1943 the press had been reporting what the new *maquis* groups were doing. The syndicated Vichy press, at the behest of the Germans, called them bandits and terrorists. They painted them as groups of communists eager to bring the country under the control of Moscow. These *maquisards* were more dangerous to the French way of life than the occupier, or so the press would have readers believe. The public were also told that they were all foreign, Jewish and morally bankrupt. Beginning in December 1942, just after France had become fully occupied, a handful of men under the command of Georges Guingouin had begun a concerted campaign to thrust a spanner in the works of the Vichy–German machine. It began with the partial destruction of an aircraft factory, and the sabotage of a series of baling machines in Eymoutiers, east of Limoges, with a view to stopping hay being sent on to the Soviet Union to support the Nazis in their battles on the Eastern Front.

Left-wing tracts asked young people called up for work duties to disperse, and even called for 'careful and discreet actions' – an early call for restrained sabotage or striking. Letters found their way to town halls calling for internal sabotage of the running of *la Relève* and a battle against governmental initiatives. Beginning in the Corrèze and moving into the Haute-Vienne and Dordogne, the *préfectures* bemoaned the rise in 'acts of terrorism', recognising that 'the population, which is at least a little scared, can see these actions as a reaction to the German occupation' rather than the behaviour of small numbers of delinquents. This was, of course, dangerous for public opinion vis à vis local police forces. Nevertheless, at this early stage it was claimed that 'the population would like […] that severe sanctions should reprimand such injustices and abuses'. The prefect's report continued to claim that the majority of the population had 'lost interest in propaganda relating to the *Révolution national*, instead only interested in an end to the hostilities which would improve their famine'.[2]

By the autumn of 1943 some 40,000 to 50,000 men had joined the *maquis* in France, still just 20 per cent or less of STO *réfractaires*. Some joined *maquis* groups in the countryside which, if nothing else, seemed to promise shelter, food and an occupation; it was, after all, an alternative to the *chantier de jeunesse* and subsequent probable deportation for STO. Police authorities were having some difficulty in defining what the groups were trying to achieve, other than to live a life of outlaws. They knew that many *réfractaires* were, in some respect, being led by the underground Communist party through its new mouthpiece, the *Front national*, because of 'its words of order and construct of the future world'. The same authorities also worried that the Communist party was one that 'trains these young men, providing them with a strict discipline and associating them with acts of terror' such as 'burglary, arson, armed robbery and attacks involving explosives'. It was felt that these young men would soon have low morale due to rain or illness that would no doubt accompany their stay 'in the *maquis*'.

Prefects reported on such '*defiants*' who were obtaining material by robbing town halls, shops' stocks or *chantiers de jeunesse* for materials but, significantly, by July 1943 public opinion had begun to turn towards helping the young men, who the public did not want to see leave for work service. They noticed 'that the population is complicit with them or at least […] watch what they are doing in a rigorous silence. In Haute-Vienne and Creuse, two people who provided accommodation to *réfractaires* were each hit with an administrative fine of 10,000 francs.'[3]

There were no *maquis* groups in the immediate vicinity of Oradour-sur-Glane. Several young men from the village or nearby went into one *maquis* or another, and we know of some individuals with links to nearby *maquis* groups or Resistance networks. The village was not immune, however, from the anger that some *maquisards* provoked. Some criminal elements used the novel existence of the *maquis* as an excuse to carry out infractions. These *faux maquisards* were largely dealt with by true *maquis* leaders on the spot or in the months that followed liberation. But it was important for *maquis* leaders that their cause retain the support of the population. In some quarters, particularly during 1943 when they were still a new concept and portrayed as communists attempting a power-grab, they were initially equally feared and despised.

Some *maquisards* certainly behaved better than others. Jeanne Crombé's December 1943 letter clearly attests to *maquisards*, or at least young men claiming to be *maquisards*, coming into Oradour to commit robberies:

> We are on a farm, but it is known that here there are only refugees, the workers are Lorraines, and us ... the boss [Picat] lives in the village! Twice, the tobacconist has been held up at gunpoint, two months in a row, and they have not managed to punish them. It is a bit crazy that nobody is armed anymore, because if that were the case that might put a stop to it.[4]

André Desourteaux, grandson of both of Oradour's wartime mayors, also talked anecdotally of these events,[5] calling them 'bits of tomfoolery', but if Jeanne Crombé's view of the *maquis* reflected that of even some of the inhabitants of the village and its surrounds, the *maquis* was anything but universally popular even just six months before the Allied invasion of Normandy.

Stolen Youth

A short section of moving footage[1] from the summer of 1943 shows carefree young couples swimming in the gentle waters of the Glane, then sunbathing in each other's arms, before wandering uphill towards a small but impressive church with a four-sided sloping steeple. The sun is shining and the pleasure seekers from Limoges follow the edge of the tramlines that pass the church and head through the village towards the north-west of the department of the Haute-Vienne. The couples would have arrived on the morning tram that day and would probably be on their way back to the tiny station, from where they would take the evening return towards Limoges. They would not have stayed overnight. They might have secured some vegetables and a little meat to take back to the city with them, but the restaurants in the *Hôtels Milord* and *Avril* would have been closed.

Just a few kilometres away from the couples arriving on the tram, 14-year-old Albert Valade would already have spent hours in the fields around the hamlet of Le Mas du Puy. Carrying a stick made of hazelwood which he had carved and stripped of its bark with his penknife, his job was to ensure that the cattle did not stray once he had led them to good pasture. Hedgerows bordering roads, and unmarked fields meant that animals could easily wander.

From time to time he was kept company by his friend René whose own herd was sometimes kept in a neighbouring field. Albert often looked on in awe as René's dogs hunted and killed hares. Under German occupation, hunting – a major pastime in the Limousin – had been banned and ownership of firearms strictly prohibited. The banning of hunting left a significant hole in the life of youngsters like Albert, as well as his father:

> The game had become abundant and we all became poachers. Sometimes I went out with my neighbour, an old man named Matthieu. He taught me how to lay traps, he was a specialist. He would often catch rabbits around their warrens in the woods of Puy-Imbart.[2]

Poaching had taken the place of hunting.

Whether it was a weekend or not made little difference to peasant farming families. Boys from such *paysan* backgrounds rarely continued with schooling beyond the *certificat d'études*. Albert had begun work looking after the family's herd of cows in May 1943, just as soon as he could get away from school. Teachers allowed *paysan* children to sit their *certificat* early so that they could be available in the fields sooner. Even before children like Albert left school, they would have helped during the summer holidays, at weekends and at the end of the school with tasks such as pulling up potato plants when the time came for harvest. His herd of 'around twenty cows, four bulls and two heifers, all with a red coat' was typical of Limousin cattle. 'You had to watch them permanently, but it was not hard,' he recalled.[3] The minding of the herd was not physically demanding so it was a job reserved for the youngest member of the family capable of full-time work, or the grandfather. As there was no grandfather in the Valade household, and no brothers, the job fell to young Albert and his dog, who would run towards any animal threatening to cross a boundary, and persuade the beast to return.

Albert loved and respected his sister Germaine, a decade older than him: she was a 'good person, and she was my godmother'.[4] She was totally committed to her family and 'never left the home'. Like Albert, Germaine's adult, working life had begun early. She had married Jean Couvidou, nine years her elder, in nearby Veyrac in October 1934, just weeks after her fourteenth birthday. She had already given birth to a daughter five weeks earlier and the couple settled with Germaine's parents at La Barre, near Veyrac. Later, the whole family moved to Le Mas du Puy, which looked over the eastern edge of Oradour. Even before that move, the Couvidou couple had already added to their litter. Yves was born eighteen months after their wedding day and Edmond a year later. Edmond was the only one of Germaine's four children to be born in the environs of Oradour, in June 1941. Germaine had four children of her own by the age of 25. 'After they got married we all lived together, without fuss.' Germaine had been delighted at the arrival of her little brother and had mothered him. 'I remember her beauty and I remember the depth of her expression, somewhat sad,' Albert recalled.[5] As well as maintaining the household, helping in the fields, rearing children, cooking meals and procuring and selling produce, women old and young also brought in extra by sewing gloves. Albert's mother and Germaine both contributed in this way.

Vichy saw young people as the best hope for the future, untouched by the values that it claimed the Third Republic had destroyed. Through youth

groups, schooling, posters and leadership schools, Vichy promoted a vision
of what French men and women should look like and how they should
act. Honesty, discipline, family values, clean living, early marriage and large
families all fitted into the Vichy vision. But peasant families like that of Jean
Valade had been living like this for years. The National Revolution did not
really ask much new of them, other than a devotion to Pétain, which they
never really managed.

For youngsters in urban areas, even including large villages such as
Oradour, occupation brought with it far more change. Young people had to
live their lives worrying about food shortages, aerial bombing, STO call-ups
and occupation by a foreign power.

There remained few opportunities for the young people of Oradour or
elsewhere to enjoy themselves once the lavish town balls disappeared, funds
dried up, refugees filled the communal spaces and priorities changed. French
policy, introduced in 1940 and 'developed by Vichy, was that as long as
France was in mourning for its defeat and the absence of its loved ones in
German POW camps, concentration camps or German factories, modesty
and decency should be cultivated and dancing banned'.[6] In the cafés, alcohol
could only be served on certain days and the Vichy 'return to earth' and
'return to family' mantras led to many fearing being frowned upon for living
an existence reminiscent of the 'debauched' France of the Third Republic.

As a result, impromptu *bals clandestins* (illegal dances) sprang up. Events
were held in sheds or barns and attended mainly by younger people desperate
for some social contact beyond the café. Music would be supplied by a soloist
or perhaps a small group. These occasional get-togethers were tolerated by
gendarmeries, despite Pétain considering that young people should be doing
more productive things and subsequently prohibiting all forms of dances.
Elsewhere in the country, *bals clandestins* were both an expression of youth
culture and a political statement. What better opportunity to refuse to follow
the Vichy line than by enjoying oneself?

Occasionally a film show was held in one of Oradour's hotels and some
TSF radio sets were finding their way into homes. A visit to the cinema was
only possible for those who worked in or were able to stay over in Limoges
because, by 1943, the trams were limited to two per day. Robert Hébras
managed it occasionally. But it was also expensive. 'Just when the return to
the land is being preached, all entertainment is being totally abolished,' two
young men told the prefect of the Indre-et-Loire. 'Can peasants go to the
cinema? Do they play boules or cards at their age? Of course not. That is why

A group of youngsters. From left: Irène Redon, Roger Barthélémy, Francine Brissaud, Henri Bouchoule, Angèle Bois, André Desourteaux, Francine Pinède, Pierre Dupic. (Collection Angèle Valladeau)

we are asking you to allow dancing for a few hours on Sunday afternoons.'[7] Permitted it was not, but it came to be ignored as long as it was out of sight. If *gendarmes* found out about the *bals clandestins*, they would often ensure that word reached the dancers of their 'raid' well before they arrived.

A New Girl

A new girl appeared in and around Oradour during the late summer of 1943. Slender and dark-haired, her classically beautiful face surpassed her young age. Her name was Marguerite Simon.

In the hamlet of Les Bordes her uncle, blacksmith Hippolyte Redon, lived with wife Louise and a son called Pierre, who was approaching school-leaving age. They ran an *auberge* and Hippolyte cycled to work in Oradour each day. He was one of four children of Pierre Redon, who had died when Hippolyte was just 10 years old, just after his wife Maria had given birth to their fourth child, a daughter.

Hippolyte also had two brothers, one of whom had by 1943 joined the Resistance in the countryside around Limoges. The other was a baker in Limoges. During her youth, his sister, Emilie, had met a Breton man called Jean Simon, later discovered to be a small-time criminal. They married in Oradour in December 1927 before moving to Paris, where they set up home. They had a daughter in September 1932 called Marguerite. The child hardly knew her father at all because Jean was locked up. Emilie set about bringing up Marguerite alone. She doted on her little one and nicknamed her 'Guiguitte'.

When the Nazis occupied the city in the early summer of 1940, life had become harder and less safe. Life in the 15th *arrondissement* of Paris was tough anyway. Emilie sent Marguerite to *L'Oeuvre des Saints Anges*, a Catholic school set up a hundred years previously to help girls who were orphaned, abandoned or poor. Its aim was to prepare them for the professional world. Soon food became even more difficult to come by and cases of severe malnutrition of children in the poorer areas of the city, combined with the threat of aerial bombardments, persuaded Emilie to send her daughter to the safety of the provinces. Marguerite left Paris during the summer of 1943, not long before her eleventh birthday. Emilie had turned to her oldest brother, Hippolyte, in the safety of the village of her childhood. Her own widowed mother lived with the family so the girl would be with her grandmother too.

Marguerite joined the *École des filles* in Oradour at the start of the new school year, September 1943. She was clever, assiduous and excelled in a Vichy-designed curriculum, designed to prepare the girls for successful lives as housewives. There were lessons in housekeeping and dressmaking, as well as mathematics and French. Marguerite also attended catechism with *l'abbé* Chapelle. She made cards for her mother which she posted back to Paris along with pieces of her work. Her uncle Hippolyte and aunt Louise kept a box of Marguerite's papers that included schoolwork for Emilie to see later. They wanted to ensure that those valuable memories, like her daughter, were kept safe from the bombs expected to fall on Paris. The precious documents and letters from Marguerite to her mother, back in Paris, attest to the life of an intelligent, pretty, funny and loving young girl.

Also new to the school for girls in the autumn of 1943 was teacher Denise Bardet. She had moved back to Oradour to be close to her mother, Louise. Both of Denise's parents were peasant farmers. Not long after marrying, Louise and her husband Germain inherited a farm from his mother, along with a significant string of debts. The farm quickly became unprofitable and the couple were forced to move out when Denise was 1 year old. They moved in with Louise's own mother at her farm in a hamlet called La Grange de Boeil, 2km outside Oradour.

Five years later, a brother for Denise was born, called Camille. After three years of happiness and hard work, tragedy struck. Denise's father's health had

Widow Louise Bardet sacrificed everything to give her children, Denise and Camille, a good education. Denise, a teacher in the girls' school, turned 24 on the day of the massacre. (Collection Jean Bardet)

already been failing badly. He had never fully recovered from his experiences in the trenches of the First World War, where his lungs had been ravaged by gas. He died in 1929 when Denise was 9 years old and Camille a toddler. Louise set about raising her children alone, alongside running the farm with her own widowed mother.

Louise was determined that her children would have better prospects than she had ever been able to enjoy. She worked hard so that both Denise and Camille were able to attend school beyond the elementary stage. Denise proved to be exceptional at mathematics as well as French and at 12 years of age she was sent to *l'École primaire superieure de filles* in Saint-Léonard, east of Limoges, as a boarder. She stayed for five years and thrived. Most weekends she returned home and helped Louise with tasks on the farm. Camille helped too, but otherwise their mother was left alone, once Denise's grandmother had died. Louise tended to the animals daily and took them to pasture. Alone she planted the wheat and weeded around the crops, financially stretched and going without so that her children might flourish. She even spent her meagre earnings on books for Denise, who responded by reading to her a wide range of literature during long evenings while Louise made or mended clothes.

Denise won her place on a teacher-training course in Limoges and seven years later Camille followed his sister along the same path. Denise disliked the training period, regarding it as three wasted years while her intellect matured. Her first proper teaching post, in Chéronnac, was a distance of 45km from her mother. During that period she used her spare time to write down her thoughts on literature, philosophy, history and even Germany's position in the world. In a series of school exercise books, she also expressed her innermost feelings. She cared deeply for the children at school, but ideally she wanted to teach at a higher level to avoid the monotonous drawl of the primary stages of education. She loved the cultural and political history of Germany and was disturbed by the onset of Nazism. She wished the country to return to the greatness reflected in its writers of literature and philosophy.

Beautiful as well as bright, marriage was proposed to her a number of times. She wrote of her suitors as unsuitable and occasionally ridiculous. Eventually she did find love and got engaged to Georges, a young man from Limoges. Highly intelligent and well-read, Denise knew that she owed her education to her mother. In the autumn of 1943, back at La Grange de Boeil, she was happy to see her mother and brother each evening. Some days she cycled home to eat lunch with them before returning to Oradour for afternoon school.

Link and Filter

Mathieu Borie was a builder and stone mason. Originally from a small Haute-Vienne village, he lived with his wife in Saint-Junien but kept his equipment at a workshop in Oradour, where he had friends and an aunt, Jeanne Mercier, the grocer.

Borie was certainly a member of the Resistance in some capacity. He was not a member of the *maquis*, but in a notebook that he wrote and kept to himself and his family[1] for many years later, he outlined work he had done from his parental home in Boissournet, a village near Peyrilhac. He 'slept occasionally' in this house and 'gave meetings to volunteers who wanted to join the *maquis* and to *réfractaires* who did not want to go [to Germany]'. Though only 16km north of Oradour, that area was *maquis* territory, extending to Cieux where the 2409th Company of the *Francs-tireurs et partisans français* (FTP) was camped. In 1943, through friends at the football club which he had joined, David Jakobowicz, whose Jewish parents had brought him and younger sister Sarah to the area, had begun to engage sporadically in some activity with a small FTP *maquis* that existed in semi-clandestinity in Saint-Victurnien. The group was linked to the much larger group further north. That group conducted operations on both the railway and the roads,[2] and in time David became a fully committed *maquis-ard*, though he still lived at home for most of the time.

After the implementation of STO, and throughout the second half of 1943 and first half of 1944, some *maquis* groups were inundated with young men wanting to join. But it was rarely possible simply to walk out to a *maquis* camp. The communist-backed FTP were particularly conscientious when it came to security. They had to guard against infiltration by the *Milice*, the Gestapo or the *Groupes mobiles de réserve* (GMR), police paramilitary groups created by the Vichy government often tasked with finding and eliminating the *maquis*. They also had to limit numbers because they could not feed, clothe or arm large numbers of men. The FTP struggled to get any sort of weaponry and usually relied on guns or ammunition from the Great War or hunting rifles, collected from sympathetic *paysans* or former military men where there was not an *Armée Sécrète* (AS) *maquis* to join.

Borie's role was that of a *légal* – no less dangerous than that of a *maquisard* – who carried on with a normal working life while being a point of contact and a filter mechanism for those who expressed a wish to join the *maquis*. The FTP also gave to these *légaux* responsibility for finding hiding places for *réfractaires* who wished to join the *maquis* when they were required. Groups had to be limited in number for reasons of secrecy and mobility, but the *réfractaires* hidden in farms and villages throughout the land needed to be ready for when the call came because the leadership of the FTP were very much hoping to spark an national insurrection when the time came.

Men like Borie may have participated in *maquis*-type activities, especially during night-time. They sometimes partook in small-scale sabotage, infiltration into factories or railway stations, or delivery of messages, weaponry or materials. Borie also explained in his notes that he 'made false identity papers' and distributed clandestine newspapers to *réfractaires*, of which there were several in Oradour. Most days he shared a table with the Beaubreuil brothers while taking lunch at the Mercier grocery store.

In his notebook Borie mentions a Resistance group in Oradour. He gives the name of textile merchant Jean Dupic as 'in charge of the Resistance in Oradour' and also that of Marcel Pascaud, the young pharmacist, who is described as a '*résistant* in my Oradour group'.[3] For there to be a small group of like-minded men in a village the size of Oradour is thoroughly unsurprising. Quite what their work as *résistants* might have been is less clear. There was certainly no armed Resistance in the village so the likelihood is that these were individuals, and there were probably others, who met occasionally to discuss the future and who were happy to distribute some propaganda. Both Dupic and Pascaud saw a lot of customers and Dupic, in particular, had links with Saint-Junien. Tickets for the cycling race at the time of the town festival, for example, were always available from him, as well as from an outlet in Saint-Junien. Neither Dupic, Pascaud nor Borie are listed on official Resistance lists. A great many people contributed towards the Resistance, whether as *légaux* or in a capacity like Dupic and Pascaud, without ever receiving any official recognition.

Odette

On 17 November 1943, an inspector came to visit Oradour's school for infants, the former presbytery building purchased in 1862. It was run by Raymonde Vincent, an elegant, smiling and active young woman in her early twenties originally from Limoges. Relaxed and casual to the outsider, Madame Vincent was devoted to the children in her classes. The infant school was a dependency of the school for girls, so her role was that of schoolteacher and deputy to Andrée Binet, head of that establishment. The class the inspector visited was a mixed group of children, boys and girls, who would, the following year, go to either of the main schools to begin their primary studies properly. He was not impressed with the school buildings but was much more complimentary of Raymonde Vincent herself, to whom past inspectors had been less kind. She had, he said, 'managed to reduce the poor-quality surroundings of the classroom [...] by making an effort with its decoration, putting up a number of children's drawings, and a motto in red letters on a blue background'.[1] What was more, he was pleased with the physical state of the children which reflected well on her as a teacher.

The following January, Andrée Binet was forced to take an extended leave of absence due to a difficult pregnancy. Nobody knew quite how long she would be away for, nor did many know of the reason behind it. Raymonde Vincent would have to step up as acting head of both schools and a replacement teacher had to be found for Binet.

The young teacher who came to replace Andrée Binet was called Odette Couty. When offered the post, Odette had been only too delighted to accept. Oradour was closer to home and easily reachable by bike or electric tramway.[2] During the week she would stay at the *Hôtel Milord* and return to her parents' home on weekends. Very little was known of the pretty blonde supply teacher who worked at the girls' school alongside Denise Bardet for the first half of 1944. Less still of the brave existence from which she had arrived.

Saint-Sulpice-Laurière is a small town 40km to the north-west of Limoges, where predominantly working-class families derived their income from one of the privately owned rail companies. The Paris–Toulouse railway line met with another that stretched east towards Guéret and

*Odette Couty was due to finish her teaching
placement at the girls' school on the day before the
massacre. She agreed to stay on the extra day because
of a planned medical visit. Her father, a railwayman in
the Resistance, was arrested the following day. (Centre
de la Mémoire, Oradour-sur-Glane)*

Montluçon. Many trains stopped at its station alongside a sizeable marshal-
ling yard where wagons were joined to other rolling stock.

It was there that, on 31 May 1921, Gaston Couty and his new wife
Marie-Louise celebrated the arrival of a daughter who they named Odette.
Gaston was a *mécanicien* employed by the *Compagnie d'Orléans*, which, at
the end of 1938, would be one of the major train companies nationalised
under the *Front Populaire* into the SNCF. The job of *mécanicien* on a steam
train was that of the driver, responsible for the safety of the passengers and
rolling stock, while the *chauffeur* had an altogether different role, keeping
the furnace red and hot by feeding it coal.

Gaston's employment eventually led to the couple and their daughter
moving to northern Limoges, to a *quartier* near to another station where the

streets were packed with *cheminot* families. Here they built their own small house – an achievement at the time – on the *rue du Grand Treuil*. Intelligent and eager to succeed in her dream of becoming a primary-school teacher, Odette worked hard and won a teacher-training place. By early 1943, she was in a position to enter the profession early as a supply teacher, and she applied for placements. She travelled in her new role almost as much as her father who, by then, manned the line towards Angoulême from the main Limoges–Bénédictins station, so Marie-Louise looked after the home and did all she could to fit around a lifestyle that saw all of them rarely together at the same time.

Gaston's job as a railworker saw him spend his days in a highly politicised workplace. He became a member of the *Résistance-fer* movement. Mainly transporting documents and passengers over the demarcation line, this also involved low-key sabotage which was remarkably dangerous for Gaston, an employee in plain sight.

In September 1943, Odette was contacted by an aunt Marthe with an invitation to apply for a job. The head of a local school, Marcel Villégier, had, since 1941, been supporting a nearby home for Jewish children. As more and more Jewish families had arrived in France from occupied countries, children had been split up from parents. The Parisian *Organisation de secours aux enfants* (OSE) had brought children into the non-occupied zone where they had been setting up homes, often based in old manor houses. Originally run like camps, Jewish adults provided religious instruction and teenagers were recruited from nearby towns to act as monitors. One was *le château du Couret*, less than 1km from the village of Vistrat, and Villégier's own school.

Villégier's school was almost oversubscribed with two classes of thirty children. But, knowing the secular curriculum leading to the *certificat d'études* was vital for pupils at the age of 14, he sought out the leaders at Le Couret, whose pupils, mainly girls, were given only a basic education, and offered help. He agreed to take some children for parts of the day to help them prepare properly. Girls began walking to classes in the village school buildings to receive proper preparation. Many had come from families of intellectuals and thrived despite having arrived in France from Poland, Austria, Romania and Germany with limited spoken or written French. Meanwhile, the centre at Le Couret continued to grow, taking on full-time housekeepers and a cook. More girls went to Villégier, including some who were behind in their studies and needed, and wanted, to catch up.

Eventually he had to cede to a lack of space, as well as resistance from unhappy local parents. Religious observations meant that girls were not being sent on Saturday mornings, which Villégier felt was unsustainable. On behalf of the staff at Le Couret, he pushed the municipality for a third class for his school which would be based at the *château*. Surprisingly he succeeded and two Catholic teachers were taken on to school thirty children. The chief rabbi from Limoges, whose sister was part of the school's staff, came weekly to provide religious instruction to help the children to retain their religious identity despite deepening Vichy anti-Semitism. The pupils were housed and fed; the chef was renowned for her quiche Lorraine. All teachers who observed Jewish rituals lived in the *château* or nearby.

November 1942 and full occupation of the country by the Nazis threatened the haven of tranquillity. Roads passed almost underneath the school's walls carrying German vehicles on a daily basis. Round-ups had become more frequent, and sometimes children disappeared in the night, either taken by the *Milice* or sent away by staff to more secure locations. Others arrived in their places and the numbers were maintained at around thirty, but in July the regional authorities decided to disband the class rather than stand between the Germans, the Vichy authorities and the increasing pressures of round-ups.

Many girls were sent away to the Alps or to safety elsewhere, but by September more than a dozen remained. Villégier decided to keep the class open for a little longer but received no interest from potential replacement teachers. Villégier was at a loss when his housekeeper mentioned her niece, a supply teacher as yet unassigned. She called her Dédée and her real name was Odette Couty.

Odette began the job at Le Couret in October 1943. She had only recently become engaged to a young Limoges schoolteacher. She shared a room at the manor with the other remaining teacher, Marcelle, and taught there until the class was wound down by the following Easter. For five months she was loved by the children into whose lives she had appeared, and whose existence was threatened on a daily and nightly basis. Odette would have been under no illusions that her position was not only irregular, but also put her in harm's way, though neither she nor Villégier would have known quite how much. Odette stayed until the class finally had to be disbanded and the children sent elsewhere. She returned to her family home and awaited her next assignment which happened to be in Oradour-sur-Glane.

1944

In his famous diary of life in Saint-Amour, Léon Werth notes the certainty of the townsfolk and people of the villagers all around that above all they would not allow themselves to starve. The tide had turned against Vichy collaborationist policies and against the authority of the government and its National Revolution. Men like Laval were hated, Pétain less so. Very few had chosen to resist, very few to collaborate. Many were happy to break the framework of the law as much as they needed to allow themselves to survive; the authority of Vichy was over.

Most people were concerned with food supplies, the level of taxation and the potential requisition of livestock. One of the peasants about whom Werth writes is a former tenant farmer called Laurent who had moved into the small-scale dealing of farm animals, just like Fernand Hyvernaud in Oradour. Though a devoted Pétainist, Laurent had become very concerned, even something of an anglophile, when it seemed that Germany might take all his animals. When the requisitions turned out to be less extreme than he imagined, he settled into an attitude reflective of most in his position: a dislike of the government coupled with a 'wait and see' attitude. Underpinning all this, however, was his trust in Pétain.

According to the Limoges office of the *renseignements généraux,* (information services), reporting at the beginning of March 1944, 'Farmers have made significant profits. They seem to be driven solely by the spirit of monetary gain. The people of the cities are resentful of them.'[1] 'Country prices' were the result of the peasantry selling their produce above the low prices set by the government, but less than where middlemen were out to make profit as black marketeers. In and around Oradour, pigs were slaughtered illegally and clandestinely, meat shared and sold locally. Offal was made into charcuterie and other preserves. This and any home production of food all undermined the local Vichy-appointed bureaucracy, pleasing to both the peasant who made money from it and the local consumer for whom products were not only available but reasonably priced. East of Limoges, Georges Guingouin's *maquis* took the authority of Vichy away by policing marketplaces and ensuring that reasonable prices set and displayed under his name were adhered to. In areas such as Oradour, where the *maquis* was less prevalent and had different

priorities, this did not happen. But whether Limoges' citizens were resentful
of country prices or not, they continued to come to Oradour and its environs
to secure the goods that they could not obtain in town.

Aside from schemes that avoided handing sales tax to the state, and a growing avoidance of escaping requisitions, the majority of *Radounauds* were
otherwise indifferent to whatever the Vichy government did or said. Most
people struggling to make a living did not act against their better conscience.
There is no evidence of letters of denunciation from businesses whose rivals
may have been dipping into the grey market. The relatively open existence of
réfractaires, communists[2] and Jews invited no betrayals of community.

Once demobilised, Albert Mirablon had rejoined his former employer
Crédit Lyonnais in Limoges, where he lived with his wife and son. His mother,
Anna, lived nearby. It was not long before he heard talk of opportunities to
work for the Resistance. Having travelled Europe extensively, he was ready to
do what he could, however small, to help undermine the Vichy government
and the German occupiers. An early contributor, he joined the *Libération-sud*
group in October 1941. Responsibilities included the distribution of clandestine newspapers, for which he ran the *Limoges-sud* sector. He also used his
photographic skills to great effect, taking photographs for use in the newspapers as well as taking photographs of machinery and other materials stolen
from the Germans, supplying these documents to the *Service de renseignements*
and to his contacts. He did the same for publications produced by the other
two main Resistance movements, *Combat* and *Francs-tireurs* after the groups
combined under the banner of the *Mouvements Unis de la Résistance* (MUR)
in January 1943. By then Mirablon was also involved in more active work for
Combat, which pre-dated the *maquis*, by carrying out sabotage raids and theft
of German equipment. Registered on 1 April 1942 as a *sous-lieutenant* in the
Kasanga network, he was listed as an agent P2 of the FFC, *Forces françaises combattantes*. His work continued into June 1944. His mother Anna felt disturbed
by Allied bombings in Limoges and moved to Oradour for safety, away from
the city and near her sister Maria and Albert's cousin Fernand Lesparat.

Resistance organisations had relied heavily on clandestine propaganda to
communicate anti-Vichy ideas. Leaflets, newspapers and tracts were widespread in towns and cities after 1942, though even there they hardly littered
the streets. Camille Senon, living in Limoges but returning to Oradour
each weekend to a particularly politicised family, did not see much clandestine propaganda at all in the countryside. Despite the work of the likes of
Mirablon and even the presence of what amounted to a Resistance committee in the village, clandestine newspapers did not find their way to the general

population, most of whom were not interested in receiving them. Camille's visits home always included Saturday evenings spent with neighbours who owned a TSF radio set. There they listened to *Radio Londres* followed by *Radio Moscou*. They listened to information about Russian progress on the Eastern Front as well as news from London. They gathered news from the mainstream censored newspapers, recognising the biased reporting of Resistance activities which boosted their spirits. The press continued to report a narrative of a Moscow-driven effort to install communism after the war. But Gaullist Resistance had made huge strides since the creation of the MUR in 1943, uniting its diverse elements. The peasantry of the countryside was increasingly on the side of the *maquis*, whether Gaullist or FTP. This meant supplies of food and shelter, storage spaces and sometimes protection for new arrivals parachuted in from Britain.

According to a March 1944 report there was a 'growing disarray, a growing weariness, discouragement and scepticism' in the population. It states that the promise of an Allied invasion (*débarquement*), as reported on the radio and through airdrops of leaflets and British newspapers, was weakening 'a good and healthy understanding of the efforts of the government to retain for our country its honourable place after the war'.[3] For the people, however, they wanted only an end to restrictions and to see the back of the Germans, as well as the vicious *Milice*, GMR and French Gestapo agents. Their hunting of *maquisards*, whatever a person thought of either side, had created in southwest France a feeling of an oncoming civil war such as had been lived in Spain. Nobody wanted that.

Brehmer

At the end of March 1944, a German division led by General Walther Brehmer was sent to south-west France with the simple order of eliminating as much of the increasingly troublesome *maquis* as possible. It moved through the Dordogne, Corrèze and Haute-Vienne leaving such a trail of devastation and brutal reprisals in its wake that even Guingouin, and other local leaders, knew that they had to take some responsibility for the lives and livelihoods of the ordinary French people who were targeted. Brehmer's orders were to target civilians for brutal measures, and in doing so communities would turn against supporting the *maquis*. This was accompanied by further propaganda campaigns, calling on good French patriots to refuse to support the bandits and terrorists who were bringing the wave of terror on to France with the sole purpose of setting up a communist state.

Brehmer did not spend much time searching for *maquis* units, other than by setting fire to forestry to flush them out. A month earlier Field Marshal Hugo Sperrle had issued orders relating to dealing with guerrilla fighters.

The death of innocent bystanders would be entirely the fault of the 'terrorists'. Houses from where shots had been fired should be burnt to the ground and all civilians should be taken into custody. Decisiveness and speed of action were to be paramount, and indecision on the part of troop commanders, putting troops' lives at risk, would be punishable. Lastly, 'given the present circumstances, measures that are subsequently regarded as too harsh cannot provide ground for punishment'.[1]

The Brehmer operation led to mass arrests and killings of civilians with tenuous links to the *maquis*, as well as Jews. 'Never before has the climate in the region been so anxious,' reported the prefect Marc Freund-Valade[2] to Pierre Laval, then holding the post of Vichy's Minister of the Interior. 'Terrorism, German reprisals, the prospect of a civil war and that of deadly bombings which now appear to be fatally linked to an allied invasion attempt. Everything contributes to a deep depression of spirits.'[3]

On 28 April 1944, Jean de Vaugelas, chief of law and order for the Limoges region, placed a message in all of the Vichy-administered local newspapers to all people of the area. De Vaugelas had been brought to Limoges just twenty days earlier after having served as regional chief of the *Milice* in Marseilles, as well as being commended for his brutal action against the *maquis* of Glières. His printed orders painted the *maquis* in no uncertain terms. These were, he claimed, one of three types of individual:

> Honest young men who believe in good faith to be making amends for defeat by serving in the camp of the Resistance [...] Former soldiers who are obeying through a sense of discipline orders by certain ambitious leaders devoid of any political meaning and therefore traitors to their word and to their country [...] Workers thirsty for social justice who are preparing you to become slaves to international communism.[4]

The language used was provocative, particularly following Brehmer. He offered an olive branch for those who renounced their past actions and who had not engaged in 'terrorist' acts. However, for him there was:

> no such thing as a GOOD or BAD *maquis*, but only gangs of rebels. Furthermore, those responsible for killings or sabotages, whether ringleaders or accomplices who have ordered, given advice or material aid, or directed or facilitated terrorist operations, will be struck without mercy. Those found with arms or explosives would be brought before a court martial and, without recourse of appeal be judged within twenty-four hours.

Those who stayed out of the way of *maquis* activity would, he said, have nothing to fear. At the first sign of trouble, people should 'stay inside their houses, keeping doors and windows closed [...] ready to respond to any summons or requisition. Any hostile protest or shelter of persons outside the law, will bring with it immediate and serious sanctions for those responsible. The part of the population acting correctly will not be punished.'[5]

In the weeks immediately before and after the Allied landings in Normandy on 10 June 1944, *maquis* operations, such as sabotage of bridges and railways and ambush of troops, multiplied. But before that, Guingouin's *maquis* – the biggest and most redoubted in the region – became particularly inactive. One of the former teacher's major successes had been to establish links with the Special Operations Executive (SOE) in London, becoming one of the few FTP-backed *maquis* groups to receive weapon drops. But Guingouin, who had been acting independently from the FTP's central command as well as London for some time, changed focus. Following Brehmer, his *maquis* slunk into the hills and woodland around Châteauneuf with the intention of protecting it until the Germans were far more stretched.

The German High Command had desisted from listing the area to the east of Limoges as a *maquis* hot spot. Whereas the earlier Brehmer operations had targeted the Guingouin area, later 'clean-ups', such as the one that was brewing in the area around Montauban, did not.

For the period of April to May 1944 the *gendarmerie* of Eymoutiers recorded no acts of 'terrorism' that included attacks against railways or roads, or industrial sabotage. By then many *gendarmeries* were supportive of the *maquis* so small operations may have gone unreported. However, the report indicates numerous examples of thefts of *tickets d'alimentation* from town halls, attacks on public banks or thefts from shopkeepers or farmers.[6]

Some rural villages became so entirely dominated by nearby *maquis* groups that secrecy became a thing of the past. Sussac, central to Guingouin's area, became such a place, as did Siorac-en-Périgord in the Dordogne, where one local communist was so prominent and influential that the curate was happy to hide armaments in the church tower. But this was not the norm. In most places a fear of denunciation prevented open support of the Resistance. Such was the case in Oradour. It had, however, already moved beyond the excesses of denunciations and xenophobia, perhaps because of its own experiences with outsiders such as refugees. Its close links to Limoges provided by tramway or bicycle meant that a great many outsiders came from the city. It was rural but not hidden in the hills. With the Gestapo so nearby, people knew what they could and could not get away with. No arms were hidden there for any nearby *maquis*, nor was there even a *maquis*. It would have been folly for any group to be visible in or near such a community.

A Summer of Outsiders

During the month of June, the Limousin countryside was in full bloom. Family gardens, worked on with extreme diligence and care, already offered up scented flowers and tasty vegetables.[1]

This was how a local journalist described the early summer in and around Oradour. The European war was approaching a climax – Germany's second front was due to open up on the French coast at any time – yet life in the village went on. Rooms were full in Oradour's hotels even if nobody, except for their long-term residents, used their restaurants. At first, they had homed evacuees and refugees from Alsace-Lorraine before their places were taken by people who could afford to pay from all around the country. Owners of hotels tried to be self-sufficient. Most owned a cow and some poultry.

Nathan 'René' Lévy was a Rennes dentist born in April 1896 in Metz.[2] He was married to Lucie Mina Bloch, ten years his junior. The exact details of Lévy's passage to Oradour are unclear, but anti-Semitic laws would have resulted in him losing his practice and his place on the registry of dental practitioners. He left for the south with Lucie and they managed to get across the demarcation line together, apparently with a young daughter in tow.[3] Somewhere along the line the family separated from each other, René heading for Limoges and his wife to Grenoble. On 16 February 1944 Lucie arrived in the Drancy camp, having been arrested at 32 *cours Jean Jaurès*, Grenoble, where she had been living under the name Lucie Cleny.[4] She was then sent to Auschwitz on convoy number 69, on 7 March 1944, where she was killed on arrival, just five days after departure.

Even by June 1944, René Lévy would not have known that his wife was already dead. There are no traces of their daughter who, it can only be hoped, escaped transportation having been sent somewhere safe. René Lévy left few traces of his life in the Limoges area. He lived clandestinely under an assumed name. In April 1945, the newspaper *Sud-Ouest* published an interview with a survivor from Rennes which must have been him. He was, he claimed therein, registered in the *Hôtel Avril* under the surname Lacroix. The hotel register was destroyed in the massacre so we will never know when he arrived.

He had not, according to a different source,[5] come to stay in Oradour by accident. The quiet, well-provisioned village had been recommended to him by one of his clients who lived very near him in Rennes. Knowing that he was Jewish and looking to flee south, she had told him where her mother was staying and asked him to call in on her if he made it over the demarcation line. The client's mother, twice-widowed Jeanne Leroy, was 61 and had three daughters by her first marriage to a director of a fabric company. Her second husband was the owner of a shoe-making company in Saint-Malo. Oradour had been recommended to her by friends from Paris who had settled there, writing to her often and recommending its tranquillity, its excellent position and the fact that one could live well there.[6]

Jules and Jeanne Lang, an older Jewish couple from Caudéran, a suburb of Bordeaux, had come to Oradour for safety and also lived in the *Hôtel Avril* temporarily before finding a place in the lower village. Gabriel Delvaille, the mother of Robert Pinède who lived next door, was also a resident. The hotels relied on long-term residents for their business during the period. Jewish individuals or families with the ability to pay their way fared better at a time during which they felt terrorised by feverish anti-Semitic policy that had become Nazi in nature. Those without money would have been hiding out either in the countryside or under false identities in the larger towns and cities, where they could melt into obscurity. Some, who may have been left over from the GTE that had existed near Oradour until 1942, would have been agricultural workers. Jean Jackow, for example, was a Polish Jew, 38 years old and a father of two, who was living and working at a farm in Le Masférat. He, like many other Jews in the countryside, had managed to escape detection.

The countryside and villages such as Oradour played temporary home to Jewish children. In southern France, small communities often helped protect Jews once it became clear after 1942 that the government was actively persecuting them. The fact that the Pinède, Kanzler and Bergmann families were Jewish did not seem to bother anybody much.

David Jakobowicz's activities with the Cieux *maquis* were, however, putting his wife, their new baby Michel, his sister Sarah and his parents, all at nearby *Maison-Blanche*, in considerable danger. By the spring of 1944, a Pétainist veteran lived in a flat above them who was known to host collaborators, *miliciens* and even Germans. By May 1944, David had also been involved in several close shaves between the *maquis* and *miliciens* in the area around La Malaise.

Through his contacts in the Resistance, David knew Martial Machefer, the former paper worker who had set up as a cobbler in Oradour. He also knew that the Kanzler family had lived there without any bother for several years. David first found a safe place for his baby son, Michel. Pierre and Anna Gabriel lived in a hamlet called Chez Lanie just outside Oradour and Anna agreed to nanny Michel for the months to come. Though childless themselves, they had a *pupille de l'assistance publique* living with them. Yvonne Delavault was a 12-year-old who had been there since April 1942 and would help to look after Michel.

Machefer agreed that David's 14-year-old sister Sarah could stay with him, his wife Anna and two children. Given her status, Sarah would have to stay hidden, and Machefer did not wish to have any further attention drawn to him. He had already helped to house a 10-year-old Jewish boy called Raymond Engiel, finding him lodgings with a nearby farming family. 'Machefer was like that,' André Desourteaux told me. 'He said nothing. We just didn't know.'[7]

Other youngsters had been sent to Oradour entirely legally because it was safe and offered a good lifestyle at a difficult time. Alphonse and Andrée Lévignac and their two boys, Serge aged 16 and Charles almost 12, were faced with expulsion when the Germans occupied Alsace-Lorraine in the summer of 1940. Oradour had received many French speakers from the Moselle but the Lévignac family found themselves in Avignon. Alphonse had worked as a wood merchant before becoming an insurance salesman and he found work, while his wife Andrée found a primary-school teaching post. Friends wrote to Alphonse and Andrée about the quaint village of Oradour, where food was relatively easy to come by, they felt welcome and, above all, they felt safe. Through these contacts, Alphonse and Andrée organised summer placements for their two boys and they would stay in Avignon so that Alphonse could continue to work.[8]

Sixteen-year-old Serge would go to a farm about a quarter of a mile from the village centre just over the River Glane. Nearby a fallen tree bridged the span of the stream providing quick access. His hosts at Le Masset were the Villéger family, tenant farmers. They had seven children: four boys and three girls. Serge would spend his time in the open air of the countryside helping the two oldest boys, Guy who was 16 and Henri who was 15. The Lamige family in the village would look after Charles.

There were also Spanish children in the village. Some Spanish families had never left even after the 643rd GTE had been moved in 1942 to another nearby town. Fourteen-year-old twins Pilar and Francisca Gil Espinosa, originally from Alcañiz, were at the school for girls. Another pair of sisters, Emilia and Angélina Masachs, aged 11 and 7 and from the Sabadell area of Barcelona, were also students there. Their father, Joan, a spinner by trade in Spain, like all the Spanish fathers of Oradour, fled after fighting in the Republican army. As part of the 643rd GTE he was assigned to work in quarries and in carpentry details while his wife of twelve years, Emilia, tried to make a home in La Fauvette.[9]

One Spanish boy called Mario Escamilla, born in Barcelona in 1932, had crossed the border in 1937 with his parents. In April 1944, 12-year-old Mario fell on to potato-harvesting equipment and cut his forehead. His mother took him to see Doctor Paul Desourteaux, who was apparently less warm with refugees as had been his mayoral predecessor Joseph Beau.[10] Mario's wound was stitched up without too much attention to hygiene. Several days later the injury became infected and 'resembled a melon'. Mario was taken to hospital in Limoges and his condition worsened. He remained there until 17 June 1944. Ultimately this would save his life.

The previous winter Robert Hébras had seen a crate of grapes in a shed. They were grapes for eating rather than winemaking, not only rare but expensive. Where they had come from, he did not know, but he was told that they were for Oradour's Spanish families. On New Year, each person would eat twelve grapes at midnight to bring them luck for the year to come. That they were there, and that they were being stored, says much for the ingenuity of whoever bought and brought them for the Spanish children.

PART TWO

THE TENTH

If, one day, God asks us to sacrifice our lives, be true to him, and let us go to heaven together.[1]

The words of Jacques Lorich during his sermon in Oradour on Sunday
4 June 1944

Gatherings

L'abbé Chapelle had, for years, feared that his *Radounaud* parishioners were losing their faith in God. Numbers at regular worship had fallen, despite the arrival of the Mosellans. The people did, however, still attend the significant events and festivals. On Sunday, 11 June 1944 the festival of the *Fête-Dieu* would take place in honour of the *Saint-Sacrement*. The plan was that a procession would follow a church mass, always far better attended than normal. *L'abbé* Chapelle would be at the heart of the procession behind children carrying processional banners and some of the choir. The priest, under a four-cornered canopy and with a statue of the Virgin Mary, would follow a transparent case displaying the consecrated host. The congregation would follow a trail of stations, stopping before each one for a moment of adoration. Young girls would

2 Environs d'ORADOUR-sur-GLANE (Haute-Vienne)
L'Eglise

Edit J. H. Beau

The church of Saint-Martin. The main entrance is on the right; the lower door to the sacristy on the left. In front is the roof of les halles. *(Centre de la Mémoire, Oradour-sur-Glane)*

scatter flower petals. The procession would attract a good crowd, which would follow behind. On the morning of Saturday 10 June, some of the children of the primary school would spend time creating bonnets and posies for the day. By Saturday the church had already been decorated in readiness for the event.

Word had been coming in all week about the successful Allied landings that had taken place earlier that week. Everybody knew that there was still a long way to go, but an end might finally be in sight. Throughout south-west France, Resistance leaders were busy putting plans into place for the weeks to come. Marie Hébras had more pressing matters to which she needed to attend. She had to prepare one of the *reposoirs* (altars) to be placed along the route of the procession for the Sunday festivities. On top of a white tablecloth into which she had sewn seasonal flowers, bouquets sat beside statuettes of the Virgin Mary and the Saints. The altar would then be placed at a nearby cross-roads next to the town's *bascule* (weighing scales), operated from her window by Marie 'Titi' Valentin. At this intersection, Titi's husband Jean had his barber shop, and the couple also had their precious garden. The road to Saint-Junien passed by the farm of La Lauze, outside of which a cross completed the station, and other significant sites would be similarly decorated.

By May 1944 the frequent Allied bombing on the outskirts of Paris had forced former GTE chief warden Jean Henry and his Mosellan wife Gilberte Biver into action. The couple decided to take their 2-year-old daughter Michelle by train to the relative safety of the rural south, to the village where they had first met. After acquiring a certificate of voluntary evacuation, they made the journey to Oradour, arriving on 18 May. They moved into the small home in the lower village with Gilberte's mother and her stepfather Louis Perette, and stayed for several weeks.

Gilberte, by then 22, planned to stay on with Michelle. Jean had enjoyed the break, but the time had come for him to return to their home in the Paris suburb of Sartrouville, where he was a music teacher. Travelling was, however, complicated by the Allied landings on 6 June. At first, he discovered that he could not take the train because the route was blocked at the demarcation line.

Marcel and Henriette Joyeux had come to Oradour to visit Henriette's parents, Fernand and Marie Hyvernaud, and her siblings. They had brought with them the newest member of the family, 6-month-old René. Henriette's two much younger sisters Raymonde and Yvonne would have loved having their new nephew around for the weekend but would have to wait until the end of the school day to play with him. Sixteen-year-old Albert was kept busy by his father in the fields outside the village but both were due home for a Saturday lunch with the rest of the family. Their brother Marcel, 21, had been called up to the STO. The next oldest was René, 19, who had set off early to work in their fields at Saint-Gence that day. His intention was to return to Oradour that afternoon to see baby René. Henriette's other brothers were small children themselves. Gabriel had turned 6 four days earlier, while Roland was 4 and André just 3.

Christiane Villatte, née Praline, her husband, Amédée, and their
2-month-old son Christian were staying with Pierre and Mélanie Villatte
on the day of the massacre. (Collection Benoit Sadry)

As well as being *président* of the *Légion*, which, by 1944, had become almost inactive, 47-year-old Jean Roumy was a seed seller with a son who was away having volunteered for *operation Todt*. On that Saturday he was also a father-in-law-to-be, looking forward to introducing his son Albert's long-term girlfriend to family as his future daughter-in-law. Twenty-three-year-old Albert had come to Oradour that morning hoping to take Ginette Couturier[1] to see his grandmother, and he also had a friend coming to his home for the weekend. It would be a few days of celebration for the family. Albert and Ginette had arrived the previous evening on a tandem bicycle purchased for them by Ginette's father.

Tobacconist Pierre Villatte's son Amédée had, two days earlier, celebrated his first wedding anniversary with his bride, Christiane. Seven weeks earlier the pair was delighted at the birth of their first child, a boy called Christian. Pierre and Mélanie Villatte were doing all they could as grandparents to support the young couple. Christiane, a striking woman with dark hair piled atop her head, had insisted that the young family come to stay with her parents-in-law because she feared getting caught up in the Allied bombardments of Limoges. She was not the only one. Albert Mirablon's mother Anna had also returned to the village for the same reason.[2]

Early Risers

An escaped prisoner of war who had never known the identity of his real father, Daniel Senon had developed an appreciation for life since returning to Oradour three years previously. When he was a boy his mother had married Denis Mercier, brother of Eugénie Brandy, who ran the café-bar in the village. That marriage had given Daniel a half-sister, 19-year-old Yvonne, and an extended family. In his early thirties, he was finally enjoying himself as a free man, and had recently begun seeing a local girl.[1]

He woke early that Saturday morning and got out of bed feeling happy. Despite the early hour he felt content for mundane reasons: 'I felt happy because it was the last working day of the week before Sunday and for us, the younger generation, Sunday was a day of fun.'[2] First, though, Daniel had work to do, delivering post throughout the *commune*. Being a Saturday, the town's mail would arrive by train at Saint-Victurnien and he needed to be there to meet it. He got on his bike and peddled to the station to wait for its arrival, due at nineteen minutes past six. François Darthout, his 46-year-old workmate, was waiting for him. The men chatted with a tramway worker who was also waiting for the slow train that they called the *tacot*. They discussed the reported landings on the Normandy beaches. Soon they were joined by tobacconist Pierre Villatte.

When the train finally arrived, they picked up the mail sacks between them and were happy to see that the expected bags of tobacco were there too, for that Saturday's tobacco distribution day. Men from all around would be eager to collect their allowance. Senon and Darthout were given permission by Villatte to let people know that the distribution would take place as expected that day. Senon and Darthout made their way slowly along the steep and winding road from Saint-Victurnien to Oradour. They crossed the Glane and climbed the *rue Emile Desourteaux* to the smart post-office building alongside the tramway station. Postmistress Odette Bouillière was waiting along with another PTT employee, Marguerite Gourceau. Twelve-year-old Robert Lavisse, Odette's nephew, was still sleeping in the flat above. He was staying there with her and his grandmother. For the boy it was a short holiday away from the 5th *arrondissement* of Paris.

Odette had taken over the post office in 1941 having grown up in Eymoutiers, on the other side of Limoges. She was in her late thirties, childless, and had seen the move to Oradour as an opportunity for a fresh start. Her mother, Marie-Rose, had later joined. Odette wanted to get through the morning's work as quickly as she could as she intended to spend time that day with Robert. The sorting of the mail began in earnest and was completed by a quarter to eight, at which time Darthout and Senon set off to do their rounds. Senon headed for the village of Les Bordes, after which he would go to the hamlet of La Croix des Bordes.

With the line back to Sartrouville temporarily blocked, former 643rd GTE guard Jean Henry had contacted the *Académie de Limoges* and managed to get a short extension to his stay in Oradour approved. He knew, however, that his absence could not extend to a further full week. He thought that the route north must finally have cleared so, early that Saturday morning, he kissed his wife Gilberte and their 2-year-old daughter Michelle and boarded the tram for Limoges.

Alphonse Lévignac was also an early riser that day and he set off to catch the same morning tram that would take him the seventy-five-minute journey to Limoges. He was preparing to leave, having spent four days visiting old friends while his sons, Serge and Charles, settled in for the summer holidays.

His wife had stayed behind in Avignon while he took the opportunity for a short break. The three of them had got on a train to Limoges on 6 June and then the tram to Oradour. It was time to return home, so that morning he was heading to Limoges where he planned to look around the city and find out about train services. He planned to take the early evening tram back to Oradour, where he would spend some time with his sons before travelling back to Avignon.

His eldest son, Serge, had started equally early. He would spend the morning at work with his hosts' two eldest sons Guy and Henri Villéger. The three boys had been given packed lunches and their instructions for the day. Firstly, they were to cross over the Glane in an ox-drawn cart and head for Bournet beyond the other side of the village. Their job, which would take until the afternoon, was to cut hay to be used as bedding for the animals. They also had to collect sticks and make *fagots* (bundles of kindling wood), which they would then need to load on to their cart. They would not be finished until the afternoon, by which time Jean Villéger would come to collect the hay in a second cart. He would set off around eleven o'clock, leaving his wife Marguerite in the Masset farm with their three daughters. The eldest, 14-year-old Renée, had completed her schooling, while 9-year-old Odette was off sick with an eye infection. The family's youngest member, 2-year-old Hélène, was asleep in her bed.

Gilberte Biver was a refugee before meeting GTE camp commander Jean Henry and moving north to the Paris region. The couple had a 2-year-old daughter called Michelle. (Centre de la Mémoire, Oradour-sur-Glane)

Jean Hébras had, since his retirement from working on the tramways, often helped out in the fields for the Georges family. He had spent the previous day doing so, and that Saturday he had headed off early in the morning to take some animals from Orbagnac to Saint-Victurnien. The animals had been requisitioned by the occupant and there was a market for requisitioned beasts taking place there that morning.[3]

Fate

Everything was completely normal for Emma Lebraud who, at the age of 18, was already running her own dressmaking business on Oradour's main street in a tiny property she called *Chez Emma*. Each day she travelled the 6km from her family home in Charratt to her small workshop by bicycle. Primary-school teacher Denise Bardet also cycled to Oradour that morning, kissing her mother Louise goodbye before setting off from their farm at La Grange de Boeil. Louise was looking forward to clinking glasses with her daughter at lunchtime, when Denise cycled home. Saturday 10 June 1944 was Denise's twenty-fourth birthday.

Young teacher Odette Couty, Andrée Binet's replacement, was preparing for the final day of her contract at the girls' school. She had been set to leave the previous day, but a medical visit had been announced and Odette was happy to agree to do the extra day's work. At half past four that afternoon she would leave the school and move on to the next chapter of her life. To celebrate, she planned to meet a friend at the *Hôtel Milord* for an early lunch before returning to class for the afternoon. She would say goodbye then get on her bicycle, which she left outside the hotel, and head home to Limoges.

Meanwhile, 24-year-old Marguerite Villemonteix had arrived at the bourgeois home of Doctor Paul Desourteaux and his wife Marie to start her day of work as a domestic help. At the age of 15, dark-haired Marguerite, from a peasant family, had married Léonard Thomas, a 30-year-old farmer and widower from Oradour. After she gave him three children, he abandoned her. She moved back to her family home near Cieux, travelling to and from the Desourteaux house daily.

Spanish refugee Carmen Espinosa had also emerged from a very difficult few years. She had come to the region with relatives and her husband, Alberto, who had been assigned to the 644th GTE in Saillat-sur-Vienne, just west of Saint-Junien. Unfortunately, her marriage broke down, so she decided to move to Oradour where she knew some familiar faces who had been accepted into the community. She found happiness while living in the village. As well as finding steady work in a butcher's shop recently established by Gabriel Maire, a *mosellen* refugee, she found love again. Her new fiancé, Esteban Herrero Perez, was originally from Castilla y León and like many Spaniards had been keen to avoid forced moves from GTE camps to

Annie Ratier pictured on the steps to the bureau de tabac, *run
by Pierre Villatte. The tram rails lead westward past the main*
Champ de foire, *the station and the post office.
(Collection Benoit Sadry)*

organisation Todt installations or to the Reich. He had joined up with the
French Resistance. On 10 June 1944 Carmen was two months pregnant.

That Saturday the shops would fill up. Tobacco rations and tickets for other
foods were due to be distributed. Jean Jackow left his wife and two children
in the hamlet of Le Masférat. He may have been collecting tobacco but, as
an unregistered Polish Jew who may not have had the correct paperwork, he
probably went to the village that morning to collect essential food. Likewise,
a Spanish family originally from Zaragosa, consisting of three generations,
would arrive that morning. Forty-five-year-old Juan Téllez Domínguez[1] had

previously been assigned to the 643rd GTE, possibly alongside Jackow, and assigned to work in nearby Bellac. That Saturday he went to Oradour with his second wife Marina, sixteen years his junior, and his 72-year-old mother Ramona.[2] The couple had three children. Miquel was 11 years old and Harmonia 7, who were both at school that day. Twenty-one-month-old son Llibert was also with his parents in Oradour. On most Saturdays, Francisca Espinosa Magallón of the Gil-Espinosa family, originally from Aragon, took her twin daughters Francisca and Pilar to see their father Joaquín Gil Egea wherever he was working. He happened at that moment to be very nearby in La Valade. That Saturday, however, they did not go to see him, but went to school for the medical visit. Francisca had also promised to take one of the children to the pâtisserie after school, where she sometimes helped out behind the counter.

Eight-year-old Roland Bricout was a *pupille de l'assistance publique* who had recently arrived in the area. He had been placed with Louise Ousta, and her husband Pierre, who was a sawyer and specialised in cutting long planks from whole tree trunks by sawing lengthways. Roland had caught scabies on 25 May and was sent by Doctor Desourteaux to Limoges hospital for isolation and treatment. He was certified well on 6 June, the day that the Allies landed in Normandy, and had returned to school in Oradour just two days earlier.

Over the Threshold

It was eight o'clock when Albert Valade returned to the farmhouse in Le Mas du Puy for some breakfast. He had already done his early shift in the field with the family's herd of cattle. Each Saturday the family expected at least some city dwellers to come to them looking for vegetables or eggs. The tram from Limoges would bring some and they would come to their hamlet on bicycles or foot. That would happen much later in the day. As Albert ate he watched his sister, Germaine, a decade older than him, deal with her four children. She was not tall, but still bigger than Albert who was a particularly small boy. Her dark hair was pulled back as always, and her sunken eyes and pronounced cheekbones decorated a wide but elegant face. Three days earlier Albert had celebrated his fourteenth birthday. He was pleased to have his family so close to him.

Georgette, Albert's oldest niece, was 9 years of age, and as tall as him with 'long, light brown hair and big velvety blue eyes'.[1] She carried her books in a leather satchel and, that day, was wearing a pretty flowery dress. She had only recently returned to school after badly cutting her knee in a playground accident. The wound had become infected, placing her lower leg in danger. That morning only one of her brothers would be accompanying her on the walk to the village. Eight-year-old Yves was still asleep in his grandparents' room having spent the night coughing, while Lucien was just 3 so too young to attend. His mother was struggling to wean him away from the breast and he would yell when he did not get offered it.

Edmond, the middle of the three brothers, was ready to go with his older sister. Brown haired with 'always smiling' grey eyes, he also had dimples in his cheeks. He was the favourite grandchild of 47-year-old Jean. Edmond was no fan of school and preferred the garden, where he would help his grandfather plant beans. He was scared of aeroplanes, fearing them all to be German bombers. That Saturday morning, he put on his backpack and open sandals, having finished with wearing wooden-soled clogs at the beginning of that week. Germaine and her mother watched the children join six friends for the short walk downhill to the village and looked at the sky. None of the children were wearing raincoats because the morning showers had cleared and the sun was trying to shine through the clouds, promising a fine day ahead.

A mile to the north, in the village of Les Bordes, Martial and Maria Deglane were getting their youngest child René ready to join a group of other children on the walk to school. The family home was fuller than normal because René's oldest sister was heavily pregnant and had come to stay. Jeanne, who usually lived in Limoges with her husband, had decided several weeks earlier that she wanted to have her baby at home where her parents and two sisters could help. She feared the bombardments that were predicted to come down on the city of Limoges and had craved the calm of the countryside.

One of her sisters, Solange, was 16. The other, Andrée, was 22 and would be heading to Oradour that morning where she worked for Michel Avril, a local wood merchant. She enjoyed helping to look after her employer's 8-month-old boy and was well prepared for the arrival of her sister's baby. Foremost in her mind, however, was a planned lunchtime walk with her boyfriend Daniel Senon, the 26-year-old postman who lived in Puy-Gaillard. She often passed him on her way to work as he set out on his rounds.

Little brother René picked up his satchel and left the house holding hands with Madeleine Tomasina, a pretty dark-haired 8-year-old girl, first sent from Paris to the Limousin countryside by Maria's sister when it looked as though Paris would be occupied. Madeleine's father, a Parisian of Italian descent, agreed with his wife's prudent and heart-breaking decision that their only child should be brought up in the peaceful and warmer climes of the 'free zone'.

In the same village 12-year-old Aimée Ballot set off for school with Irène Bonnet, two years her junior. Irène was actually Aimée's niece, her 31-year-old mother, Marguerite, being Aimée's oldest sister. But in large Limousin families generational divisions often blurred. Marie, mother of Aimée, had given birth eleven times, though four of her children had not survived beyond the age of 2. Her husband, Jean Ballot, was a handsome man at 64 years of age, with neatly parted hair and a dark moustache. He continued to belie his age by working on small building projects and headed off to Oradour where he was working on friend Fernand Hyvernaud's new barn. Usually he and eldest son André, who also worked in town as a notary clerk, would walk home together for lunch. During the warmer months Marie took a picnic to Oradour where her daughter Aimée and granddaughter Irène would join her on the grass. Marie would carry the remnants of the picnic home for her husband, and whichever of her other children might be around. That Saturday Georgette would be there but Léon, their oldest son, was a prisoner of war in Dantzig, and Emile was in Upper Silesia having been called up for STO.

Antoine Lavergne had spent three years as a prisoner of war and had been released the previous year for health reasons. He had returned to his wife,

Louise, and son, Gilbert, at their farm in Theineix. His own father Jean was also a veteran and had fought as an engineer in the Aisne. He had lived with his son and Louise since his first wife died and was valuable help on the farm.

Just as Gilbert had headed off to school, the two men set off to a nearby field where they needed to weed around potato plants. It was an arduous task and they were joined by their regular labourer Adrien Duvernet and, a little later, by Jean's brother-in-law Antoine Montazeaud, who arrived by the morning tram from Limoges. A veteran who had lost an eye to a shell at the Somme, Montazeaud would be accompanied by his own son-in-law for what would be an arduous day's work shared amongst extended family, as was the Limousin way.

Thirteen-year-old Gilbert had been blessed with light brown hair, dreamy eyes and a cheeky lopsided smile. He had continued his schooling beyond the *certificat d'études* and had been given responsibility for the school library. That afternoon he was due to go to one of one of Tournier's music lessons, but not before coming home for lunch with his mother, who was taking a break from the fields afforded to her by the extra pairs of hands. The men would eat later because the day was precious. They took with them a horse and cart, and a second cow-pulled cart that contained fodder for the cattle. Gilbert set off to school on his bicycle.

In exchange for looking after a herd of cattle for her neighbours, Marcelle Bureau had managed to get her hands on some white bread and vegetables. She was 36, and she and her husband Barthélémy lived with her farmer parents Jacques and Marie Descubes in the hamlet of Le Repaire. Also living with them was one of her sisters, Eugénie, who had turned 30 that spring and was as tall as her father. She had straight dark hair pulled across her forehead and had her hands full looking after her 5-year-old daughter Renée; her husband Jean Faucher was a prisoner of war.

Because she had looked after the cattle, Marcelle was able to give a piece of white bread that morning to Renée and to her own 8-year-old boy Fernand. Both children were setting off to school with others from the village. She told them to put the bread in their bags and keep it for recreation.[2]

Clouds in the Morning

Mathieu Borie arrived in the village early, disappointed that the falling rain would disrupt the cement laying he was meant to be doing that morning at his aunt Jeanne Mercier's grocery store. Deciding it was worth the risk given that the rain should clear, he left his parents' home in Boissournet where he had been staying since news of the Allied invasion of Normandy had come through. There had been Germans in Saint-Junien too and his wife told the 34-year-old Borie to stay away. He travelled the 11km south by bicycle to get to his workshop in Oradour.

Borie, known to his friends as Mathis, picked up tools and materials and left them at the shop, before heading to the Brandy café to have something to eat with two friends. Aimé Renaud, the 30-year-old mechanic and son-in-law of the owner, joined him. A little later wheelwright Fernand Lesparat also sat at the table. He was agitated:

Fernand Lesparat, who worked as a wheelwright alongside his father. On the morning of 10 June, he is reported to have been anxious about a possible round-up and wanted to take to the maquis. (Archives départementales de la Haute-Vienne, 201 W 59)

If you want, guys, we could take to the *maquis*, all three of us together. We could go with you, Mathis, because, you know, you're a *maquisard*. But we have to go this morning because this evening it's going to get dangerous and it will be too late. I've been told that something bad is going to happen.[1]

Lesparat said nothing more. Later in the day he would see Albert Mirablon, his first cousin who lived in Limoges and was heavily involved in the Resistance. A few days earlier Lesparat had told Renaud that they should hide each day. 'I'm worried,' Lesparat said at the time. 'We would do well to join the *maquis*, and till then we should go off to the lake each day, early in the morning [...] We can just fish and be safe. I really believe that something is wrong.'[2]

Renaud had told Jeannine, the oldest of the Brandy sisters, what Lesparat had said. The couple and their daughter, Any, lived above the café from where Jeannine ran her hairdressing business. She was supportive of her husband's wish to join the *maquis*, or at least to flee, hide and remain safe.[3] But Renaud could not just abandon his job. He worked as a mechanic in Limoges and mechanic's jobs were no longer easy to come by. It may have been that Lesparat had been told about STO round-ups and identity checks by his cousin. The *Milice* and the Gestapo were actively looking to arrest anyone with links to the *maquis*, as well as men fit to deport. Joining a *maquis* was also not easy. Contacts were needed and most *maquis* groups were not well enough supplied to take in more men.

'We have to wait a few more days,' replied Borie over breakfast. 'I'll let you know as soon as I can. I haven't had an order yet, but as soon as I've received it we can go.' Outside the café they saw some people from Saint-Junien who, like Borie, had left the town when the soldiers had arrived. Like him they wanted to go back as soon as it was safe.

Just as Borie was ready to start work it began to rain again. He decided to use the time by going to Puy-Gaillard just across the Glane, where his aunt Jeanne lived with Matthieu Mercier, the former postman. By then René would be at their grocery store, and Madeleine Bonnet, the orphan who had been taken in, would be able to help too. The hidden Beaubreuil brothers could look after themselves but René and Madeleine would ensure they were fed.

Borie needed to pick up poles, empty bags and a tarpaulin in order to complete the work at the shop. His aunt was at home, where she also ran a small bar. 'Stay and have a drink,' she said. 'Come on, it won't kill you.' He agreed. 'Every day here, in the bar, I hear people talking about some sort of *clean-up*. That really would not be good,' she said. She thought Borie might know more. He did not. He had only heard the same from Lesparat that morning.

There were rumours, and round-ups and identity checks were happening all over the region.

'You should not believe all that,' he said. 'It's a crock of lies.'[4]

He headed back to town with a cart full of equipment and, on the bridge that crossed the River Glane, saw two of his three nephews, René and Marcel Hyvernaud, who were on their way to school.

At half past nine at La Croix des Bordes, Andrée Deglane saw her beau, Daniel Senon, approaching. The pair embraced and chatted for a while before making arrangements to meet at ten minutes to two next to the Lanot abattoir, provided the rain held off. Senon continued his round, remembering to let everybody he saw know about the important tobacco distribution,[5] while Andrée headed off to work in the village.

When Albert Valade came back to the farmhouse briefly at ten o'clock, he had been surprised to see his 20-year-old second cousin Marcel – the STO evader with whom he had become firm friends – in the house. Marcel had told him at breakfast that he was going in to Oradour to try to get his hair cut. The rain had, he said, put him off, and he would instead go in the afternoon.

His aunt teased him, 'You wimp, scared of a couple of drops of water.'[6] Marcel smiled and made the excuse that he would need first to inflate the tyres of his bicycle.

In Le Cros, 2.5km from Oradour, Aimé Faugeras was reminded by a neighbour that there would be a distribution of tobacco, and ration tickets for food. He had set off quickly for Pierre Villatte's *bureau de tabac* to make sure he got hold of his *décade* – his ten days' supply – as well as his father's. While there, he had been tempted to stay and get his hair cut but, acting on his father's plea to return and take lunch with him, he turned around and headed home. Martial Ledot, the 63-year-old husband of Léonarde, like so many farmers from the hamlets all around Oradour, went to the village that morning too. Most would be back by lunch but missing the tobacco distribution would be disastrous.

Just before midday Daniel Senon got back to the post office, where he left his postbag. Odette Boullière was still there, but Marguerite Gourceau had finished her shift at eleven o'clock and had headed home for lunch.

'See you Monday,' said Daniel to Odette as he set off along *rue Emile Desourteaux*. He headed downhill past the *Champ de foire* and all the various shops and businesses. He stopped off to see Andrée Deglane to confirm that, given the improved weather, their date was on. He strolled on through the lower village and past the church, crossing the river, then strolling the short

Matthieu Mercier on his bicycle outside the post office. After
retiring as a postman, Mercier helped run a grocery store.
(Collection Benoit Sadry)

incline to his family's farm at Puy-Gaillard where, after delivering the remaining letters of his round, he was to dine with his family. On that day all the family were together for their meal, including Daniel's grandmother. Once finished, he got back on his bike and set off to meet Andrée for their walk. His colleague at the post office, Marguerite Gourceau, got home to the family farm in the hamlet of Les Rentiers in plenty of time to have lunch with her youngest sister Andrée who was just 9 years old. After they had finished Andrée headed back to afternoon school. Marguerite was due to return to the post office at half past three so she picked up a pitchfork and took to the fields to help her parents who had begun the harvest.

Pierre Tarnaud, a 35-year-old former prisoner of war, had spent the whole morning in Saint-Victurnien with his wife. The couple had taken several animals for requisition and slaughter. It had been an early morning and they were looking forward to getting back to their farm in Le Theil, 2km north of Oradour. To get home they had to pass through the village centre. Everything was entirely normal when they travelled through sometime between half past twelve and half past one.

The morning tram had brought people from Limoges who were using their Saturday to do some food shopping, but the village was not bustling. The sun was shining after the morning rain, and the Limousin air was clear. The bright sun had brought out the glorious colours of early summer, gleaming off the red roofs and silver tram tracks that ran along the gritty road towards Limoges. Aimé Renaud had finished lunch with his wife Jeannine and daughter Any. He lazily climbed Oradour's main street towards Hubert Desourteaux's garage, where he had agreed to help that day. His friend Fernand Lesparat walked alongside him. They chatted about the *maquis* and whether they might ever join. Renaud got on with some work while they carried on talking.

Robert Hébras should have been working at his employer's garage in Limoges. The day before, his boss, unhappy at the workload of requisitioned vehicles, had got into a dispute with a German officer. Robert was told that it would be safer for him, given his age, to stay away in case the garage got targeted for round-ups. Robert remained at home and fitted an electric socket for a neighbour who had been given a small electric stove. He had finished a lunch shared with his mother and two of his three sisters.

Robert's sister, Georgette, a 22-year-old nurse, had also come home to Oradour from Limoges because she felt uneasy about possible aerial bombings. Their father was in Saint-Victurnien that morning and had yet to return. Their 9-year-old sister Denise had finished her meal and was preparing to go back to school. Martial Brissaud, wheelwright, football teammate and childhood friend of Robert arrived at the door. He and Robert chatted in the warm sun about the following day's match. Under the watchful eye of her mother, Denise kissed her big brother at the doorstep and headed back to school.

Sixteen-year-old Yvonne Gaudy, who lived on her parents' farm in the village of Theineix, 2km north-east of Oradour, decided that she would take a post-lunch walk to deliver some gloves that she had finished. Her agent, Yvonne Bardet, ran a family farm in the hamlet of Villa-Andrée on the road to Saint-Victurnien. Yvonne would walk through Oradour, cross the Glane and join the road at a set of crossroads in Puy-Gaillard. On her way she saw her young neighbour Gilbert Lavergne who was heading back to school. She liked Gilbert, admiring him because he had stayed on at school after getting his *cértificat*. He told her that he had a music lesson later that day and asked if she needed a lift. She happily hopped on to the pannier rack of Gilbert's bicycle and they giggled as they headed downhill towards Oradour.

Arrival

On the other side of the River Glane, east from the Saint-Martin church and the rest of the village, several farms overlooked Oradour from an elevated position. A number of fields sloped down from the farm buildings to the river and its tributary where a fallen tree provided a well-trodden makeshift crossing. At one of these farms, Les Brégères, 18-year-old Marcel Bélivier was getting himself ready to go to a music lesson which would be held in the music room above the Dagoury café. He had eaten with his parents, his two sisters and his grandfather. His younger sister, Marie-Louise, had already left for school and his older sister, Alice, was getting ready to help their mother in the fields. His older brother, Lucien, had been called up for STO and the family did not know exactly where he was. Marcel, striking, dark-haired and a footballer, was already running late when his father asked him to accompany him to the stables to feed a calf. Farm work took precedence over anything else.

On the other side of the Glane, separated by the stream, the Villéger family were getting ready for their afternoon at the Masset farm. Fourteen-year-old Renée had left her mother with her sister, Odette, who was poorly that day. She went out on to the steps of the farm and looked out over the fields towards the village. The sun was out and she peered in the direction of the western edge of Oradour. Earlier, her father had gone in that direction to join her two older brothers and their new lodger, Serge Lévignac, who were cutting hay and twigs. Her other two brothers were in school in Oradour. Meanwhile Daniel Senon and Andrée Deglane were passing very nearby having met at an abattoir on the eastern edge of the village. It was a perfect day to walk. 'Together we set off. Just after the abattoir we took a right along a route which led towards Les Bordes past the Masset farm.'

At around two o'clock Marcel Bélivier and his father heard the noise of loud engines. They left the calves that they were feeding and saw three open German trucks arrive from the direction of Saint-Victurnien.[1] Marcel and his father walked to the corner of the property to get a better view, as did a neighbour at the farm next door. Daniel Senon and Andrée Deglane heard the same: 'When we reached a level just a bit higher than the farmhouse, we noticed a powerful rumbling of motors.' Vehicles were few and far between due to the restrictions on movement and petrol. 'Knowing that no cars were allowed to be on the road, we stayed there for a moment to listen.' Suddenly shots broke out, coming from the bridge over the Glane, echoing around the sloping terrain – the direction from which they had come.

It had gone two o'clock when Renée saw soldiers walking up the field below her from the direction of the stream they had just crossed. She thought they might be members of the *maquis* who, she had heard, sometimes came to farms to get food supplies.

Yvonne Gaudy, carrying her finished gloves and accompanied by Gilbert Lavergne pushing his bicycle, approached the village. From Theineix, they reached a crossroads opposite the church. On their approach they heard the rumbling of motors, so loud that Yvonne guessed it must be an army convoy. They stopped and looked towards the river where they saw automatic machine guns mounted upon half-tracked vehicles and a truck carrying German soldiers. Some 'were wearing a multi-coloured outfit, others were dressed in a green-grey'. All seemed to be armed. Yvonne lowered her head so as not to be noticed. Then 'My young friend Gilbert left me to go back to school'.[2] Her 10-year-old brother Pierre was already at school, having stayed through lunch.

At the Morlieras' *Café du Chêne*, Joseph Bergmann was the barber most popular with the young men who played for the football team.[3] One of the players, Jean-Marcel Darthout, had wandered to the church square and was waiting for the afternoon opening when the low groaning sound of heavy vehicles approaching from the Glane rattled the window frames.

'I saw between five and eight vehicles arrive, notably trucks and half-track troop carriers though I cannot be precise. All of the vehicles carried lots of soldiers who were pointing their weapons in all directions.'[4] Jean-Marcel noticed light automatic weapons, maintained in a firing position, fixed on the front of each of the half-tracks. As the vehicles climbed the *rue Emile Desourteaux*, it passed the church and the *chêne de la liberté* and Jean-Marcel was glad to be let into the barber's salon.

Aimé Renaud, stood with Fernand Lesparat, watched the German convoy roll past the Desourteaux garage. As well as the armed soldiers aboard trucks, he saw what looked like an ammunition carrier, and a truck with a flat deck carrying soldiers. He thought there were about twenty soldiers on that transport:

> They were in a firing position, their arms pointed either at ground level or at the first floor of the buildings. Behind […] came two more non-armoured

trucks, filled with troops, also armed with submachine guns and rifles. They all seemed ready to open fire. They passed right in front of the garage where I was working.[5]

Martial Machefer knew that he was in particular danger as he was already under surveillance: 'My wife insisted that I leave the house, being already strongly suspected by the Gestapo.'[6] She kissed him and told him that she would look after his two children, 11-year-old Yvette who was at school, and 16-month-old Désiré. The presence of their other house guest, Sarah Jakobowicz, made it doubly important that Martial make a break for it. 'After burning all papers which might compromise me, I left the house [...] and took the Saint-Junien road.'

When the convoy passed the Hébras home, Robert remained calm. He saw soldiers every working day in Limoges and was relaxed. It was unimaginable to him that Oradour could be in danger. For him, the look on the faces of the soldiers was one of sheer indifference. 'I see them every day in Limoges,' he told his friend Martial Brissaud on the doorstep of his home. 'They won't eat you!' No German soldiers had been in Oradour since a convoy passed

Martial and Anna Machefer with their daughters, baby Désiré and Yvette. Martial had strong links with the Resistance and fled when the SS arrived. (Collection Anne-Marie Loison)

through the night after Germany invaded the free zone in November 1942. Brissaud, spooked, decided to flee and hide.

A little further on, Jewish sisters Jacqueline and Francine Pinède were standing in front of their house with their younger brother and mother. 'During the year that we stayed in Oradour, we had never seen a German and [...] my parents were, I think, the only ones to worry about doing so given that they had taken an apartment opposite the house.' Their father, Robert, had seen the arrival of the convoy because it was Saturday and he was at home. He told his children to hide in the meadow because he didn't 'know what was going to happen'. The girls would have to look after their young brother. 'As a refugee in Oradour [...] we lived in a constant state of alert.'[7] After a short time, Robert found his children and told them that they were not yet sure whether the Germans were simply carrying out manoeuvres and it was better that they find somewhere to shelter and hide. 'Do not go back to the house,' he told them. Hearing a half-track in front of the house, he went to find his wife while the Pinède girls and their brother found a place to hide under a set of steps made of reinforced concrete behind their home.[8]

Intentions

Renée Villéger understood very quickly that the soldiers approaching the Masset farm were dressed in German uniforms. One of them dropped to his knee and pointed a rifle towards the farmhouse so she rushed inside to tell her mother what was happening.[1] Renée yelled that the soldiers were coming to kill them. 'I did not even think about leaving, but then machine gun fire hit the shrubs.' She looked out of the window and saw 'around fifteen "*Boches*" running up the hill towards the house'.[2]

Lacking the time even to grab her handbag, Marguerite organised her children. Renée scooped up her baby sister, and Odette followed them out of a back door with the family's little dog. They were not to know that the SS command had identified the farm as a suitable headquarters for the operation that was to follow. The soldiers smashed the door in and looked for the girl and woman that they had seen. But they, and their dog, managed to get to a small field separated from the farm by just one wall:

> We were crouched in some shrubs and it is a miracle that they did not see us because they came within two steps of us. We were dying of fear, and we expected to be killed as the bullets flew all around us.

They could hear the SS searching inside the house. But the shrubbery kept them hidden. They got into the densest section they could find, huddled together and waited in silence. No sound came from the children, nor from the dog.

Having seen the German convoy, Daniel Senon and Andrée Deglane stopped their walk when shots rang out, echoing around them. 'I looked at my watch, it was ten minutes past two. I asked myself what devil this could be? An encounter between the *Boche* and the *maquis*? This seemed to us the most plausible answer. But as far as Oradour was concerned, there was no resistance organisation there and the nearest *maquis* was quite some distance away.' Fearing the bullets, whatever distance they were being fired from, they set off to get as far away as possible from the zone of fire: 'We got to the first houses of the village of Les Bordes when suddenly we heard cries of terror coming from near the houses, followed quickly by some rounds of fire.'

Pierre Joyeux was on his way to Les Bordes when he heard the first bursts of gunfire from automatic weapons. 'Soon afterwards I saw a tracked vehicle appear and turn at [the hamlet of] Le Mas de l'Arbre, only around two hundred metres from where I was standing. I can't say how many soldiers there were, but I saw only two. The vehicle immediately turned towards Oradour.' He watched as soldiers began fanning out around fields in nearby Theineix, La Tuilerie and La Croix des Bordes. 'They picked up five people who were working in the fields and whose homes were in Theineix. They were not allowed to go back to their homes.' The SS had established a cordon inside which inhabitants would be rounded up and taken to the town centre.[3]

In the tiny hamlet of La Tuilière des Bordes, farmer Jean Courivaud and his wife Mélanie were preparing their 9-year-old daughter Paulette for a trip to see relations in Mélanie's hometown of Compreignac. Jean would accompany her to Limoges and put her on a train so that she could stay there for several days prior to a family wedding.[4] She had gone to school that morning to say goodbye to her teacher, and to let her know that she would be back the following Monday. Her brother, Maurice, was 24 and an apprentice butcher working for Gabriel Maire. Maurice had fought in 1939–40 before being demobilised. He would not be accompanying his family but instead would stay in Oradour for work. When Mélanie went to collect her daughter from school at lunchtime the pair had called in to see him, and Maurice passed his mother a packet of cigarettes that he had collected for his father that morning. When Jean and Paulette set off to leave, they heard the first shots ring out.

Postman François Darthout was making his way back towards the village where he lived with wife Anne, his two sons, including Jean-Marcel, and his daughter-in-law:

> I came across a young woman who told me that the *Boches* were in Oradour-sur-Glane and that they had made her turn around and come back because it was not permitted to go into the *bourg*. Straight away I got onto my bike and hurried to complete my deliveries so that I could get back and find out what was going to happen.[5]

Darthout had left his colleague, Marguerite Gourceau, at the post office that morning. After lunch with her parents she had been using the hours away from the post office to work in the fields around Les Rentiers. Using a pitchfork, she had been tossing the wheat in the fields before she was due to get back to the post office. When shots rang out from the direction of the village,

Marguerite and her parents were 'struck with fear, feeling that we were all in danger'.[6] Their thoughts turned quickly to Andrée, Marguerite's sister, who was in school. On her parents' insistence, Marguerite put down her equipment and headed to the village. She should, they said, collect Andrée and take her to the safety of the post office. As the firing became more intermittent, Marguerite set off on foot.

Once they reached the main *Champ de foire*, some vehicles slowed down and most of the soldiers got out of the trucks. Several vehicles continued on as far as the western edge of the village while two turned around and headed back down the slight incline of the main street, back towards the church and the river. Those vehicles returned with depleted crews. Maria Demery, who had two sons in school, was in her farm's washhouse situated in their small field, about halfway to the hamlet of Lalande. From an elevated position she had a perfect view of the road that ran out of the centre of Oradour northeast towards Javerdat. She put her laundry down and watched. Men got out either side of the vehicles and took up positions at what would become the eastern limit of an interior cordon of the village. They 'deployed themselves to either side of the road in a firing position, encircling the village towards which they began to move across the wheat fields. Others took up position along the road itself as far as the edge of Lalande.' A second outer cordon had also been established. 'I saw them lie down at the roadside, some pushed up on their elbows, other laid flat on their stomachs.'[7]

The arrival of the vehicles, and the subsequent about-turn at the western edge of the village, had been watched with concern by Marguerite Rouffanche. *Chez Gaudy*, the farm at which her family were by then tenants, was perched on a hill just a stone's throw from Puy-Gaillard, where operational decisions were being made. Being so close to the village perimeter, Marguerite saw three soldiers approaching the farmhouse. Dressed in camouflage gear, as had been the many soldiers that the family had seen entering the town on the back of the trucks just minutes earlier, these soldiers were carrying light machine guns. They said little to the family, other than directing them to leave with the words, '*Raus, tous au place du march*.'[8] The family were not permitted to organise any provisions and left as they were. Marguerite's husband Simon, her three grown-up children and her baby grandson made their way through the village centre.

The operation seemed to those who would later testify to be well-organised, allowing for large families to be gathered in relative calm. Doors and windows were, however, being broken down in order for soldiers to gain entrance to properties, and it was clear that it was a major operation. At the

Chalet Saint-Vincent, 0.5km along the Limoges road, Hubert de Lavérine and his wife dropped what they were doing as soldiers urged them to leave their large villa. They had been living there since Hubert had been released from a prisoner-of-war camp two years earlier. His wife Antoinette and their two elegant brunette teenage daughters followed. Their son, 9-year-old Hervé, was in the medieval town of Sarlat where he was being schooled at a Jesuit institution. Their domestic servant Jeanne Chastang followed too. She was a single 56-year-old housemaid from Corrèze with the use of only one hand due to a bite from a pig some years earlier.

Setting Up a Cordon

Having witnessed the German convoy crossing the Glane, Yvonne Gaudy had left her neighbour Gilbert Lavergne. He had followed the imposing vehicles towards the boys' school which was near the *Champ de foire*. Trying not to worry, Yvonne crossed the square in front of the church where many towns-folk had gathered. Eager to get out of Oradour, she hurried in the direction from which the vehicles had travelled. Beyond the bridge, she climbed the short distance to Puy-Gaillard where she stopped to look back. Matthieu Mercier, and Léonard Bichaud, a road worker who, like Mercier, lived in farm buildings just outside the main town, were talking but she could not quite make out what they were saying.

Yvonne felt torn as to what to do. She wanted to get to the Bardet farm, where she could leave her glove work, then go back home through the vil-lage. Any route that did not pass through Oradour was much further and she had no wish to clamber through fields. Having paused for a minute to try to eavesdrop, Yvonne heard a further roar of engines. The same two half-tracked armoured vehicles had come back from the village and were headed towards Puy-Gaillard. She heard Mercier and Bichaud agree that they should hide, so she decided to try to get away from Oradour, hoping that the soldiers would ignore her. She set off south towards Ville-Andrée, moving to the left-hand side of the road. She could hear the engines nearing her and at the last moment she leapt into a ditch at the side of the road to escape the huge wheels of one of the trucks. The vehicles sped off, ignoring the frightened young woman.

Marcel Bélivier saw the German truck swerve towards Yvonne from the farm at Les Brégères, and was relieved to see that she had managed to step out of its path. He abandoned any hope of leaving his family to go to his music lesson as he watched with his father as a column of soldiers appeared from the direction the vehicles had disappeared along. They wore camouflage uniforms, were all armed and numbered, he thought, 'around sixty men'. They went into the next farm and disappeared behind its barns. Marcel and his father rejoined their family and watched as the soldiers were ordered into three lines, 'back to the road, facing us'. They were within earshot and listened as orders were yelled at the men in German. The groupings gave the impression of some sort of military exercise.[1] Marcel's father, a veteran of the First World War, ordered his family to return to work. 'Leave them alone,' he said, hoping to avoid appearing too curious. 'You do not know what they are capable of.'[2]

Marcel went back to the stable to continue feeding the young cattle. His father headed to a field near the road, which he would need to cross. The Germans gesticulated towards him, telling him to approach, so he headed back quickly to his son. He did not know what they wanted with him, but he was scared. Marcel told his father to stay with the family before his mother arrived running, panicked because the soldiers were heading towards the farm. 'Marcel, hide yourself. They'll take you away,' she told her son, who was prime age for STO. Two soldiers arrived at the stable quicker than Marcel could find a hiding place. 'Komm raus!' the family was ordered. His mother shifted her position and blocked the soldiers' view just long enough for Marcel to hide amongst the straw bedding. His father and younger sister were rounded up along with his mother, grandfather and older sister. 'I had to stay behind the animals for a long time without budging. Through a door that led to another barn I could see and hear them. They were searching everywhere for me.'[3]

When their backs were turned, Marcel rushed to an old barn alongside their farmhouse, where he climbed into a hayloft. He crouched amongst some bales. 'From there I saw my little sister Marie-Louise who was just 14 years old. She came into the barn terrified and in tears.' The soldiers had sent his sister to tempt him out of hiding. He knew he had to resist. 'She climbed the ladder and called to me.' Marcel's father arrived behind her and called her down. 'Come on,' he told her. 'There is nothing to be afraid of.' They left with the soldiers, leaving Marcel alone with sentries posted at the door of the barn.

Meanwhile, Yvonne Gaudy approached a junction where she meant to turn right and head south towards the Bardet farm. A guard appeared and called her over to him. He was polite, called her 'Madame' and instructed her to wait on the side of the road. Nervously she did as she was told until 'fifty or so'[4] soldiers appeared in the fields either side of her. They were all armed and had fanned out, heading towards Oradour. She noticed one 'officer who appeared to be in charge of operations. At that moment he was giving written orders to his men and seemed to be organising what amounted to the occupation of Oradour.'[5] She wondered whether they might also be preparing an operation against the maquis despite having 'never heard talk of a maquis in that part of the countryside'. The officer came to a group nearby and she saw some small pieces of paper in his hand, on which she thought she could discern 'a map, and I thought it looked like a plan of Oradour'.[6]

Another twenty or so troops hurried past her towards the village. In front was Jeanne Mercier, the grocer and café owner who was struggling to keep up with the pace of the tightly packed column of soldiers behind her. She jumped into a ditch at the side of the road to let them pass but was grabbed by others behind who told her to continue alongside them. A soldier in one of the groups told Yvonne to accompany them back towards Oradour, which she did without question, followed by Madame Mercier.

At Puy-Gaillard an officer stopped Yvonne and asked to see the young woman's papers. She told him that she did not have them but lived in Les Bordes. The officer paused, then told her that she was to head back in the direction that she had come from until she reached the N141, the *route nationale*. As instructed, she left the others and headed south again until she came upon another group of people. Once again, soldiers were behind them, propelling them forward. That group contained the Bardet family, to whose home Yvonne had been headed. As well as Madame Bardet and her husband, the couple's two children aged just 7 and 8 were in the group, along with the children's grandmother and some of the domestic staff of a neighbour, Monsieur Lamaud. Once again Yvonne was stopped and told to join the group which she did before they seemed to change their minds and told her to carry on. The road to which she had been told to head was a long way on foot so Yvonne decided to get as far as the Bardet farm and wait there. Just a little further on another group appeared, this time including the Lamaud family, who beckoned her to join them. At that moment, scared and alone, 16-year-old Yvonne wanted nothing more than to be with people she knew. She did not want to cross a countryside full of soldiers. She took the arm of Madame Lamaud's elderly mother Marthe and headed back towards Oradour.

They Have Killed One of our Soldiers

Marguerite Villéger, her three daughters and their dog were trembling with fear as they waited and watched their farm being made into the headquarters for the Oradour operation. They huddled in bushes together, hidden from view. Suddenly a sustained bout of gun fire crashed against the other side of the wall. Marguerite told her children not to shout, nor to cry, even if they got hit. Eventually the shooting died down but further away she could hear more, accompanied by the sound of explosions. Still, the children, including 2-year-old Hélène and their little dog, remained perfectly still and perfectly silent.

Had Martial Machefer not come across a group of Alsatian soldiers, it is unlikely that he would have managed to flee Oradour. The papers that he was carrying, issued by the Resistance, were false:

> Just as I was leaving the outskirts of Oradour [...] I ran into a group of some thirty Germans [*sic*] who stopped me and asked me who I was. I told them that I had been crippled in the war, that I was out of work, and that I was on my way to a neighbour's field to lend him a hand. The Germans demanded my identity papers. I only showed them my card certifying that I had been incapacitated in the war. They made me take off my shoe to show my wound and the man who questioned me gave me back my card and said in French, 'Go ahead'. One man amongst the thirty in the group called out that I should return to Oradour, but as the rest waved at me to go on, I moved forward. As I did so I heard one of them say in perfect French to the one who wanted me to return, 'Let him go, there will be plenty as it is'. A rattle of machine guns took their attention from me and I was able to leave the neighbourhood without further trouble.[1]

Jeannine Renaud had been curling the hair of Marie Gougeon when the Nazi column rumbled through town. She watched with interest as neighbours emerged on to their front steps to watch what was going on.[2] She continued her work for ten minutes or so but, when two of the vehicles returned to the lower part of the village having dropped off troops, her customer became alarmed. Marie Gougeon was the wife of Fernand, teacher of the children in the school for Moselle refugees. She and her family had already been exiled from her home by the Nazis.

'Madame Gougeon told me that she was going to warn her husband and tell him to let the children go home to their parents,'[3] said Jeannine in her testimony. 'She left running, my comb still in her long hair that ran down her back, and rollers in her hair.' Jeannine, suddenly, was alarmed that her husband Aimé might be vulnerable as he was working that day at the Desourteaux garage. They had talked about the real prospect that he might be arrested and taken to work in Germany. She had even given him her blessing to go with Lesparat and Borie to join the *maquis*. 'I went downstairs to the kitchen in my mother's place and told her that I was going to warn my husband and advise him to hide because he had been expecting from one day to the next to be called up for the STO.'[4]

Jeannine Renaud, née Brandy, and her sisters Antoinette and Andrée. Jeannine ran a hairdressing business in the same building as her mother's café. (Collection Anne-Marie Rigon)

'I left, my little Any, who wanted to come with me. But I said to her, "No, stay there, I will be right back".'[5] Jeannine left her daughter in the care of her own mother and two sisters. As she left, one of her sisters, who was standing in the entranceway to the café, pointed out that a round-up was indeed taking place. 'My grandfather's family, made up of eight people were already being led into the village with other people who lived in the farms of Puy-Gaillard, five hundred metres beyond the Glane Bridge.' This was the group that contained the Rouffanche family. 'They were surrounded by soldiers, with an armoured car in front and another behind, climbing the hill into the village.' Jeannine decided to cross the square and take a back route to the Desourteaux garage:

> I took off like a shot, running quickly between the first armoured car and the hostages [...] As I rushed across the road, the Rouffanche boy who was part of the group shouted to me not to run like that as they were going to shoot me, meaning for the Germans to hear. Monsieur de Laverine, another of the hostages in the group called to my mother to not lock the door as the Germans 'would break it down', but I saw that my mother was already closing the door to our café [...] even as I ran away. Just then I heard the calls of Germans who were spreading out around us. 'Raus' came the shout from just about everywhere.[6]

As she took the back lane, Jeannine noticed that one of the soldiers was following her:

> Passing in front of the Hyvernaud's home I heard my friend Henriette [Joyeux née Hyvernaud] shout out to me 'Where are you going so quickly, Jeannine?' I did not answer. After the crossroads the soldier no longer seemed to be following me. Perhaps he had gone into the Hyvernaud's home? I heard Henriette call out 'Maman!'[7]

At Puy-Gaillard Yvonne Gaudy saw the bright flash of a white flare before noticing the same soldier who, earlier, had sent her on her way. He was standing under a lime tree and noticed her. He came towards her.

'You shouldn't be here I told you, you need to get onto the *route nationale*,' he said.

'I don't know where that is!' she replied, tearfully. He told her that she just had to keep going along the Saint-Victurnien road, but Yvonne gasped that it meant that she would be far from home. She told him that she feared her parents would be rounded up elsewhere, that she would be put into a different group and separated from them. He asked her to remind him which village she was from. On hearing 'Les Bordes' he reassured her that that would not be the case.

'But you must get on that *route nationale*,' he said. 'Do you understand?' He added that she could not go back for two or three days.

'But I have to go back tonight!' she protested.

'Well, just for this once, that is too bad,' he snapped. His French was very good, much better than that of any of the other soldiers she had encountered.

'They have killed one of our soldiers,' he began, 'so, if you get what I mean ...'

'Yes,' replied Yvonne.

'If you stay here,' said the soldier, 'they *will* kill you.'[8]

He allowed Yvonne to turn around and head away from the village. She passed trucks pulled up alongside the carriageway. On one of them she saw what looked like a large pile of shoes, with laces hanging from each one. She dared to look back to the soldier and saw him talking to another on a motorbike. They both looked towards her, so she quickly bowed her head and quickened her pace. As the motorbike approached, she felt her shoulders tighten and her heart beat as fast as it ever had. She hopped into the ditch on the side of the road hoping that it would pass her but froze when it stopped alongside. She looked up and the soldier told her to approach. She could tell that he spoke no French. He told her to walk, and to keep walking. The motorcyclist accompanied her as far as the main junction where one final large group of six German soldiers stood before her. 'Oh mademoiselle, oh mademoiselle,' they said, smiling. Yvonne was allowed on her way.

Hiding Places

'Something bad is happening, I know it,' said Fernand Lesparat to Aimé Renaud on the pavement outside the Desourteaux garage. 'Listen, I've got an infected boil on my knee so I'm going to get into bed and I think the Germans will see that I'm ill and leave me alone.'[1] Renaud watched as people milled around. Emile Desourteaux, grocer and brother of his employer for the day, pulled down the metal shutters on his shop front. Marcel Pascaud, the chemist, did likewise. Some had retreated into nearby shops or businesses, or quickly set off in the direction of their homes. Not long after Lesparat left, the wine merchant Léon Denis passed the garage and told Renaud that he was not scared of the Germans: they were 'men like us'. Renaud suggested that he join him to hide but Denis laughed the offer off: 'I am old, I fear nothing, I am going to carry on about my business.' According to Renaud, Denis had long been associated with Pétainism and even of having associations with the *Milice*. He was, in fact, a known Pétainist but had no *Milice* links. Renaud decided that he had seen enough, and that he would take the advice of Lesparat and find a hiding place.

When the empty vehicles descended back down the street, Jean-Marcel Darthout's wife Angèle, upset that her new husband might be taken away, ran to the barber shop where his hair had just been cut. 'Come quick, the Germans are bringing people from Bellevue,'[2] she said, begging him to return home. The Germans were surrounding the town, she told him, from the lower and upper extremities of the main street. Darthout paid for his haircut and hurried home. Once there he tried to make a quick exit via his back garden. He was more confident than his wife that he had nothing to worry about as he was beyond the age of the prescribed STO call-ups, and his papers were perfectly in order. Yet it had seemed 'prudent for me to get out of there'.[3] When he saw a German soldier burst into his kitchen, however, he returned and waited with his wife and mother. The soldier pushed them out on to the street 'unceremoniously' with the barrel of his rifle.

Twenty-five-year-old farm labourer Clément Broussaudier had also come to town to get a haircut at *Café du Chêne*. Like Darthout he had arrived early and had waited on a bench on the side of the road. The wide branches of the ancient oak sheltered him from the sun. Once open he had gone inside and waited his turn to see Joseph Bergmann. Lucien Morlieras had gone to collect his tobacco ration. The customers watched the procession of vehicles climb the street then return. Broussaudier watched in confusion as the vehicles moved slowly past the shop window. The clients chatted, wondering whether the Germans had come for *perquisitions* (searches).[4] Jean-Marcel Darthout had already left when a soldier appeared at the window aiming a sub-machine gun at those inside. A second soldier entered the shop and grabbed Broussaudier roughly by the shoulder, pulling him to his feet. Broussaudier's request to be permitted to secure his bicycle was ignored and he and the others were pushed into the street. With a yell of '*Raus*' each man, including Joseph Bergmann, was pushed in the direction of the *Champ de foire*.

In the Doutre household, 20-year-old Paul had been hiding for three months without anyone in the village knowing, save for his immediate family. His carpenter father Martial was concerned for the safety of his son. 'As I was a deserter from the *chantier de Jeunesse*, I had no papers whatsoever.'[5] As far as the Doutre family were concenrned, the Germans' arrival could only be an identity check, but Paul was vulnerable. If found he would certainly be shipped off to work in Germany, or incarcerated. A plan had long been in place for Paul to escape via the back garden to the countryside, where he would have to wait until checks had been completed. 'My mother put some pieces of sugar into a little drawstring pouch, my father a taste of rum in a hip flask,' but then 'my father went to look and said, "you cannot leave, it's surrounded. They are everywhere." [...] He told me to get into a trapdoor under the machines in the workshop.' Paul did what he was told and waited, while his family complied with the round-up.

STO evader Robert Besson had been opening up his family's textile shop near Pierre Villatte's *bureau de tabac* when the soldiers arrived.[6] He was alarmed at the sight of butcher Gabriel Maire being ordered to follow one of the soldiers. With his brother Abel already a prisoner of war, his mother told him to go and hide.[7] Peering through blinds, he saw 'a small and stocky German who was walking up the street at a quick pace'. He seemed to be leading a procession of people from the surrounding villages. 'Either side of the column, other soldiers were emptying houses and shops, including the barber opposite the "great oak". They were demolishing what they could, including a letter box, with an iron bar.' Besson rushed into Marie Mosnier's home. She had been hiding her nephew Jacques Garaud, also a *réfractaire* from STO. 'We need to hide!' Garaud said. His aunt added, 'Yes go and hide! I will come and look for you when it is safe.'

Housekeeper Françoise Verny watched the arrival of the SS from the residence of her employer, Léon Denis:

> After finishing lunch Monsieur Denis had gone for a walk around the village, just as he had been in the habit of doing for a long time. I was doing the washing up when, while looking out of the kitchen window, I saw the Germans arrive [...] I did not pay it much attention at that time as I was about to set off home to feed my rabbits.[8]

Françoise set off along a back route parallel to the main road and, as the Germans had at that point driven to the upper village, she saw none of them as she walked the short distance to her home. On her way back towards the lower village, she saw several soldiers accompanying two or three women:

> That scared me, and I went to hide, behind a garden wall at the bottom of the property of Monsieur Maire, the butcher. I was also alongside the road that bypassed the southern side of the village. I covered myself with foliage, flowers and plants to camouflage myself.

Françoise was not noticed despite several soldiers passing by. 'Other Germans were posted in fields behind the village, and I could see them from where I kept myself hidden. They were all armed and were watching the immediate outskirts of the locality.'

Hubert Desourteaux had stayed in his garage when the Nazis arrived. Aimé Renaud had stayed with him:

> Not knowing what was going to happen but wary of the manoeuvres of the Germans and supposing that they were going to round up the area's younger people, I tried to get out of there with my mechanic.[9]

At first, they left via the walled garden at the back of the property which led on to a south-facing field, but the encirClément of the village had been well planned and well executed:

> When we got to the field entranceway, I heard Germans coming, and they seemed to be running and firing. They didn't get us. We understood then and there that they were going to surround the village, so the two of us turned back to the garden.

There they found Jeannine Renaud and Étienne Desourteaux[10] who worked alongside their father as secretary to the mayor. Handsome and bespectacled Étienne, after Hubert the next youngest of the Desourteaux brothers, followed the family vocation as a trained physician. He had brought with him Marie Robert from the nearby hamlet of Mas-de-Glane, who was in the village to do some shopping. Hubert locked the back door to the garden, and the garden gate. Desourteaux told Jeannine Renaud to stay where she was. '[He] said to me, "You need to stay and hide with us, if you go back out you risk getting us all caught."'

Martial and Marcel Beaubreuil had climbed into a cubby hole in the Mercier grocery store:

> At the first sight of the German vehicles slowing down my aunt advised me to get into the hiding place that had been prepared in advance, and which was accessible only by a trap door hidden in the corner of the kitchen. It is fair to say that I was in rush to do so. I was hidden for only ten minutes when I heard a soldier come into the room saying, 'Everybody outside'.[11]

Their aunt's maid, *pupille de l'assistance publique* Madeleine Bonnet, followed the family. Waiting in the dark, the brothers heard more soldiers arrive and listened incredulously as the business was stripped of its assets:

> I heard them sawing wood and pulling out nails. I heard several men coming and going, in and out of the shop. They rummaged through everything, they removed everything. I heard them carrying boxes, the till, dragging it out. They cleared the whole shop and must have loaded it onto a lorry.[12]

'The *Boches* are Here!'

Before beginning his work for the afternoon, farrier Hippolyte Redon had passed by the *bureau de tabac* in order to collect his tobacco allowance. He had cycled from his home in Les Bordes, where he left his wife Louise and their son Pierre, who had left school that summer. His young niece from Paris, Marguerite Simon, had gone to school. Redon was due to spend the day fitting Persian blinds to the windows of a property in the village that belonged to a friend and, from his position up high, noticed the approaching column of vehicles from some way off.[1] Redon said later:

> Monsieur Villatte told me that there were five German trucks at the town hall, which was in the upper village, next door to the home of the Mayor delegate, Monsieur Desourteaux.

At the age of 43, he did not consider himself a target for STO, so he decided to take a look. Clearly a round-up was gathering momentum. His own workshop was on the other side of the square:

> Standing at the entrance to the *Champ de foire*, with my blacksmith tools, I saw two trucks arrive, filled with Germans who were all armed. One of them was walking behind Monsieur Binet, the husband of the Head of the School for Girls [and] an employee of the army supply corps based at the *La Visitation* barracks in Limoges. They lived in Oradour. The Germans led him in the direction of the town hall. Monsieur Binet was talking with the German while walking alongside him. I should say that the trucks were climbing the street very slowly and Binet, accompanied by the soldier, was following closely behind.[2]

Redon decided that he should make his way back down the hill towards the site he was due to work at later that day, against the flow of the round-up. He paused outside the school for girls and looked back up the hill to see the German who had been walking with Binet, by then some 50m away, gesticulating to him. He decided to turn around to get back to the *Champ de foire*, where he planned to get to his workshop and let his aunt know that the Germans were rounding up the town's men.

Mathieu Borie had been laying cement at the Mercier grocery store when the German convoy had rumbled past. He watched the trucks and vehicles that had come back from the western edge of the town pull up just beyond the bridge over the Glane, 0.5km from the perimeter of the eastern edge of the village. Soldiers got off the vehicles and set off by foot towards the nearby farms and hamlets. 'Bit by bit as they advanced they gathered everyone together, big and small, old and young, all from Oradour, to take them to the *Champ de foire*.'[3]

Borie, in one of the easternmost buildings, was amongst the first to be picked up. Soon afterwards he heard the town drummer, Monsieur Depierrefiche, announce that all inhabitants, without exception, were to make their way to the assembly point. To Borie the soldiers seemed 'feverish, cynical, gesticulating and shouting'. The population, however, seemed docile to him as they were led towards the *Champ de foire*, despite the sound of gunfire in nearby fields.[4]

When Borie arrived at the assembly point, the sight of the soldiers arming their weapons was intimidating: 'They wore expression of tense fighters, awaiting orders to fire.'

On his way to hide, Martial Brissaud came across the schoolteacher Léonard Rousseau. He was talking with Paul Desourteaux, the mayor.[5] 'I'm going to hide,' said Martial rushing off, not sticking around to hold a conversation with anybody. 'Come and tell me all about your hiding place tomorrow,' teased Rousseau.[6] Martial avoided the main road to get back to his home on the westernmost edge of the village near the Dagoury café-restaurant. He found his mother going about her normal housework and his 20-year-old sister in the courtyard, near the road. His wooden-legged First World War veteran father was resting amongst a pile of wood shavings in their workshop. Martial and his father were both wheelwrights and they worked together in the village where Martial had been born and brought up. He had turned 17 the previous January and had completed his apprenticeship, but neither he nor his sister had left home.

Peering out of the door he saw his friend and neighbour Paul Teyssaud, who worked at the Dupic shop a few doors away. Both young men were fearful of deportation so they decided to grab tools and make for the fields, hoping that they would be taken to be farm workers. But outside they saw German soldiers scouring the fields, waving weapons their way. All around gunfire crackled, irregular and dispersed but coming from all directions. Teyssaud decided that his best bet would be to get back to his employer. Martial decided, despite his father's protestations, to hide in the attic of the house. Just minutes after finding a place he heard the sound of soldiers who had come to look for the occupants of the buildings. In the street Martial could hear his sister ask his parents, 'what is he going to do all alone up there?' His father answered, 'Well, he'll have to manage ...'[7]

Had news of the previous evening's events in the Corrèze town of Tulle, just 120km south-west from the village, travelled quickly enough, people may have been more wary and certainly less calm. Following *maquis* activity, ninety-nine civilian men had been hanged from lampposts and 149 others deported. But news did not travel fast enough.[8] During the Oradour round-up some women were nervous for sons or husbands who may have been hiding, involved in some kind of illegal trading, or who were just the right age for deportation. Some would certainly have been less fearful than others depending on their experience of the German army which so far had not had reason to visit the sleepy village. Robert Hébras' mother was concerned for her son, who she feared would be deported. She told him to hide behind the house. But he was unconcerned. People on the pavement had already said that it was an identity check. Some soldiers had already indicated this. Panic was avoided and most people followed the orders without question. Hébras had experience of German soldiers. He went to the round-up with minimal fuss or concern, so laid back that he did not even remember to take his identity documents with him. He accompanied his mother and sister on the short walk to the assembly point.

In the street Maurice Picat, land agent and owner, marched up and down calling 'Everybody to the town square'.[9] When Robert got there he paused at the sight of four heavy machine guns, which had been set up around the open area, while other soldiers carried lighter weapons. He was surprised to see four more soldiers hiding behind bundles of firewood. They seemed to have grenades with them.

The sound of the convoy filled 70-year-old Marie-Thérèse de Laverine with dread. She knew of a Jewish couple who were hiding in the village, in a rented house near to her home, the *Café du Chêne* and the church. Jules and Jeanne Lang had come to the village from a suburb of Bordeaux. Though only a few hours' drive west of Limoges, Bordeaux was on the other side of the demarcation line, which was still used since full occupation as a major checkpoint. The western coast was full of Nazi activity as defences were installed along its stretch.

The *Boches* were bursting into open houses, then guarding the exits. They made everyone come out, directing them towards the village centre under the pretext of checking their identity documents. Two SS soldiers pushed open our doorway and hit the interior door over and over shouting '*Mossieu, Mossieu*'. Then they doubled their efforts. *L'abbé* Lorich, the priest from Lorrain, lived in one wing of the building. I heard him call 'One minute, one minute, we are coming!'. He opened his door. Immediately, without giving him time even to collect his hat, they grabbed him, his sister and a friend who had come from a neighbouring village with three children and led them to the town centre.[10]

Marie-Thérèse de Laverine's house backed on to a garden near to the Thomas bake house, a building set back from the bakery shop and apartment above, which she owned. She saw her tenants Pierre and Marie-Louise Raynaud and she beckoned them to follow her, along with the Lang couple who had gone there to join them. Jules and Jeanne Lang had to be kept away from the identity check. She intended to wait for the trucks to move away, so she took them into her wine cellar. She was not concerned about her nephew and his family at the Chalet Saint-Vincent, her former home, as it was located well outside of town. She had no idea that they had already been rounded up. They waited a while, but Marie-Louise Raynaud grew more and more concerned as the noises outside changed in nature and time passed. Their daughter, 7-year-old Irène, was in school.

Dentist René Lévy had also made a quick exit:

a little before two o'clock, two guys burst into the room in the *Hôtel du Champ de foire* where I was playing billiards. 'The *Boches!*' they shouted. 'The *Boches* are here!'.[11]

[...]

I understood immediately that it was better to not have to show them my false identity documents.[12] I left the hotel and took a passageway which, from the *Champ de foire*, led out of the village. A patrol saw me and I only just escaped a hail of bullets. I was, however, able to reach a little bit of woodland on the edge of the Glane.[13] From there I noticed a sentry who was, by then, guarding the entrance to the path that I had taken.

Lévy settled where he was and waited.

Gunshots

At Le Mas de l'Arbre, Marguerite Laplaud was celebrating her sixty-eighth birthday. She lived alone in nearby Les Bordes, so she had walked to the home of her daughter, Marie Boissou, for some lunch. The cordon of the SS round-up did not extend as far as Les Bordes, but it did take in La Croix des Bordes and Le Mas de l'Arbre. Sitting at the table was Marie's 16-year-old son Jacques, who had been taking a break from the fields to dine with his parents and celebrate his grandmother's birthday. The meal finished, he had decided to get some fresh air while his father took an aunt home. His grandfather was still in the house with his mother; several builder's labourers who were working for 71-year-old Léonard Lachaud were also milling around.[1] Suddenly Hippolyte Redon, the blacksmith-farrier who lived in nearby Les Bordes, appeared, peddling at full speed. 'Get to safety! Get away quickly!' yelled Redon. 'The Germans are in Oradour and they are arresting everyone.' He explained that he had managed to escape the attentions of the ever-closing cordon but, as he cycled out of town, he had been spotted speeding along the route towards Les Bordes by sentries on the bridge over the Glane. Their bullets had crashed into the hedgerows but somehow missed him and he was warning everyone he could as he rushed towards his home in Les Bordes. 'They are right behind me,' he insisted.

Redon's story may have appeared far-fetched to the gathered family, but Jacques' grandfather[2] decided that it would be best for him to go straight to Oradour to collect Jeanette, his youngest grandchild who was 9½ years old and at school. Jeanette had insisted on going back to school despite protestations from her mother that, since it was Saturday and a special celebration, she could stay at home. She had, however, been working on some writing and was desperate to finish it. Fearing for her safety, Jacques set off at speed but did not get far before bursts of gunfire forced him to turn back to the farmhouse. The whole family decided that they needed to hide as quickly as they could.

Marie-Anne Deschamps had moved back from Paris to see her parents in Les Bordes. Hearing 'bursts of gunfire and isolated shots from the edges of the village of Les Bordes on the road from Oradour', she rushed outside to see what was happening. 'I saw the population coming together, asking if anyone knew what was going on. Just then I noticed old Lachaud who lived in the first house as you come into Les Bordes when arriving from Oradour-sur-Glane, who had gone out into the middle of the wheat field to shout out to us to save ourselves. He was waving his arms, gesticulating at us to flee.'[3]

A moment or so later, no longer hearing the rumbling of motor vehicles or the crackling of gunfire, she walked towards the farms at the hamlet of Le Mas de l'Arbre. Several women told her that a German column had arrived near their houses but had then left again after firing machine guns towards the fields and the woods. About to go further to see if she could find anyone hurt or requiring assistance, she heard vehicles approaching again:

> I saw a tracked vehicle open fire and this time old Lachaud, who was return-ing to his work […] was shot down in the fields. I had heard them shout '*halte, halte, halte*' several times but without waiting they just fired.[4]

Hippolyte Senon also saw the shooting of Lachaud not far from the Boissou property. He saw the whole family rounded up along with the two remaining labourers, Marguerite Laplaud and her daughter.[5] Daniel Senon and Andrée Deglane, the young couple who had been on their lunchtime walk when they had heard gunfire, looked on aghast:

> The *Boches*, intent on finishing off their victim, did not notice us passing by, around 150m from them. Numb with fear we got to the centre of the village where groups of people had already gathered asking what could be going on.[6]

Jacques Boissou left his hiding place but as he crossed a field he was surprised by the arrival of more vehicles and again he ducked into a hedgerow. One of the vehicles left but three soldiers got out of the other and began search-ing for Boissou. When he felt that they were close to finding him he made a break for it, sprinting as fast as he could and managing to avoid the bullets that were fired in his direction. He managed to catch sight of the soldiers and noticed how young they were, almost as young as himself.[7] He reached a wheat field and paused, believing himself to be safe. But another group of sol-diers had spotted him and again fired his way. He avoided the bullets, despite his wooden-soled clogs, ducking and weaving in the crops and dropping to the ground from time to time. Eventually he reached woodland where the soldiers lost sight of him and gave up the chase.[8]

A Round-Up

Armand Senon was laid up in his bedroom. Known as Jean-Blanc, he was a tall, solidly built, square-jawed member of the football club's first team. The previous week, however, he had broken his leg. This would not just be a blow to the team, who were due to play the following day, but also to his employer the Bouchoule bakery. The Senon farm, owned by the Mosnier family but rented to Senon's father and uncle, was situated right on the corner of the *Champ de foire*. He had just finished his lunch, brought to his room by his mother, when the convoy climbed the main street and turned on to the *Champ de foire*, over which he had an almost complete view. He watched the soldiers gather and the first people arrive. To him, even the earliest to arrive appeared panicked.

> My mother came up to see me in my room to tell me that they were gathering everyone together in the *Place du Champ de foire* in order to carry out identity card checks.

He had heard gunshots in the countryside but he thought they were coming from fields on the other side of the Glane:

> One of my aunts, who was visiting that weekend, told my father and my three uncles, all of whom had just got in, to get themselves away. They climbed out of a window at the back of the house but did not get far before some Germans who had circled the town opened fire on them. One of my uncles [Martial Senon], who was a veteran of the 1914–18 conflict was injured by one of the bullets.[1]

Senon's family made their way outside to join the growing throng on the *Champ de foire*, leaving his injured uncle downstairs where he received treatment from his wife and Senon's grandmother. They washed the blood away and did what they could to stem the bleeding. Senon remained upstairs. He had already decided that he would show his plaster cast when and if the soldiers searched the buildings. Soon he heard a soldier and the sound of both women being pushed out of the door. His uncle loudly protested that he had been shot by them in his own garden and would therefore be unable to join the round-up

ORADOUR-SUR-GLANE (H.-V.). - Place du Champ de Foire.

A view of the Champ de foire *looking towards the rue Emile Desourteaux. It was here that the population was gathered on 10 June 1944. (Collection Benoit Sadry)*

unless his wound was tended to. Nobody went upstairs so he stayed and watched through the thick window. His injured uncle limped out of the door in order to join everybody else. He watched as his mother tried to return to the house, probably to tell Senon to join them, but she was stopped by one of the soldiers who were fastidiously keeping the population together in that one place. He saw soldiers banging loudly on doors in and around the square, and he watched as their owners did their best to intervene by offering to open them so that the doors themselves would not be demolished. Neighbours gathered together as the *Champ de foire* filled up. Jean-Marcel Darthout looked on:

> I saw women in tears whilst others who were carrying their babies were braver and seemed more confident. Many women arrived with prams. I remember seeing an old man arrive who had to be held up and who seemed to have been brought from his bed. The men seemed to be have been surprised at their workplaces. Their clothes gave away their professions. I remember seeing, amongst others, the baker who had put his singlet back on but whose torso was semi-naked, all white with flour.[2]

Martial Brissaud could see nothing from his attic hiding place, and he was frustrated at not being able to shift himself into a position to be able to see what was going on outside. Shots were being fired all around the village, but they seemed distant enough. All seemed calm in his house so he decided to venture downstairs:

> I had just climbed down the ladder from the attic when I heard the hob-nail boots of a German who had come in downstairs. He went into every bedroom and tried to get into a closet into which I had just climbed. The door was broken and condemned so he did not try that hard before giving up. Then he went back downstairs. During all that time I could hear what seemed to be about ten other Germans down there. I listened as they smashed up all the furniture, even the tiles.[3]

Brissaud quickly climbed back up the ladder so that he could find a safer hiding place.

Jeannine Renaud, with her husband and three others in the Desourteaux garage, thought that she had heard crashing noises from her friend Henriette Hyvernaud's home nearby. She had passed by the property on the way to the garage but, not wanting to draw attention to herself, had chosen not to respond when her friend had called out to ask where she was going:

> I definitely had the impression that they broke down the door of the house where the Hyvernaud family lived. It was next door to the garden that linked to the garage [...] I heard shouting and children crying and I defi-nitely heard a shot fired in that house.[4]

All five adults at the garage had been looking for a suitable place to hide. Jeannine Renaud and Marie Robert hid together amongst some pea plants but 'when we heard bullets whistling around us we decided that we needed to find shelter, so we huddled up against a henhouse before getting inside it'.[5]

The Desourteaux brothers hid together in the bushy arbour of a tree while Aimé Renaud hid in a small ditch behind some nettles. The garden was shut behind high walls and a locked door but even so the three men felt exposed, especially when bullets whistled by. 'When I understood that the Germans were rounding up the Hyvernaud family, my neighbours, and that they had already tried my garden gate which they had found locked, my brother and I decided to hide inside,' said Hubert Desourteaux. 'My brother went up into the attic, or in that direction anyway ... I was not able to see. I hid in a dark corner of a neighbouring building that was still under construction.'[6]

The children were next to be brought to the *Champ de foire* and they were rounded up in exceptional order. The sounds of gun shots had already been reverberating in the countryside all around, particularly on the eastern edge of the town near Puy-Gaillard, a short walk from where the infant and refugee schools stood, and the Masset farm that overlooked it. The temporary building that housed the class for refugees had been built from cheap materials so Fernand Gougeon, their teacher, fearful of stray bullets, took his pupils into the infants' classroom next door. The walls of the former presbytery were made of solid stone.[7] The infants had finished their lunch break and were in the course of returning to class at half past two, by which time the round-up was well under way.

Roger Godfrin was a pupil in the school for refugees. Crouching down, he did not see the soldier who burst in and beckoned to their teacher to bring the children, shouting 'Raus'. As the classroom was evacuated, however, the 7-year-old did exactly as he had been told to do by his parents. The German army had expelled them from their homes in the Moselle region of Alsace-Lorraine four years earlier. He had been told that he should fear the German army: 'I remembered what my mother said one day when we were sat at the table, that if we saw the Germans we should run away into the woods.' Roger's sisters, 12-year-old Marie-Jeanne and 11-year-old Pierrette, were there too and 'I told them that we had to save ourselves by getting away from the Germans, but they did not want to follow me'. Roger acted upon the instincts of a child based on an 'understanding that the German was going to take away all the children'. He was right. 'I slid away quietly and, seeing no other German, I hid in the garden behind the school.'[8]

Most were quite happy for the break in their school day. The soldiers were careful not to scare them but were firm with the teachers who, in turn, told the youngsters that there would be a school photo opportunity. When the little ones arrived at the square, walking hand in hand and in rows, parents looked nervously for their children. Many had no parents on the *Champ de foire*. The schools were filled with children belonging not just to villagers, but also to families in Oradour's surrounding hamlets, some of whom had no idea what was happening in the village centre.

The space of the *Champ de foire* opened up beyond a narrow entranceway off the main street. At the other end, the Senon farm and other barns stood alongside a path that led from the cemetery to the *bureau de tabac* in the lower village. A stone well that had served generations of *radounauds* was a centrepiece, still serving its original purpose. The village's water supplies were limited to that well, another in the Picat farmyard and three water outlets on the *rue Emile Desourteaux*. The SS gathered the population just inside the main entrance off Oradour's central avenue. More and more people arrived and stood outside Marcel Pascaud's pharmacy and Compain's pâtisserie.

The school children arrived in their rows, led respectively by their teach-ers. Odette 'Dédée' Couty, soon to leave Oradour, and Denise Bardet, on her twenty-fourth birthday, led the girls. Léonard Rousseau and his wife Jeanne led the boys, including their own son Pierre, who was larger than the other boys and with severe learning difficulties. Raymonde Vincent led the infants, including Jean-Pierre Binet, son of Andrée Binet, permanent head of the girls' school. Madame Binet eventually arrived in her nightdress and dressing gown; her husband Jean was already there. One smaller line of pupils arrived led by Fernand Gougeon. These were refugee children from Alsace-Lorraine. One boy was missing but if Fernand Gougeon had noticed he did not let on.

As the sun did its upmost to burst through the clouds, an armoured car arrived, filled with people who had been picked up in the surrounding fields. It dropped them off before turning around to collect more who had been arrested in this way.[9] Others had been shot on the spot. Marguerite Rouffanche remembered, 'men, women, children, schoolchildren, babies of all ages, three priests and the armed Germans, some flat to the floor behind their automatic weapons, others stood up surrounding us on that square.' Then a period of waiting began, which seemed 'to last forever'.[10]

Robert Hébras was glad that he was wearing only a singlet when the sun finally broke through the humid heat that had been building. He was sure that the identity-checking operation – for that was surely what this was – would be quickly over. He was struck at the sight of a young girl of around 5 get-ting dragged to the assembly point by a soldier who had hold of her ear. Near him Maurice Compain, the *pâtissier* whose business was on the square, asked a soldier whether he might go and check his oven so that his cakes did not burn. His wife was in Limoges and not due back until the evening tram. He was told that this was not permitted and that the cakes would be taken care of. Hébras noted that the soldier spoke excellent French.

Marguerite Rouffanche recalled that 'the conversations that were happen-ing between the groups led us to suppose that the Germans were perhaps there to take hostages, and that others would be taken to concentration camps'. But the choice of Oradour seemed odd since it was 'a peaceful town, [and] knew neither *maquis* nor armed Resistance'. Clément Broussaudier thought that everyone was being gathered together to be kept safe while an operation was carried out against the *maquis*, despite knowing 'that no "*maquis*" group, nor armed Resistance group existed in Oradour'.[11] After a wait of an hour or so an officer, assisted by an interpreter, asked for the mayor delegate of the *com-mune*. Seventy-one-year old Doctor Paul Desourteaux stepped up.

The Sounds of Separation

Yvon Roby was an 18-year-old who worked part-time as a postman and helped on his father's farm. He lived well outside the village so when his father asked him to collect his tobacco that Saturday lunchtime, he hopped on to his trusty Peugeot bicycle. He planned to use the opportunity to catch up with some old friends. He peddled through La Plaine to Puy-Gaillard from where he could see the church steeple. Just then a soldier who had been behind a hedge on the side of the road jumped out and pointed a gun at him. He yelled to Roby to stop. Roby was ordered to get off his bike and lean it against a nearby telegraph pole. Then the soldier whistled and another soldier appeared. Roby, anxious that he would be taken to Germany, was directed by hand signals to collect his bike and continue to the village centre.

He set off slowly, thinking of ways that he might get away, but a motor-cyclist followed him until he got to the bridge over the Glane where several trucks stood waiting. Soldiers dressed in long camouflage coats and carrying weapons were sitting atop and standing alongside the vehicles. Roby was forced off his cycle by one of the soldiers who got on it himself, riding away to the upper village. Another soldier took over, kicking Roby in the posterior, yelling '*Raus*' and pointing him in the direction of the *Champ de foire* where he joined everybody else.

Rumours had begun circulating that the Germans were there to make requisitions. A familiar motorcar rumbled down the street. Doctor Jacques Desourteaux, son of the mayor and the town's other physician, pulled up nearby having completed his rounds in the nearby villages. Alongside him was a German soldier who had brought him to the spot once he was through the barrage in the road at the western extremity of the village. Jacques Desourteaux got out and joined everybody else, apologising for his tardiness. He had been at the birth of a child in the nearby hamlet of Le Chatre.[1] He abandoned his *gazogène*-powered car in the middle of the main street.[2] By the time his son had arrived, Paul Desourteaux had already been talking to other town notables, members of the *délégation spéciale* of the municipal council. These included Jean Roumy and Léon Denis, the wine merchant. Other respected professionals such as Pierre Montazeaud, the village notary, were also involved in discussions. Marguerite Rouffanche strained to hear what was being said, but could not quite make it out.

A German officer announced to the men that they would be remaining where they were. They were told to turn around and face the wall. Once again, Robert Hébras noticed that the officer who gave the order to separate them spoke very good French. 'All the school children stayed with the women and girls on the right side of the square as you look at it from the main street. The men and boys of around 14–15 years or over were put on the left hand side.' For Jean-Marcel Darthout 'this was the moment that I kissed my wife and my mother for the last time'.[3]

'I had to leave with the women and children,' recalled Marguerite Rouffanche. 'There were heart-rending scenes of farewell. The Germans tolerated, or perhaps could not prevent, us embracing our loved ones. It all happened very quickly.'[4] As the women and children were led away, the men were not permitted to turn around but Darthout could not help himself:

> I turned my head to see the column leave. It was a very sad sight. Some women and children let out harrowing cries. We could feel how worried they were for their fathers, husbands or sons. I saw women faint. Others helped them up to take them along with the column as it left, which was well surrounded by armed Germans.[5]

Armand Senon, still in his bedroom, had withdrawn from his window when he heard the cries from women and children outside his window. Unable to see, he wondered whether the soldiers had begun to gather hostages. Suddenly he heard clicking as a gun was manipulated downstairs, so he kept as still as he could. Once the noise stopped, he crept back to his vantage point and saw the group of men sitting along the verge of the square, guarded by soldiers with light machine guns. Then he saw pharmacist Marcel Pascaud walking back from the upper town. Senon wondered whether he had been subject to questioning.[6]

From the dark corner of a half-completed extension to his garage, Hubert Desourteaux could hear events outside as people passed in front of the building. He heard villagers talking and the voice of Germans 'in a relative calm'. Hubert stayed still, standing upright in the corner of a room. 'I managed to create a small hole in the wall which allowed me to see out onto the street. I saw Germans with automobiles which they were using to move young villagers from the village. I saw four cars pass, one belonging to Monsieur Picat [...] and another belonging to Monsieur Montazeaud, our notary. They were taking them towards the lower village, onto the Limoges road. I recognised one of the youngsters as 17-year-old Paul

*Armand Senon worked in a bakery and played for
the football team. The week before he had broken
his leg and was laid up. He remained undiscovered
and witnessed events from his bedroom in the
family farm on the* Champ de foire.
(Collection Camille Richard)

Doutre.' In fact, he had seen Paul's younger brother Charles, who was 17.
Paul Doutre was hiding at home.

Columns of children began passing by:

> I was not able to see them, but I could see the Germans accompanying
> them.[7] Shortly afterwards it was the turn of the women. I saw them go by,
> also surrounded on all sides. I did not see any crying. They seemed to be in
> no doubt as to what might await them.[8]

No other witness has described the women and children walking separately. It
is probable that the children in the first column were those from the villages
and therefore unaccompanied. The second column probably consisted of
children with mothers present, though Desourteaux would have been unable

to see them in any detail. This would have accounted for the lack of tears and upbeat manner, parents and teachers making light of what was happening so as not to cause upset.

Meanwhile on the *Champ de foire*, Mathieu Borie stood waiting with the other men. Paul Desourteaux returned from the town hall and took his place alongside the rest. 'He appeared extremely brave, but he did not talk to us,' said Borie.[9] 'Two Germans arrived and asked for the owner of a car parked in the garage of Monsieur Denis, the wine merchant. Monsieur Denis set off with his son-in-law (Monsieur Henri Texeraud) and the Germans, but rejoined us later.' The men were told that they were permitted to sit on the floor and they did so with little said. 'Though we had begun to wonder what the Germans were going to do with us,' said Darthout later, 'we were all hopeful.'

Half an hour or so passed[10] before the German officer returned with another French-speaking soldier. All men were told to stand up and were put into a row, three wide. The French-speaking interpreter who, according to Yvon Roby had only a light accent, spoke: 'It seems that there is a munitions depot in the town, left here by the *maquis*. Is there anybody here who knows where it is?' When nobody spoke, the interpreter continued, 'Does anybody here own personal armaments?' One man said that he owned a 6mm rifle but the soldiers showed no interest in that.[11] Neither did they appear interested in the admission by farmer Jean Lamaud that he too owned a rifle at his farm in Bellevue.[12] The commanding officer, together with the interpreter, crossed to Dr Desourteaux and asked the mayor if he had chosen fifty hostages.[13] 'I harbour no complaint against any of my people here,' said the mayor, 'and therefore I cannot designate fifty hostages!' The mayor told the officer that he would offer himself and, if necessary, his close family members. 'So many decisions,' replied the officer and, according to Borie, he began to laugh.[14]

The men were informed that they would be divided into groups and taken to barns. There they would be guarded while searches were carried out. 'We will search all the houses,' said the interpreter. Jean-Marcel Darthout was not concerned by this. 'They can look as much as they want,' he said to a friend, 'but there is nothing to find.'[15] Before being divided up they were told to make a half-turn to face the wall. 'Anyone would have thought that they wanted to shoot us from behind,' said Robert Hébras. 'Their rifles and machine guns were trained on us, and just behind where we stood.'[16] But after a few minutes of waiting, and sweating in the hot sun, the men were told to turn back around to face the square.

Armand Senon watched on as the men were grouped:

Paul Desourteaux, mayor at the time of the massacre, with his sons. Émile is missing, banished and probably living in Limoges. (Collection André Desourteaux)

I saw four groups of about fifty men each and they were led one after another, each guarded by armed Germans carrying rifles, machine guns, light machine guns or revolvers. One of the groups was led into my father's barn,[17] just about 40m away from where I was.'[18]

Clément Broussaudier was struck by how organised the operation seemed to be:

All movements were executed by the Germans in a most disciplined and correct manner, that is extremely militarily. But once we left the square, if any person was not following the group quickly enough there would be no hesitation in hitting them with the butt of a weapon or aiming a kick into the legs.[19]

The Barn

After waiting in the hot sun with the others, it was Yvon Roby's turn to follow one of the columns of men. 'They made us leave, one after another. A German led our group. Several others guarded us on each side. You had to walk quickly.'[1] Jean-Marcel Darthout was part of the same group heading towards the lower village and was 'pushed forward roughly' by one of the Germans so that he would walk more quickly. Darthout saw a machine gun placed in the centre of the street, level with the point at which the first group had been assembled.[2] Roby and Darthout's group also contained Robert Hébras, Clément Broussaudier and Mathieu Borie. 'On our way along the main street some Germans smashed windows with their rifle butts, one of which was a window belonging to Dr Jacques Desourteaux, the son of the mayor. This was a house that was undergoing repairs.'[3]

Hubert Desourteaux watched from his hiding place in the dark corner of that very same half-built garage building:

> Later I saw a group of men pass. At the front of this group was the owner of the barbershop, Monsieur Morlieras[4] who was smoking a cigarette and joking with the person behind him who I did not recognise. They were being led towards the lower village […] As they all marched pass I could make out banging against doors coming from everywhere, and I could hear the noise of tiles falling and the like […] but it was not upsetting as such just then.[5]

The men had been divided into six unequal groups. They were led to locations scattered around the village. At the upper end of the *bourg*, they were put in a coach house and a wine storage shed. A little further down the main street more men were packed into part of the Desourteaux garage. At the lower end of the village, almost overlooking the River Glane, but with its doorway facing the church, was the shed belonging to the baker Bouchoule. The final location, visible to Armand Senon from his window on the *Champ de foire*, was a the Laudy-Mosnier barn.

Having been led there by way of the main street, that group, the largest, had left the *Champ de foire* last and had passed the Desourteaux garage where most of the men appeared unconcerned. Robert Hébras said later:

All along the breadth of the doorway, men were leaning against each other nonchalantly. There was no sign of worry on their faces, despite the installation of a machine gun on the pavement on the other side of the road. It was ready to fire and attended to by a soldier.[6]

They first turned left and headed in the direction of the church and the lower village. After a short walk 'we were made to stop opposite the barn that belonged to the Laudy-Mosnier buildings, known locally as "Le Blanc"'.[7] Hébras looked towards the lower village, utterly deserted, the women and children nowhere to be seen. 'There was nobody there, no dogs, no chickens, no people.' He remained calm and felt that most of the others in the group were of the same state of mind. They had, after all, been told that once the searches were finished everybody would be free to leave.[8]

Yvon Roby watched a German soldier unsuccessfully try to open the door to the barn. 'This was fortunate for me because there was no way out of there and I would never have succeeded in getting away.'[9] Instead the men were taken to a courtyard attached to the property, where, set back, was a warehouse rented to Jean Senon. It was cluttered with barrows, carts, wood and hay, so three men were told to clear sufficient space. One of them, Monsieur

A view of the main street leading westward from the lower to the upper village. On the left is the Desourteaux grocery store (épicerie). The tram rails can be seen in the road. (Collection Benoit Sadry)

Duquéroix, had a daughter who lived in Limoges and was rumoured to acquaint with Germans. Once the clutter was cleared, a soldier found a broom and swept an area in front of the warehouse before setting up a machine gun and training it on the crowd. A second was set up and behind them two soldiers adopted a firing position. Two others held rifles while a soldier who appeared to be the leader of the small detachment had a revolver.

A simple open-fronted stone-walled barn with a roof made from the same red-clay tiles that adorned the majority of the buildings in the area, it was a place they all knew well. The narrow entranceway led to the lane at the back end of the *Champ de foire*. Its far wall backed on to the same row of shops that the men had just passed. Within the courtyard, opposite the main barn, stood a row of stables with a door to the same main building, a block of stables, that the soldier had been unable to kick open. They remained unused. Once space had been cleared everyone was told to gather in the shade of the open warehouse. The machine guns blocked the opening through which the group had passed, 7 or 8m from them. Just a courtyard separated the men from the soldiers and their weapons, and an open patch of ground alongside the barn sloped upwards to the outer walls of another property. The buildings were packed closely together and offered little room for manoeuvre. They were tall and any chance of escaping over them was reduced to zero by their sloping roofs. Elsewhere in the other barns, stables and warehouses, all the men of Oradour, some still teenagers, waited.

The Service Tram

Before Jean Hébras had brought his family to Oradour, Marcelin Chalard held the post that Hébras would fill. When he had been reassigned to Limoges, his apartment had become the Hébras family's first home, and it was there that Robert was born. As such, Chalard still had many ties to the village where he had spent many years of his working life. That Saturday, he asked his supervisor at the Limoges terminus if he could accompany a maintenance trip as it would give him an opportunity to stop off in the village and try on a suit at Jules and Paul Santrot's tailor's shop. His plan was to be dropped off, try on the suit and get collected by the tram on its return trip.

Like Chalard, Martial Dauriat was a long-time employee of the *Compagnie des Tramways Départmentaux de la Haute-Vienne* (CDHV). It was he who was asked to take a maintenance tram along line three to Bussière-Poitevine. Louis-François Tabaraud would accompany him. One man would drive, the other would identify issues on the line. There were no passenger cars attached.

That mid-afternoon, the tram approached Puy-Gaillard and began the descent towards the church. As they slowed they noticed a dozen or so military vehicles parked along the edge of the road, one behind the other, over a distance of some 250m. The trucks were surrounded by soldiers, some of whom signalled for the tram to stop. Tabaraud, who was not driving the tram, remarked that they were 'armed with rifles, light machine guns and revolvers, and were in camouflage with helmets. The outfits were, as far as I remember, a sort of iron grey.'[1] He estimated between sixty and a hundred men, or more. Some were on the road, many more in the surrounding fields.[2]

The tram was made to wait for a quarter of an hour before fifteen or so soldiers appeared who were 'leading a column of about thirty people, like a herd. They were all around them.'[3] The group was told to stop near the tram. The soldiers began to inspect the engine. All three of the tram engineers were told to get off and join the group that was being led towards the bridge, but they retorted that, since the tram was on a slope and the electricity supply had been cut, it needed to be secured so as to avoid an accident. The uniformed Tabaraud and Dauriat were allowed to proceed but Chalard was told to join the group of men and women of all ages. They recognised Jean Baptiste Lavergne and his 17-year-old son Jean who, that morning, had gone to Oradour from their home in Limoges on bicycles to buy food. Both were CDHV employees. They asked Dauriat to look after their bicycles, which were loaded on to the tram. Chalard was allowed to put his bicycle back too, but was told that he must join the rest of the group.

The soldiers glanced over the tram while the group was told to move towards the village. Tabaraud and Dauriat asked some sentries if Chalard could return as they needed him for the safe operation of the tram. 'One of these soldiers spoke good French. He told us that he could not do anything, but if we were wise we should listen to him, insist on nothing and go straight back to Limoges.'[4] The two men watched as their colleague was led away towards the bridge. He was walking alongside Monsieur Lavergne and, after 20m or so, Chalard turned around suddenly to look behind him. Immediately two shots rang out. Chalard stumbled away from the column and grabbed a railing, wailing and howling in pain. As his legs buckled, he was shot twice more and he fell, killed instantly, at the edge of the bridge across the Glane.

Seven-year-old Roger Godfrin, whose sisters had refused to flee with him, decided that he needed to leave the school garden where he had been hiding:

I took a path towards some woods by the Glane. I ran very quickly and [...] lost one of my sandals, the left one, but I did not stop to pick it up because I knew I did not have time. I went through thorns but I did not stop to think about the pain. Before the woods I saw Monsieur Marcellin Thomas, the baker, my father's boss. He was with a lady by the name of Dalstein, a refugee from Lorraine and a girl called Françoise Bertrand, who was 14, and who I knew quite well. They were hiding behind a bush.[5]

Octavie Dalstein, a 67-year-old widow from Rupigny, a hamlet next to Charly, had agreed to look after her great-niece Françoise when the child's parents had died in the 1930s. Aunt and great-niece had been among those expelled from Moselle:

I was probably there for about five minutes. But then I saw two Germans on the other side of the same bush. They were armed with machine guns. I thought that if I stayed, I would probably be killed quickly so I made a run towards the woods [...] The grass was high, and I got caught up in it. [It] tangled between the toes on my bare left foot, because I had lost my sandal. I fell over. The two Germans had seen me trying to escape and I saw them laugh. Another German who I had seen [earlier] was stood near the cemetery. When he saw me, he whistled to me, but I got out of sight behind the houses.[6]

From their hiding place amongst the brambles and ivy of a wall in an abandoned garden, STO evaders Robert Besson and Jacques Garaud had heard rounds of firing that sounded like they were coming from a farmyard. They saw little Roger Godfrin make his getaway, and looked on in horror when, after seeing a soldier aiming a rifle in what they thought was their direction,

Madeleine Bonnet, a ward of the state who lived with and worked for Jeanne Mercier. Madeleine managed to get back to the grocery store before being discovered by the SS.
(Collection Denise Gally)

the shots brought down a young woman whom they had not seen nearby. This was likely to have been young Françoise Bertrand. Though the boy did not see it, the soldiers who had been on the other side of the bush also executed her great-aunt Octavie Dalstein and baker Marcellin Thomas on the spot.

At the Mercier grocer the Beaubreuil brothers stayed still in the space that had been prepared for them. They heard movements in the shop above. The soldiers had come back. They remained for a while, going up and down the stairs to the bedrooms, possibly taking linen or other goods. When they happened to be upstairs the boys heard the sound of somebody else. It was Madeleine Bonnet, 17-year-old orphan and employee of their aunt. Somehow, she had evaded both the round-up and the march to the church, which was just across the square from the grocery store in which they were hidden. They could do nothing but listen:

> [She] crossed the shop and ran out into the garden, calling for my aunt. We heard her talk with another woman who was saying to her 'my poor little one, it's terrible, it's over for us.' Then there was a burst of machine gun fire […] A little later my brother found them both killed at the doorway to the cellar.[7]

Sanctuary

The centuries-old church, small and dimly lit, was packed with women, schoolchildren, toddlers and babies in arms or in their prams. The pews clogged up what available space there had been. After the march down the main avenue they had passed the old oak tree that stretched out next to the market hall and the *Café du Chêne*. The outer doors had been locked. 'Before we knew it, it was full of women and children. Schoolchildren and toddlers of all ages were squashed up close to mothers who had pushed prams into that sacred place.'[1]

As time passed quiet descended. They were told nothing, as the wait went on and on. Many children whose parents were in the surrounding villages, had the female teachers as their sole source of comfort. *L'abbé* Chapelle had not been allowed to accompany the women to the church. The Moselle vicar, Jacques Lorich, had also been kept with the men, but his sister Angélique was there, as was Odile Neumeyer. Her brother Emile, by then a 21-year-old theology student, had been visiting Odile for the weekend and had been caught up with the men. The women and older children did their best to reassure the little ones that they would soon be out.

As the noise quietened down, Marguerite Rouffanche looked around and found her family members:

> I found myself reunited with my two daughters and my 7-month-old grandson. I watched as my little niece, who was 5 years old, slept [...] She was the only child of my sister-in-law from Orbagnac [...] and went to the village school.[2]

Marguerite's daughter Amélie whose husband, a plumber, was working outside of town that day, held her baby, 6-month-old Guy. Her teenage sister Andrée did what she could to help. The church had become stuffy.

The three women were preoccupied with thoughts of what might be happening to the girls' brother, Jean, and their father, Simon. Some women muttered but were careful not to alarm the children. Crammed in and uncomfortable, almost 250 women and over 200 children were packed into a space designed to hold no more than 350. Most, however, felt safe in the sacred place. Occasionally one of the two exterior doors would crack open and a soldier would look inside. Little was audible from the village, but the crackle of gunfire seemed more and more sporadic.

Roger Godfrin kept running:

> I got as far as the woods and headed down to the Glane. Some more Germans, six of them, saw me when I was coming out of woodland. They called to me and whistled, but I ran away as fast as I could. They chased after me but I got to the other side of the river by wading through the water

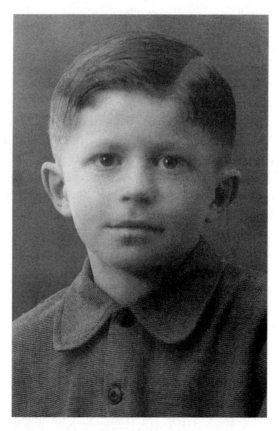

Roger Godfrin, the only schoolchild present in class to escape with his life. As refugees from Alsace-Lorraine, his parents had told him to run when they saw Germans. His two sisters declined to follow him. (Centre de la mémoire, Oradour-sur-Glane)

which only went up as far as my knees. On the other side, I hid behind a tree. The Germans left me alone for a minute, so I headed back towards the woodland. I crouched down behind a tree and I was able to count the six soldiers who had followed me. I saw them fire a volley of bullets towards me.[3]

Roger looked up to see that the bullets had killed a dog called Bobby that had followed him as far as the edge of the river.[4]

A little later Roger was found by road worker Pierre Gabriel, who took him to the Pincemaille household in Laplaud where the family cared for his wounds and removed the thorns from his feet, bathing them in *eau de vie*, a strong locally produced spirit. A doctor was called and Roger was checked over. Then the Pincemaille family, who had come to Oradour from Alsace-Lorraine and knew the Godfrin family, spent the night in some nearby woods before returning to the house the following day.

The Laudy-Mosnier Barn

Robert Hébras was not panicked by the firing stance adopted by their guards. He did not doubt that everybody would be set free once the searches of the village were complete. Even older veterans were relaxed,[1] some thinking of little but the thirst brought on by the heat.

Some of the younger men gathered towards the rear of the warehouse and chatted a little about what was going on. Darthout was quick to point out what seemed obvious, that the soldiers could not allow the searches to be interfered with. 'They are guarding us, what do you think?' He felt more uneasy than Hébras, however. One of the soldiers chewed sugar cubes from the pocket of his tunic. Yvon Roby was feeling anxious too as he watched another restlessly handling his gun. Roby, who lived well outside Oradour, felt like something of an outsider as groups slowly gathered, so he pushed himself further back. The soldiers told one man who tried to sit down near Darthout to get back to his feet.

They waited for half an hour or so and all the while Yvon Roby could not take his eyes off the soldier fiddling with the weapon. He 'really caught my eye. Beginning to fear for my life I slowly moved myself out of the line of fire.'

Darthout looked up from a conversation that had begun with his football teammates to see several officers approach. Too far away to hear what they were saying, they appeared to be talking primarily to the gunners.

Joseph Bergmann turned white. 'They are going to kill us,' he spat out. The apprentice barber, born in Ickern, had never let on to his friends that he spoke any German, always maintaining the impression that he was Austrian.

'Stop it, Joseph,' came the reply from Darthout and the others. 'Stop talking such nonsense. Stop it now.' Bergmann persisted. 'Stop, Joseph,' spat out Darthout, 'they have other things to do.' But Joseph Bergmann had heard the soldiers talking about the next stage in the operation.[2]

'We suddenly heard what sounded like the firing of a cannon,' said Yvon Roby. 'It could have been the sound of a tank's gun. There had been a tank near the *Champ de foire*.'[3] 'That explosion, which was loud but not close enough to make the barn shake, seemed to be the signal for the shooting,'[4] said Clément Broussaudier. Next came the sound of machine guns firing which, according to Mathieu Borie, 'seemed to come from the Desourteaux

Widely assumed to be Austrian, Joseph Bergmann was a German Jew whose family had moved to Alsace-Lorraine. He worked as a barber in the Café du Chêne *and played on the football team. (Collection Association Nationale des Familles des Martyrs d'Oradour-sur-Glane)*

garage.[5] Immediately the soldiers yelled out and 'on [this] brief command the six Germans discharged their arms onto us'.[6]

Roby had moved far enough back into the crowd and towards the open room's extremities. This probably saved his life:

I was last to be shot. Seeing the men at the other side of the room fall I had the presence of mind to throw myself down to the ground, flat on my stomach, thus turning my back to the Germans. The bullets screamed in from everywhere, ricocheting off the wall next to me. The splintering of mortar and rock covered me with dust. After several rounds of machine gun fire I could no longer breathe, suffocated by the dust.[7]

Mathieu Borie also threw himself to the ground and played dead until 'nobody showed any sign of life [when] they stopped firing at us'.[8] During the onslaught, Broussaudier had dived to the ground and Darthout had been hit during the first round of fire by two bullets, one in each calf. As he went down, two further bullets hit his thighs. Whether he dived or was knocked down by the impact of the bullets, he had no idea: 'In several seconds I was covered with bodies.'[9]

Postman François Darthout, Jean-Marcel's father, was still on his round delivering post near Le Repaire, 3km from the Laudy-Mosnier barn, when he heard muffled explosions, 'the result, no doubt, from the detonation of grenades and followed by an intense burst of gunfire'. Later he supposed that it must have been the beginning of the massacre and he had no idea that his eldest son had just been thrown to the ground by bullets, nor that his wife and daughter-in-law were locked in the church.

Jean Valade was asleep, head resting on the kitchen table, when his son Albert returned from minding the cattle to take a late lunch. Suddenly Jean's head shot up. 'Did you hear that?' he asked, in a daze. 'That was machine-gun fire.' Albert was used to hearing hunting rifles but had never heard the firing of military weaponry. Jean, on the other hand, was a 1914–18 veteran. He knew the sound of weapons of war. Outside, in the lanes and courtyards of the village, rumours began to circulate as neighbours called in on each other, before the sounds gradually died down.

Tabaraud and Dauriat, the two tram drivers who had been waiting in their locomotive, also heard the terrible sound of automatic gunfire. 'They must have been killing the victims,' said Tabaraud. 'We didn't hear a single human cry over the bursts of firing.'[10] Much nearer to one of the execution sites, Jeanne Lang was hidden in the cellar of Marie-Thérèse de Laverine's home. She heard gunfire come from a nearby storeroom: 'Suddenly from the Milord shed, which was 6m from the house where I was hidden, harrowing cries and panicked screams rang out, punctuated by rounds of firing.'[11]

When the shots had come, Robert Hébras, who like Yvon Roby had moved back into and behind the crowd, immediately dropped to the hard floor. He was injured in a knee, above his left breast and five times in his right wrist. Two further bullets had grazed the left side of his forehead. 'The bullets had passed through the others and by the time they reached me they no longer had the power to go in deep [...] They were explosive bullets.'[12]

As Jean-Marcel Darthout lay collapsed on the ground, he expected to be given the *coup de grace*: 'I listened to the cries of the injured. It was not shouting but muffled gasps. I was smothered underneath the injured, flattened out and covered with blood that was pouring out of other men.'

Clément Broussaudier had to hold himself still as one of the soldiers stepped on his ankle:

A friend was laid across my chest and his blood was soaking me […] I heard the breech of a gun click as it was armed and then a muffled blow. The injured man atop of me was thus killed. I felt him shudder, tremble, then nothing more.[13]

Yvon Roby lay trembling under a pile of bodies as the soldiers looked for dying men:

The injured were crying out, howling, some calling for their wives and children. Seeing this the Germans, who were wearing heavy boots, climbed onto the bodies to finish them off with a revolver […] Personally, I was injured in the shoulder by one of these gun shots. [One] of the men's bodies was covering me totally. That is what saved me. I was hurt at the same moment that the injured man lying on top of me was exterminated out-right. Somehow I managed to continue to simulate death.[14]

The soldiers set about the task of covering the bodies with whatever combustibles they could find. First, they spread hay and straw from the barn. 'One of the Germans was using a steel pronged fork,' said Mathieu Borie, 'and I could hear it as he sank it into the dead bodies beside me.' Next the soldiers threw on bundles of kindling wood followed by another layer of straw and twigs. 'Rails from carts, logs, a very big ladder and even wooden crates [were] thrown haphazardly on top of us. One crate smashed into my head. I will remember the shock of that for a long time,' said Roby. Once finished the executioners left the courtyard presumably to receive new orders, find more combustible material, or to take a break. They left no sentry. 'As they left, they were laughing amongst themselves,' said Darthout.

The soldiers were away from the carnage for about fifteen minutes. During that time Darthout heard sounds suggesting others were alive. Despite severe pain, Darthout attempted to change position so as not to suffocate under the weight of bodies. 'I touched the hand of the man next to me. It was Monsieur Alliotti.[15] He told me that his legs were broken.' The two men whispered a little. Alliotti always came to Oradour to see his wife and child on weekends, during which time he played football alongside Darthout. He said that the Germans were going to burn them but Darthout reassured him, telling him that they would get out. 'Alliotti must have suffered enormously,' said Darthout. 'He called out for his wife and his children, then he said, "Adieu". As for me I felt as though my legs had been paralysed.'[16]

'I heard them opening bottles in the next building,' said Mathieu Borie. 'They got the TSF radio set working at its maximum volume. They were laughing and shouting amongst themselves.' Marcel Brissaud, wheelwright father of Martial who had hidden, was the first to speak audibly. He already had an artificial leg after having lost it in the First World War. 'My other leg, it's gone,' he groaned. The soldiers had fired low and then high and Brissaud's leg had been all but severed. Pierre Duquéroix, who had helped prepare the barn, replied that his arm had gone. Father of seven and garage owner Pierre-Henri Poutaraud was unhurt. He hissed at everyone not to move at all. Men were dying, some managing to lift their heads through the straw, all soaked with blood. Joseph Bergmann said a few words to Mathieu Borie, but it was too late for the barber. Duquéroix and the tailor Jules Santrot also spoke but they too were dying.

Witnesses

Dauriat and Tabaraud had been waiting in their tram for the electricity to be re-established so they could return to Limoges. Dauriat had become increasingly concerned that the tram may not hold on the slope without additional blocks under the wheels. He was looking around for someone to ask for permission to get out on to the road when a patrol of five soldiers approached.

They 'led me, with my colleague Tabaraud and three other people from the surrounding countryside who arrived with a harvester hitched to cows, towards the centre of the village'. They passed Chalard's body which had been left on the side of the road. On the walk up the incline of the main street they noticed that most of the doors of the buildings were shut but for a few in which soldiers were seemingly conducting a search. They did not appear to be pillaging.[1] Along the pavement the men, terrified and forbidden to look around, noticed rectangular cardboard or wooden grocery boxes but were unable to see what was inside them. They got to the pharmacy where an officer checked their papers. 'One of the men with him explained the situation in German and he seemed to understand when Limoges was mentioned.' Since the men were employees of the tramways their papers were in both French and German and explained that they were not from Oradour. Tabaraud's attention was drawn to a soldier behind the officer who was showing off a woman's handbag. He wore it across his shoulder and pulled out of it 'a bloody handkerchief which he waved around saying '*Mouchoir Fraülein!*'[2]

Near the spot where they had stopped, Dauriat watched soldiers busily piling up 'small grey or yellowish packets into similar boxes in front of doors, noticeably right in the centre of the village'.[3] These were the only civilian witnesses to this systematic placement of incendiary devices. 'The officer spoke to us in French,' said Tabaraud. 'He told us to go back as quickly as we could, and to leave the scene without looking either right, or left. We were to jog.'[4] They ran as far as the church 'but, seeing other armed patrols in front of us,' said Dauriat,[5] 'and fearing attack from them in case our running gave them the impression that we were escaping without permission I advised my companions to continue on at a walking pace.'

They saw no other civilian during their brief visit to the centre of the village. 'They all must have been shut away or already shot. I had heard shooting and bursts of automatic fire numerous times while I had been forced to wait by our tram, before getting to the bridge,' said Dauriat later. 'I did not notice any other dead body. I did not hear any cries for help or moaning, nor shouts nor complaints. In my opinion everyone must have already been dead or playing dead.'[6] They got back to the waiting tram, accompanied by the three farmers and their cows. When they boarded the tram they found that the electricity had been restored, and at around a quarter past five they set off for Limoges.

During the time that the tram drivers were in the town centre and the men lay dying in the barns, Marguerite Rouffanche and her family waited anxiously in the packed nave of the church. 'After an hour-and-a-half the Germans opened the door[7] and started to empty that part of the building of people. Some women and children were put outside. Two Germans, aged around 30,[8] forced a gap between the women and children so that they could get through and brought in a box about 0.8m long which they put down in front of the communion table at the far end of the nave. It must have been heavy because it took two of them to carry it, and had lots of white strings hanging out.'[9] They put the box on to two chairs.[10] Marguerite, standing quite nearby, could see inside it when it was opened by two soldiers. 'Soon afterwards the Germans left, without having said a word to us and without, seemingly, to have given us a second thought.'[11] This time the men left via the small door in the Sainte-Anne chapel. Marguerite was alarmed by what she saw. 'I found myself imagining that they were going to blow up the church with us inside,' but most people remained calm. Outside in the square SS-Sturmbannführer Adolf Diekmann stood, arms crossed, while his second-in-command SS-Hauptsturmführer Otto Kahn directed operations.[12]

The soldiers returned to the Laudy-Mosnier barn having drunk wine and champagne at the Villatte bureau de tabac. Talking loudly amongst themselves, they took several moments to release livestock tied to buildings near to the barn. Then the sound of the striking of matches signalled the start of the inevitable fire. 'Just before, they threw a powder on us which must have been sprayed given the noise made by the machine they used,' said Mathieu Borie.[13] The fire spread rapidly, and Darthout decided that he would try to escape the heat:

I could feel fire licking my hair and, trying to protect my head with my hands, they too were burning. My clothes caught fire so, feeling the flames around my shoulders, I called to my comrades for help to get out.[14]

Mathieu Borie, 'suddenly aware that there were no more Germans guarding us', freed himself from the stacks of wood by using sticks to push burning wood away from his face and stepped over bodies in order to get out of the barn and into the courtyard:

> I saw Santrot senior[15] and Brissaud senior begin to burn. They had been down there beside me, still alive but too injured by bullets to move [...] I spoke to them and they told me that they could not move and that I should flee.[16]

The Sacristy

Marguerite Rouffanche would be the only witness to what happened within Oradour's *Église* Saint-Martin:

> Several moments later a muffled detonation came from within the box and before long a black, acrid and burning smoke began pouring out of it, filling the entire church. That smoke was asphyxiating so women and children began screaming and crying for help. Everybody was panicking and trying to get clear. All the schoolchildren were there with us, including the 13 and 14-year-old boys.

What made the panic worse was the lack of space. There was nowhere to get away:

> At that moment people were climbing over each other, whole families, school children, not to mention mothers carrying babies.[1]

Marguerite Rouffanche led her family towards the only place that she could think of: 'I found some protection from the asphyxiation near the sacristy where I sheltered with my two children and some neighbours.' The sacristy door was locked but the strength of dozens including Marguerite forced it open. The room was small with a wooden floor and benches around the outside. Wooden steps led down to a storage space with a door to the outside, where soldiers had gathered. It was locked anyway. Marguerite knew that their only chance of survival would be to stay still and hope that the soldiers did not look in. She pushed herself into a space at the top of the steps where she crouched alongside her youngest daughter, Andrée. Her other daughter, Amélie, held baby Guy close to her and found space on the other side of the sacristy.

> The screams and shouting were getting louder which must have annoyed the Germans who unleashed bursts of machine gun fire through the windows of the sacristy.[2]

Once the suffocating gas had killed most people, soldiers entered by the main door and fired on those still alive. They sprayed bullets, firstly in the direction of the Sainte-Anne chapel where scores of people had gathered trying to get to the smaller second exit on the other side of the building, and also into another chapel on the northern wall. The shots killed anyone still alive, splintering the plaque commemorating Oradour's ninety-nine 1914–18 war dead. Then bullets were fired into the sacristy from the nave as well as through the window from outside. Marguerite could only watch as Andrée was shot through the neck, dying instantly. Marguerite, frozen with fear, lay down and played dead.

Incendiary grenades were thrown into the main church, and then through the lower door of the sacristy, creating a furnace below. Marguerite, unable to move for fear of being shot, could only look on as explosions brought down the floorboards of the sacristy and all those hidden inside, including her eldest daughter and her grandson, who fell directly into the furnace below. 'More than half of those people were burnt alive,' she later claimed.

In the cellar of Marie-Thérèse de Laverine's home, a stone's throw from the church, Marie-Louise Raynaud had heard too much and needed to know that her 7-year-old daughter Irène was safe. Terrified, she no longer wanted to be there with the Lang couple, Marie-Therèse and her husband Pierre, the baker. Then it got worse. 'A terrifying sound erupted from the direction of the church which was just a few dozen metres from us,' said Jeanne Lang afterwards. 'Detonation followed detonation; then an immense clamour and terrified cries. Machine guns fired, and a cloud of smoke rose up. Still so many cries! We stayed completely silent; frightened, appalled and horrified. There was no doubt! A terrifying massacre was being carried out just a few metres from where we were.'[3] Pierre Raynaud, still covered in flour from a morning spent in the bakery, agreed to go looking for Irène. The couple kissed goodbye and, checking that the coast was clear, Pierre left his wife behind.

Miraculously Marguerite Rouffanche, curled up in the sacristy of the church, had not been hit by any bullets. Lying as still as she could and holding the hand of a dying woman, she could just about make out what was happening in the nave: 'Soon after the firing had stopped some Germans came inside the church and built a pyre. They brought in straw and firewood and turned over the church stalls and chairs. Then they set fire to all of it.' Two men brought firewood to the doorway of the sacristy threatening to block her path, so when they went to get more her instinct for survival pushed her to act. Using the pyre and its smoke as a hiding place, she ducked behind it and headed towards the only part of the church with large windows: the eastern wall behind the altar.

'I noticed a stepladder usually used for lighting candles and I got up onto it to get up to one of the windows, the one on the left-hand side.[4] I threw myself through it.' Marguerite had managed to find a window made of reinforced glass and a lead frame, which had already been blown out by one of the grenade explosions. The metal grill could be pushed away to forge a gap. She forced her way through and fell 3m on to a steep banking below, managing to steady herself to avoid further injury. 'A neighbour, Madame Joyeux,[5] aged 22 or 23, who was a mother of a small baby of around 7 months, followed me through the window. She tried to pass her baby to me but I was unable to catch him and, hearing the bullets all around me, I got back to my feet to find shelter in the garden. Madame Joyeux must have been killed as she was getting out of the window.' Henriette Joyeux, in town to visit her mother and father Fernand and Marie Hyvernaud, had done her best to save her baby, René, whose father Marcel had already been taken to one of the barns.

Marguerite's escape had not gone unnoticed. She staggered around a steep grass verge, trying to reach the presbytery. She reached *l'abbé* Chapelle's vegetable plots. 'I got as far as the peas when I was shot five times in my legs and shoulder. I felt my shoulder blade splitting.' She fell amongst the vegetable plants, her would-be assassins assuming that they had killed their target.

Marguerite Rouffanche, the only survivor from the church. She escaped through a window after witnessing her two daughters and grandson die. She also lost her son and husband. She lived with the memories until 1988. (Collection Benoit Sadry)

The Cyclists

According to Léonie, regional commander of the MUR, Albert Mirablon was sent to Saint-Junien in order to undertake a mission on 10 June 1944. Quite what the mission entailed is unknown. It may have related to the delivery of documents or newspapers or it may have been a photographic mission. With elements of the SS *Das Reich* division in Saint-Junien for the previous two days it is unlikely, though not impossible, that it related to sabotage. More probably, as someone who knew the area well, he had been sent on a mission of reconnaissance. How many men were left there? Which routes were they taking? What was the state of their equipment?

He travelled on his beloved cycle and likely had done all he needed to do by lunchtime. By then, his mother Anna lived in Oradour near his aunt and his cousin Fernand Lesparat. He would have been unaware, as he approached the village in the mid-afternoon of that Saturday, that the smoke arising was a warning to stay away. No doubt people from surrounding villages would have told Mirablon to go no further – that the men of Oradour were being rounded up. Knowing he had more reason than most to take a turn and head as far from Oradour as he could, he must have known that he had to go to the village where his mother was. Whether he thought too, at that moment, of Fernand Lesparat and his aunt we will never know. Had he planned to go to the village and see Lesparat on that Saturday? Nor will we know whether he had already done so during the days that preceded. We do know that Lesparat was almost obsessively concerned about something that might be about to happen. He had said so to his friend Aimé Renaud that morning, when his friend had asked him what was behind his worries:

> I asked him to tell me what he knew. He told me that, what he knew, he had got from a good source. He added that he would tell me the following morning, Sunday [...] He said we would have more time to chat about it then.[1]

By then Fernand Lesparat would have had more time to speak to Albert Mirablon who may have indicated that he would be calling in to visit.

What is undisputed is that by the time Albert Mirablon, arrested somewhere on the outskirts of Oradour, was brought to the *Champ de foire*, his cousin was already dead. From his bedroom window Armand Senon had witnessed the round-up, the departure of the women and children towards the church, and the partition of the men into groups. He had also seen the last group of men outside the warehouse, part of his family farm and just across the square. 'I heard the shooting coming from the barn. It lasted several minutes. As soon as it had finished the Germans went into the stables to release the livestock, wishing to save them the fire.'[2]

Not long after that shooting had died down he witnessed the arrival of a group of seven or eight men, accompanied by Germans, at the *Champ de foire*:

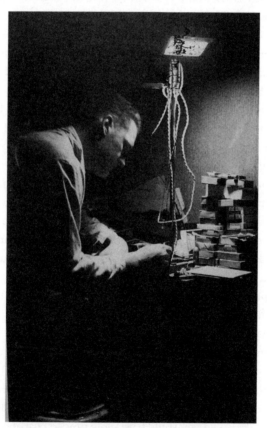

Schooled in the United States, Albert Mirablon was a keen cyclist, photographer and a member of the French Resistance. His mother had moved to Oradour and he called in to see her on the day the SS were in the village. (Collection Claude Mirablon)

It must have been people who were not from the *commune* who were just passing through. Most of them had bicycles with them.[3]

Senon did not recognise any of the men, including Albert Mirablon.

> The Germans guarded them for a short while, and then one of the chiefs arrived. Without proceeding to any verification of identity papers or bothering to check who the people were, he gave an order to the soldiers with them who were carrying automatic weapons. They made those with bicycles lean them up against the Beaulieu building.[4] Then they made the civilians line up in front of that building's forge and, from a distance of 10m, one of the men fired at them. I could see the executioner in front of the hostages. He shot along the row in a sweeping motion. The men fell straight to the ground. Then I watched as he aimed his gun towards the ground and continued shooting at these civilians. Dust was whipped up from the ground.[5]

The bodies of the victims were then added to the others already in the Beaulieu forge.

Armand Senon understood at that moment that the Nazis were killing all of the village's men. For a reason he never fully understood, he made the decision to struggle down to the *Champ de foire* and give himself up to the soldiers:

> I was going to give myself up in order to be shot, just like the others. But when I got to the *Champ de foire*, in front of our house, I could see no Germans anywhere nearby. So, I decided to hide in some bushes behind the house. My leg was in plaster so I had to crawl along the ground, dragging my leg until I got to the undergrowth.[6]

From there he heard a loud explosion – probably the device set off in the church, or perhaps a little later when the SS set off further detonations to speed up the destruction of the building. 'I thought that they had blown up the bridge because it came from the direction of the church.' It didn't occur to him that it might have been the church that was destroyed. Anna Mirablon, the Oradour girl who had gone to America, her sister Marie Lesparat and Albert's mother and aunt were also dead.

Dying of Thirst

For Robert Hébras, somehow still alive in the Laudy-Mosnier furnace, nothing seemed real.[1] He thought he was the only survivor. 'The progression of the fire was quick. I tried to resist for as long as I could by protecting myself behind the bodies of those who were already dead. I did not hear the soldiers leave.' Extricating himself from the tangle of bodies with strength he did not know he had, he stumbled to the back of the shed expecting to be shot. No bullets came. At the rear of the barn a small door promised an escape. He was surprised to find that it opened, but it only led to a small enclosed courtyard.

Stepping over bodies and shielding himself from flames, he went into the main courtyard. From there he heard voices and footsteps in the alleyway that led back to the *Champ de foire*. It would be folly to walk into the path of the same soldiers whose gunfire he had just escaped. Instead, he traced his way through the thick smoke to the stables that had not been used. Pulling open one of the doors, he slid into a dusky murkiness. As his eyes adjusted, he saw a human figure on the other side of the stable. Panicked, he shot back outside and hugged the wall as he made his way around the outside of the structure. As the ground sloped up to the final stable he heard hushed voices. The words were French and the intonation, he was sure, was Limousin. In a gap between buildings he found Broussaudier, Borie, Roby and Darthout. Three of the men were carrying injuries, but Darthout looked particularly badly hurt.

There was no escape route, other than by the main entranceway. They could not pass that way. A window into a building a little further on looked promising until they saw that it was barred with metal, and on the other side of it a stack of wood was piled high. Hébras watched as builder and stonemason Borie climbed up to a small piece of damaged wall, about a metre and a half off the ground:

Well understanding that the barn and its adjoining stables would burn, I got straight to it. I set to work alone with a view to getting out of there. Some stray bullets had lodged in the wall, alongside a hole that I was making with my knife. I thought we could get through to the next barn.[2]

Borie had seen that the stones in one of the walls were badly joined. 'Stone by stone he made a hole big enough for a man to get through,' said Hébras.[3] Borie climbed through first. 'I ended up in the corner wall of a barn belonging to Monsieur Thomas who owned the café-restaurant.'[4] It was their only hope so they all decided to give it a try. 'We all slid through one after another,' said Hébras, 'and fell into another barn. Darthout was struggling with his injured legs so the others helped him.' Darthout was barely able to use his bullet-damaged legs: 'We climbed up the wall. Somebody pulled me from above, somebody pushed me from below, and we fell into a barn, onto a hay loft.'[5] All around they could hear rifle fire, machine guns and incendiary grenades exploding in the surrounding buildings.

Borie climbed from the elevated loft on to the top of a large stack of firewood, shifting three bundles so that he was hidden from sight. He got out his flick knife as a means of defence. Then, seeing Hébras, he pulled him into the same hiding place. Broussaudier followed and hid in a corner, and Roby came next. 'Darthout was bleeding from everywhere [...],' said Roby, 'and he begged me to help him to move and then to hide him.'[6] They buried themselves in straw cut from bean plants, managing to get completely out of sight. They listened to the explosions of gas bottles, tiles falling from roofs and the continual firing of guns and cannon. Broussaudier tried to speak and was told to be quiet by Borie. The Germans must, he said, be nearby. All five men were desperately thirsty in the unforgiving heat.

They had hardly settled when the door to the barn opened and two soldiers came in. 'One of them went straight back out,' said Borie, 'but the other climbed the ladder to the hay loft, his rifle strapped onto him.' The ladder passed right between the hayloft and the stack of wood on top of which Borie and Hébras were hidden. 'He was just a metre from us,' said Hébras. 'He struck a match which immediately went out, but was luckier with the second. The straw that was hiding our friends went up immediately.' The soldier, who Borie believed to be no more than 18 years of age, looked around and saw nothing out of the ordinary so he stuffed some of the straw on top of the stack of wood where Borie and Hébras were within arm's reach, before climbing back down to ground level. Before leaving, the soldiers fired incendiary grenades into the roof of the barn. 'The flames shot up underneath the tiles and the slats and rafters began to burn,' said Borie. Along with Hébras, Borie climbed across to the hayloft by crossing through flames that were leaping higher than them. They could not stay where they were.

Broussaudier and Roby decided to take their chances by going back through the hole in the wall by which they had arrived. 'Soon afterwards we hid in a hutch next to the hay barn,' said Roby. 'I made a hole with my foot and my one remaining good arm and covered myself with manure.'

Hébras remained with Borie and Darthout but it was imperative that they move. Borie loosened boards, allowing him to lower Darthout to the stable below. But they could not stay long. 'The ceiling was beginning to crumble,' said Borie. 'The smoke […] was suffocating us. It was impossible to resist any more and once again we had to get out.'

The door of the stable did not fully close and they could see that it opened on to an edge of the *Champ de foire*, almost opposite the Senon farm. They watched as two sentries walked up and down the pathway, a distance of about 100 paces. 'The heat was terrible, but next to the building there were three lean-to hutches: the first, the nearest, was a rabbit hutch, the second was for pigs and the third was a hutch for chickens.' They squeezed into the first, made of brick and with a tiled roof. There was just about enough room to stand and Borie watched at the door as two red-eyed rabbits watched them. He could see a good route to the cemetery. Four soldiers arrived from the lower village with a horse and cart. Borie recognised it as belonging to a wine seller from another village who had been making deliveries. The horse belonged to Jean Thomas, owner of the bar, *l'Estaminet du centre*. Borie watched the soldiers release the animal from its harness, encouraging it to move away and escape the flames by kicking its rear.

A wind was picking up that was worsening the spread of the flames. They could hear the smashing of falling tiles and the groaning as beams gave way. Four more soldiers came along the road from the cemetery towards the lower village, two of whom turned around and traced their route back in the same direction. Borie wondered whether they would ever leave.

Darthout's condition, meanwhile, was worsening: 'I had a fever, I was thirsty, I was suffering.' But the men could not stay where they were. 'A wave of heat from the barn had reached that first hutch,' said Borie. 'The blaze was almost upon us. A ladder that was up against the door caught fire, the door too. We began to choke on the smoke and we were dying of thirst.' Borie and Hébras dragged Darthout into the furthest hutch from the furnace, normally full of chickens. There was some water left out for the animals and Darthout drank first, followed by Borie. 'Just then the hen arrived in front of the door with her chicks. They paced up and down, calling out and scratching at the door.' The men could not let the birds in for fear of being seen.

The figure that Hébras had seen in the dark of the first stable had been Poutaraud, the mechanic. His body was later found tangled in a fence on the left-hand side of the lane that led to the cemetery. He had tried to make a break for it by the main entrance and was spotted, pursued and shot.

Tough Decisions

Pierre Joyeux had been watching events from the village of Les Bordes:

> There had been no end to the isolated firing and bursts of automatic gun-
> shot throughout the afternoon, coming from just about everywhere [...] At
> between four and half past four we saw smoke rising from the lower end of
> the village. From Les Bordes we could not see the upper village. We thought
> that there must have been some sort of encounter between German troops
> and the *maquis*.[1]

At around half past four Albert Valade decided that he needed to take his
herd to drink at the edge of the Glane. On his way out he passed his sister,
Germaine, who was sewing gloves by the window. She wore a cream dress
with grey stripes and a pink crepe headscarf. 'Don't take them too far that
way,' she told him. 'Head to the other side,' she continued, gesturing away
from the village.

He had only just arrived at the field where his cattle could eat lush grass
and drink from the river when he heard, and felt, an explosion. The sound of
guns restarted, this time for longer periods. He was alone but for his herd of
cows. 'I was scared because, as the crow flies, it was coming from not far away.
The sound of those weapons ... the noise, you could feel it in your chest.'[2]

While he was in the fields his sister Germaine had also heard the noises.
Out in the pathways between farms, rumours were circulating about the
round-ups. Sitting on a bench in silence, she was desperate to go to Oradour
to get her children. One of her friends, whose husband was a prisoner of war,
had a 5-year-old son at school and another had two of her four children there
that day. As soon as one of the young women said she should go, the other followed. Seeing them leaving, Germaine could not stay where she was. 'If you
only know them like I know them, you wouldn't go,' said her father, recalling
his experiences of the trenches. She grabbed her bicycle. 'Yes father, but I am
going. Don't say anything to mother.'[3] With that she joined the others.

René Hyvernaud approached Oradour by bicycle, having spent most of
the day working in Saint-Gence. 'I noticed thick smoke rising from my home
village. A guy told me that Oradour had been set alight by the Germans who

were burning everything.'[4] Hyvernaud continued as far as La Plaine where villagers persuaded him to go no further. He turned back towards Saint-Gence with the intention of warning the farm labourers and spending the night there. He went first to Veyrac, a different route to Saint-Gence, but while there he heard the rumbling of a motorised column of vehicles heading his way. He decided to stay where he was until the danger had passed.

In La Malaise, just 5km from Oradour, word had reached David Jakobowicz, his wife Anna and David's parents Aron and Golda. David's sister Sarah, and his own baby Michel, were hidden right where the SS were conducting round-ups and burning property. Sick with worry, David and Anna set off on foot across the countryside. They would pick up baby Michel from the Gabriel couple before establishing whether Sarah was safe. They slipped past several soldiers on their way and had no idea that the farm that they, and Golda, had visited many times over the previous weeks to see their son was within the southern extreme of the cordon. Describing the events many years later, David recalled the farm was deserted. He recounted that Anna was alerted by the sounds of her child and David broke down the door of the cellar. They collected their baby and returned to La Malaise.[5]

Hippolyte Redon had arrived back at the small boarding house (*pension*) that he and his wife called home in the village of Les Bordes. He was shaken up, having witnessed the round-up and been shot at, but he had issued warnings on his route back. In his wife's restaurant he found wood merchant Michel Avril who told him that he needed to get home. Redon tried to persuade Avril he should stay away from the village centre until more was known about what was going on, but Avril was desperate to find his wife and their 8-month-old son Georges. Telling Redon that he would take no chances, he left his bicycle there and told him that he would find a route across the fields.

Earlier, Redon had seen André Foussat, member of the *délégation spéciale* and leader of the theatrical society. Redon had equally done his best to persuade him not to go to the village. Foussat, a miller who lived and worked in Le Repaire south-west of the village, happened to be on the wrong side of Oradour. Not knowing of the horrors that were taking place there, he felt he had a civic duty to be in the village. He also wanted to get word to his wife that he was safe.[6]

The Old Man

STO evader Paul Doutre was still under a trapdoor to a storage area under the work benches of his father's carpentry workshop. His father had told him to stay until the coast was clear but his family had not returned to tell him what was happening. He had heard firing from all directions, and a crackling noise had just started, coming from above. 'I opened the trapdoor and looked through. The whole house was on fire.'[1]

He climbed out and went into the alleyway between the workshop and the house, looking to save something, anything, from the flames:

> Suddenly I heard machine guns firing, and I went straight back inside the workshop. They were shooting to prevent me getting out of there. They threw incendiary grenades towards me. I didn't know what to do [...] my hair was burnt.

The soldiers stayed and watched, ensuring Doutre could not escape. Taking a side door, he managed to evade them and hid in a vegetable garden from where he could see the soldiers, camouflage netting in their helmets, who were watching the workshop burn, waiting for him to die. 'They had, I believe, already burned down almost all of the houses [...] it was all burning [...] the workshop was burning. There must have been some doing the burning, some doing the killing.'

Doutre was worried about his 17-year-old brother Charles who had already been rounded up. The soldiers did not stay long, but his position remained perilous. When the roof of the workshop, in which the soldiers believed he was trapped, collapsed they finally left. 'They came as far as the fence and one of them said, "*kapout*".' Waiting a little, he looked up and was amazed to see a face:

> I looked up and I saw old Litaud, our neighbour, who had come to the [upstairs] window of his house. I called out 'Monsieur Litaud, come down you are going to burn. Your house is on fire.' He answered, 'Is that you Charles?', I said, 'no it's me Paul.' He said, 'How can that be?' and I said,

'Three months ago I deserted the *chantiers de jeunesse* and my parents have been hiding me all this time.'

He begged Litaud for any news of his family:

'Oh my poor boy', he said, 'they've killed everyone, burnt everything.' Litaud came out to the garden. I did not know what to do. He helped me to cut through the fence, and then he camouflaged me in the greenery. He said to me, 'Stay there, I'm going to see whether I can see them. If they kill me, it is alright. I am 84 years old, it does not matter.'

Paul begged him to reconsider but the old man went in search of news or survivors.[2]

Smoke was billowing throughout the house and into the roof space where Martial Brissaud was concealed on the western edge of the village. He had no idea what had become of his family 'so I quit my hiding place and I peered out of a window onto the garden. There were four Germans carrying machine guns. I looked out of a fanlight in the roof onto the main street and saw another German with a light machine gun guarding the road into Oradour.' He stayed in the ever-thickening smoke until the soldiers left the garden carrying bundles of what looked like stock from the Dupic textile merchants next door. 'The Germans had moved away, but I could see that all the houses were already aflame and starting to crumble.'

Maria Démery had seen the soldiers arrive from her wash house in Bel-Air. She had determined that she had to collect her two boys, André and Ernest, from school. Leaving at around half past four, she came across no soldiers on her way. 'All the houses in the upper village were already on fire,' she later testified, except for the house belonging to Monsieur François Dupic, the textile merchant, next to the Brissaud house. 'All along the road I saw pieces of blackened bread and modern-looking five-litre petrol cans which had been left at intervals.' She also saw chains and mechanic's tools scattered all around. 'In the distance I could see Germans climbing about the windows of the house belonging to the other textile merchant Jean Dupic, brother of François, whose place was a bit further on than the town hall.'

That Maria had not been stopped was miraculous:

When I was passing in front of the house belonging to the wheelwright Brissaud, I heard my name called out. I struggled to see who it was, and the voice was definitely calling me: 'Maria, Maria'. Then I saw young Brissaud on the roof of his house, balancing on tiles and hidden behind the chimney.[3]

She told him that she was going to look for her children but Brissaud told her not to go into the village because the Germans were burning everything and shooting people. 'I told him that I could see them and they were quite a way from where we were. He climbed down from the roof, his house already on fire. Flames were coming from inside, getting bigger all the time.' Determined to find her children, but unsure whether she could proceed, she paused. 'Just then a youngish man, the younger Nicolas from Javerdat[4] arrived on a bike. After finding out what was going on, and that the Germans were in the village, he insisted that I leave for home [...] Brissaud remained, trying to get clothes and linen out of the house.' The thickness of the smoke had saved her. 'I could certainly see them in that street, but they did not notice me.'[5]

After a while, old man Litaud returned to the garden where Paul Doutre was hiding. He said that he could not see anyone:

He helped me to get through to a neighbour's garden and I crawled as far as the cemetery where I knew there was a little building. I climbed along a furrow almost all the way and, once there, I hid in a family tomb that was in the course of being built. I stayed for, I don't know how long, pulling the door as far as I could behind me, so I was out of sight. Later I went to Les Bordes, 3km away. I was looked after by some girls who I knew from school and who had stayed in Les Bordes that day [...] As for my family [...] my father, my mother, my grandmother, my brother, my 5-year-old niece. I never saw any of them again.[6]

The Burnt Page

Hubert Desourteaux had lost all notion of time as he waited in the dark of his incomplete garage extension. Earlier, 'from a garage space just a single doorway away, where my brother normally parked his car, there had been machine gun fire ten to fifteen minutes in duration almost without pause [...] I heard no human cry and I had no concept of what had happened.' Desourteaux did, however, hear the many single shots, the *coups de grace*.[1] 'After the shootings, the Germans came into the building where I was hidden. They did not go into the room where I was. When they saw that building was unfinished and empty they went straight back out.' But they had not quite finished. 'They climbed up into the garret. I smelt gasoline; no doubt my hidden store. They must have punctured it [...] I heard someone scattering something.' Afterwards he found that it had been charcoal thrown on the corpses.[2] A little later, around five o'clock,[3] he smelt smoke which very quickly became overwhelming. Hearing the crackling of flames above him, he went out to the garden, where he crouched in a small courtyard among walnut trees. 'I understood just then that the whole place was in flames [...] I watched, alone, as the village burned.' Later he could clearly see flames rising from the steeple of the church.

Jeannine Renaud had waited in the chicken coop:

> A thick smoke was flooding in, burning my throat. Prone as I am to bouts of coughing, I knew that I'd be unable to put up with the smoke any longer without coughing. It would, I decided, be better to be taken by a bullet than to die suffocated. I poked my head out and saw a German soldier walking the interior of the garden. I pulled back quickly and he did not notice me. Not long afterwards Madame Robert and I were forced to leave our hiding place because of the considerable smoke that was enveloping us.[4]

They joined Aimé Renaud in his hiding place. 'The German [...] was nowhere to be seen,' said Jeannine.

> The house and the Desourteaux garage were, by then, in flames. We heard the loud machine gun fire in the garage but had no idea that it could have

been what it turned out to be. We had heard no cries from any victims who, from what I later learned, were rounded up and massacred right beside us.[5]

At the Mercier grocery store in the lower village, Martial and Maurice Beaubreuil had been forced to creep out of their hiding place. 'Two soldiers came into the house and climbed into the attic coming back down a couple of minutes later.'

Their departure was followed by 'a loud crackling, which sounded to me like fire,'[6] said Martial. The air turned black and it was impossible to breathe. 'I managed to get out of my hiding place, not without difficulty, and stumbled across the wooden flooring, which was in flames. I went out into the garden and fell onto my stomach, where I remained, still, in a passageway.'

Martial led Maurice past the body of Madeleine Bonnet. 'From there I could see a machine gun, seemingly pointed in the direction of the bridge over the Glane, and two soldiers patrolling on the *Place de l'église*.'

The machine gunner had not seen the brothers, so they leapt over a wall and ran towards the Glane. 'I jumped into a ditch which seemed deep enough to keep me out of sight of the Germans.'[7]

The men stayed in their hiding place until the early hours of the morning, watching as the village was destroyed. René Lévy, the Jewish dentist from Rennes, was also in the ditch behind the *Hôtel Milord*. He had crawled there before his escape route had been cut off by a sentry:

> I heard a succession of machine gun fire and explosions throughout the afternoon which were destroying the houses. Around seven o'clock[8] the flames were climbing into the sky from the church bell tower, and a little later the whole village was ablaze.[9]

Maria Démery was not finished with trying to find her two children. At around half past five she set off again, this time with a friend, a Madame Faucher, whom she begged to accompany her. This woman, whose home was just 300m from the western edge of the village, had been told by Martial Brissaud that everything was burning but, like him, had believed that the people must be safe. The two women reached the village's western edge unimpeded and managed to find their way through the thick smoke to the boys' school.

'The town hall was already completely burnt down. The school was empty. There was nobody anywhere, and no trace of any children in the vicinity. 'Inside one of the classrooms a table had caught fire,'[10] said Maria Démery.

Madame Faucher saw 'one of the classrooms in flames, the tables on fire. The roof of the town hall [next door] was beginning to cave in. The school-bags belonging to the children were still hung up on the wall.'[11] They knew they had to get out. At the Brissaud house they again saw Martial, who had returned to try to save what he could and was piling belongings into a wheel-barrow. 'He did not seem to think that his family had been killed and thought that they were probably in the fields.' Martial Machefer appeared nearby and went with Brissaud into the last house of the village which belonged to an elderly former woodcutter, widowed Pierre Giroux, who had been paralysed for twenty years. They found him already dead in bed, the fire just taking over the property. When Machefer spotted a soldier, the small group made a quick escape. In doing so they passed Marie Ducharlet, who had come on a similar mission to find her grandchildren and would not be talked out of it. They heard her being shot behind them.

Sometime after six o'clock, a dark, thick smoke began to appear all around Albert Valade as he nervously kept watch over his cows. Soon the smoke obscured the light of the sun. Tiny pieces of burned paper and cloth, no more than ash, gently drifted on to the grass around him. With a slight gust of wind, a blackened sheet of paper, not entirely burnt, landed at his feet. The markings were legible. It was a page from one of the many books stored at the church for catechism lessons, the type each child who attended *l'abbé* Chapelle's course knew well.[12] Nearby, in Le Mas du Puy, Jean Sergue[13] was pulling up beans. He was 16 and a ward of the state. He was working alongside his boss and guardian. They had heard the firing too. They also experienced the strange dark rain of ash and saw pages from the same books. Uninformed as to events in Oradour, they did not want to believe what they suspected: that Oradour's church was burning.

At around half past six André Foussat, known by many as comedian Monsieur Dédé of the pre-war Oradour variety concerts, set off with his friend, Pierre Joyeux, and Joyeux's wife. Foussat, determined to go into the village, rode his bicycle, and the Joyeux couple were on foot. Within minutes they reached La Croix des Bordes. They did not know that they had reached the limit of the outer cordon, inside which houses were to be emptied of people for the round-up. All properties within a second cordon, closer to the village centre, were to be destroyed. Foussat decided to peddle ahead:

> He had only just left us when and was about two hundred metres ahead. He quickly pulled up on the left-hand side of the road and I saw him wave his handkerchief. This was undoubtably to signal to the Germans guarding the

road at that spot that he meant no harmful intent. Straightaway, he was cut down in a hail of bullets.[14]

The firewood merchant Michel Avril, who had left Hippolyte Redon's home earlier, never made it back to the village and his body was later found in the countryside, near a hamlet that fell within the outer cordon. His wife and baby son had already been taken to the church. Foussat's wife Valérie, whom he was keen to get news of, had not been amongst the women rounded up that day as she had been attending a hairdresser's appointment in a neighbouring village. Germaine Couvidou, sister of Albert Valade, along with her two friends Lucienne Thomas and Léonie Vevaud, had got as far as the village to look for their children. The bodies of all three were discovered within the village confines.

The Evening Tram

Camille Senon had been looking forward to spending Sunday with her parents after a long working week in Limoges. That Monday, 5 June, had been her nineteenth birthday and, despite the era of restrictions, she was hoping to bake a cake when she got home to her parents' small, rented house in Le Repaire. The week had taken on a new level of excitement on the day after her birthday when news of the Allied landings in Normandy spread through Limoges.

She was excited at what she might hear by way of war news. She had secured a new, better job and the liberation must, she thought, be just weeks away. She had signed paperwork to begin at the social security offices, revulsed at the section in which she had to attest that she was not a Jew nor did she have any Jewish ancestry. She was so 'green' to the ways of the world that the anti-Semitic legislation of the Vichy regime had just about passed her by.[1]

She got to the station in plenty of time and waited to board the evening line-three tram. She wondered which faces she would see that evening. Thinking back to her previous visit, the last time she had seen her parents, she almost wished she had complied with her father's suggestion of taking the week off. They had gone together to visit Raymond's grave and then to see her uncle, Lucien Morlieras, his second wife, and her cousin Irène. Later she had tried to give some reading material to another of her cousins, injured baker-cum-footballer Armand, who was stuck in bed. But Armand had been more interested in his girlfriend, Irène Redon, a former classmate of Camille's, who lived on the other side of the square and worked in the café-pâtisserie. Another of her cousins, Olga Lacroix, had just given birth to her third child, so Camille was pleased to visit the baby, Roland Jacques, five days after his birth.

The gathering crowd was large, but boarding was delayed. An employee from the tram company came and told them that the tram may not run after all.

'The Germans have been at Oradour since the beginning of the afternoon,' he told them. 'We do not know what is happening there. We have phoned several times but Oradour is not picking up!'

Camille wondered what she would do if the tram was cancelled. The station staff had been ringing the telephone exchange at the post office, but nobody was answering. In itself that was not unusual, and it seemed as if identity checks were occupying the whole village, so the staff decided that the tram would run. The passengers were allowed to board the three carriages and the electrically driven tram pulled away more or less on time.

Thinking about what they had been told, Camille was worried, and she could sense that others were too. She looked out of the windows, listening to chatter about what the delay might be due to and, as the tram stopped at various points on the western limits of the city, people got on who had that morning travelled to the city to do their shopping. The city opened up to countryside and villages along the route as the tram climbed slowly out of the city and on to the higher ground of the western Haute-Vienne.

> Halfway through the journey we noticed a big strip of black smoke against the blue sky. When the tram stopped in one of the hamlets we asked some bystanders 'What is that smoke?' We were told, 'We don't know. It is from somewhere near Oradour but we haven't seen anybody coming from that way.'[2]

The tram continued on until Laplaud, the last but one stop before Oradour:

> There, there was a young man on a bike who had come from that direction. He yelled out 'Don't go there, don't go there. They are killing everybody.' I don't know if the driver of the tram did not hear or if he didn't understand but he set off anyway.[3]

The tram arrived at Puy-Gaillard before going downhill a little towards the Glane. Gasps rang out at the activity all around. As well as the many soldiers, lots of military vehicles were parked alongside the road.

> An SS soldier climbed onto the tram and gave the order that any travellers from Oradour must get off. I got off, as did others from the other carriages. There were about twenty of us. There were three teenagers and several other children, and these were mainly people I knew. The same soldier that had got us off the tram led us away, but not to the centre of Oradour, he led us to the edge of a field.[4]

One of the passengers on the tram had been Emile Redon, the entrepreneurial owner of the *Café-épicerie* and cider press on the *Champ de foire*. He had been in Limoges on business. Camille had known the family all her life:

> Monsieur Redon [...] approached me. He had a daughter [Irène] who was my age, and I was friends with her. He came to me, a moment after

speaking to the SS man, and he said to me, 'He just told me that the women and children are burning in the church.' I looked at him, disbelief in my eyes. We had seen the church on fire, but how could women and children have found themselves inside a church that was burning down. You cannot understand that. It is beyond the realms of imaginable. It was not possible.[5]

Jean Couvidou had seen his daughter on to the train to Compiègne and the family wedding. At the station he had heard rumours of something happening in Oradour. Having no wish to wait for the evening tram, he had taken his bike with him to pedal home during the afternoon. He could not shake off the rumours about the village where his son Maurice worked. Along the way he came across several people who warned him that Oradour was in flames and that he would be at serious risk if he continued in that direction. 'But I was far from giving credence to the rumours.' He did not know whether his wife Mélanie was amongst those who had been rounded up, and he knew that Maurice must be there in the centre of everything, the bakery being so central. 'I was terrified for the lives of my loved ones, nothing would have held me back.'[6]

He was in view of Oradour at around half past six. At La Plaine he was stopped by Mélanie Milord whose husband was in the village in advance of the baptism of their nephew, due to take place the following day. He had gone ahead of her from Limoges while her two daughters, Nicole who was 4 and Marie-Claude who was just 4 months old, were already at the *Hôtel Milord*, where they had been staying with her mother-in-law. She followed close behind Couvidou until they got to Puy-Gaillard where they saw a tram waiting. She held back. 'Quite a few of the passengers had been lined up on the side of the road, others were still in their seats inside the compartments,' said Couvidou. 'Those who had got off were from Oradour, or from very nearby. Several Germans, armed with machine guns, were guarding both the passengers and the convoy.'

The soldiers stopped Couvidou, shouting in French, 'Are you armed?' When he replied that he was not, they searched him before pushing him into the rows of passengers from Oradour. Just then Mélanie Milord arrived on her bike. Couvidou looked up and saw her assess what was ahead of her. Instead of carrying on towards the tram where she would be arrested, she veered right on to a track leading to Les Brégères. 'As soon as she left the road to get onto the path to the farm, they fired. Madame Milord was shot down by sentries posted to guard all the intersections of roads and pathways.' Her body was later found in a farm courtyard under a cart of manure.

Also aboard the tram was Alphonse Lévignac returning from Limoges. He planned to see Serge and Charles in Oradour before heading home to Avignon. He did not live in the village so had not got off the tram. After two hours of waiting, during which time he saw the village being set alight, the tram was sent back to Limoges. Lévignac looked back at the flames, desperately hoping that Serge and Charles had not been caught up in the violence:

> I had the impression that incendiary grenades were being thrown inside the buildings. I saw Germans approach several nearby homes and almost instantly the buildings were in flames. There could not have been anyone inside because I saw nobody leave those buildings. Neither were the Germans firing their guns. This is what led me to assume that all the people had already been rounded up.[7]

The group of passengers confirmed as native to Oradour were led over fields to the Masset farm. They crossed the farmyard seeing none of its occupants. Instead soldiers were bringing large pieces of bread and pots of charcuterie outside and making sandwiches. 'They were eating and laughing,' recalled Camille. The peasant farmers had been making provisions ready for summer works. 'Bread enough for three weeks had been made. A pig had been killed, and charcuterie made from it.'[8]

Marguerite Villéger, her three daughters and their dog continued to wait in silence on the other side of a wall that the group from the tram passed near to. Cattle had been released into a field right next to where they were hidden. Thirsty, scared and suffering from the acrid smoke inhalation, they could hear the shouting and laughing from their home.

The field into which the group from the tram were led ran parallel to the Les Bordes road:

> We were, perhaps, a kilometre from Oradour and a kilometre from Les Bordes. From the field itself we could not see the road. SS soldiers guarded us and further on another group were digging the ground. We did not know why. Presently one of those who had been digging came over to us and counted us before heading back. We were horrified at what that could mean. All we could do was wait.[9]

The sun was going down and the day was getting cooler:

> As evening approached the same SS soldier who had told Monsieur Redon that the women and children were burning, came back to us. He taunted us. 'Are you trembling? Are you cold? Are you scared? There is nobody left alive in Oradour.' It chilled my heart, and I thought that they were going to kill us [...] we were all thinking the same.[10]

The Miraculous

Not long after the tram arrived at Puy-Gaillard at around seven o'clock, Mathieu Borie decided that it was time to attempt an escape. The noise of firing had died down and, with Robert Hébras, he had been counting the gaps between the passing by of the sentries. They were unable to see around to their left which was the open area of the *Champ de foire* where, earlier that day, the whole village had been assembled. But the lack of noise from that direction suggested that most of the activity there was over. It would be risky, but the smoke in the air offered some obscurity and Borie had an idea. Directly opposite the hutches was the Senon farm, alongside which was a gated gap leading to a wall. If the men could get through that gap without being noticed they would stand a chance of following the wall to the cemetery which could then serve as their next hiding place. Beyond that was woodland and potential safety.

Borie was fifteen years older than Hébras but the two had been friendly for some time. Borie's experience, however limited, of real-world danger with a Resistance group allowed him to think clearly. His quick thinking and leadership had already saved lives that afternoon. Crossing the *Champ de foire* would be a calculated risk, and if they were seen they would be shot at or pursued. He took it upon himself to lead the way. 'I saw a dog which belonged to Monsieur Senon. It was imperative that it did not bark.' He pointed to the gap that he knew was there, but which was hidden by a high stack of tree trunks that had been prepared for sawing. It was high and wide and Borie warned Hébras that, when he followed, he must ensure that he go around them. He would be too visible if he climbed them. Borie promised to wait for Hébras and Darthout, who was gasping breathlessly. He took off his wooden-soled shoes: 'I crossed the *Champ de foire*, barefoot. I made my way to the gate and opened it. The dog looked at me as if he understood what I was trying to do.'

Hébras was to follow, but first he had to wait for the sentries to approach and leave again. 'Robert, leave me,' said Darthout. 'I might ruin your escape. This is getting more and more painful. So, go on. Try your luck and think of me!' Hébras knew that the fire would soon consume the last hutch. But he knew that he had to try to save himself. Injured himself, he had no strength to carry his friend. 'Go on,' said Darthout.

With no idea if soldiers had arrived at the other end of the *Champ de foire*, Hébras was petrified. He would have to time his run perfectly. 'The thought of a sudden brutal death paralysed me. Would I suffer? I failed to leave several times and had to wait again. Suddenly I felt deep within me a strength that told me I had to hurry. I could delay no further. I turned towards Darthout [...] 'Adieu. As soon as you can, go! Be brave! Good luck!' He smiled at me.'

Hébras pushed the door open slowly and crept forward. 'Panic took hold of me. I could not believe that I was having to play this game of Russian roulette, so heavily fixed against me. The person holding a weapon in this case was risking nothing.' He ran as quickly as he could and managed to look left. There was nobody there, but the houses, shops and buildings of Oradour were in flames. Remembering to go around the tree trunks, he arrived at the gate at the edge of the Senon farm. Borie, true to his word, was waiting for him behind the wall. Without a word, the men crept forward along an open and visible expanse of grass keeping low and close to the wall. Finally, they reached the gates to the cemetery. 'Is Darthout coming?' asked Borie. 'No he couldn't,' said Hébras.[1]

As they pulled open the gate to the cemetery it squeaked loudly so they rushed into the one part of Oradour that remained untouched. Hiding between the headstones, they made their way to the far wall and climbed over it. They were into the woods that bordered the northern edge of the village, and from there they could make their escape.

The men passed very near to the spot where Armand Senon was hiding in a bush, having crawled there earlier, dragging his broken leg behind him.[2] During that time Armand heard the sounds of the destruction of his home village as well as the footsteps of soldiers nearby:

At one point I saw a head covered with ginger hair not far from me; it really scared me. I thought that I had been discovered because I couldn't make out what was happening. This person sat right next to me, without seeing me. I could not see who it was. The person went off again groaning in agony because he had been hurt. I could not see his clothes and I still believed that it was a German.[3]

In fact it had been Darthout who had not given up hope of staying alive. Soon after Hébras had left, Darthout had decided to summon up the last of his remaining strength and follow, having relieved his friends of the danger of trying to look after him. Halfway across the *Champ de foire* his legs had given way and he had fallen to the ground. But fear forced him onward and he crawled across to the edge of the open square. He got to the wall opposite and climbed to his feet, managing to hang on to a house that was in flames. 'Some towels were drying on the line. I took them and I used them.'[4] The elementary dressings probably saved his life. He waited a little while longer until he had gathered his breath and some strength before once again dragging himself as far as a bush, where he dropped and hid.

In the bushes behind the Masset farm, Marguerite Villéger, her three daughters and their dog still waited, moving just a little from time to time to prevent their limbs from seizing up. The singing and laughing from the courtyard continued, and by now a table had been set up there. The pig that the family had butchered two days earlier had been entirely consumed. The night was not very cold but they shivered through fear and shock. The cries that they had heard from Oradour would never leave them; now the darkness of that night seemed to last forever.

Camille Senon and the other passengers shivered, all the while looking at the makeshift grave that had apparently been dug for them:

> The night was approaching. It was around ten o'clock German time. An officer arrived and, since I lived in Limoges, I had my *carte d'identité* with my Limoges address. I rushed towards him and said, 'We are not from Oradour, look at my address [...] we are from Limoges, we are only here to spend the weekend in the countryside. I'm here to go to another village, Les Bordes.' I don't know if he understood, I don't know if someone translated for him, I really do not know and can only suppose. However he said sharply, '*Papiers!*'. Everyone got out the identity papers, but he did not even glance at them. Instead looking annoyed he said, '*Raus.*' We understood that that meant 'leave' and we all left, going in the opposite direction to Oradour.
>
> When we arrived at the village of Les Bordes there were lots of people on their doorsteps and they rushed towards us. 'At last, someone who has come from Oradour. What is happening there? Where are our little ones? Our children haven't come home from school.' Of course all the children from the commune were at school at Oradour-sur-Glane and had not come home. These people were dying with worry. We said to them, 'No, we know nothing. We were in the tramway from Limoges. We don't know what has happened in Oradour.' We did not tell them what the SS had told us because we could not believe it. We did not want to believe it.[5]

The villagers invited the group into their homes, and they offered shelter for the night. Everybody began to talk to each other:

The lady whose home I went to said, 'Listen, this morning I went to do my shopping in Oradour. I saw your Papa.' That Saturday my father had been working in the centre of the village, working on the roads. She told me about the conversation that she had had with him. I was thinking that those were perhaps the last words of my father and that she was reporting them to me. Then she told me that she had also seen my aunt [...] 'Your cousin Irène [Morlieras] was there too.' I did not know what to think. That had all happened in the morning but we still did not know what had happened in Oradour in the afternoon. Who was still alive? I was so worried. At around midnight trucks filled with soldiers passed through the village without stopping. That was that. We spent the night there.[6]

Irène Morlieras was the daughter of Lucien and Catherine and worked in their café. She had never wanted to move away from them and ran the café almost on her own. Irène was first cousin to Camille Senon. (Collection Marcel Lenfant)

A Path

After returning from the cattle requisition in Saint-Victurnien to their home in Le Theil, Pierre Tarnaud and his wife had watched and waited all day. The firing from the village had been relentless. In the middle of the afternoon two young women arrived with their younger brother, who Tarnaud could see was, in some way, disabled. They told the farmer and his wife how their father had urged them to hide because they were Jewish, and that their surname was Pinède. They told them that they had managed to escape from a cellar through a window. They had seen a soldier take away their father, whose hands had been in the air. A little later a boy of around 16 had come to the house in order to find refuge. He had been tracked by the Germans, having escaped when they had arrested his mother, grandmother and other people from his home. Tarnaud had in fact seen the mounted machine gun that had followed the boy before losing him. It had not come as far as Le Theil. The boy told them how he had been shot at by machine-gun fire but had not been hit. The undulating ground had, said the boy, saved him by allowing him to get away unsighted. The boy was Jacques Boissou.

Late in the afternoon Robert Hébras and Mathieu Borie had stumbled on to Tarnaud's land. The hair on both of their heads was badly singed:

> Hébras was badly burned on one arm and was carrying bullet wounds to his shoulder and arm. Blood was flowing from them. They seemed panic-stricken and did not want to stop and deal with their injuries. They told me that they had managed to get away from the flames, saying that the Germans had shut them and the other men in a warehouse and fired rounds of machine gun fire on them, piled straw and sticks on them and set them on fire. We were not able to keep them there with us, so dazed were they by what they had seen.[1]

Tarnaud offered them wine to quench their thirst. They accepted, though Hébras would have far preferred water. While Borie and Hébras were with them, Tarnaud saw livestock arrive in the wheat fields behind the farm. Smoke and huge flames were already rising from the village.

After leaving Tarnaud, Borie and Hébras walked late into the night, determined to get as far from Oradour as they could. They avoided roads and kept to woodland, all the while heading in the direction of Borie's parental home in Boissournet. It was a walk of some two and a half hours at a good pace. They stopped from time to time to drink from streams before eventually approaching the village of La Martinerie, by which time all was dark:

> We approached slowly, and carefully. In the absence of suspicious noises or shadows we knocked on the door of the only bourgeois house in the village. The door swung open and a huge man asked us bluntly what we wanted. His cold and abrupt tone did not feel at all welcoming.[2]

The house belonged to a well-heeled couple by the name of Barataud who owned and rented out several farms. Borie and Hébras had walked into an area in which the Cieux *maquis* were active and all bourgeois houses would have been used to the visits, often unwelcome, of local *maquisards*. The two men at the door, shockingly bedraggled, covered with dry blood and black with smoke, must have worried the owner. 'What must you have done to them for them to attack you?' he said.[3] Many thought that whatever had happened at Oradour must have been the direct result of reprisals. Hébras' heart sank at the man's reaction but then he heard a friendly, familiar voice – that of a young woman. 'What are you doing here, Robert?' The Pinède girls and their brother had found their way to the same house. He and André Desourteaux had always called their friends '*Les petites juives*' and somehow he had stumbled across them at the end of a hellish night. They told him how they had left their hiding place underneath the *Hôtel Avril* and had come across two SS sentries. Whoever those sentries were, they had allowed them to get away.

Hébras stayed at the house that night, though he refused to sleep indoors, as he would for months afterwards. Before that, Jacqueline and Francine Pinède helped him clean his wounds, and even removed a bullet from his shoulder.

After leaving Hébras, Mathieu Borie was determined to carry on to his mother's home in Boissournet. A friend cleaned him up and, with a good slug of *eau de vie* to strengthen his resolve, he set off again. In the hamlet of La Banèche, he went to his youngest sister Louise Vareille.[4] Along with her husband René, she offered him respite, but Borie refused, saying he needed to reach their mother. Seeing her brother in such a state, crazed even, she asked a villager to accompany him a little way. An hour later Borie was in Boissournet. But with his mother's home just 200m away, he was struck by the fear that he may have been followed. He climbed under a hedge and slept for several hours, until hunger and cold forced him inside. It was still early morning, and he bandaged his wounds, which were not severe. He told his mother about what had happened in Oradour, then ate a little and drank water. After a brief rest he set off to Pellechevent where he had contacts in the Resistance.

Perette Sauvet and her husband, both engaged with the FTP of Cieux, had been due to go to Oradour that Saturday afternoon. They had seen the smoke, just 16km south-west of where they were, but had no idea of what had gone on. They were delayed, so Perette persuaded her husband that they should go another time, despite being due to visit the *sabotier* and his state-of-the-art mechanical clog-making equipment. Just two days earlier her group had attacked a German truck. In the days that followed the massacre those in the FTP in the Cieux area were terrified that Oradour was just the start, and that the SS were searching for survivors. In the villages all around Oradour, many people chose to spend their nights in the woods. The rumoured survivors of the Oradour massacre were being tracked down, but this was a job that had been left to the *Milice* for reasons of completion.

It was late morning, around eleven o'clock, when the Sauvet couple saw their friend approaching, limping slightly:

> As he approached us he was saying 'The planes! The planes!' Then he came inside and took shelter in our house. We could hardly understand what he was saying [...] He repeated the phrase 'They are looking for us.' My husband and I thought he was mad [...] It was then that we saw his injured arm and back. I tended to his wounds and in dribs and drabs, he told us about the Oradour tragedy.[5]

At first they found it hard to believe, but as he gave details they thought about how many people that they knew who might have lost their lives if the story were true:

> It may be stupid but my mind turned to two pretty girls at the café where we always went; two beautiful girls of the Limousin of whom I had always secretly been slightly jealous, two such luscious girls so full of life ...[6]

Perette was thinking of Andrée and Antoinette Brandy, both of whom died with their mother Eugénie in the church.

Perette and her husband looked after their friend and sent for a young Jewish doctor called Doctor Denès who was hiding in the village and who was known to help the *maquis*. 'You were lucky,' the doctor told Borie during his examination, 'that this [bullet] did not go in. You got away with that one.'

PART THREE

HELLSCAPE

Das Reich

On 9 June 1944, the night before the Oradour events, *maquisard* Jean Canou was returning from a mission. He was a miner by trade from the village of Saint-Léonard-de-Noblat, east of Limoges, and had taken to the clandestine armed Resistance, heading up a Guingouin-attached FTP *maquis* in Cheissoux. His group, travelling in a small truck, had been following orders from Guingouin to bomb bridges over the Vienne and had just successfully sabotaged a bridge in Brignac. As they reached RN 141 in the village of La Bussière they came across a German Talbot sports car coming from the direction of Guéret. There was no sign of any support behind.

Canou's men surrounded the car before the driver, the only occupant, had an opportunity to use his weapon. Canou later testified:

> I made the car stop and we found ourselves in the presence of an SS commander. The car contained a large number of ordnance survey maps, a TSF radio set and all sorts of other documents. We put the commander under arrest and, since I did not have a second driver, we left the vehicle behind.[1]

They took off towards Cheissoux, taking an earlier turning than originally intended so as not to come across the German column that would be following the commander.

As the truck jerked its way to the *maquis* camp in Cheissoux, Canou spoke to the officer who 'spoke French quite well and I summarily interrogated him. He told me that he had been coming from Guéret where he had fought and that his orderly had been killed.' He told Canou that forty or so trucks were not far behind him. By changing route, Canou explained, he had already ensured that their paths would not cross. Canou described the officer as 'very tall. He was about 1.80m in height and was very well built. He was carved, like an athlete. I think he told me that he was 35 or 36. He said that he had already fought the Russian campaign.' Canou later claimed that he had forgotten the name of the man but he did remember 'that he belonged to the Der Führer regiment'. Another *maquisard* called Léon Vigneron was at the camp when the officer was brought in. 'He was taken by the group who captured him to St-Julien-le-Petit, and I do not know what became of him afterwards.'

The men had captured Major Helmut Kämpfe, one of the most decorated officers in the SS *Das Reich* division. He had, that day, headed up a battalion sent to retake the town of Guéret which had been 'liberated' by the *maquis*. When they got there, it had already been taken back by the Wehrmacht. Major Kämpfe had overseen the killing of twenty-nine *maquisards* in the outskirts of the town, at a place known as Poteau de Combeauvert. Witnesses to that massacre claimed that some of the men were crushed under the German half-track vehicles. The major had then received orders to return quickly to Limoges to prepare a major operation the following day. Inexplicably he had sped ahead of the rest of the convoy by a distance of around 3km, despite knowing that he was in *maquis* country.

When the column that followed came across the abandoned vehicle they found 'the commandant's vehicle on the right-hand side of the road, completely plundered, engine still running. The commandant had been about ten minutes ahead. The action carried out immediately by the commander in charge, reconnaissance patrols of the area, were unsuccessful.'[2] They left their mark by executing two farmers in a nearby field.

The PCF, the underground communist leadership that directed FTP operations, and Georges Guingouin were already partially estranged well before the Allied invasion of Normandy. When they pushed for Guingouin to commit his troops to liberating the city of Limoges as early as 7 and 8 June, he had steadfastly refused to comply. He had no doubt that early action would lead to civilian bloodshed. In Corrèze an attempt was made to liberate the large town of Tulle, which succeeded. By 9 June, however, 99 men were hanging from the town's lampposts while a further 149 people were deported, of which 101 never returned. Guingouin was furious at those who thought that Tulle could be liberated and then held by the under-armed and inexperienced FTP. To make matters worse, a new enemy had arrived, the SS Division *Das Reich*.

Guingouin, distanced from the central units of command, knew little about the movement of the redoubted armoured division which had been stationed near Montauban and ordered to make its way north. Commanded by *SS-Brigadeführer* Heinz Lammerding, the enormous division of 15,000 men and 209 tanks and self-propelled guns[3] had been in the south of France recuperating, repairing machinery and accepting large numbers of replacement men from around the Reich, including Alsace-Lorraine. Even on the advent of the Allied invasion of Normandy it was not ordered to speed northwards to Normandy, but to concentrate on ridding the southern area around Limoges, Brive and Tulle of *maquis* groups while making steady progress north. It was ordered to shatter the Resistance by 'leading an immediate and brutal strike against the gangs that have formed in the sector of Tulle and Limoges'. Its arrival in Normandy was not expected to take place before mid-June, regardless of the fact that the Allies had already made good progress when those orders were given. Its first priority was to search out the Resistance and destroy it, and if that slowed its movement down, so be it.

Spread out in several columns at a time across vast swathes of countryside, its route was directly north through Brive and Limoges. It was, however, also given the mission of ensuring that the roads and railways that followed that route, and those that passed from west to east from Bordeaux to Clermont-Ferrand and beyond, were clear so the German supplies could be kept fluid. General Lammerding had no interest in dealing with Guingouin so he did not go looking for the well-established but latent *maquis* in the eastern Haute-Vienne. Lammerding inflicted misery on his way through Tulle, Figeac and parts of the Dordogne where *maquis* groups chose to take on parts of the division with tragic results. By 9 June Lammerding had arrived in Limoges and set up a divisional headquarters there.

A column was sent to the northern part of the department to Guéret where there had been *maquis* insurgency, while two further headquarters were stationed in the western part of the departement, in Rochechouart and Saint-Junien. As such, the isolated forest of Châteauneuf and the plateau around Sussac were avoided, and the only dealings that *maquis* groups under Guingouin's command had with *Das Reich* occurred almost by accident. On 9 June, a convoy protecting the rear of a column headed further east towards Guéret found itself in Guingouin territory. One of Guingouin's most trusted chiefs, Pierre Magadoux, was concerned that the SS may discover a trail to the *maquis* camps, and he saw an opportunity to strike a blow. With the blessing of Guingouin, Magadoux took a small unit to the village of Sainte-Anne-Saint-Priest. He was under orders only to intervene should it seem that the convoy was heading in the direction of the camps. When they got there, the convoy had all but gone; however, left behind was a single mounted machine gun that had broken down. Four SS men were attempting to fix the vehicle. Magadoux and his men set upon them and captured the machine gun. Two SS men escaped but one was killed and another injured and taken prisoner. The machine gun was fixed, recovered and used later against the German army.[4]

Saint-Junien

It was only when Vichy insisted on the removal of Saint-Junien's communist mayor in 1941 that a right-wing man, Emile Gibouin, was installed in his place. The new mayor was, however, proposed by the outgoing council and was by no means supportive of the Vichy project. The Resistance found roots in areas where factory workers had already been brought on board by the clandestine Communist party and Saint-Junien, already a 'red' town, had seen support grow for nearby *maquisards*. Some factory workers considered themselves *maquisards* despite continuing to live and work in town.

Perched on the banks of the Vienne, Saint-Junien was also located on a key railway line, linking Limoges to Angoulême, and onward to the western coast. It was a line of immense importance and for this reason, once the Allies had landed in Normandy and activated 'Plan Vert' aimed at bringing the railway network to a halt, it was targeted by the *maquis*. On the first Wednesday night in June, a viaduct across the Vienne, just a kilometre outside Saint-Junien, was bombed, rendering it impassable. The rail company tried to block it with a locomotive and some wagons but doing so caused it to partially collapse, derailing the train and taking some of the wagons into the river. The following day, 8 June, local FTP *maquisards* took possession of the *mairie* (town hall) and the headquarters of the *Légion*. They also took up positions around the bridges.

With the bridge over the river rendered useless for several weeks, passengers were forced to descend from the train well before they reached the small station. With their luggage, they then had to walk a short way along the southern bank of the Vienne and take either a pathway towards the town, or another towards the station in order to meet the corresponding train for Limoges. Around seven o'clock on the evening of that warm June evening, a train arrived from Angoulême and its passengers got off before the viaduct, from where most would join the path towards the station. Among the passengers was a group of ten German soldiers. As they made their way towards the station, shots rang out. A group of *maquisards* hidden in woodland nearby had seized the opportunity to attack. Firing was returned but no *maquisards* were hurt, and they melted away into the distance. One of the soldiers was killed and a civilian was injured.

Word spread and increasingly it was feared that the incident would bring repercussions on the people of the town. Five of the German soldiers got on the train going back to Angoulême. The remaining four carried the body of their dead comrade as far as the station at Saint-Junien. There they boarded the train and took the body to Limoges. They arrived at ten o'clock that night and reported what had happened. The *Kommandantur* immediately sent an armoured train to Saint-Junien. It was full of Wehrmacht soldiers as well as Lieutenant Wickers of the Gestapo. Even as the train crossed the Limousin countryside on its 25km journey, a telephone call was made to the station chief insisting that the mayor be ready to meet the train, armed with a map of the town. Emile Gibouin was sought out at his home and the two men returned to the station. Gibouin got on the phone to the chief of police and instructed him to bring the map. At a quarter past eleven the train arrived, and the soldiers took up positions around the town. Some firing was exchanged but nobody else was hurt.

The following morning Gibouin was questioned by Wickers, but the mayor refused to give any names of known communists or *maquis* leaders. He told the Gestapo agent that he would assume full responsibility, offering himself as a hostage. Wickers demanded 100 men to assemble with shovels and picks the following morning and told Gibouin that as of two o'clock that afternoon his powers would be suspended. Anyone coming into or leaving the town would be obliged to show their papers and the town was all but surrounded. Gibouin showed the Germans as much hospitality as he could to try to stave off the reprisals that it seemed they were planning. By the evening it was clear to Gibouin that the Wehrmacht no longer had any such plans but he was aware that by the following day things could change for the worse, when the soldiers were relieved by an SS division known for its cruelty.

Around fifty men, mainly older retired labourers and all that Gibouin and the police commissioner could find, gathered outside the station the following morning at eight o'clock waiting for their instructions. The *Hôtel de la Gare* looked out over the station and Wickers joined Gibouin and gave the men their orders. Ditches were to be dug and roads barricaded with fallen trees and overturned carts. During the afternoon numerous trucks and half-tracks rolled into town and with them came some 300 soldiers led by *SS-Sturmbannführer* Adolf Diekmann, a thin and intense leader with a hard stare. With him he had brought the 1st Battalion of *Der Führer* regiment of the SS armoured division *Das Reich*. Diekmann took over and the Wehrmacht was dispatched from Saint-Junien. Immediately the people of the town were concerned to see a watchtower set up in the bell tower of the church. A curfew was imposed

The Hôtel de la Gare *in Saint-Junien where the final preparations for the operations of 10 June 1944 were made. (Author's collection)*

between nine o'clock that night and six o'clock the following morning. The sounds of patrols filled the night – of jackboots and German voices. Mothers and fathers hid their children in attics not wanting to try to flee for fear of being caught. Hardly any German presence had been seen in Saint-Junien since the demarcation line was crossed eighteen months earlier. On the night of 9 June 1944, the people of the town feared the very worst.

The dreaded round-ups never came. The morning was eerily quiet until engines started up again. People went to work, and while identity papers were checked, there was no violence. Rumours spread about a man, a Jew, shot outside the station, but nothing further. Still the people waited and watched. The town's mayor and the curate were in conversation with the Germans. More soldiers were seen at the top of the bell tower of the church. Hearts pounded in anticipation of what might happen next. At half past twelve, there was a roar of activity and vehicle after vehicle left, some carrying troops, others machine guns. The soldiers were, for the moment, going away. By the evening of 10 June all Germans had left Saint-Junien.

It was from Saint-Junien on 10 June 1944 that the 3rd Company of the 1st Battalion of *Der Führer* Regiment of *Das Reich* Division, under the command of *SS-Sturmbannführer* Adolf Diekmann, set off for Oradour-sur-Glane.

Numb

When morning finally came 14-year-old Renée Villéger, who had been keeping her 2-year-old sister warm, told her mother that she needed to find out what had happened in their farm. Little Hélène needed milk. The oldest daughter crept around the wall that had saved their lives to what remained of the Masset farm. Fire had destroyed it all, buildings and belongings. There were remnants of what had been food in the yard as well as broken crockery, and the fire was still burning in places. One stable had been spared and Renée approached it. There was no sign of the pigs or cattle, all of which had been freed. A farm dog lay dead on the ground. Renée went into the stable where a solitary cow had come back for shelter, and to feed. She calmed the animal and took a little milk which she rushed back to give to her sister.

It was six o'clock in the morning, and the sun had barely risen, when Léon Sage, who had been on the evening tram and had narrowly escaped with his life the previous evening, was awoken by François Barataud. The old man was frantic about the fate of his wife, daughter and granddaughter, none of whom had returned. Sage, who had been staying in his country home with his family at La Croix des Bordes, had provided a bed for Jean Pallier, an SNCF engineer from the Paris area. Pallier's wife, Françoise, and three children were in Oradour, where they had been staying at the *Hôtel Avril* to escape the Paris bombings. She also had her 10-year-old niece Jacqueline Guionnet with her. On an assignment to Limoges, Jean had asked permission from his bosses to call in and see them on the Saturday evening and stay all day Sunday with them. Colleagues had driven him by car to Oradour until they were stopped. They arrived at Puy-Gaillard just before the tram, having earlier had to load and unload the car. A good knowledge of German had probably saved Pallier as he was able to explain his mission, but he was added to the group of passengers from the tram. His colleagues in the car were allowed to return to Limoges unharmed.

Camille Senon and some of the other passengers of the evening tram who had been given shelter for the night in Les Bordes had also gathered together early. They discussed whether they should go to Oradour or walk to the other villages and find out if the women and children had been taken somewhere else. What the SS officer had told them the night before still seemed far-fetched. Camille was one of those who decided to go to Oradour and near the village she spoke to Pallier.

On the short walk to the village they came across Jean Courivaud, who the previous day had seen Mélanie Milord shot dead on a bicycle in front of him and Jean Guyonnet, a 65-year-old farmer also from La Croix des Bordes. They passed the Masset farm which had been burnt down. 'Numerous cartridge cases, of English origin, were scattered over the road,'[1] said Sage later. Guyonnet reported seeing plenty of evidence that the property had been used as a headquarters for the whole operation. 'There were lots of traces that led us to believe that the Germans had stayed there and had eaten there. There were chicken feathers.' Something else disturbed them. 'In a bush fifty metres or so from that place alongside a ditch was a fistful of the long hair of a woman. It was light brown in colour.'[2]

Nothing could have prepared them for what they saw when they got to the village:

> The houses were in ruins. The windowsills still had pots of flowers on them, but there was rubble all over the pavements. Cooking pots hung in the fireplaces, and coffee pots stood on the corners of the stoves. The core of each house had crumbled, and as we went on, we saw that each and every house was in ruins. I kept thinking that it was like a nightmare. I thought I would surely see a house that was intact, someone alive or a familiar face. But no, it was just ruins and more ruins.[3]

Camille's father, Martial, had been there just like all the others, but there was no sign of any of them.

'We got to the crossroads, next to the freedom oak and opposite my aunt and uncle's house, which was in ruins.' It was there that Camille turned left to cross the bridge out of Oradour to make her way to her parents' home:

> In Le Repaire I found my mother. My father had not come home. He had, as suspected, been killed. My grandfather had also been killed, as had his wife. The sister of my father, her husband, their daughter [...] they had all been massacred, along with so many other cousins. Some were close, some more distant, but we all saw each other all the time because that is how it was. Everybody knew everybody else. The youngest of my little cousins was 12 days old[4] and he had a brother who was 3 and a sister who was 2 years old. They lived in the hamlet of Puy-Gaillard. So their father, their mother [...] all five were mown down.[5]

The road that goes to the hamlet of Les Bordes, immediately after the massacre. The infants' school and the school for refugees were both on the left of the road. (Centre de la Mémoire, Oradour-sur-Glane)

The others went on, unsure whether the soldiers had even left. 'When we went into the village it was still in flames and the heat was hardly bearable, so we had to walk quickly.'[6] Near the home of Doctor Paul Desourteaux they found two bodies, carbonised, and small enough to suggest that they were the remains of children. At the western edge of the village, near the Dagoury café, lay the body of Marie Ducharlet from La Valade, who had been shot through the head. Jean Courivaud looked into the Desourteaux garage where he saw many bodies, some still just about recognisable. Among them he recognised his son, Maurice, former soldier, apprentice baker.

They could not stay for long. A group of soldiers appeared behind them and were catching up, though they had yet to notice the men. Courivaud

saw the two small bodies, and that of Madame Ducharlet in houses that were
burning. They were then spotted, and were called and questioned. Courivaud
showed his identification documents that showed his Limoges address, and
Pallier showed a work permit detailing why he was working in the area.
Again, Pallier was able to explain in German. The same two documents had,
the previous evening, contributed to their lives being saved. The men were
told in accented French to leave quickly. It was eight o'clock in the morning
when they left Oradour.

After giving milk to her sister, Renée Villéger had carried on searching
what remained of the Masset farm. She went to a tiny outbuilding where
sometimes the chimney sweep, Jean Ito, slept. Inside, she found some stale
bread. She was about to take it back when she heard footsteps, so she rushed
into a field of cabbages and hid. When she heard French voices, including
words in the local patois, she approached them. They were people who had
been to Oradour and what they told her she knew that she could not report
to her mother. She went back to her family's hiding place and shared out
the bread. Renée told them that it was safe to emerge but, unconvinced, her
mother Marguerite took them to a thicket where she found an empty bottle
and collected water from the Glane for her children and the dog to drink.
They would spend a further night in amongst the trees.[7]

In Lalande, 60-year-old Arthur Senamaud, a former shopkeeper, had hardly
slept the night before and he had ventured out into the early morning sun.
He had been stopped during the round-up but told to return home. Through
the course of the day, he had heard the firing and explosions but had not
understood what any of it meant. When smoke rose from the direction of
the village, he and others who had gathered thought that the woods around
the area had been set alight, to flush *maquis* groups out. In the early morning
gloom, smoke still hanging in the air, women from all over had begun arriving in the hamlet, eager to go on to Oradour to find their children who had
not come home from school:

> The night before, Madame Ducharlet had stood in the ditch opposite me
> for about an hour. She had wanted, at all costs, to go into the village to find
> her little ones. I had just been told that she had been killed. Her body had
> been found alongside the road at the entrance to the village.[8]

Arthur Senamaud dissuaded the parents in Lalande to go further. He had
heard that the Nazis were still in Oradour and he begged them to wait just a
little longer.

That same morning, a *château* owner from Queyroix picked up Robert Hébras from the Barataud house in La Martinerie where he had stayed overnight with the Pinède family. Hébras was loaded on to a horse and cart and taken to a doctor in Cieux, a large village under the control of local *maquisards*. His wounds were tended to, and he received a shot in the belly to stave off infection. He was returned to the house where he stayed for a while with Jacqueline, Francine and André Pinède. Locals came asking Robert what had happened in Oradour and he was forced to retell the story of his escape many times. Then, with the Pinède girls and their brother, Robert set off to the home of his sister Odette and her husband in Le Pouyol, to the east of Oradour. They walked across fields, avoiding roads. Robert half-expected to find his sisters and mother there, as well as his father. But when he got there, he found out that the women and children had never arrived. Jean Hébras already knew that his son had survived: he had heard so from a number of people. He had, however, heard nothing of his wife, Marie or Robert's sisters – 22-year-old Georgette and 9-year-old Denise – all of whom were still missing.

Georgette, Marie and Odette Hébras. For days after the massacre Robert Hébras and the Pinède siblings stayed with Odette and her husband while their father, Jean, tried to establish what had happened to his wife, Marie, and daughters, Georgette and 9-year-old Denise. (Collection Robert Hébras)

A Key with No Door

It had been a long shift at the Limoges sorting office of the PTT for 18-year-old André Desourteaux. He had worked an eight-hour shift beginning at midday on the Thursday, then Friday had been a day of rest and he had spent it in Oradour, his home. Then he had travelled to Limoges to begin what was known as the *grand service*. This prolonged shift required stamina. Beginning at five o'clock in the morning, André would work until midday, then rest in a room provided at the Limoges office until seven o'clock in the evening when the shift would begin again, lasting until five o'clock the following morning. This meant that when his family, including both his grandfathers Joseph Beau and Paul Desourteaux, were being rounded up and taken to the *Champ de foire*, André was fast asleep 20km away. He began the second part of his shift but there were murmurs around the sorting office about what had been happening in Oradour. He was permitted to finish early, so he readied himself to go home. There were no tram services that would get him near to Oradour as they had all been suspended so he decided to take the train from Limoges to Saint-Victurnien. He could cycle from there.

The train set off along the course of the Vienne, following the winding valley. Once in Saint-Victurnien and in the chill of the early morning, André readied his bicycle for the slow climb to the higher ground that would take him the 7km to his home.

'The first thing I saw was smoke pouring from the bell tower which was missing its top.'[1] He made his way through the wreck of the village. Many buildings were smoking, and some still burning. He got to his father's shop around half past eight that morning. 'I had the key ready but there was no door left. There was nothing left.'

The girls' school next door, into which he used to peek as a child, was also smouldering. There was no sign of anybody, civilians or soldiers:

I crossed the town and went out into the fields that overlooked the village. There I found a man from Oradour and I said to him, 'we have to go back, we have to find the people.' You see for me, they had burned the village, but they had not burned the people. He said, 'You can't go back there, the *Boche* are still there.'

The church after the massacre. The roof and the bell tower collapsed and the bell itself melted in the heat. On the left, the door to the sacristy shows evidence of a targeted furnace. The collapsed roof of the marketplace is in the foreground. (Collection Gontard, Centre de la Mémoire, Oradour-sur-Glane)

The sentries who had remained in town overnight had already begun to dig communal graves for bodies not totally consumed by fire. At the moment André had passed the freedom oak on his bicycle, they must have been in an area behind the church. In a daze he looked around, sticking to the western upper end of the village where his family's homes had all been. Later that morning, men and women he knew, and who lived nearby, began to arrive.

Robert Besson and Jacques Garaud had spent the night in Les Bordes. Early the following morning they returned to the spot where they had hidden and where young Roger Godfrin had briefly paused before running for the woods. Near to the wall that had obscured them, they found the bodies of baker Marcellin Thomas and refugee Octavie Dalstein stuffed into a wheelbarrow. There was no sign of Jacques Garaud's aunt Marie Mosnier, with whom he had been staying and who had told them to stay where they were until she returned. During their search they also found the corpse of Pierre Poutaraud, the garage owner, tangled in a fence on the side of the lane towards the cemetery – a lane along which they had initially planned to escape. Had Poutaraud survived his escape attempt, he would have been faced with the death of his wife Renée and six of his seven children, all under 12 years of age. Only one daughter survived because she had been staying with her grandmother in Ambazac.

There was no sign of Robert Besson's mother or father. Some time later, however, when the devastation was removed, Guillaume Besson's place of

The view from the main door of the church back towards the wreckage of the covered marketplace and, beyond that, the Café Central *that had belonged to the Brandy family. (Collection Boye, Centre de la Mémoire, Oradour-sur-Glane)*

death was established because a wedding ring was found alongside the scissors that he always carried.

René Hyvernaud had spent the night in woodland near one of his family's properties in Saint-Gence having never made it home for the family gathering. At half past six that morning, an armoured tracked vehicle, a side car and a motor car had approached the farm where he had hidden. The cars turned around when they were near the farm. Fearing that they were prospecting the area and ready to attack it as the next place along the line, René decided that it would be in his best interests to get back to Oradour. He did not know what had happened there but figured that, as the troops had already been there, he would be safer at home. He got to Oradour at around ten o'clock but, seeing three trucks parked under some horse chestnut trees at the bridge into the village, he decided that it would be wise to take a detour. He hid his bicycle under the bridge. Bicycles and motorcycles that had been thrown on to the banks and into the waters of the Glane were strewn everywhere. He also saw the body of Marcelin Chalard, the tram worker, which had also been thrown into the river from the bridge. He waited a while and, when the trucks pulled away, he made his way to his family's home which was tucked away behind the church. He was amazed at the destruction. He went first to his grandmother's house. It was still standing:

> Smoke was starting to pour through the roof. I went closer to see what was happening. The doors and windows were wide open, and furniture had been ripped apart. In the kitchen, in front of the window I could see, alongside a bicycle and the trapdoor that led to the cellar, the body of my grandmother […] Her body was partially covered with the belly of a cow.[2]

The corner of the Champ de foire *following the destruction. Marcel Pascaud's pharmacy is a burnt-out shell. The car belonging to wineseller Henri Texeraud remains in the same spot to this day. (Collection Association Nationale des Familles des Martyrs d'Oradour-sur-Glane)*

He went into the church where 'I was met with an horrific spectacle. Inside, several metres from the main entrance, I saw the body of a woman laid out, completely unclothed. It looked as though her clothes had caught fire.' Further into the church, about 4 or 5m in, he saw a pile of bodies, around 1½m high and 2 to 3m in diameter. 'The whole thing was a reddish blaze from which smoke billowed. You could still definitely make out the forms of bodies due to the skeletal structures. Other bodies, mainly children and half burnt, were strewn across the nave.'[3] He went further into the church where he saw two children, both shot dead, legs intertwined. He wanted to separate them but he could not stand the thick smoke and the 'nauseating odour which suffocated me'. Before leaving he saw that 'the floor of the sacristy had crumbled and that, below, fire was still blazing'.

Hyvernaud next went to La Plaine to spread the news of what he had seen. Several days later, when he returned and searched through his grandmother's home, he found the hide of one of the family's cows that had been killed and butchered for meat by the soldiers who had been there. The belly – all that remained – was what had been thrown on top of his dead grandmother.

André Desourteaux was told of one person who had survived the shootings in the barn and who lay badly injured in the hamlet of La Fauvette. The survivor was one of his friends, Jean-Marcel Darthout, and he was being looked after in the home of an aunt. Eager to know more, Desourteaux headed straight there. 'He was more than injured. He was in a hellish state. He managed to say a few words to me. He said that they had killed everyone. I started to understand.'[4] André's worst fears before then had been that most of the village had been taken away and deported, but it became clear that the men at least had been killed. 'I decided to head home, but I couldn't. If you ask me what I did that day … well I can remember very little.' Darthout's brother Aimé, who had escaped the massacre because he was not in the village, arrived. He offered to look after André, taking him to a different aunt who lived in Saint-Victurnien. That night, and for days to come, André neither slept nor ate.

Darthout had been found in bushes near to the Senon farm. During the course of the night he had heard voices coming from the nearby cemetery path and, recognising some words spoken in *patois*, he had called out. Some villagers looking for their loved ones found him, barely alive, and put him into a wheelbarrow. They pushed him back to one of their houses, each bump causing him excruciating pain.[5] They cleaned his wounds and tried to get him to sleep there but he refused, telling them that none of them was safe in the farmhouses. They all went into nearby fields wrapped in blankets, and Darthout spent a sleepless night wracked with pain and cold. The following morning, they left him in the field and sought out postman François Darthout, his father, who arrived several hours later shedding tears of joy to see his son alive. He had heard news that his other son had been seen in Saint-Victurnien too. But as for the women and children, there was still no word. Both men had lost their wives in the fires of the church.

Having spent an entirely sleepless night at *Maison-Blanche* in La Malaise, David Jakobowicz had waited until first light before making the journey to Oradour in order to try to find his 14-year-old sister, Sarah. In sight of the devastation, he could see some fires still burning. He believed that all women and children must have been led away into fields where, he assumed, they would have spent the night huddled together. Approaching from the south, he saw that there were still soldiers in and around the lower village. He, like other villagers he saw on the roads and fields, would have to wait it out.

At two o'clock in the afternoon Arthur Senamaud finally went to Oradour after managing to wait for word that the soldiers had left. He went with other desperate parents, passing the spot where Madame Ducharlet's body had been earlier in the day. Rumours had spread that François Dupic's house and shop had been spared but, by early afternoon, it too had been set alight. In his testimony Arthur Senamaud was not the first to speculate whether that house had served as a second headquarters on the other side of the village from the Masset farm. Empty bottles lay strewn behind the property which suggested that it been used for something.

Amongst the devastation, Senamaud saw human remains and charred remnants of animals all along the main thoroughfare. Inside the church he saw the same horrors as those who had gone before, and noted that 'the left alcove', which was where the confessional was located, 'must have avoided serious fire damage [...] because the confessional box, though scorched by heat, had stayed standing'.[6] Inside were the bodies of two boys. Sitting with each other, their bodies were not damaged by the flames, their faces only lightly blackened:

> One of them was sat, back faced to the nave. He must have been around 12 years old. The other, a little older, was sat facing the church in a crouching position, arms pressed down onto his thighs, face looking to the floor with head having fallen forward.[7]

There was nobody in the priest's side of the box.

Marie Hyvernaud, the other of Mathieu Borie's younger sisters, lived with her husband, Jean Hyvernaud,[8] in the hamlet of Mazenty, south-west of Oradour. Two of their three children had, the day before, been at school. René was 10 and Marcel 8. Their youngest child Albert, who had just turned 6, was left with his grandmother and two younger cousins in Mazenty because his shoe was broken, meaning he could not attend school.[9] By four o'clock rumours had reached them. Oradour, they learned, was on fire. They had looked out to see the thick smoke above the village. Jean tried to get to the village immediately but was pushed back by the cordon. At first, he assumed the church was being used to shelter everyone from the destruction. Believing that the women or children would probably have been kept safe, he was forced to turn and head for home. Just at that moment, around five o'clock, he saw the clock tower collapse.

The couple talked and decided that the children must have been put with their teachers at a safe distance from the fire. They were sure that they would have been looked after, and that they would have their children returned to them at sunrise. They waited impatiently all morning and received no news. In the early afternoon, word spread that the women and children had been in the church when it had been burned. They still did not want to believe, nor could they allow themselves to do so. Finally, word reached them that one of their sons had just been identified in the church. The couple left for the village, numb with fear, and got there at half past four in the afternoon accompanied by several neighbours. They found the body of 8-year-old Marcel, laid out on his side. 'It certainly was my little one. His mouth was open, he seemed scared [...] his foot was broken and twisted around. I was still able to give him a kiss.'[10] The child was still wearing one clog. Jean and Marie wrapped his small body in a bed sheet that they had brought with them. They could not find the body of their oldest son, René. Later, they buried Marcel in Mazenty, using a coffin that Jean built himself.

Discoveries

Sick with worry about his boys Serge and Charles, Alphonse Lévignac, who had returned by tram to Limoges the night before, first approached Oradour by foot at around nine o'clock on the morning of 11 June. 'I noticed that the Germans were still in the village. As well as automatic machine guns there were sentries placed all along the edges of the village.' He waited and returned at half past eleven, by which time there was some movement. The machine guns were being moved and Lévignac, who had gathered with several people from the outlying hamlets, noticed a vehicle belonging to one of the village's merchants that had been requisitioned by the troops. The convoy was heading in the direction of Limoges, via Veyrac. When it passed through the village of La Plaine the car hit a telegraph pole. It was damaged so the troops lobbed incendiary grenades into it to burn it out, before moving on.[1]

A farmer in La Barre de Veyrac called Justin Darthout had, the day before, seen an SS motorcyclist who had stopped at his door and written on it in chalk. The marking read 'K 3/1' followed by a large arrow pointing in the direction of Nieul. Darthout had tried to speak to the soldier but had received no response other than a 'threatening glare'.[2] Soon afterwards the motorcyclist returned heading up a convoy of around twenty vehicles, and stopped at the intersection ensuring they all took the correct turn for Nieul. Darthout saw several cars in the convoy belonging to residents of Oradour, including that of Dupic, the textile merchant, and a van belonging to Léon Denis, the wine merchant. On many of the trucks Darthout saw bicycles piled up, and one soldier playing the accordion was balanced on top of one of the trucks that was loaded with soldiers, bags and bundles. The following day when Darthout got as far as the Chalet Saint-Vincent belonging to de Laverine near Puy-Gaillard, he saw soldiers still guarding the route. Another man who had been talking to the soldiers, asking if he could go and find his father, approached Darthout and told him that the soldier had simply said, '*tous kapout*', while showing the man his watch, pointing out eleven o'clock.

David Jakobowicz made his way back to the village during the late morning, desperate to find his sister Sarah. He happened across Martial Machefer, his contact through the Resistance who had been hiding Sarah for more than a week. Machefer was terrified at what might have become of his wife Anna, and their two children, not to mention Sarah. He told David that he had heard rumours that the women and children had been taken to the church but that he did not think Sarah would have gone to the round-up given that she was in hiding. David waited until the evening then went into the village, passing a little way through the hellscape to reach Machefer's home and shop in the lower village. Within the destroyed flat he found a metal bed frame, under which were the remains of his sister.[3] He wrapped her in some bed linen and buried her in a vegetable patch that his father had been renting near a house in woodland on his way home.[4]

At around half past one Lévignac finally made it into Oradour. He was accompanied by mechanic and survivor Hubert Desourteaux. Along with Aimé and Jeanette Renaud, and Marie Robert, he had finally decided to flee at two o'clock in the morning. 'We managed to get out of there via fields, and got to the hamlet of La Plaine, in the commune of Veyrac, without coming across anyone. We still had no idea that the population had been massacred.' At the edge of the village they saw the body of Chalard, the tram driver, whose

Sarah Jakobowicz, a 15-year-old Jewish girl who was being hidden in Martial Machefer's home. She did not go to the round-up for fear of being deported. (Collection Hervé Machefer)

head had been shot through and whose body was partly lying in the Glane. 'The village itself,' said Lévignac, 'was completely destroyed and still burning.'

At around three o'clock Lévignac was still searching for any trace he could find of his two sons. As he passed behind the presbytery, he heard faint calls. In amongst a bed of peas he found 'an older woman who was begging me to throw her in the Glane, to let her die because she was in so much agony'. This woman's 'legs were burnt up to the knees. She told me that she was seriously injured but had escaped from the church.' Lévignac called for help. He had found Marguerite Rouffanche, who had watched her two daughters and baby grandson die in flames. Alphonse Lévignac would never, however, find any trace of either of his sons.

Monday and Tuesday

Two nights after the massacre a friend of the Villéger family of the Masset farm, Monsieur Javelaud, heard that Marguerite and her daughters were still in a thicket of trees between the River Glane, a stream and the Masset farm. He led a group to collect them and took them to his home at Le Moulin de Bordes. Two-year-old Hélène had had little more than several sips of river water to drink for two days. Marguerite insisted on going to Oradour to look for her husband and four sons.

The two cows that had led the cart taken by 16-year-old Guy, 15-year-old Henri and 16-year-old Serge Lévignac on the morning of 10 June had wandered back towards the remains of the Masset farm, as had the two that Jean Villéger, Marguerite's husband, had led later in the day. They were found at the edge of the village, near the bridge over the river. Fourteen-year-old Renée, who had bravely been the first to leave the hiding place in the bushes behind the farm wall, went into the village with her mother. The two carts, emptied of their contents of hay and fagots of kindling which had been used to light fires, stood in the lower *Champ de foire*, near the church. 'I could not believe my eyes, it all seemed madness to me,' wrote Marguerite Villéger later:

> It was more madness than I ever wanted to see. I searched amongst the ruins and I recognised something. I found my husband's *gilet* and there you have it, Monsieur. In this hell I lost my husband, my four sons, my house and now I have to have courage to simply live.[1]

That day more people came into the village to look for their loved ones. Jean Courivaud, who had been one of the very first into the church on the Sunday morning, returned at around half past one that Monday:

> I went into the church where I saw the burnt bodies, what remained anyway. The evening before the Germans had been in and made most disappear, in particular those bodies that were not entirely destroyed by flames. They had buried them in a ditch next to the church.

Martial Machefer had seen his friend Aimé Faugeras in the village on the morning of the massacre, when the farmer had been sent by his father to pick up their tobacco. Faugeras had rushed back home for lunch, narrowly missing the round-up. From the hamlet of Le Cros, Faugeras and his father had heard the sounds of the massacre. On Monday morning, Machefer and Faugeras set off, hoping to perhaps find survivors or to help in whatever way that they could. On the way they chatted about what might have caused the SS to come to Oradour. At the church Machefer showed Faugeras where Madame Rouffanche had been found the previous day. While there, they noticed that the toilet next to the vegetable garden and behind the church had not been burned. Thinking that there could be someone inside, they went in. At the back of one of the stalls Faugeras found the body of a baby, wrapped in its swaddling. The baby, a boy, had received mortal gunshot wounds.

Léonarde Ledot, wife to Martial Ledot, a woodcutter and farmer, also headed for the centre of the village on the afternoon of Monday 12 June. Her husband had gone in search of his tobacco ration and she felt sick at the thought of what she was about to find out. Widowed twelve years previously, she had found happiness again with Martial, himself a widower. They both had children by their previous marriages and had married in May 1938 before setting up home in Le Repaire. As well as worrying about her husband, she also feared for her daughter from her first marriage, Marie, wife of cattle trader Fernand Hyvernaud. She had heard awful rumours but could not compute the possible consequences. Her granddaughter, Henriette, had married Marcel Joyeux eighteen months previously and had given her great-grandson René at the age of 59. She knew of the family gathering and her daughter's other children, of which seven were potentially in the village.[2]

On her way to the village somebody had approached and told her the news that she had been dreading. Earlier in the day, she was told, the body of a baby had been found by Aimé Faugeras and Martial Machefer and it had been identified as 7½-month-old René. Stoically she made her way to an area behind the church where the baby's body had been laid out. She recognised the child at once and immediately sought authorisation from the town's new mayor to take him away for burial. She also found the body of her own mother, 78-year-old Françoise Devoyon, covered with the cow belly and, with the help of members of the Red Cross, she arranged for her mother to be recovered. Later she was told that her granddaughter Henriette's body had been found in a shallow ditch near the toilet block where little René had been discovered. Their brave escape attempt was later confirmed by Marguerite Rouffanche. Léonarde was also able to identify her daughter, mother of eight

Germaine 'Marie' Hyvernaud, who was found just inside the vestry of the church, where the burning floor had crashed into the cellar. Léonarde had lost another six grandchildren that day. Two grandsons remained, including René who had been working in Saint-Geste. Her husband Martial, she learned, had been shot and burned in one of the places of execution.

The morning after the massacre Léon Beaulieu, a manager-engineer for the TPE (*Travaux publics de l'état*), heard the rumours of what had happened in Oradour. He was horrified because he knew of four men who lived in or near the village – road workers for that sector. He spoke to his chief engineer on the Monday morning, and both men decided to go there. When they arrived, locals advised them to turn around because the Germans were still there. They returned instead the following morning, and they managed to get into the village. Beaulieu found out that one of his men, Léonard Bichaud, a man a few years younger than himself who was married with a son in his early twenties and who lived in Oradour, had perished along with his family. He asked after Martial Senon, a man a few years older than him who, like Bichaud, had fought in the First World War. He hoped that Senon, who lived

The ruins of the rue Emile Desourteaux, *looking downhill towards the river. The steps to the* Villatte *bureau de tabac are on the left. (Collection Benoit Sadry)*

in a hamlet called Le Repaire just outside of Oradour, might have escaped. He learned, however, that on that fateful morning Martial Senon had been going about his business in the village, keeping the streets clean and tidy. Others had spoken to him and he, it seemed, had not escaped. Léon thought of Martial's poor wife Catherine. The couple had lost a son, Raymond, five years earlier and it had hit Catherine hard. He wondered about their daughter Marie-Marguerite, known to most as 'Camille'. She, he knew, worked in Limoges and travelled home for Saturday evenings. Léon only hoped that she had not arrived in time.

Léon Beaulieu saw sights that had hitherto been unimaginable to him. Teams would need to be sent by him, he thought, to work through the debris and human remains in order to make the streets passable. There was some good news, however – a crumb of comfort in the circumstances. He got news that two of his men had survived. One of these, Pierre Gabriel, a man of his own age who lived with his wife Anna and looked after a *pupille de l'assistance publique* in a tiny hamlet just outside the village, had survived. The news was tempered by the discovery that the girl that they looked after as their own daughter, Yvonne Delavault, had died in the church. Pierre with his wife, who he later learned had also been caring for a Jewish baby,[3] had found the one surviving child from the schools of Oradour. He had come across a young boy, not yet 8 years old, shivering and hidden in some bushes, and had taken him to safety. The young boy was called Roger Godfrin.

Destinies

It was only in a letter sent from Limoges on 1 July 1944 that Amélie Simon received confirmation that her 'Guiguitte', 11-year-old Marguerite, who she had struggled to bring up alone, was dead. Amélie responded on 8 July – probably the date she received that missive – writing directly to her brother Hippolyte Redon. He responded by answering questions regarding formalities that were to come and providing a new address which, because it included 'par Javerdat' rather than Oradour-sur-Glane, would ensure that post would

Marguerite Simon had been brought up by her mother in Paris before being sent to her uncle Hippolyte Redon in 1943 for safety. (Collection Benoit Sadry)

arrive a little quicker. The box of flour that he had readied to send her had been destroyed at the post office in Oradour. He would, he said, send some of theirs. He included a photo of his son, Pierrot, and of 'the poor little martyr', Marguerite. He described the search for recognisable bodies in the remains:

> They are still searching for bodies amongst the rubble. They have just removed some men from the village who were in the old Beaulieu forge. They found glasses belonging to J[ean] Dupic, Valentin, Chapelot, Nicolas or Beaubreuil. I do not recall who the others were.[1]

Nobody survived from the christening gathering at the Milord household, nor the Roumy engagement party. Of the Hyvernaud family gathered to see the new Joyeux baby, everyone was killed. In the Villatte family, baby Christian and his mother Christiane were among the dead. Those children who had been looking forward to the celebration of the *fête-dieu* the following day by making bonnets, died. Large families were wiped out. Four-year-old Simone Poutaraud lost both of her parents and six siblings.

None of the Vichy-installed mayoral team was spared. According to some witnesses, even those who showed their papers to soldiers on the *Champ de foire* to demonstrate their various allegiances were laughed away. Former GTE camp warden Jean Henry, who had left the village that morning by tram to find out whether trains were running so he could return to his teaching job near Paris, later discovered that his wife Gilberte and 2-year-old Michelle had been killed. The Lévignac children, left in Oradour for the summer, died. No Parisian families or children placed in the safety of the countryside survived. Nor did the refugees from Alsace-Lorraine or Spain who were in the wrong place at the wrong time. Provenance, political belief, age or religion made no difference. The priests were killed, babies were killed, old men and women were killed. Parents who had come to the village to look for their children were killed. Cyclists just passing through on a Saturday ride were killed. Shoppers from Limoges, only in the village because they were desperate to find food, were murdered – no opportunity given for them to show their identity cards.

Albert Valade's sister Germaine and his young niece and nephew died, as well as his cousin Marcel, there to hide from STO. Camille Senon's father, grandfather, aunt, uncle, first cousin and many other relations died. Robert Hébras' mother and two sisters died. All family belonging to André Desourteaux, who lived in Oradour, except for Uncle Hubert, died. He lost his parents whose romance had stoked the flames between the two political giants Joseph Beau and Paul Desourteaux, both of whom were killed. All of the teachers were killed – Léonard and Jeanne Rousseau along with their two children, Denise Bardet who was celebrating her birthday, Raymonde Vincente, Andrée Binet, Fernand Gougeon and Odette Couty on her last day in post. They all died. Odette's father Gaston, who was in the Resistance, was arrested and deported the following day not knowing the fate of his daughter. He died in a concentration camp in 1945.

Giuseppe Miozzo had come to France from Padova in 1927 with his family for a better life as a tenant farmer but had been deported in March 1941 because he had refused to sign up to serve militarily under Mussolini. In September 1943 he was deported to Germany. After the war he would find out that his 39-year-old wife had been rounded up and killed along with seven of their nine children. His eldest daughter, who was already married and had moved away, and 15-year-old Angelina, who had run away when she saw a soldier approaching, were the family's only survivors.

After burying his 14-year-old sister Sarah, and telling his parents of their loss, David Jakobowicz took to hiding in the fields around Saint-Victurnien. Antoine Bardet, the mayor of the village, had agreed to hide his wife and child while his parents stayed on at *Maison-Blanche*. David spent some evenings with them but *Milice* activity in and around the area was intense, especially as the German army moved through. Eventually David took his entire family to Cieux for a short period until the region settled down.

A few weeks later, late at night, Perette Sauvet, to whom Mathieu Borie had gone at the end of his mammoth walk following the massacre, was home alone; her husband was at a parachute drop. A knock came at the door of their house. Isolated and wary, Perette let two men in. They were looking for her husband, code name 'Camille'. She did not know them and took the precaution of isolating them at gunpoint until her husband returned. These men were Robert Hébras and André Desourteaux, who had come to join the *maquis* of Cieux. That *maquis* had established some element of control in that area. *Le Commandant* Bérnard and his lieutenant Gaston Texier, originally from a hamlet just outside Saint-Victurnien, knew Jakobowicz and they did what they could to keep the family safe, first in Cieux, then back at *Maison-Blanche*, while the battle to liberate the region began. After the liberation of Limoges and the rest of France, in September 1944 the Jakobowicz family moved Sarah's body from the temporary grave dug by David on the evening of 11 June to a Jewish grave in Limoges.

A Question of Survival

Nothing could have prepared Camille Senon for the days that followed the massacre. She went back into the village to help where she could as a massive recovery and clean-up operation began:

> Those few days were terrible because the occupation forces did not let the search and rescue or the catholic theology students sent to help, into the village to begin the clear up. They only let them in on the follow- ing Tuesday so, with the exception of the church and the barn […] the places of execution were not known. They only found those by going from building [to building] in an effort to find human remains. The people from the surrounding villages, particularly the parents of schoolchildren, were coming to try to find things that had belonged to their children; pieces of

Searching the debris and wreckage of homes for belongings. (Collection Association Nationale des Familles des Martyrs d'Oradour-sur-Glane)

clothing [...] or where bodies had fallen one on top of the other and not completely burnt.'

Bodies were found in the well of the Picat farm but they were not identified. Similarly, bodies were found in the oven of one of the bakeries. The charred remains of a baby were found in a metal dustbin:

> One day there was a mother; she picked up a hand which looked like the hand of a young girl; well looked after. She said, 'This is my daughter's hand, I recognise it', and she took it home with her. And then, two years later she said, 'I have no proof that this is my daughter's hand', and she brought it back and put it into one of the two glass-topped coffins that sit atop the tomb.

The day after the massacre, the sub-prefect took Jean-Marcel Darthout to the hospital in Saint-Junien but it was there that they found out that Gestapo agents, probably French *miliciens*, were trying to track down survivors. For safety, he took Darthout instead to the hospital at Confolens. On arrival he went into surgery to remove lodged bullets. He was left there under a cloak of secrecy to begin his recovery. Marguerite Rouffanche had been taken to the large *Château de Laplaud* where the owner had given her first aid for several days while the rumours abounded that survivors were being tracked. Eventually, on becoming very ill she had to be sent to the hospital in Limoges where she remained until late October.

Whispers

An ordinary, peaceful large village community, Oradour had never become a place linked to Resistance. It was no Sussac, or even Cieux. If anything, such places were to be avoided by Nazi commanders hoping to carry out a short, sharp hit with no material losses. In terms of its selection for a 'brutal and lasting strike' that would scare the population into retreating away from any support of the Resistance, the village of Oradour-sur-Glane fulfilled a host of criteria that sealed its fate. It was easy to surround, with little likelihood of any resistance from within, or from any significant *maquis* group near enough to respond quickly. It was on a planned route for the next stage of the SS division's move north and it was quick to reach. In the course of one afternoon, it was chosen as an ideal marker. Moving northward, it wanted the people ahead to remember the example of what might happen to them: the village that had been wiped from the map, the one that used to be called Oradour-sur-Glane.

Closer to the centre of the tragedy, on a personal level and without that historical perspective, the people who had suffered most wanted answers. Who or what had caused their community to be chosen? At a time when French people were split and informers despised, the families and friends of victims, survivors and people who had lost everything they owned needed someone to blame. The soldiers had been faceless hordes; there must, some thought, have been a reason for what had happened to their village.

At first there were whisperings, and survivors interviewed during the inquest in November 1944 put forward their own ideas. None would hold up under the weight of examination, but they are interesting when considering the state of mind of those left behind. Southern France was, by September 1944, well used to the retaliatory justice being meted out in the full force of the *épuration* (purge).[1] Moreover, the French were used to the idea that they had just as many French enemies as German. They were used to the young men, and sometimes young women, who had been recruited by the *Milice,* carrying out identity checks of their own authorisation, strutting around towns in their uniforms usually in the safety of numbers. They were used to French men making arrests alongside the Gestapo and openly boasting about their engagement in the despised organisation. They were aware too of young men and women who saw fraternisation with the Germans as an opportunity. For men, it was an opportunity for quick advancement in the occupier's infrastructure, material gain and safety from any reprisals.

By the summer of 1944, the course of the war turned in favour of the Allies. These youngsters felt under pressure, knowing that they might have to flee with the Germans in order to ensure their own survival. Equally there were women who had taken to enjoying the company of German soldiers. Later, during the course of the *épuration*, these women would be heavily punished by *maquisards*. The women's behaviour was known as *collaboration horizontale;* this was just about unheard of in Oradour because so few Germans or even *miliciens* ever went there, but one young woman's name was immediately mentioned.

Jeanne Duquéroix was already suffering extreme grief when she was arrested by members of the FFI on 22 August 1944, along with her aunt in whose Limoges home she was staying. During the massacre she had lost her father, Pierre, in the Laudy-Mosnier barn, her mother and her sister Angélique, who was 23 at the time, just a year older than her. Jeanne was born in Oradour and had lived there until the family uprooted when she was 11 so that her father could serve as a private valet to a Jewish family in the 12th *arrondissement* of Paris. The family returned to the village in June 1940, joining the exodus south, once again taking up residence in the house that they already owned. Jeanne, Angélique and their parents lived together and also provided lodgings for a little boy called Jean Carrignon, a refugee from Paris who was 5 years old when he arrived and 8 years old when he died in the church. Angélique stayed in Oradour but Jeanne wanted to train as a secretary, and managed to secure a job in Limoges where, during the next three years, she fulfilled several posts. She also became involved with one of her bosses, a Monsieur Delbourg, becoming his mistress. She was arrested on suspicion of collaboration with the Germans but she and her aunt were quickly acquitted of any wrongdoing. This accusation, she claimed, must have been the work of her former boss Delbourg, spurned when she moved jobs, who she suspected denounced her and her aunt of links to the Gestapo.

The story did not, however, end there for Jeanne Duquéroix. Whether she admitted to her FFI interrogators or not, her September 1944 statement regarding the massacre at Oradour was unambiguous about how she, albeit after the massacre, *had* become intimately involved with a German Gestapo agent. On 27 June 1944, just two weeks after the drama in which her family had been killed, she received a knock on the door:

Around eleven o'clock at night. Two Germans in uniform came in who, I would later find out, were from the Gestapo. One of them, called Meyer, spoke French fluently. They interrogated me for around half an hour, asking if I had been the mistress of Monsieur Delbourg and if I knew Alice Pommier (my aunt).[2]

The two men showed Jeanne an anonymous letter claiming that Alice Pommier had been in relations with the *maquis*. Jeanne told Meyer that she believed the letter to be the work of Delbourg, in retaliation for her ending their former affair.

Delbourg was instead arrested by Meyer on charges of false denunciation and for wasting his time:

Following that he [Meyer] came several times to my office with the pretext of interviewing me. He had no other motive than to procure my favours and, afraid of being sent to Germany for STO or deported or imprisoned by Meyer I ceded. As a result, at the restaurant La Chaumière, in Limoges I twice had sexual relations with this German policeman.

Jeanne would have felt under considerable duress, and many young women would have found themselves in similar situations. How she must have felt on discovering that her name was being linked to the destruction of Oradour is difficult to conceive. There may be aspects of her personal story that are disturbing, but as she stated in her September 1944 interview:

I feel sick that I am suspected of having been something to do with this massacre. I too am a victim, having nothing left at all. If I had had something to do with this do you not think that I would have done something to save my own family?

Jeanne reported that, during the course of her conversations with Meyer, she had asked why Oradour had been annihilated. It is quite likely Meyer would not have known himself. According to Jeanne, she explained to the German that Oradour was her home, to which he responded that:

the people of Oradour killed some young SS men when they arrived there with their units. The women of the village then danced on the soldiers' bodies. This unit had just returned from the Russian front and when their friends heard about the death of their own men they were disgusted and set fire to the village.

Nothing in Meyer's version, as reported by Jeanne Duquéroix, rings true but it is possible that it was the version of events which had been communicated to him:

I must say that I did not believe Meyer's words but I did not insist on the matter, nor protest to him. On another occasion I tried to question him about it but he told me to talk no more about it, nor did he provide any motive as to the massacre of the people. He did not want me to question him on the subject.

The interviews conducted during the inquest by the 20th *Brigade régionale de police de Sûreté* provide an insight into some of the other stories doing the rounds. By the time the interviews took place, enough time had passed for the survivors to have exchanged ideas. Interviewees were asked about possible links to the *Milice* that might explain the choice of Oradour. It is no slight on these witnesses who gave their thoughts, reflective of a lot of hearsay and rumours. One interviewee who had lost his wife and two of his daughters had, on the day of the massacre, been in Saint-Victurnien. As this particular interviewee was not a witness to the events of the day he was not asked to testify at later legal proceedings:[3]

I don't know what could have caused this tragedy. I was present, however, sometime during last Spring, at a conversation between several clients of the *Café du Chêne*, run by [Lucien] Morlieras in Oradour, all of whom died during the massacre, and François Desourteaux, a son of the doctor and delegated Mayor, a notary clerk in Paris. This man had come to Oradour for a holiday with his family. In my presence he said the following to those present: 'Personally, if I was Pétain, there would already have been forty men shot in Oradour'. Monsieur Hyvernaud the elder, since deceased, asked him for the reasons and pressed him for a response. Just then the owner intervened and prohibited the conversation from continuing. It stayed there.

The witness' version of events, which he had seemingly made known to plenty of people since the day of the massacre and had even reported to the FFI and other investigators, was heavily contested by another witness. Adrien

Aymard, a mechanic who was also present, confirmed that the conversation had taken place, but that it had happened a year earlier than claimed, in 1942:

> We were in the kitchen of that café and the discussion turned to the politics of Marshal Pétain. At some point, François Desourteaux gave his opinion, directed at Fernand Hyvernaud:[4] 'If the Marshal was as bad as you seem to claim you would have been shot.' The discussion was about to get animated when the owner intervened and personally, I did not want the discussion to continue.[5]

Aymard quoted another witness to events and said that everyone was aware of what was being said about the incident, but that he denied it thoroughly. He also said that, as the incident had occurred so long ago, and that François Desourteaux had rarely visited the village since, he was sure it had nothing to do with what had transpired.

The exchange is representative of the strength of support for, or rejection of, Pétain in 1942 and 1943. Many former conservatives, including Hyvernaud it seems, had by then turned against the regime and even the marshal himself. That Lucien Morlieras felt it best to put an end to such a public discussion is also telling. It is suggestive of a fear of an overly interested public audience.

Clearly young François Desourteaux was Pétainist at that moment, but many people changed their opinion over the course of the war. His father, by then the delegated mayor, was known to be supportive of the regime. As has already been described, Oradour was typical in being politically split, and the Desourteaux family represented the right. On the day of the massacre, political allegiances meant nothing. François Desourteaux was at his home in Paris. He lost most of his family in the massacre too and died at the age of 63 in 1971.

The same witness, when asked it is assumed, also spoke about the Roumy family, even going so far as to suggest that the homes of Roumy's friends were avoided in the round-up. Jean Roumy, an agricultural vendor in the centre of Oradour, was another Pétainist. But having faith in the marshal and his policies, even into the final months of the war, did not make a person an active collaborator. The witness suggests that Roumy may have known that something was about to happen in the town. He mentions a visit paid to his widowed mother-in-law Marie Blanchon, accompanied by his son Albert, on the morning of the massacre. According to this story the men had been to visit a farm that they owned in order to visit tenants. On their return they called on Roumy's mother-in-law to give her part of a pig. Albert, it was claimed, was heard to say, 'Father, we need to be on our way to see what is going on in Oradour. It is really unfortunate for the young people who will have to go to Germany.' Quite who claimed to have overheard the utterance is not mentioned.

The story only added to rumours that the Roumy family had been aware of a round-up of forced labour planned for that weekend. Fernand Lesparat, through his cousin Albert Mirablon, might also have known something. The truth is never likely to be known. Marie Blanchon herself made a statement, however, that is tellingly different. She gives far more detail about her son-in-law's weekend, adding that she had been visited not only by Jean and

Jean, Albert and Marie Roumy. A trader in agricultural chemicals and seeds, Jean was head of the Oradour chapter of the Légion. Albert, assumed to be a milicien, was nothing of the sort, and was in Oradour to celebrate his engagement. (Collection Benoit Sadry)

Albert, but by one of Albert's friends, Pierre d'Albois who was staying with the Roumy family in Oradour because he was unable to get home because of train trouble. According to Marie, it was Jean who made the comment that would be later misconstrued:

> My son-in-law must have had a premonition, because at one point he said, 'Well my boys, we must get going, you never know what might happen. I fear for the kids; if someone came, they could be taken off to Germany.'[6]

Such unhealthy and unhelpful rumours propagated at a fast pace. The mention of the Roumy family lasted well beyond the trial that would take place in 1952. In the mid-1980s Paul Doire, a baker who at the time of the massacre was in northern Haute-Vienne, was interviewed on camera. He had lost a 17-year-old daughter in the massacre. In the interview,[7] he claimed that it was a good thing the Roumy men had not survived as they would have been killed afterwards. His belief was that young Albert Roumy was a *milicien*. He was not alone in describing Albert as such.

Marie Blanchon explained what amounted to a simple misunderstanding of what her grandson did:

> I know about the rumours surrounding my grandson, Albert Roumy, as being a *milicien*. I was never aware of him being part of such an organisation and I do not believe it. The truth is that in order to escape the possibility of being taken by STO, he enrolled himself in the *formation Todt* where he worked as a deputy superintendent at the 'SET in Bordeaux'.

Albert had made the choice to work for the *organisation Todt* in Bordeaux from where he would be able to return occasionally and see his fiancée rather than risk being sent away to work in Germany.[8] Albert had been issued with a uniform which he had, rather inadvisably, worn in Oradour in the past. That those who had seen him in it could not tell the difference, of course, further suggests that real *miliciens* were rarely if ever seen in the village.

Clearly Jean Roumy visited his mother-in-law on the morning of 10 June. And he had of course led the Oradour branch of the *Légion*. But by that time the *Légion* had all but disappeared. He had rejected two of Vichy's central policies. He was no virulent Germanophile nor was he an anti-Semite, having befriended Robert and Carmen Pinède, who he well knew to be Jewish. He may still have believed in Pétain but that did not mean that he would have had reason to be involved in the planning of a massacre. Indeed, that weekend his son was home to celebrate his engagement to Ginette Couturier. Friends, such as Jean d'Albois, had been there too. It was a special weekend for them. Léon Couturier, father of Albert's fiancée Ginette who lived in Limoges, had got to know his daughter's future father-in-law Jean Roumy well:

> I had had the opportunity to talk with him about international events and I can affirm on my honour that Monsieur Roumy, father, was far from being a collaborator. The son, Albert, was not a *milicien*. If it was his uniform that led some to suppose the opposite, that was his uniform of a 'supervised worker'. He had been living in Bordeaux since 15 June 1943, the date that he should have left for Germany […] He had been on leave for a fortnight which should have ended on 11 June. But I gave him advice, I told him to go with his friend to Villemonteix to hide, so as not to be picked up by the Germans. My daughter was going to have to return home alone, the Tuesday morning, by tramway.[9]

Albert's friend Jean d'Albois had arranged to meet his parents, who lived in Compiègne, on Monday 12 June in Paris, assuming the trains were running. He never arrived because, like his friend Albert, he was murdered in the massacre. Jean Roumy also died, as did his wife Marie, and their daughter-in-law-to-be Ginette Couturier who was in the church. Jean Roumy's remains were identified in the Desourteaux barn.

On 2 November 1944 the newspaper *La Marseillaise du Centre* published a 'clarification':

> The lieutenant commanding the *groupe Marc, groupe de police, 2ème bureau* in Bordeaux, certifies that Albert Roumy of Oradour-sur-Glane, general deputy superintendant at the SET in Bordeaux, was part of a Resistance group. He rendered us, amongst others, significant services by facilitating our access to the Saint Jean station, providing us with documents of admission onto the trains, and providing information that was precious for our services.

There were undoubtedly other families who were fully behind Pétain or who might have expressed their views openly in the past. But expressing right-wing opinions and actively collaborating were poles apart. Most of Oradour's population, like most people in southern France, were living their lives apolitically, trying to keep their heads down and putting food on the family table. There is evidence of only one letter of collaboration received by the authorities from an Oradour resident in November 1941. This did not stop further rumours, in the months that followed the drama, that somebody local had brought the tragedy on the village.

The Barthélémy family was the subject of rumours. On 1 April 1944 the couple had begun preparations to relocate north by travelling to their 'villa' in Montlouis in order to clean it. 'I decided to stay there alone,' said Marcelle in her later interview,[10] 'to avoid the house being requisitioned as a shelter for the victims of the Tours region, given that we had all decided to come home for good once my son had finished his studies.' One *paysan*, 38-year-old Marie Roby from Les Bordes, told investigators that the 'family, refugees from Paris' often came to see her for vegetables. Albert Barthélémy had last come on 2 June when he told the neighbour that he was going to leave Oradour to go home to Montlouis and that it was his son's examinations that had prevented him from doing so beforehand:

> He added that he was due to go home and leave Oradour-sur-Glane behind on Tuesday 13 June 1944. He had explained to me some time before that he had managed to find a way of sending his possessions, notably his valuables, to his home in Mountlouis by truck, adding that he had even sent potatoes.
>
> During the same conversation he had added, 'you people simply do not know what war is, but we might all yet learn'. He added that he said that, being 'well-informed'. I thought that he wanted to scare us because he was an avid Anglophobe.

Marie Roby also claimed that she had heard, second hand, that 'because he was not liked in the community, he said he would have revenge on its inhabitants'. She said that the garage in which he had left his two cars had not been burned, which is certainly inaccurate.

He was a man who had made some enemies. Not only did the same witness say that he was 'clearly a collaborator' but another neighbour from the same village, Martial Thomas, told investigators that he, along with Monsieur and Madame Roby and another villager, had signed an FFI joint statement against him when they had visited after the massacre. Thomas described him as a:

> fervent collaborator who never missed an opportunity to praise the work of the Germans. He said to me sometimes, 'Don't believe Hitler wants to hold dominion over us if he wins the war. He will have far too much to do and will not have time to worry about us.' He was always praising Hitler's regime, he kept on at it and told us that if we were unhappy, it was just our

fault. He told me once that in Germany there was a factory which, instead of making packaging for butter was really making aeroplanes [...] he told me that he knew that war was going to break out and in order to place his money somewhere safe he had bought a property [...] he did not hide that he had transferred his account from Paris to the bank in Bordeaux, and some to Limoges.

Pierre Tarnaud had for a long time sold milk to Barthélémy. 'I chased him away one day when he said that we needed Germany to win the war so that a new order could be imposed on us. From that moment on he was not welcome in my home.'[11] Aimé Renaud said that Barthélémy was 'known as a big collaborator within the village'. Fernand Lesparat had told him that Barthélémy:

had filled up his car with petrol and blown up his tyres. This information is definitely true. He [Lesparat] believed that Barthélémy was informed on events and at the least was preparing for his departure whatever the event that was to come might turn out to be. At that time, we feared the *Milice* as much as the Germans, they were constantly checking everyone's papers.[12]

Why Aimé Renaud would claim this, given that *miliciens* rarely, if ever, came near to Oradour, is unclear. Tram passengers to Limoges, however, did often get their papers checked.

Clearly feelings ran high towards some individuals prior to the massacre, and these sentiments were only strengthened by the tragic events. Knowledge of the fate of these families would have been incomplete, only adding to suspicion. At the time of the depositions, there were still suspicions that Barthélémy had escaped with his son, quit the region and joined up with his wife. It emerged that only Marcelle Barthélémy, still in Monlouis-sur-Loire, was living. Alfred was killed along with his son Roger, who had just discovered that he had passed his exams and was celebrating his nineteenth birthday before preparing to rejoin his mother. Marcelle's mother had also died. Marcelle had received a letter informing her that her son had passed his examination and that her husband, son and mother would join them on 15 June, nine days after it had been posted. By then they were dead but news spread so slowly that it was 1 July when she received another informing her that she had lost her family. She collapsed on her doorstep and was taken inside to be cared for by neighbours.

The region around Tours, liberated in September 1944, had been badly affected by bombing, making travel difficult but Marcelle finally travelled to Oradour on 12 October 1944. On arrival she was arrested by the FFI who took her to their barracks in Limoges for questioning. After a severe interrogation she was freed but told to return the following day for further questioning, after which she was interned and accused of being an agent of the Gestapo. They told her they believed her husband had fled prior to the massacre and demanded that she must know where he was. It took eyewitness accounts of Barthélémy being present at the round-up on the *Champ de foire* to convince investigators.

> In preparation for our upcoming move, my husband had made preparations. He was so happy to be leaving Oradour where lately we had been suspected of being collaborators, which is absurd. People there could not understand how we were able to live there for so long without working and claimed that we would not have been able to do so if we had not been receiving money from the Germans. These suspicions really affected us since we had no relationship, direct or indirect, with any German service nor any agent, German or other-wise. In truth we lived very modestly in Oradour, from our own savings that we had made out of our business and linked to our property in Paris.[13]

The Inspector of Police in Limoges gave her several photos, bank notes, a letter and an identity document belonging to her son. There was also a small wallet that belonged to him. All had been half burnt. The Barthélémy bodies were never identified.

Wine merchant Léon Denis' name was also sullied. Denis owned the build-ing in which his family and the Barthélémys lived. They shared a garden and Pierre Tarnaud claimed that the two men were seen daily talking in their garden.[14] 'These two men spent lots of their time discussing politics. Someone told me that Monsieur Denis had in the past belonged to the Croix-de-Feu.'[15]

During investigations most people said they had no idea why Oradour had been targeted. Others came out in support of Barthélémy and Denis, having heard the rumours. Simply more outspoken than others, there would certainly have been plenty of other Pétainists in Oradour, just as throughout Vichy France. Françoise Verny, the widowed housekeeper to the Denis family who had worked for the wine merchant for fourteen years prior to the massa-cre, told the investigators how she believed the rumours had been overblown:

> I certainly never saw any Germans at Monsieur Denis' home, and I do not believe that [he] had any link to the occupation troops. But there is one thing of which I am absolutely sure. Madame Denis could not stand the

sight of them, nor bear talk of them. She really did not like them. I did
not know that the Denis family was known as one of fervent collaborators.
Nobody ever said anything about it to me.[16]

Had Verny been giving a statement laced with personal loyalty, or could it
have been that these men's political views were subsequently overblown?
She continued:

> I also knew the Barthélémy family, Parisian refugees, and Monsieur Denis'
> tenants. These two families got on well when they met up, but this was not
> that often. Their relationship was cordial; I never noticed Messieurs Denis
> and Barthélémy spouting any propaganda in favour of Germany. Sometimes
> they met in the garage but I never overheard them.

Léon Denis died in the massacre, as did his wife Marie, daughter Simone and
son-in-law and business partner Henri Texeraud with their children, 8-year-
old Josette and 2-year-old Jean Claude. Léon Denis was shot in his own barn,
along with Texeraud, after doing all they could to buy time by providing the
Germans with motor cars while gathered on the *Champ de foire*. In the 'Chai
Denis', a recognisable though mostly carbonised body was found – that of
Doctor Paul Desourteaux. Léon Denis' tobacco card was also found there.

Patry

In August 1944, Georges Coudert and a friend were having a drink in a bar in the *Café Gambetta*, in central Limoges. They began chatting to a man called Patry who was sitting alone, drinking at the bar. 'In the course of telling us about all the operations he had done with the Germans, he told us that he was not at all as nasty as was made out by others.' He told them about an old woman who he had intervened to save in the town of Blond, without giving any specific details. He also boasted that he had intervened with some soldiers who had stolen some sugar ration tickets in the same region, a known *maquis* area. Then he told them that he had been at the massacre of Oradour-sur-Glane:

> This sparked my interest because my fiancée, a primary school teacher in the village, had died there. I quizzed him further. Patry said that, during the massacre he had asked the commanding officer whether he might have permission to save a young girl whose father he knew well and with whom he was friendly. The officer told him that if he insisted, he would be shot himself. [1]

Patry had been talking to Georges Coudert, police inspector and fiancé of Denise Bardet.

By the time he was interviewed, Eugène Patry, a 31-year-old interpreter for the Gestapo and father of two, had been arrested by the FFI and interned ever since. He claimed that he had not been at Oradour but the new revelation brought forward by Coudert was followed up by the police commissioner. This time he admitted the conversation with Coudert and acknowledged the story he had told. 'It is however,' he told his questioner, 'absolutely false that I participated in any manner whatsoever in the massacre. I can only maintain my previous testimony [...] and underline once more that I have never been to Oradour-sur-Glane and that on 10 June I did not leave Limoges.' He said he had been on leave, his wife ready to give birth. 'I wanted to sound important and interesting, but it was not my intention nor wish to provoke a reaction from the two men.' [2]

Strangely, this was not the first time Patry had told the story. André Joyeux was a tobacconist in Limoges who had lost his mother Catherine, a divorcee who had moved from Paris to be near family. One day, during the weeks following the event, he had shown some photographs of the ruins to a client in his shop. The photographs showed charred bodies amongst burnt-out buildings. At that moment another client, who happened to be an agent of the French Gestapo, arrested Joyeux and took him to the Villa Tivoli, headquarters of the *Milice*. First, he was questioned by a German general called Meier then passed to a French agent who spoke French fluently with a German accent. This agent, who Joyeux described as having greyed brown hair, a wide jawbone and a square chin, slightly slanting eyes, slightly stooped and with an unwelcoming appearance, was Eugène Patry. The agent asked Joyeux why he had been showing the photos, to which Joyeux responded that he had lost his mother, but that in showing the photos he had made an error in judgement. Patry took him aside, into a cloakroom, and told the story of the young girl he had tried to save. 'I am also a father of two children,' he told Joyeux. 'I was there at the massacre of Oradour-sur-Glane. I saw men, women and children killed. I had a friend, an Alsatian, who worked at the barber shop belonging to Monsieur Morlieras.' Joyeux told Patry that he had known this man personally. Patry continued, 'Since this young barber was married with a kid, I tried my best with the officer in charge of the column to get permission to adopt the little girl. That officer […] turned to me and said that if I carried on I would be shot myself. I left terribly upset.'

What Patry had been trying to achieve with his false story, beyond self-aggrandisement, is hard to say, but it does suggest that he may well have been to Oradour in the lead-up to the event and that the barber in question, the German-born Jew and popular member of the football team Joseph Bergmann, was either under surveillance or really a friend of Patry. He did not, however, have a little girl, but a young son. Patry's story may provide evidence that Oradour-sur-Glane had been discussed as a target during meetings that he had attended on 9 and 10 June in Limoges and Saint-Junien.

Filliol

Jean Filliol, originally from the Dordogne, was known as '*le tueur de la Cagoule*' (the killer of the Cagoule), having played a role in several crimes for that far-right group, including the assassination of two Italian anti-fascists in 1937. Interned in the Limousin camp Saint-Paul-d'Eyjaux by order of Pierre Laval in November 1942, he was released in the spring of 1944 when old friend Joseph Darnand decided that he wanted him to lead the *Milice* under Jean de Vaugelas, who had just been named *directeur général du maintien de l'ordre* for the region. From May 1944, Filliol was the *directeur général* of the *Deuxième service*, the 'action and information' service – a kind of Gestapo of the French *Milice*. He operated under the name Deschamps and gathered around him a small team, including Eugène Patry, Camille Davoine and Jean Thomine. They set up in *la caserne du petit séminaire* where they questioned and tortured suspected *maquisards* on the second floor of building B, room 19. On 10 May 1944 they had participated side by side with the Germans in a round-up of suspects in an area around Périgueux. They had also arrested, among others, Victor Renaud of the Alliance network. A witness recognised Renaud and lived to tell the tale of the behaviour and cruelty of these Frenchmen:

> Throughout several night-time sessions he also was taken to room 19 for countless interrogations carried out by Filliol and his torturers. Some nights we were taken there together. He displayed an indomitable bravery, revealing nothing [...] of his patriotic commitment, nor of the help he had provided to the F.T.P. [...] He entrusted his watch to my brother to be handed over to his little François [...] and on June 23, 1944, at about 4:30 pm, he, with our two comrades and two other young maquisards of the Limousin [...] were shot under the walls of *la Maison d'arrêt* de Limoges, 11 bis, place du *Champ de foire.*[1]

Jean Filliol, who escaped justice at the end of the war, attended a meeting on 9 June in Limoges, to which other *miliciens* were summoned. He was tasked with designating four teams of four to accompany the SS on a mission the following day 'in the course of preparation, to take place in the area around Saint-Junien'. One testimony was provided by Camille Davoine, a 26-year-old former hairdresser originally from northern France who had also served alongside Joseph Darnand and had been placed in Limoges as a result. For several months he had been serving in Vichy and then Limoges as a *milicien* and inspector for the *Police aux Questions juives*. It is quite evident from his testimony and the testimony of the survivors of Oradour that no *miliciens* were present at the massacre. None were seen in the village or its environs. Instead they had that morning been rerouted to other operations in the area. Filliol told them during the meeting of the ninth that their role would be to 'curb the excesses of the Germans'.[2] On the mission to which Davoine had been assigned, there is no doubt that he was given clear opportunity to do this when a single man out of fifty was beaten up. We know little more about these operations, but this may all have been part of the planning.

After much more questioning Eugène Patry decided to give a further revised statement. He had been lying about so much more than the story of the girl he claimed to have tried to save. He had not been on leave and had been part of the delegation that had been sent to Saint-Junien on 8 June 1944 following the shooting of a German soldier near the railway station on the banks of the Vienne. His testimony confirmed the events of the following day and a half. He attended the meeting with Filliol and was part of one of the teams brought to Saint-Junien for a second time on the morning of 10 June. He had not been sent to Oradour, however, but had been sent on the same mission as Camille Davoine, to a village called Saillat-Chassenon, which was surrounded and men from a local factory rounded up because the factory manager was rumoured to have been supplying oil to the *maquis*.

That operation had taken place at the same time as another unit of the SS *Das Reich* was in Oradour. Patry had seen *SS-Sturmbannführer* Adolf Diekmann in Saint-Junien before the massacre and again when they returned before departing to billet in Nieul. According to Patry, nobody from the SD, the SS's own Gestapo, or the French police or *miliciens* had been sent to Oradour. It is highly likely that the Frenchmen were included in the meetings that led to the selection of Oradour-sur-Glane, and perhaps even in supplying local information, but it seems Diekmann decided that he wanted no civilian Frenchmen there, probably to avoid slowing the operation down, and to avoid future eyewitnesses.

According to Patry, he had been told that an operation would be taking place due to events that had occurred in Oradour-sur-Glane:

When we arrived in Saint-Junien, Lieutenant Kleist [of the Gestapo] went to get instructions at the HQ of the SS in the hotel opposite the station which we had been in the night before. I then saw the Commanding officer of the SS division Das Reich […] This was the officer that I saw again in Limoges, at the Gestapo HQ, the day following Oradour-sur-Glane. I'm not sure of his name.[3] Kleist was with him for about an hour. When he came back to us he told me that the *maquis* had attacked a car occupied by twelve SS men, and these twelve, which included a lieutenant, had been taken prisoner, taken to Oradour-sur-Glane and hanged, except the lieutenant who had escaped. He [Kleist] added that he did not want to follow this commander as he intended to take forty hostages in Oradour-sur-Glane and that he did not want to be present at these executions.

Patry could well have still been lying but in this, his third deposition, he had given a multitude of information that proved to be correct. If he is to be taken at his word, a web of lies was in the course of construction, stories that could easily be spread by hearsay.

It is very unlikely that Kleist would or could have chosen not to follow Diekmann, but more likely that he had been told to take the *miliciens* on a different assignment. Oradour-sur-Glane was going to be destroyed in its entirety. The story that was apparently given to Patry was a patchwork of lies based around the kidnapping of Kämpfe and the escape of *SS-Obersturmführer* Karl Gerlach who had been picked up by the *maquis* near Peyrilhac but managed to escape and return to Limoges on foot dressed only in his underwear. He had been taken to a village later claimed to be Oradour-sur-Glane, but that was part of the fabrication. Patry went on to give details of the reunited battalion's evening in Nieul, and an operation the next day in which the *château* of Morcheval was burned to the ground.

The Cathedral

Word had already spread about what had happened in Oradour but the local, regional or national press were not permitted to carry news of it by German censorship in Limoges. Even as seminarists and Red Cross teams travelled to and from the remains of the village for weeks after the massacre, details of what had happened remained sketchy in the extreme. On 21 June 1944, there was to be a service held in the cathedral of Limoges at half past nine in the morning, at which the Bishop Monseigneur Rastouil would speak in memory of the 'dead of these recent days'. Unable to publish details of the plans for the service in the press because of the lockdown on news of the massacre, Rastouil ensured that all churches in the diocese made their congregations aware of the plans. On hearing of these plans the Gestapo and *Milice* set about spreading the rumour that those who attended would be putting themselves in danger. They drip fed the word that caverns underneath the cathedral would be mined. When the day approached roadblocks, chicanes and security checks were set up in case any Resistance forces made a move on that poignant occasion.

During the course of his interview Patry confirmed that plans had been in place to carry out an attack:

> When the religious service was going to be conducted in Limoges Cathedral in memory of the victims of Oradour-sur-Glane, a former air force sub-officer by the name of Schmitt [...] from Châteauroux where he is well known, gave the orders to two Gestapo informers [...] to blow up the cathedral by placing a bomb in the underground passages of the cathedral. The bomb was going to be supplied by Schmitt who was chief interpreter and in charge of informants for the Limoges Gestapo.

The bomb never exploded. Additionally, two further Gestapo officers, including Joseph Meyer, were charged with attending the service and providing reports on the sermon given by Rastouil and other dignitaries. In the case that his or others' speeches used language that was deemed 'against Germany, they had to stop the service. The car that was to take him [Rastouil] was ready in front of the building.' Despite the presence of troops Rastouil spoke out against the 'acts of indescribable savagery committed by Hitler's "panzers", massacring hundreds of innocents'. The day was declared a day of mourning, and all shops, cafés and restaurants closed. At once it would be a 'grandiose demonstration of sympathy to honour the martyrs of Oradour, while at the same time a protest against the barbaric Germans'.[1]

Public buildings and the offices of the newspaper *Le Courrier du Centre* put out flags ribboned in black and at half mast. Journalist Pierre Poitevin, who had spent the final two years of the war recording some of the Nazis' worst crimes in the area, often clandestinely and from as close a standpoint as he could manage, described the event: 'Despite the fear and the terror that the Germans provoked, despite the possibility of incidents which kept many women, young ladies and children away, an immense crowd gathered that Wednesday morning in the cathedral.'

This crowd of 'twenty thousand, more perhaps', noticed that, as the solemn high mass was ending, Rastouil did not deliver the prayers of pardon, instead bringing the service to a premature close. The prefect, Freund-Valade, had got up to warn Rastouil that the police had arrested two men, and found some unusual tunnelling in a nearby building. There was a very real fear of explosives underground. The archbishop slowly finished off the service so as not to evoke panic in the crowd. The congregation, some of whom had heard the rumours started by the *Milice*, knew that the service had been ended early and dispersed, but did not panic. That same afternoon another service, again attended by Monseigneur Rastouil, the Protestant pastor Chaudier and the regional prefect Freund-Valade, took place in the ruins of Oradour itself. Written copies of the speeches were disseminated by the Resistance. News of the massacre also travelled through a letter, reproduced identically, always beginning 'Dear Aunt' and containing a full account of the massacre in the words of a loved one so as to circumvent the news censorship.[2]

Twenty days later, Rastouil, with whom the *Milice* were furious, was finally arrested – this time because he had refused to play his part in a religious service in honour of the Vichy minister Philippe Henriot who had been assassinated. Neither did he attend a ceremony organised in honour of Henriot at the *Monument des Morts*. He was taken away at eight o'clock the day following the ceremony, arrested as a criminal and put under house arrest in Châteauroux.

The Same Question

'I was a quite shocked to find out that there had been some escapees from that village because we left on the principle that, as far as we knew, there were no survivors.'

'Did you think, thank God that someone survived?'

'No. Honestly I did not think that, at least not at the time. I have to be completely honest.'

Heinz Barth, East Berlin, 1983

The question that survivors were asked more than any other was always the same. Why, in your opinion, was Oradour destroyed?

'I still ask the question, why this massacre,' said Robert Hébras who, at the time of writing, still works hard representing Oradour's past and is the last remaining of only five survivors of the shootings:

Why this massacre of innocents? If this had been a place where there was Resistance, well that would have been one thing. That would have been dramatic, but this is the only place in France where it was simply a crime. There were no German soldiers, there was no Resistance, there was nothing around.

If you take all the others; If you take Ascq, if you take Maillé [...] in all the others there was an attack on the German army and reprisals. In Oradour that was not the case. It was a *'crime gratuite'* [...] If there had been the least thing we, the people, would not have gone to the assembly point like a flock of sheep [...] On the *Place* we were just chatting; we did not think for a single second about death. That might seem odd, but that is how it was. Before that day there was perhaps 50 per cent of the population, and I am being modest, who had never seen a German in their lives.[1]

Camille Senon has had over seventy years to consider why her family's home village was chosen for destruction: 'We had absolutely no idea why this massacre took place. We still do not know.'

At the *procès de Bordeaux*, which took place in 1953, and at which Camille testified along with many of the other survivors, none of the officers that gave any of the important orders were present. The men that attended were, on the whole, 'foot soldiers', and none had had any say. The man probably most responsible, *SS-Brigadeführer* Heinz Lammerding was protected from extradition in the RFA (West Germany). His immediate superiors, *SS-Standartenführer* Sylvester Stadler, *SS-Hauptsturmführer* Otto Kahn and *SS-Untersturmführer* Heinz Barth, were all absent too. They had already ensured, through carefully planned narratives, that *SS-Sturmbannführer* Adolf Diekmann was the man inculpated, almost entirely, and fortune favoured them when he was killed in battle in Normandy just weeks after the massacre at Oradour. What angers Camille Senon is that the politics of entente intervened and deprived the victims and the survivors of Oradour of their justice. 'We were not allowed to know the reasons, the pretexts, for this massacre.'[2]

This is perhaps where justice failed. Had Oradour-sur-Glane not been chosen then another place would have suffered instead. But an honest post-war statement from the likes of Lammerding, rather than a half-baked insistence on blaming the action on largely unrelated events such as the kidnapping of Kämpfe or Gerlach meant that the *Radounauds* would always be suspected of armed Resistance in the village. Even when two French journalists managed to track Lammerding down in Germany for an interview, prior to writing a book in 1969, Lammerding stuck to his story.[3] That questions would hang over the people of the village for having had some role in their own destiny; that there might have been *maquis* activity or explosives stored there, or that an SS officer was taken there. All hokum, and all theories that fed straight into the hands of revisionist historians or sensationalist journalists.

In the weeks that followed the massacre, Robert Hébras and the other survivors went into a kind of semi-clandestinity, but Hébras did eventually join the *maquis*:

> I stayed with my sister for eight days or so before going into the *maquis*. I was told that the *Milice* were looking for six survivors; the five men and Madame Rouffanche. I heard this through an intermediary of Monsieur Barthélémy. They had asked if I was at work. Darthout was in hospital and Madame Rouffanche too.

For him the Resistance became a place of refuge:

In a way the Resistance came to save me. I stayed there because I was alone. I did not have a home to go to. I went to the Atlantic front, to Saint Nazaire. I wanted revenge. I asked twice for a transfer to the First army, but I was twice refused. The colonel said to me, 'you, you stay with me.'

Camille Senon stayed with her mother Catherine in Le Repaire, where she tried to come to terms with the loss of her father, grandfather, aunt, uncle and countless cousins. She was and remains a strong woman, forceful and driven. Helping the teams to clear the site and find bodies is proof of her inner mettle. The work was horrific. Her mother, whose life had always been at home, had never really got over the death of Raymond. In Le Repaire, her life had consisted of sewing for some extra income and tending the few chickens and rabbits that they could afford while her husband Martial went out to work on the roads. She looked after the small garden and cooked meals. She had found satisfaction in Le Repaire before the killings. When Camille told her mother that she would need to go back to Limoges to resume work, her mother knew that she did not have enough income to cover the rent of her home. Very little state aid was forthcoming because a war was still on,[4] so her mother moved in with Camille in Limoges in September 1944. The shock of losing so much had affected Catherine very badly, and she became progressively more ill.

In late 1946 Camille applied for a position with the PTT in Strasbourg, and she was successful in the *concours*. Her mother, still quite ill, joined her three months after she got there. While both women had a fondness for the people of Alsace and Lorraine, having both got to know many refugees who had come to Oradour during the war period, neither had been aware of the story of the *malgré-nous*, which they learned during the three and a half years that they spent there before moving to Paris. They learned about the suffering of the people of the region during the annexation by the Nazis, and of the violence with which Germanisation of the region had been applied. How the French language had been prohibited in all places with dire consequences for those caught speaking or writing it. That names of places, and people's own family and first names had to be Germanised, and that even the *beret basque* had been banned. Camille felt a very real solidarity with the families who had been forced to live under such tough conditions, and learnt how many such families had undergone plundering of their own young men, boys even, to go and fight with the German army in the final years of the war. This, for most, was not a choice and they had to go '*malgré-eux*', despite themselves.

Despite this knowledge, and this affinity with the people of that region, Camille was shocked in 1953 when called to give evidence in the *Procès de Bordeaux*. Of those twenty-two men standing trial for their part in the massacre, fourteen were from Alsace-Lorraine. Thirteen of these young men had, the court learned, been *malgré-nous*. Camille was brought to tears by this:

> I was shocked and confused that Alsatians, whose sufferance I knew and understood, had been able to be part of the SS, that they had been able to participate in the massacre. But when I thought about it, and when they said that they had been sent by force it changed, for me at least. At the end of the war they were recruiting youngsters, younger and younger all the time. It was easy to pressurise them, and to threaten reprisals on their families if they refused. It was easy to make them 'have to' join against their will.[5]

The very idea of Frenchmen carrying out the massacre added a different dimension to the 1953 Bordeaux trial, a military tribunal. One of the soldiers convicted in 1953 was found to have spent a year in the village with his family as a refugee in 1939. These *malgré-nous* were then almost immediately pardoned. Relations between the survivors of Oradour, the people of Alsace-Lorraine and the French government were strained to breaking point as a result. Robert Hébras was called to give his testimony, but he just had to stand and recount what he had already said before. During the week-long trial the witnesses' role was extremely limited, and this frustrated Robert Hébras and Camille Senon, both of whom testified. 'I was not allowed in because I was a witness,' says Robert Hébras. 'I was told by the president,' who was Marcel Nussy Saint-Saëns, nephew of the great French composer, '"Monsieur Hébras, mention the facts, only the facts and be brief". The whole thing lasted about ten minutes.'[6]

According to *Life* magazine, 'the spectacle of French criminals lumped with Germans so incensed deputies from Alsace that they talked of quitting the assembly. And France had to face the fact that the most vicious of Oradour's slayers had escaped.'[7]

'It was a tragedy, this business with Alsace because there was a deep rift between the people of Limousin and the people of Alsace,' says Camille Senon. 'On one side, the Limousins who said that they [the accused Alsatian *malgré-nous* SS soldiers] had participated in the massacre and they were guilty. The amnesties that were given, it was like our loved ones were killed again. But then you think of the Alsatians, they were saying that they had been victims too, that they had been annexed.'

The trial took place against the background of street protests in Strasbourg where the *monument aux morts* was veiled in black. 'The officers who had ordered the massacre were dead or unreachable, as were most of the Third Company, *Der Führer* Regiment, *Das Reich* SS Division who carried it out,' reported *Life* magazine. 'France could only enter the names of 44, believed to be fugitives in Germany, and try them in absentia with the second-string murderers it had been able to bring to the dock.'[8]

Two men were condemned to death. One, called Karl Lenz, was German and he admitted to killing in cold blood. Georges René Boos was the only Alsatian who had joined the SS of his own accord and his behaviour on the day had been deplorable on many counts. He was a sadist. When the thirteen Alsatians had their light sentences overturned by order of the French *assemblée nationale*, and the two death sentences were changed to prison sentences, the people of Oradour were angered, claiming that they had been martyred for a second time. A delegation from the *Association National des Familles des Martyrs*, led by André Desourteaux, returned the *Croix de la Légion d'honneur* to the prefect. They returned a bronze plaque presented in the name of the Republic by President Charles de Gaulle. The mayor later returned the *Croix de Guerre* that the community had received in 1948. The Communist party in particular led the protests and the names of the assembly members who had voted for the amnesty were displayed outside the *village martyr*.

Camille Senon sheds a tear when talking of the tensions between the two places and peoples that she knows so well: 'And now today, it really is the case that the generation who lived through 1944 need to disappear entirely. There are not many of us left now. But the wound is still deep, open and painful.'

Smokescreen

This is what Hitler's hordes are capable of!

The SS of 'Der Fuhrer' found it easier and less dangerous to attack a defenceless population than to face up to the maquis, who would have been capable of responding.

MUR pamphlet,[1] June 1944

Ector O. Munn was an American who worked for Supreme Headquarters Allied Expeditionary Force (SHAEF). He took photographs and wrote a report in the autumn of 1944 having interviewed survivors of Oradour himself in situ. In his very early but remarkably prescient appraisal he stated what was even then the most plausible reason for the choice of Oradour-sur-Glane:

The destruction of the lower village. (Collection Association Nationale des Familles des Martyrs d'Oradour-sur-Glane)

Oradour was small and easy to handle. It was prosperous and worthwhile looting, was located off the main highway, and was easy to reach from Limoges, where the battalion was spending Friday night, June 9th. If an impression was to be made on the countryside it would therefore serve as well as any other place.[2]

Simply put, Oradour-sur-Glane, unlike the much bigger Saint-Junien, had no *maquis* immediately nearby. One local who lived in La Plaine, near Veyrac to the south-west of Oradour, described the situation during an inquest:

In the month of June 1944 I was perfectly up to date with the location of the *maquis* groups in the region. There were those that we used to call the *maquis de Blond* which were stationed in the territory around the communities of Blond, of Cieux and of Peyrilhac. Another *maquis* group was camped in the region of Brigueil, about twenty kilometres from Oradour.

Subsequent research has found this mechanic, Adrien Aymard, to be correct:

Oradour was perfectly calm and there was no *état-major* (headquarters) installed nearby on 9 June. What is more I was perfectly aware of encounters between the *maquis* and the Germans in the area around Oradour and, to my knowledge, no German officer was taken prisoner in the surrounding area and taken to Oradour. It could not have been otherwise because as I said before there were no organised elements of Resistance in our communities […] The locality was perfectly calm during the entire day.[3]

Aymard was being interviewed in response to claims made by Major Otto Weidinger, in his regimental history of *Das Reich*, in relation to which his Oradour justifications made little sense.

The destruction of Oradour was quickly condemned by the German High Command, even before Pétain wrote to them to protest. There had been a recognition that soldiers were becoming undisciplined and 'attributing the fault to inhabitants judged responsible for an intolerable situation'. This was leading to exaggerated actions from soldiers. 'It must not be the case that women and children be affected by combats or that farms be burned where there has never been a terrorist, or that men be killed because of this.' It was felt that the behaviour of the Germans in Oradour had been 'shameful' and an 'insult to the traditional good name of the German soldier who fights honestly and distances himself from all reproach'. These messages did not sit well against the Sperrle orders, which had allowed for commanders to carry out reprisals without danger of consequent punishment for an overzealous approach. It all highlights how, after a task such as Oradour had been carried out, the people in charge needed to find a scapegoat fast, as well as a framework on which to build their defence and to which they must stick, like a brotherhood, over the decades that followed.[4]

The disappearance of Major Helmut Kämpfe has, over the decades, been given as a prime reason for the destruction of Oradour. This rumour, first propagated by the German High Command directly after the massacre, was instigated in an attempt to shift some blame for the tragedy on to the actions of the Resistance. While timing links the events, the 'arrest' of Kämpfe had no direct effect on the choice of Oradour. It simply presented an opportunity for the German High Command who had already decided that a whole village or small town would be wiped off the face of the Earth. Kämpfe's disappearance was a pretext on which the operation could be hung. That Diekmann was a personal friend of Kämpfe was extremely useful. Those higher up the chain of command, such as Lammerding and Stadler, knew that an upset Diekmann would carry out the task. He was a man who had already proved himself capable of such work. He lacked scruples, was reliant on alcohol and followed orders without question. His death weeks later was perfect for the story. The Oradour operation was always going to happen somewhere.

The search for Kämpfe was primarily conducted to the north and to the east of Limoges, near to where the ambush had happened. During one of the searches on the morning of 10 June 1944, SOE operative Violette Szabó was picked up and arrested. *Maquisard* Léon Vigneron testified later that, on 10 June, 'I heard that a car containing civilians carrying a white flag was driving around Saint-Léonard and the surrounding region asking where the officer was. They were offering other prisoners in exchange.' This last-ditch resort was attempted by Lammerding because his division had been ordered to depart for the north of the country. A prisoner who had been a *légal* by the name of Laudoueneix was tasked with finding the leader of the local Resistance, offering fifty *maquis* prisoners held by the Gestapo in exchange for Major Kämpfe. Guingouin was ready to accept the offer, but when he heard about the twenty-nine *maquisards* killed at Combeauvert and the destruction of Oradour, he ordered the execution of Kämpfe. It is probable that Kämpfe was killed on 11 June 1944. It is also possible that Guingouin was not even aware that Kämpfe himself had ordered the Combeauvert executions.

Kämpfe's killing was, therefore, a result of and not the reason for the massacre of Oradour.[5] The regional chief of the *Milice*, Jean Filliol, announced during the course of the meeting with four *miliciens*, in the late afternoon of 9 June, that a 'significant operation' would be taking place 'the following day in the Saint-Junien area'. Filliol had attended a meeting with the Nazi and SS general staff earlier that day at a hotel in Limoges. He had been informed that the German plan consisted of launching a 'brutal strike', as had been indicated in an order from higher up the previous day. That order predated the capture of Kämpfe, as had the meeting attended by Filliol.

The *Wehrmacht* had not dared proceed with major reprisals against the population of Saint-Junien following the attack on the German passengers on 8 June. It had been clear by looking at the town plan provided by the chief of police that by engaging in such an operation somewhere there were *maquis* groups nearby and even possibly in the town at that moment, they would suffer losses. The elements of *Das Reich* that were sent to the town the following day probably intended Saint-Junien to be destroyed. On arrival a close examination of the maps, conversations with locals and a look from the church bell tower convinced them that even they would not be able to conduct the quick strike that they wanted without a significant fightback.

The town of Saint-Junien was too large for them to be able to destroy completely – it would require too many men, too much explosive and the round-up itself would probably not be clean enough. Too many people would be likely to escape, and word would spread quickly to the *maquis*. Another location had to be found, but the German commanders had a pretext. That Major Kämpfe was being held by the *maquis*, albeit many miles away, gave them a further excuse. What they were about to do had enough of an element of 'reprisal' about it, and the excess could be blamed on an overzealous commander on the ground, given the character of Diekmann. *Miliciens* were involved in planning a meeting in the *Hôtel de la Gare* in Saint-Junien on the morning of 10 June because local knowledge was vital for what they planned to do. They may well not have told those *miliciens* that they planned to kill everyone. That order may even have been given directly to Diekmann later, even as late as the journey between Saint-Junien and Oradour when he is known to have taken an order by radio. However, the *miliciens* were involved in the selection of Oradour-sur-Glane and helped in planning the round-up. Later claims that the choice of Oradour-sur-Glane was due to a mix-up on the part of the commanders who meant to target Oradour-sur-Vayres, a small town some 40km south-west of Saint-Junien, which had become something of a hotspot of *maquis* activity, is unbelievable. The German commanders were perfectly capable of using a map; they relied on such detail on an hourly basis. The similarity in names may have entered the train of thought, however, when considering how they might later explain the choice of a village that they knew was peaceful. This kind of detail may have been pointed out to them by *miliciens*.

That round-up in Oradour-sur-Glane had to take place in a state of calm. Oradour-sur-Glane was chosen because it was very easy to surround, of the right size for the numbers of soldiers involved and located between Saint-Junien and the battalion's next stop in Nieul, just a short distance north-east. The men of the battalion would have been compliant, but a good number were 'green' having recently joined following training near Bordeaux. These included *malgré-nous* from Alsace-Lorraine. Some of the SS certainly considered themselves French. They were, however, SS soldiers and a refusal to follow orders would result in arrest, court martial, execution and possibly the arrest and deportation of their own families. These men had to be managed, though some commanders saw the operation as a good opportunity to 'blood' these men who had not been present during the division's earlier operations in Eastern Europe, where the massacre of civilians had been commonplace. In Poland, two years to the day before Oradour, a series of atrocities were carried out by the same division following the assassination of Reinhard Heydrich. In Lidice, Poland, an almost identical event had taken place, though that time under the auspices of a reprisal for hiding one of Heydrich's assassins. Existing footage of that day could be mistaken as footage from Oradour. In Lidice, the women were not burnt in the church but sent to death camps. The division carried out countless other atrocities on a smaller scale as it travelled through France. Other divisions, whether SS or regular *Wehrmacht*, also killed civilians.

In order to keep the population calm during the round-up, civilians were told that it was an identity check. Once the population had been gathered together no papers were looked at, but instead they were told that a search was being carried out for stores of weaponry and explosives – another fabrication. It did ensure, however, that there was no fightback and that the men could be kept placid on their way to the barns. When they were told to wait for the search to be carried out they did so calmly and in an orderly fashion. The officers in charge had to ensure everyone remained in the same place so that the task of killing everybody could be carried out with maximum efficiency and minimum fuss.

The scale of the event, in its own smaller, is more contained way, no less shocking than the Holocaust. The soldiers that came that day had no intention of leaving any survivors, so 643 people were killed, including 255 women and 207 children, locked in the church where some would still have been alive when the flames engulfed them. Their remains were unrecognisable to family members who survived them, so parents of schoolchildren who lived outside the SS cordon were left to survive their children without having bodies to bury. This was the salt that the SS wanted to rub into the wounds. Many men were also alive as they were consumed by fire.

Those in charge of the operation wanted to leave no survivors that day. There were to be no witnesses of any kind – man, woman or child – to the wiping of a village from the Earth. In the days to come, some soldiers returned to dig mass graves, perhaps to cover the crime, but more probably to add a further element of total annihilation.

In East Berlin in 1983, the trial of the most senior former SS officer ever brought to account for the events at Oradour took place. He was finally arrested in December 1981, but extradition was never an option under a new atmosphere of European detente. His trial that year saw Heinz Barth receive a life sentence, and the only regret he expressed was being unable to regularly see his grandchildren. Barth had been living under his own name and in his home town since the end of the war, easily managing to escape the attentions of the authorities.[6] Survivors were taken to East Berlin to testify, and gave their stories of horror and loss yet again. They were treated as VIPs and offered the opportunity to speak to Barth directly. Jean-Marcel Darthout publicly asked Barth whether he could sleep at night knowing what he had done. He received no response. Barth was a man who had been utterly persuaded by Hitler's policies and had killed freely whilst in the SS. He was released in August 1997 due to supposed ill-health but survived for a decade afterwards.

In 1985, an inquest was called into what had happened to Otto Kahn, Diekmann's second-in-command at Oradour, who had previously been presumed dead until it then emerged that he may still be alive, hidden in Germany.[7] It was quickly established that Kahn had indeed been alive, and hidden, until his death in April 1977.[8] General Heinz Lammerding had returned to Düsseldorf where he had built a successful engineering business, despite being condemned to death *in absentia* in 1953. He lived in comfort, free from the danger of extradition, until his death in his bed in 1971. Before that, however, he sued a German publication for defamation because its journalist had claimed that he had massacred hostages rather than *résistants* in Tulle and Oradour.[9]

Conclusion

One thing that is not so well known is the suffering, and how long that lasted, for the people of the villages. The hamlets were not destroyed; they were intact. But there were no more children. And that is no exaggeration. There were no more children.

Albert Valade, 1930–2019

The massacre at Oradour continues to make news outlets. In March 2014, an 89-year-old man was investigated by German anti-war-crime investigators who travelled to the ruins and reinvestigated the case. In February 2015, the French magazine *Paris Match* located Georges René Boos, one of the more notorious officers still alive in Alsace-Lorraine from where he had been

Charles de Gaulle, then Chairman of the Provisional Government of the French Republic, visiting the village on 4 March 1945. (Collection Association Nationale des Familles des Martyrs d'Oradour-sur-Glane)

voluntarily recruited. This man, who had had his death sentence overturned, had been believed dead. He had served his sentence, released after fourteen years. He died in 2016. The same journalists located another Alsatian the following year and interviewed him. Interesting though these stories were, they offered nothing new. Both men had been subject to criminal procedures half a century previously. Shockingly, graffiti was sprayed on the walls of the visitor centre in the spring of 2020, referring to the name of a far-right revisionist whose conspiracy theories regarding Oradour have been often disproved. The vandalism made newspapers and television news bulletins around Europe, and was universally condemned.

In the decades that followed the Second World War, Oradour-sur-Glane became a memorial to France's sacrifices during the dark years of the occupation. Charles de Gaulle visited and saw the devastation at first hand. In 1946 it was agreed that the ruins be preserved so that future generations could see and feel the scale of the event, and pay homage to this 'village martyr'. Its people, who had lived normal but very different lives had died together, whatever their beliefs or past experiences, because the Nazis who commanded the operation that day decided that there would be no survivors. As such they all became part of the martyrdom of Oradour-sur-Glane, and became entwined in France's attempt to represent its wartime experience as a unified suffering. For several decades, France was represented as a country that had suffered, and resisted. The individual stories of the people of Oradour, of the local politics, of its difficulties and peculiarities, became lost in the burnt-out shell of a tragedy in which all of France could share.

Despite the projected Gaullist view of France as a nation of Resistance, any links between the story of Oradour and the story of Resistance would suggest something other than total guilt on the part of the perpetrators of a 'crime gratuite', and rightly so. Over time the village took on an almost mythical image in France's commemorative process – a place that was 'untroubled, self-contained, and quintessentially French'.[1] This village and its community represented the many other villages or small towns that, in the late 1940s, presented for the French a compelling vision for a nation that was rebuilding its walls and its pride. Despite the religious connotations of the word martyr, with which its name became permanently linked, Oradour fitted into the mental picture of a peaceful, idyllic location of undeniable and comforting 'Frenchness', whether as 'cradle of the secular republic' or as one of many places 'at the heart of an eternal France of conservative values and morals'.[2] Oradour has, on a regional and national level, become an important aspect of France's wartime memory and subsequent commemorations. What Oradour

One of the two classes of the girls' school in 1942–43. (Collection Association Nationale des Familles des Martyrs d'Oradour-sur-Glane)

actually was – a complicated mix of people and politics with aspects of its past that challenged France's own vision of itself – was lost in all of this.

In the 1970s, Robert Paxton began to question France's image as a nation of Resistance. Further work by other historians brought some of these questions further to the forefront of the minds of French people. Several key points emerged, not forgotten so much as not recalled by Gaullist historians in the years following the liberation of France and the subsequent end of the Second World War.

Firstly, the Vichy government was responsible for the implementation of a number of measures that persecuted minorities such as Jews, Freemasons and gypsies independently of Germany.

Secondly, the suppression of other political parties which became vital to the assumption of power by Philippe Pétain had begun even before France had entered a war with Germany. The Communist party had been made illegal in 1939, and many militants had been interned as a result. This had forced politics underground, and the arrival of Pétain at the head of a government ready to work and collaborate with Hitler's Germany, had happened against the background of a rising right-wing nationalism that included anti-Semitism and xenophobia at its core.

Thirdly, while France had become something of a preferred destination for refugees in the late 1930s and in 1940, Vichy's dealings with exiled people had not been handled well.

André Peyroux, André Dagoury and his mother Mélanie Dagoury outside her business, Le Restaurant de la Promenade. *(Collection Benoit Sadry)*

All of this was central to France's difficulties with coming to terms with its past, as the period was closely re-evaluated and examined. Even its politicians had to come to terms with France's past. There had been resistance in France, and it had contributed to the country's liberation, but France was not a nation full of resistance. Numbers of participants in resistance activities were actually very small. Numbers of active collaborators were equally small. Most people had looked on, sometimes hedging their bets, but mostly just trying to survive and get by in life. Further debates have raged amongst historians as to what resistance actually means. There were certainly a great many people who knew of illegal activity yet remained quiet. There were others who housed young men who refused the call to work in Germany, or sheltered Jewish families, but these people were not counted in official post-war Resistance numbers, nor in many cases did they wish to be. There were people who passed on messages, tampered with postal bags, distributed illegal propaganda, held back agricultural produce that should have been requisitioned. Were these people part of the Resistance? Certainly, they were not part of the armed force, but they were important in their own way, and they cannot be ignored, nor can those who provided food for the *maquis*. Most towns and villages had these sorts of people and Oradour-sur-Glane was no exception.

Similarly, most places had supporters of the Vichy regime, right wingers, people ready to denounce, active supporters of groups loyal to Pétain. Oradour had these too. These are the nuts and bolts that made up the internal workings of the town. And then there were the outsiders: Spanish families left over from the forced labour battalion, Jews in hiding, refugee families, *réfractaires* from forced labour in Germany staying with relatives, refugees from Alsace-Lorraine, to name but a few. Recognition that these people were equally among the martyrs of Oradour was slow to come as they did not fit into the narrative of the idyllic French village, but just like the mist that has risen on many aspects of France during the four years of occupation, details of Oradour's lost awkward memories have emerged too. Oradour was representative of the rural Limousin, a microcosm of society, and just like every other place had exceptions to every rule.

The existence of the Resistance made reprisals throughout France inevitable. Requests for FFI fighters to be recognised as soldiers rather than insurgents were flatly denied by the German High Command. As one historian puts it:

> The position taken by the German military regarding the armed struggle with irregular fighters was simple. For them, this was a phenomenon contrary to international law which had to be reprimanded and punished without pity.[3]

The SS *Das Reich* division was well practised in dishing out severe reprisals, as were other SS and *Wehrmacht* divisions. What marks out the massacre of Oradour-sur-Glane is that it was not a reprisal, despite being painted as one almost retroactively. It was a demonstration of force, even if it was a *'crime gratuite'*[4] that served to send a message to the inhabitants of the region and indeed to the rest of France that resistance of any kind, including aiding and feeding the armed *maquisards*, must stop. On the other hand, it served to strengthen the feeling in central France that resistance should continue and the *maquis'* most influential period was to follow, when the dice of Oradour had already been rolled. The German High Command had not understood that their ever more aggressive tactics, particularly towards civilians, would 'provoke a spontaneous and justified Resistance'.[5] The massacre of Oradour-sur-Glane was a war crime, just as was the implementation of Hitler's Final Solution to the Jewish problem. Neither had a place in the context of warfare, nor could be justified as such. Other massacres that happened nearby could not, strange as it might seem, be labelled as criminal actions despite the killing of civilians. All could be justified against criteria relating to allowed reprisals against civilians and perceived combatants.

Whereas the German aim had been to remove a village from the map in its entirety, the *Radounauds* who survived did not let that happen. They constructed a new Oradour-sur-Glane and made it their job to guard the *village martyr* as a place of memory and learning. Robert Hébras has worked particularly hard to ensure Franco-German reconciliation, as have many others who lost everything. The buildings of Oradour-sur-Glane still stand, though over time they have crumbled into shells. This lively, peaceful village contained so much more than buildings, and this book is an attempt to recognise the many people, young and old, who lived there.

Notes

Introduction

1   Mouvement de Libération Nationale, *Les Huns à Oradour-sur-Glane*, p.14.
2   Mainly by American academic Sarah Farmer and researchers Eva Léger and David Ferrer.

Part One: The Long Road

Battles of a Priest

1   Desourteaux, A., Hébras, R., *Oradour-sur-Glane: Notre village assassiné*, pp.34–7.
2   Ibid.
3   According to 1925 figures the population stood at 1,789. It had previously peaked in 1662 at 1,952 but by 1939 it had dropped to 1,574. Half of this was spread out amongst the forty or so hamlets and localities of the *commune*. As Limoges had developed into a major city and other large nearby towns such as Saint-Junien became increasingly industrialised, more and more people looked for employment there.
4   'Oradour Visages', a temporary exhibition which ran from 2014 until 2019.
5   Poitevin, P., *Dans l'enfer d'Oradour*, p.2.
6   In 1926 it was described in detail in *Bulletin de la société archéologique et historique du Limousin*, Tome LXXI Limoges Imprimerie, R. Guillemot et L. de Lamothe, 1926.
7   Full descriptions of festivals are contained in, Desourteaux, A., Hébras, R., *Oradour-sur-Glane: Notre village assassiné*, pp.66–75.

The Freedom Tree

1   Hivernaud, A., *Petite histoire d'Oradour-sur-Glane*, p.11.
2   *Bulletin de la société archéologique et historique du Limousin*, Tome LXXI Limoges Imprimerie, R. Guillemot et L. de Lamothe, 1926.
3   This *ligne électrifiée* was installed and maintained by the *Compagnie des Tramways Départmentaux de la Haute-Vienne* (CDHV).
4   Real name Françoise. It was not unusual at this time in this part of France for people to use names different to those given to them at birth.
5   Fouché, J. (ed.), *Comprendre Oradour. Centre de la mémoire d'Oradour*, p.61.
6   This was confirmed to me through conversations with André Desourteaux, grandson of both men.
7   Author interview with André Desourteaux, March 2019.

Autarky

1   Here he means the streets of the 'martyred village', still preserved to this day.
2   In the course of this book I refer to a direct interview with Robert Hébras as well as a number of his publications. This quote is taken from his book, *Avant que ma voix ne s'éteigne*, (Paris: Borderie, L. Elytel éditions, 2014), p.35.
3   This farm was where the *Centre de la Mémoire* is now located. Its buildings are the first a visitor now comes across as they enter into the ruins, on the right-hand side before reaching the village's '*bascule*'.
4   Marguerite Rouffanche would be the only woman to survive the 1944 massacre.
5   Bélivier, M., Sadry, B., *Oradour-sur-Glane: Regards et histoire*, p.226.
6   Descriptions of village life were provided to me by Robert Hébras either verbally or in his writing. He describes this dining experience in *Oradour-sur-Glane: Notre village assassiné*.
7   Fouché, J., *Oradour*, p.94.

A Well-to-do Village

1   *La Dépêche*, 23 February 1923.
2   MLN, *Les Huns à Oradour-sur-Glane*, p.14.
3   Delage, F., *Oradour: Ville martyre*, p.7.
4   MLN, *Les Huns à Oradour-sur-Glane*, p.14.
5   Poitevin, P., *Dans l'enfer d'Oradour*, p.2.
6   CDCM 1FP47 *Courriers divers de l'abbé Jean Baptiste Chapelle, curé d'Oradour-sur-Glane de 1941 à 1942 à la famille Deleuze*. Ibid. Card dates 29 March 1942.

The Way Home

1   Author interview with André Desourteaux, March 2019.
2   The 1920 census incorrectly listed him as 'grandson'. He was half French but quite what his real relationship was to Pierre and Dora is unclear.

The Entrepreneur

1   Desourteaux, A., Hébras, R., *Oradour-sur-Glane: Notre village assassiné*, p.55.

A Future of Music

1   Desourteaux, A., Hébras, R., *Oradour-sur-Glane: Notre village assassiné*, pp.55–6.
2   Ibid.

'He Knows How to Teach'

1   Mauriat, Jean-Jacques, 'Institutrices à Oradour: Brulées par les Boches 10.06.1944' in *D'onte ses: Publication du cercle généalogique historique et héraldique de la Marche et du Limousin*, No. 7 (2013), p.40.

2   Ibid.
3   Ibid. Report of a visit made by an inspector on 17 February 1937.
4   Ibid. Inspector's report made during the last scheduled visit, 19 December 1941.

Just a Road Worker

1   Perlier, G., *Camille Senon* p.26.

A Picture Postcard

1   René's father, Matthieu, a postman until his retirement and a former veteran, was a
     cousin of Eugénie Brandy née Mercier who ran *Chez Brandy*.
2   Author interview with Robert Hébras, March 2019.
3   Cathalifaud, H., 'Marcel Pascaud, pharmacien à Oradour-sur-Glane, mort dans le
     massacre de la population, le 10 juin 1944' in: *Revue d'histoire de la pharmacie*, 91e
     année, No. 337 (2003), pp.134–6.
4   Desourteaux, A., Hébras, R., *Oradour-sur-Glane: Notre village assassiné*, p.47.
5   Ibid., p.59.
6   They had two children, Solange and Pierre, neither of whom were home in June 1944.
     Solange was married and Pierre was at the *chantiers de jeunesse* in La Rochelle.
7   Poitevin, P., *Dans l'enfer d'Oradour*, p.2.

Mobilisation

1   *L'Abeille de Saint-Junien*, 26 August 1939.
2   Author interview with Robert Hébras, March 2019.
3   Desourteaux, A., Hébras, R., *Oradour-sur-Glane: Notre village assassiné*, p.80.
4   Author interview with Robert Hébras, March 2019.

Evacuees

1   *L'Abeille de Saint-Junien*, 9 September 1939.
2   'Retour sur le drame d'Oradour-sur-Glane', interview with Madeleine Wolf in *Schilick:
     le magazine d'informations municipales de la ville de Schiltigheim*, 23 May 2008, p.10.
3   Madame Boulestin's children were in school in Oradour on 10 June 1944.

Turmoil

1   For a full analysis of the *Front populaire* and its collapse see Kedward, R., *La vie en bleu*,
     pp.214–19.

Exodus

1   The story of this family was discovered in a series of letters in 2015. CDCM 1FP111 - Documents concernant deux victimes d'Oradour, Madame Brassart-Crombé et Mme Gustin – Coppenolle originaire de Roubaix: courriers, coupures de journaux.
2   Cobb, R., *French and Germans, Germans and French*, p.49.
3   Jean Baptiste Lebas was rearrested and died in Mathausen in 1943.

The Road

1   Plas, P. (ed.), *Genèse et Développement de la Résistance en R5 1940–1943*, p.28.
2   Author interview with Robert Hébras, March 2019.

'A Surly Man of Great Pessimism'

1   Author interview with Robert Hébras, March 2019.
2   Author interview with Camille Senon, March 2019.
3   Perlier, G., *Camille Senon: Survivante du tramway d'Oradour-sur-Glane*, p.26.

'*Maréchal, Nous Voilà*'

1   Author interview with Robert Hébras, March 2019.
2   Poitevin, P., *Dans l'enfer d'Oradour*, p.18.
3   Fogg, S.L., *The Politics of Everyday Life in France: Foreigners, Undesirables and Strangers*, p.23.

The Mosellans

1   Author interview with André Desourteaux, March 2019.
2   The details of this period are drawn primarily from Wilmouth, P., *Des Mosellans dans l'enfer d'Oradour-sur-Glane*, Chapter 1.
3   Wilmouth, P., *Des Mosellans dans l'enfer d'Oradour-sur-Glane*, p.36.
4   Ibid., p.42.
5   Testimony of Mme Moog, née Marie-Louise Pincemaille, June 1989, CDCM 14FP Fonds André Désourteaux.
6   Wilmouth, P., *Des Mosellans dans l'enfer d'Oradour-sur-Glane*, p.55.
7   *Ce n'est pas pour toujours* – as reported by a Mosellan who farmed in Champnétery 60km from Oradour, in Mosellan.

A Bigger Congregation

1   *Le Lien*, No. 5 February 1941.
2   maitron-fusilles-40-44.univ-paris1.fr/spip.php?article184832&id_mot=12018.

The Camp

1 Gibouin, S. (ed.), *Oradour: 70 ans après*, p.38.
2 Pascal Plas in Gibouin, S. (ed.), *Oradour: 70 ans après*, p.53.
3 Ibid.

The Shoes Scandal

1 Desourteaux, A., Hébras, R., *Oradour-sur-Glane: Notre village assassiné*, p.83.
2 Anecdotally, Desourteaux proved to be a little harder towards the plight of the refugees, but the population in general certainly softened towards their guests.
3 Author interview with André Desourteaux, March 2019.
4 ADD – 72AJ/232 Dossier 9: Archives of the Comité d'histoire de la Deuxième Guerre mondiale – Notes et rapports sur des missions et des projets d'organisation conduits dans la région du Sud-Ouest, January 1942–March 1942.
5 ADHV 986 W 461 Légion française des combattants: notices individuelles des membres des bureaux des sections comunales.
6 Fouché claims that he was a leading member but in conversations with his grandson I was persuaded otherwise. A document held in the archives lists only five members, of which Desourteaux is not one. No definitive list has yet been discovered.
7 Fouché, J., *Oradour*, p.85.

The Camp Commander

1 Gibouin, S. (ed.), *Oradour: 70 ans après*.
2 CDCM 1A3 Groupe de travailleurs étrangers dirigé par le commandant Otto à Oradour de 1940–1942: témoignage de Mr Bielsa.
3 ADHV 986 W 481 Temoignage de Mme Faucher à La Lande d'Oradour-sur-Glane, 20 July 1945.
4 Ibid.

A Return to Roots

1 Perlier, G., *Camille Senon: Survivante du tramway d'Oradour-sur-Glane*, pp.30–1.
2 CDCM 2A18 Massacre d'Oradour sur Glane, statement by Paul Veyriras regarding his school friend, Henri Bouchoule.
3 ADD D3 14 L'organisation des marchés agricoles en Allemagne.

Under Surveillance

1 ADD 72AJ/232 Dossier 9: Archives of the Comité d'histoire de la Deuxième Guerre mondiale – Notes et rapports sur des missions et des projets d'organisation conduits dans la région du Sud-Ouest, January 1942–March 1942.
2 Fouché, J., *Oradour*, p.109. Faugeras became mayor of the new Oradour after the war and ensured that the communists filled a vacuum of power left behind.
3 ADHV 1517 W 54.

4   Anecdote from a 1606 document written in the hand of Henri IV himself.

5   This is the view given to me by André Desourteaux, Robert Hébras, Albert Valade and Camille Senon.

6   Fouché, J., *Oradour*, p.110.

7   Roche died as a result of a heart attack at the end of June 1944.

8   Plas, P. (ed.), *Visages de la Résistance 1940–1944: Libération de Limoges*, p.13.

9   Ibid., p.13.

10   Registered on 1 April 1942 as a *sous-lieutenant* in the *Kasanga* network, he was listed as an agent P2 of the FFC, *Forces Françaises Combattantes*.

A Restricted Life

1   Letter written 26 March 1942 CDCM 1FP47 *Courriers divers de l'abbé Jean Baptiste Chapelle, curé d'Oradour-sur-Glane de 1941 à 1942 à la famille Deleuze.*

2   Author interview with Albert Valade, March 2019.

3   Author interview with Albert Valade, March 2019.

'The Prestige of the Marshal Remains Intact'

1   Speaking in 1988, Farmer, S., *Martyred Village*, pp.17–18 note 6, Darthout had found a job in a nearby peat farm in order to avoid the *Service de Travail Obligatoire* that, due to his age (he was 20 in 1944), would have meant him being obliged to sign up for the scheme. Had he been discovered living such a life that he would have been arrested and deported.

2   Author interview with Camille Senon, March 2019.

3   D stands for *débrouillard*, meaning 'to get by'.

4   Fogg, S.L., *The Politics of Everyday Life in France: Foreigners, Undesirables and Strangers*, Chapter 1.

5   ADHV 185 W 144 RG report to police, 24 February 1942.

6   ADHV 185 W 44 Monthly reports 'au chef du gouvernement' by prefect of Limousin – April 1942 report.

Bellevue

1   Despite searches in the departmental archives relating to children taken into care, Madeleine Bonnet's file is missing.

2   *Le Populaire du Centre*, 9 Octobre 1936, p.5.

3   In fact Marie-Louise's mother, Marie-Élise was still alive. She died in 1968.

4   Certificate of education.

5   ADHV 995 W Dossier Penot R.

6   gw.geneanet.org/oradour1944?lang=fr&pz=paul+julien+emile&nz=desourteaux&p=guy+rene&n=canin.

7   This quote would remain anonymous.

Occupation

1   Known locally as the Gestapo, this term is used in this book. In fact this was the KDS (*Kommando der Sicherheitspolizei und des SD*), the regional command centre of the

police de sûreté and of the SD (the security service of the SS often confused with the Gestapo). Initially it was established as the *Einsatzkommando* of the Sipo-SD, becoming the KDS at the end of 1943. Valode, P., Chauvy, G., *La Gestapo Française*, edi 8.

2   De Mareschal, E., 'Un des hauts lieux de résistance du pays' in *L'Express,* 8 September 2010.

3   Perlier, G., *Camille Senon: Survivante du tramway d'Oradour-sur-Glane*, p.45.

A Store Cupboard for the Reich

1   Author interview with Robert Hébras, March 2019.

2   185 W 1/44 Rapports au chef du gouvernement. Rapports mensuels du préfet régional au chef du gouvernement sur les principales questions intéressant la région de Limoges, May 1942–June 1944.

3   Fogg, S.L., *The Politics of Everyday Life in France: Foreigners, Undesirables and Strangers*, p.8.

The Tanner

1   In French, a *tanneur-mégissier*.

2   Mediterranean Jewish.

3   Report from *1941 Commissaire de police de Bayonne*. Archives Départementales des Landes, 283 W 80, quoted from maitron-fusilles-40-44.univ-paris1.fr/spip. php?article204282.

4   CDCM 11FP Fonds Jacqueline Pinède 1999, letter to Director of the Centre de la Mémoire.

5   The couple could perhaps have been David Jakobowicz, his wife and baby. Marguerite Lederberg in Farmer, S., *Out of the Picture: Foreign Labor in Wartime France*, pp.255–6.

6   Ibid., p.256.

7   Farmer, S., *Out of the Picture: Foreign Labor in Wartime France*, p.257.

The Return of Otto

1   According to David Ferrer Revull, who researched the nineteen Spanish people who died in Oradour for his book *RECUERDA: Españoles en la masacre de Oradour-sur-Glane* (Edición de marzo, 2020). Source lhistoirepourtous.over-blog.com/2020/05/l-histoire-pour-tous-n-50-deux-familles-aragonaises-victime-du-massacre-d-oradour-sur-glane.html. This is a translation of the original article, www.eldiario.es/aragon/cultura/espanoles-aragoneses-masacre-nazi-oradour-sur-glane_1_5947315.html.

Réfractaires

1   The call-up came in the spring of 1944.

2   Valade, A., *Oradour 10 Juin 1944: La page de catéchisme*, p.33.

The *Petites Juives*

1   It was a legal requirement that Jews wear yellow stars in the northern zone –
    something that Pétain managed to avoid in the southern zone. Jews were, however,
    obliged to have official papers stamped with the word *'Juif'* of *'Juive'*. It is important to
    note that the northern or occupied zone extended along the western coast of France
    to the Spanish border.
2   CDCM 11FP Fonds Jacqueline Pinède 1999, letter to Director of the Centre de la
    Mémoire.
3   Ibid.
4   The UGIF offices in Limoges were under surveillance and were closed on
    30 May 1944 by the Gestapo by order of the Paris leadership. It was hoped that the
    UGIF could be used as a 'mousetrap' to pull in family members wishing to find out
    about interned relatives. This in turn would make the arrest of large numbers of Jews
    easier, but the plan failed to receive the backing needed.

The Sign of the Gamma

1   See Millington, C., *France in the Second World War*, p.106.
2   Author interview with Robert Hébras, March 2019.
3   Kedward, R., *Occupied France: Collaboration and Resistance 1940–1944*, pp.66–7.
4   Ibid.
5   Author interview with Camille Senon, March 2019.

Watching in a Rigorous Silence

1   CDCM 1FP111 - Documents concernant deux victimes d'Oradour, Madame
    Brassart-Crombé et Mme Gustin – Coppenolle originaire de Roubaix: courriers,
    coupures de journaux.
2   ADHV 185 W 1/44 Monthly Reports 'au chef du gouvernement' by préfet of
    Limousin, July 1943 report.
3   Ibid.
4   CDCM 1FP111 Documents concernant deux victimes d'Oradour, Madame
    Brassart-Crombé et Mme Gustin.
5   Author interview with André Desourteaux, March 2019.

Stolen Youth

1   Featured in the early moments of *Oradour*: Part one, *Les Voix de la douleur*, Part two,
    Aujourd'hui la mémoire, written by Marc Wilmart, directed by Michel Follin, FR3
    Limousin-Poitou-Charente and the Conseil Général de la Haute-Vienne (1989).
2   Valade, A., *Oradour 10 Juin 1944: La page de catéchisme*, p.29.
3   Author interview with Albert Valade, March 2019.
4   Ibid.
5   Valade, A., *Oradour 10 Juin 1944: La page de catéchisme*, p.70.
6   Gildea, R., *Marianne in Chains: In Search of the German Occupation 1940–45*, p.154.
7   Ibid., p.156.

Link and Filter

1 Borie, M., Borie, R., 'Oradour-sur-Glane: notre père, ce héros!' in *La Nouvelle Abeille*, No. 1371, 12 July 2018. In fact he did his best to sell this *cahier* to the highest bidder. A letter held in the archives to journalist Serge Dobinet demonstrates that he had no intention of letting it go without due financial reward. CDCM 1FP16.

2 According to David's son Michel, quoted in Baury, M., *Oradour-sur-Glane: Le récit d'un survivant*, p.218. There are, however, major inconsistencies in this second-hand account of events.

3 CDCM 1FP 128: *Cahier de Mathieu Borie*.

Odette

1 999 W Inspection académique. Dossiers d'instituteurs: 5, 9, 79.

2 Villégier, J., *De l'honneur et des larmes*, p.69.

1944

1 ADHV 185 W 3 14 RG to Vichy weekly, 6–12 March 1944 inclusive.

2 Except one letter, explored earlier, from 1941 regarding militant communists.

3 ADHV 185 W 3 14 RG to Vichy weekly, 6–12 March 1944 inclusive.

Brehmer

1 Gildea, R., *Resistance, Reprisals and Community in Occupied France*. For a detailed account of this period of repression see Pike, R., *Defying Vichy*.

2 Marc Freund-Valade was installed as prefect of the Haute-Vienne in September 1943. Freund-Valade's character was already stained by his active engagement in deportations that took place when he was prefect in the Aude.

3 ADHV 185 W 144 Report by prefect of the Limoges region to the minister of the interior, dated 9 April 1944.

4 Archives départementales de la Dordogne, fonds de la presse PRF 1-238 (L'Avenir de la Dordogne), 29 April 1944.

5 Ibid.

6 Grenard, F., *Une légende du maquis: Georges Guingouin, du mythe à l'histoire*, chapter titled 'La lutte contre les bandes'.

A Summer of Outsiders

1 Delage, F., *Oradour: Ville martyre*, p.7.

2 Some second-hand sources suggest that Lévy had come to Oradour the morning of 10 June 1944 but André Desourteaux, grandson of the mayor, told me that he was definitely a '*pensionnaire*' at the hotel, meaning he was a long-term resident. An article in the newspaper *Ouest-France*, 5 April 1945, in which Lévy is interviewed in anonymity, certainly seems to confirm this.

3 According to books.openedition.org/pur/43321?lang=en.

4 ressources.memorialdelashoah.org/notice.php?q=identifiant_origine%3A%28 FRMEMSH0408707111282%29.

5 Some of the pieces in the puzzle surrounding Lévy were solved here. kristianhamon. blogspot.com/2015/02/normal-0-21-false-false-false-fr-x-none_6.html.

6 Another theory is that it had been Lévy who had told Leroy to come to Oradour and that he had come to see her there that particular day. The exact truth is unlikely ever to be known, but the version in the text is the most likely on examination of a range of sources.

7 Author interview with André Desourteaux, March 2019. Further information about Martial Machefer was provided to me by his son, Hervé.

8 ADHV 1517 W 424 Procès-verbaux d'audition 1944 1207/1 A. Lévignac.

9 The family had spent some time north of Lyon before being interned at the detention camp in Argelès-sur-Mer and separated with Joan until they were reunited at the 643rd GTE in Oradour. In the case of Joan, as with the Gil Espinosa twins' father, it is unclear whether the men were still in the region or had been assigned to work for the *organisation Todt*.

10 CDCM 14FP Fonds André Desourteaux Mario Escamilla 1975 interview.

Part Two: The Tenth

1 Wilmouth, P., *Des Mosellans dans l'enfer d'Oradour-sur-Glane*, p.58.

Gatherings

1 Speaking in 1988, Paul Doire said that it was as well that they had died, as the survivors could not have forgiven Albert for being in the *Milice*. Doire himself was not in Oradour that day as he was a baker in the north of the Haute-Vienne and active in the *Armée Secrète* (Secret Army). He lost a 17-year-old daughter as well as parents, grandparents, uncles, aunts, in-laws and cousins. www.oradour.info/ruined/chapter2.htm.

2 Poitevin, P., *Dans l'enfer d'Oradour*, p.96.

Early Risers

1 As per March 2019 author interview with André Desourteaux. Listed also *Liste officielle […] des prisonniers de guerre français (Reproduction numérique)*, ISSN 2391-291X, gallica. bnf.fr/ark:/12148/cb34458709m/date (Bibliothèque nationale de France).

2 CDCM 1FP26 D Senon statement, PTT documentation.

3 Desourteaux, A., Hébras, R., *Oradour-sur-Glane: Notre village assassiné*, p.103.

Fate

1 Léger, E., *Oradour-sur-Glane: On the emergence of a global site of memory in France* and Ferrer D., *RECUERDA: Españoles en la masacre de Oradour-sur-Glane*.

2 The 643rd victim of Oradour.

Over the Threshold

1 Author interview with Albert Valade, March 2019.

2 Valade, A., *Oradour 10 Juin 1944: La page de catéchisme*, pp.44–5.

Clouds in the Morning

1   ADHV 1517 W 424 Procès verbaux d'audition 1944 PV1207/3 A. Renaud.
2   ADHV 1517 W 424 Procès verbaux d'audition 1944 1207/5 J. Brandy.
3   ADHV 1517 W 424 Procès verbaux d'audition 1944 1207/5 J. Brandy.
4   CDCM 1FP 128 Cahier de Mathieu Borie.
5   CDCM 1FP26 D Senon statement PTT documentation.
6   Valade, A., *Oradour 10 Juin 1944: La page de catéchisme*, p.32.

Arrival

1   ADHV 1517 W 424 Procès verbaux d'audition 1944 1207/11 M. Bélivier.
2   ADHV 1517 W 424 Procès verbaux d'audition 1944 PV1207/34 Y. Gaudy.
3   Bergmann was in fact German by birth.
4   ADHV 1517 W 424 Procès verbaux d'audition 1944 1207/76 J.M. Darthout.
5   ADHV 1517 W 424 Procès verbaux d'audition 1944 PV1207/3 A. Renaud.
6   Machefer would later claim during the 1953 trial that his wife recognised several soldiers as having spent time in Oradour. It is impossible to know if this is true, but we do know that at least one of the Alsatian soldiers involved that day had been in Oradour during the first wave of evacuees in September 1939 to October 1940.
7   Fouché, J., *Oradour*, p.156.
8   Fouché, J., *Oradour, la politique et la justice*, p.271.

Intentions

1   Valade, A., *Oradour 10 Juin 1944: La page de catéchisme*, pp.55–7, 76–9.
2   CDCM 1FP16 M. Villéger. Taken from a statement given to journalist Serge Dobinet in 1946.
3   ADHV 1517 W 424 Procès verbaux d'audition 1944 1207/45 Pierre Joyeux.
4   Jean and Mélanie had an older daughter called Janine who was not in Oradour that day. She was 23 and married.
5   CDCM F Darthout statement PTT documentation.
6   CDCM 1FP26 M. Gourceau statement PTT documentation.
7   ADHV 1517 W 424 Procès verbaux d'audition 1944 PV1207/39 M. David, épouse Démery.
8   ADHV 1517 W 424 Procès verbaux d'audition 1944 PV 1207/25 20 September 1944 M. Thurmaux veuve Rouffanche.

Setting Up a Cordon

1   ADHV 1517 W 424 Procès verbaux d'audition 1944 1207/11 Bélivier and Bélivier, M., Sadry, B., *Oradour-sur-Glane: Regards et histoire*, p.62.
2   ADHV 1517 W 424 Procès verbaux d'audition 1944 1207/11 Bélivier.
3   Ibid.
4   ADHV 1517 W 424 Procès verbaux d'audition 1944 PV1207/34 Y. Gaudy.
5   ADHV 1517 W 424 Procès verbaux d'audition Y. Gaudy additional statement taken in 1949.
6   ADHV 1517 W 424 Procès verbaux d'audition Y. Gaudy 20 September 1945. It is important to note that no such map or written instructions were ever discovered.

They Have Killed One of our Soldiers

1 Ector O. Munn CDCM 2A23 Interview with Machefer conducted.
2 ADHV 1517 W 424 Procès verbaux d'audition 1944 1207/5 J. Brandy.
3 ADHV 1517 W 424 Procès verbaux d'audition 1944 1207/5 J. Brandy, also 1944 account Bélivier, M., Sadry, B., *Oradour-sur-Glane: Regards et histoire*, p.48 and letter to Serge Dobinet CDCM 1FP16.
4 ADHV 1517 W 424 Procès verbaux d'audition 1944 1207/5 J. Brandy.
5 In an interview given to a Resistance newspaper in late June 1944, Jeannine Renaud, née Brandy, described how she decided to leave her daughter behind.
6 ADHV 1517 W 424 Procès verbaux d'audition 1944 1207/5 J. Brandy.
7 Ibid.
8 ADHV 1517 W 424 Procès verbaux d'audition 1944 PV1207/34 Y. Gaudy.

Hiding Places

1 ADHV 1517 W 424 Procès verbaux d'audition 1944 1207/3 A. Renaud.
2 She was referring to a small village found to the south of Oradour, on the Saint Victurnien road. ADHV 1517 W 424 Procès verbaux d'audition 1944 1207/76 J.M. Darthout.
3 ADHV 1517 W 424 Procès verbaux d'audition 1944 1207/76 J.M. Darthout.
4 ADHV 1517 W 424 Procès verbaux d'audition 1944 1207/13 C. Broussaudier.
5 Paul Doutre, interviewed by France 3 in 2014.
6 The account of Robert Besson taken during the November 1944 1207/15 inquiry makes no mention of hiding with Jacques Garraud, and Garraud's account of the day given to Ector E. Munn is equally threadbare. More detail emerged of their escape together when they both gave evidence at the 1953 trial in Bordeaux.
7 Fouché, J., *Oradour, la politique et la justice*, p.279.
8 ADHV 1517 W 424 Procès verbaux d'audition 1944 1207/75 F. Verny.
9 ADHV 1517 W 424 Procès verbaux d'audition 1944 PV1207/14 H. Desourteaux.
10 Given name Louis Aimé.
11 ADHV 1517 W 424 Procès verbaux d'audition 1944 1207/70 M. Beaubreuil.
12 Taken from Martial Beaubreuil's testimony given at the 1953 trial as quoted in Fouché, J., *Oradour, la politique et la justice*, p.283.

'The *Boches* are Here!'

1 Detail provided by Sandra Gibouin who had been told by his son Pierre. It is believed that the house he was working on belonged to the pharmacist Marcel Pascaud, very near the *Champ de foire*.
2 ADHV 1517 W 424 Procès verbaux d'audition 1944 1207/28 H. Redon.
3 CDCM 1FP 128 Cahier de Mathieu Borie.
4 CDCM 1FP 128 Cahier de Mathieu Borie.
5 Although termed mayor here, he was officially Head of the Special Delegation that replaced the municipal council.
6 Hébras, R., *Oradour-sur-Glane: Le drame heure par heure*, p.11.
7 ADHV 1517 W 424 Procès verbaux d'audition 1944 PV1207/10 M. Brissaud.
8 Author interview with Robert Hébras, March 2019.

9 ADHV 1517 W 424 Procès verbaux d'audition 1944 1207/46 R. Hébras.

10 Pauchou, G., Masfrand, P., *Oradour-sur-Glane: Vision d'épouvante*, p.30.

11 This account, published in an April 1945 edition of the newspaper *Sud-Ouest* was never directly attributed to Lévy but it is almost certainly his story that is told here. Lévy had been staying at the *Hôtel Avril* but he may have been in the *Hôtel Milord*. The square on which that café was located was known locally as the old *Champ de foire*. It makes sense that he could have made an escape from that part of the village, which is much nearer than the main *Champ de foire* where the general population was being gathered.

12 Probably under the name Lacroix.

13 This 'ditch' behind the *Hôtel Milord* was the same one in which the two Beaubreuil brothers would also successfully hide.

Gunshots

1 ADHV 1517 W 424 Procès verbaux d'audition 1944 1207/17 J. Boissou and 1207/28 H. Redon.

2 François Barataud.

3 ADHV 1517 W 424 Procès verbaux d'audition 1944 PV1207/30 Deschamps, Marie-Anne.

4 Ibid.

5 Jacques Boissou would only find this out later. His brother had managed to get away.

6 CDCM 1FP26 D Senon statement PTT documentation.

7 Valade, A., *Oradour 10 Juin 1944: La page de catéchisme*, p.58.

8 CDCM 1FP26 M. Gourceau statement PTT documentation.

A Round-Up

1 ADHV 1517 W 424 Procès verbaux d'audition 1944 1207/21 A. Senon.

2 CDCM 1FP26 Fonds J.M. Darthout.

3 ADHV 1517 W 424 Procès verbaux d'audition 1944 PV1207/10 M. Brissaud.

4 ADHV 1517 W 424 Procès verbaux d'audition 1944 1207/5 J. Brandy.

5 ADHV 1517 W 424 Procès verbaux d'audition 1944 1207/5.

6 ADHV 1517 W 424 Procès verbaux d'audition 1944 PV1207/14 H. Desourteaux.

7 ADHV 1517 W 424 Procès verbaux d'audition 1944 PV1207 62. Roger Godfrin gave his testimony on 20 September 1944 alongside Alice Marty, the head teacher of the school for girls in nearby St-Gence where Roger was looked after. He was 8 years old when he gave his initial testimony.

8 ADHV 1517 W 424 Procès verbaux d'audition 1944 PV 1207/62 R. Godfrin.

9 According to witness statements these were probably peasant workers from the area around Theineix.

10 ADHV 1517 W 424 Procès verbaux d'audition 1944 PV 1207/25 20 September 1944 M. Thurmaux veuve Rouffanche.

11 ADHV 1517 W 424 Procès verbaux d'audition 1944 PV PC 1207/13 C. Broussaudier.

The Sounds of Separation

1   Poitevin, P., *Dans l'enfer d'Oradour*, p.27.
2   Contrary to popular belief, the car still visible on the *Champ de foire* is not that belonging to Dr Desourteaux but wineseller Henri Texeraud's. Desourteaux's car was removed to a nearby garage as it was blocking the road after the Germans left. This detail was confirmed to me by Robert Hébras: 'I knew Texeraud's car well enough, I had serviced it for him many times!'
3   CDCM 1FP26 Fonds J.M. Darthout.
4   ADHV 1517 W 424 Procès verbaux d'audition 1944 PV 1207/25 20 September 1944 M. Thurmaux veuve Rouffanche.
5   CDCM 1FP26 Fonds J.M. Darthout.
6   ADHV 1517 W 424 Procès verbaux d'audition 1944 1207/21 A. Senon.
7   They may have been passing by on the pavement next to the wall, too low for Desourteaux to see down to.
8   ADHV 1517 W 424 Procès verbaux d'audition 1944 PV1207/14 H. Desourteaux.
9   ADHV 1517 W 424 Procès verbaux d'audition 1944 1207/12 M. Borie.
10 This timeframe was suggested by Darthout but it is difficult to gauge its accuracy from other statements.
11 ADHV 1517 W 424 Procès verbaux d'audition 1944 PV1207/24 Y. Roby.
12 ADHV 1517 W 424 Procès verbaux d'audition 1944 PV1207/46 R. Hébras.
13 This number varies according to several reports but Mathieu Borie was stood nearby and could hear the conversation.
14 ADHV 1517 W 424 Procès verbaux d'audition 1944 PV 1207/12 M. Borie.
15 ADHV 1517 W 424 Procès verbaux d'audition 1944 PV1207/76 J.M. Darthout.
16 ADHV 1517 W 424 Procès verbaux d'audition 1944 PV1207/46 R. Hébras.
17 Senon's father was a tenant farmer, who kept his agricultural equipment in storage in the town.
18 PV 1207/21 This was the Laudy-Mosnier barn – in fact the final group to leave. Strangely it was led a long way round to the barn which actually backed on to a lane on to the *Champ de foire*, visible from Senon's vantage point.
19 ADHV 1517 W 424 Procès verbaux d'audition 1944 PV1207/13 C. Broussaudier.

The Barn

1   Roby says that he was part of the second group, but Darthout claims that he was in the final. The first group, it seems, turned right out of the square and was split across two locations either side of the road, one in the Senon garage and one in the Denis garage.
2   This is one of several details not included in his 1944 testimonies but which he talked about in *Une Vie avec Oradour*, Patrick Séraudi, France 3 Limousin, Pyramide (2011).
3   ADHV 1517 W 424 Procès verbaux d'audition 1944 1207/46 R. Hébras.
4   Lucien Morlieras, uncle of Camille Senon.
5   ADHV 1517 W 424 Procès verbaux d'audition 1944 PV1207/14 H. Desourteaux.
6   Hébras, R., *Oradour-sur-Glane: Le drame heure par heure*, p.20.
7   ADHV 1517 W 424 Procès verbaux d'audition 1944 1207/46 R. Hébras.
8   This additional detail was added by Hébras in *Une Vie avec Oradour*, Patrick Séraudi, France 3 Limousin, Pyramide (2011).
9   ADHV 1517 W 424 Procès verbaux d'audition 1944 1207/24 Y. Roby.

The Service Tram

1   ADHV 1517 W 424 Procès verbaux d'audition 1944 1207/6, L.F. Tabaraud.
2   Based on estimations supplied by both Tabaraud and Dauriat in September 1944.
3   ADHV 1517 W 424 Procès verbaux d'audition 1944 1207/6, L.F. Tabaraud.
4   ADHV 1517 W 424 Procès verbaux d'audition 1944 1207/6, L.F. Tabaraud.
5   ADHV 1517 W 424 Procès verbaux d'audition 1944 PV 1207/62 R. Godfrin.
6   Roger was accompanied during his September 1944 interview by a local teacher. He had just turned 8 when he gave it. Later versions of his story emerged with some additional details. During the first testimony quoted here, the account of his actions was probably drawn through a series of specific questions. None of these testimonies were recorded and some information may have been felt to be irrelevant by the scribe.
7   Beaubreuil, M., *La Nouvelle Abeille de Saint Junien*, No.778, 22 Octobre 2005.

Sanctuary

1   ADHV 1517 W 424 Procès verbaux d'audition 1944 PV 1207/25 20 September 1944. M. Thurmaux veuve Rouffanche.
2   Ibid.
3   There are several versions of Roger Godfrin's story, some given much later. One of these describes him being helped by Marcellin Thomas, and also playing dead in front of a soldier. For the purposes of this account I have stuck to the original testimony, given just months after the event and in controlled conditions. This was the account given again at the Bordeaux trial in 1953. ADHV 1517 W 424 Procès verbaux d'audition 1944 PV1207/62.
4   ADHV 1517 W 424 Procès verbaux d'audition 1944 PV 1207/62 R. Godfrin.

The Laudy-Mosnier Barn

1   As described by Jean-Marcel Darthout in *Une Vie avec Oradour*, Patrick Séraudi, France 3 Limousin, Pyramide (2011).
2   CDCM 1FP26 Fonds J.M. Darthout.
3   ADHV 1517 W 424 Procès verbaux d'audition 1944 PV 1207/24 Y. Roby. Whether the sound was made by a tank or not, other witnesses who were in the Laudy barn attest that the sound came from the direction of the *Champ de foire*.
4   ADHV 1517 W 424 Procès verbaux d'audition 1944 PV1207/13 C. Broussaudier.
5   ADHV 1517 W 424 Procès verbaux d'audition 1944 PV1207/12 M. Borie.
6   ADHV 1517 W 424 Procès verbaux d'audition 1944 J-M. Darthout.
7   ADHV 1517 W 424 Procès verbaux d'audition 1944 PV1207/24 Y. Roby.
8   ADHV 1517 W 424 Procès verbaux d'audition 1944 PV1207/12 M. Borie.
9   ADHV 1517 W 424 Procès verbaux d'audition 1944 J.M. Darthout.
10 ADHV 1517 W 424 Procès verbaux d'audition 1944 1207/6 L.F. Tabaraud.
11 Pauchou, G., Masfrand, P., *Oradour-sur-Glane: Vision d'épouvante*, p.48.
12 ADHV 1517 W 424 Procès verbaux d'audition 1944 1207/46 R. Hébras. One of the bullets was later taken out of his wrist and he kept it.
13 CDCM 1FP26 Fonds J.M. Darthout.
14 ADHV 1517 W 424 Procès verbaux d'audition 1944 PV1207/24 Y. Roby.
15 Felix Aliotti.
16 CDCM 1FP26 Fonds J.M. Darthout.

Witnesses

1 ADHV 1517 W 424 Procès verbaux d'audition 1944 1207/7 M. Dauriat.
2 ADHV 1517 W 424 Procès verbaux d'audition 1944 1207/6 L.F. Tabaraud. *Mouchoir* is French for handkerchief.
3 ADHV 1517 W 424 Procès verbaux d'audition 1944 1207/7 M. Dauriat.
4 ADHV 1517 W 424 Procès verbaux d'audition 1944 1207/6 L.F. Tabaraud.
5 ADHV 1517 W 424 Procès verbaux d'audition 1944 1207/7 M. Dauriat.
6 This suggests that the tram drivers were taken to the village centre after the shooting of the men, while the women and children were contained within the church. Quite why they were sent away and ordered to return their tram to Limoges is uncertain given what they had seen. It is possible that the officer felt that they may have returned having seen just what he wished them to see: an orderly search in a calm village centre.
7 This must have been the main door at the rear of the church, underneath the bell tower.
8 In a later testimony Madame Rouffanche said that the men were aged between 20 and 25.
9 ADHV 1517 W 424 Procès verbaux d'audition 1944 PV 1207/25 20 September 1944 M. Thurmaux veuve Rouffanche.
10 A detail added by Marguerite during the Bordeaux trial in 1953, Fouché, J., *Oradour, la politique et la justice*, p.335.
11 In later testimonies Madame Rouffanche mentions that she saw the 'strings' being lit, something she did not say in the first testimony given on 16 November 1944. She clarified that she did not know exactly how it was lit in the 1953 Bordeaux trial when she said, 'I don't know what sort of machine it was.' Fouché, J., *Oradour, la politique et la justice*, pp.335–6.
12 Fouché, J., *Oradour*, p.163.
13 Evidence of a similar use of phosphorous over the top of the debris and human bodies was present throughout Oradour afterwards.
14 CDCM 1FP26 Fonds J.M. Darthout.
15 The younger of the father and son team of tailors, Paul, 37, also died.
16 CDCM 1FP128 Cahier de Mathieu Borie.

The Sacristy

1 Fouché, J., *Oradour, la politique et la justice*, p.336.
2 ADHV 1517 W 424 Procès verbaux d'audition 1944 PV 1207/25 20 September 1944 M. Thurmaux veuve Rouffanche.
3 Pauchou, G., Masfrand, P., *Oradour-sur-Glane: Vision d'épouvante*, p.58.
4 ADHV 1517 W 424 Procès verbaux d'audition 1944 PV1207/25 20 September 1944 M. Thurmaux veuve Rouffanche.
5 Henriette Joyeux née Hyvernaud, friend of Jeannine Renaud.

The Cyclists

1 ADHV 1517 W 424 Procès verbaux d'audition 1944 PV1207/3 A. Renaud.
2 ADHV 1517 W 424 Procès verbaux d'audition 1944 1207/21 A. Senon.

3   Ibid.
4   The Beaulieu forge was on the corner of the main entrance to the *Champ de foire*.
5   ADHV 1517 W 424 Procès verbaux d'audition 1944 1207/21 A. Senon.
6   Ibid.

Dying of Thirst

1   Desourteaux, A., Hébras, R., *Oradour-sur-Glane: Notre village assassiné*, p.109.
2   CDCM 1FP 128 Cahier de Mathieu Borie.
3   Desourteaux, A., Hébras, R., *Oradour-sur-Glane: Notre village assassiné*, p.113.
4   CDCM 1FP 128 Cahier de Mathieu Borie.
5   1FP26 Fonds J.M. Darthout.
6   ADHV 1517 W 424 Procès verbaux d'audition 1944 PV1207/24 Y. Roby.

Tough Decisions

1   ADHV 1517 W 424 Procès verbaux d'audition 1944 1207/45 P. Joyeux.
2   Author interview with Albert Valade, March 2019.
3   Ibid.
4   ADHV 1517 W 424 Procès verbaux d'audition 1944 1207/36 R. Hyvernaud.
5   The account of the recuperation of Michel Jakobowicz is taken from an account given to him by his father David long after the event, and communicated to a second author in 2005. Some elements of the account are impossible and some wholly incorrect. For example, it claims that Anna Gabriel had been either rounded up or killed in the church when in fact neither she nor her husband were ever rounded up. The account also claims that the couple saw the execution of passengers from the tram which, again, never happened and geographically makes no sense. Whether due to memory issues or otherwise, I have taken the elements of the account that seem reasonable. It is wholly possible that David and Anna found the Gabriel couple with the baby, but this would directly contradict David Jakobowicz's account, which I did not wish to do.
6   ADHV 1517 W 424 Procès verbaux d'audition 1944 1207/33 G. Couvidou.

The Old Man

1   Paul Doutre interview with France 3, 2014.
2   Paul Doutre interview with France 3, 2014, combined with testimony published in Bélivier, M., Sadry, B., *Oradour-sur-Glane: Regards et histoire*.
3   She may well have been mistaken due to the smoke. Brissaud himself claimed that he was in the eaves at that moment.
4   It is not entirely clear who this person is. It may have been Julien Nicolas but how and why he was there at that moment is not known.
5   ADHV 1517 W 424 Procès verbaux d'audition 1944 1207/39 M David, épouse Démery.
6   Paul Doutre interview with France 3, 2014.

The Burnt Page

1   An additional detail added during the account he gave to Ector E. Munn CDCM 2A23.
2   This section is quoted verbatim from Munn's report which is written in English, therefore the translation was made by him.
3   According to Munn's report but he was wearing no timepiece so estimations of time are approximate.
4   ADHV 1517 W 424 Procès verbaux d'audition 1944 1207/5 J. Brandy.
5   Ibid.
6   ADHV 1517 W 424 Procès verbaux d'audition 1944 1207/70 M. Beaubreuil.
7   Ibid.
8   This estimate of the time by Lévy is probably an hour or so out. It is more likely that he saw these flames between five-thirty and six o'clock in the evening.
9   April 1945 edition of the newspaper *Sud-Ouest*.
10 ADHV 1517 W 424 Procès verbaux d'audition 1944 1207/39 M. David épouse Demery.
11 ADHV 986 W 481 Témoignage de Mme Faucher, 20 July 1945.
12 Author interview with Albert Valade, March 2019.
13 After the war he took the name Jean Sègue. Valade, A., *Oradour 10 Juin 1944: La page de catéchisme*, p.149.
14 ADHV 1517 W 424 Procès verbaux d'audition 1944 1207/45 P. Joyeux.

The Evening Tram

1   Author interview with Camille Senon, March 2019.
2   Ibid.
3   Ibid.
4   Ibid.
5   Ibid.
6   ADHV 1517 W 424 Procès verbaux d'audition 1944 1207/33 J. Courivaud.
7   ADHV 1517 W 424 Procès verbaux d'audition 1944 1207/1 A. Lévignac.
8   Author interview with Camille Senon, March 2019.
9   Ibid.
10 Ibid.

The Miraculous

1   The timing and content of this conversation differ slightly in the men's accounts. It is a very sensitive point but clearly Darthout was unable to carry on and certainly encouraged his friend to go on without him. At that moment a young Robert Hébras knew that they would be better separating to stand any chance of survival.
2   He would remain in the same spot until the following afternoon.
3   ADHV 1517 W 424 Procès verbaux d'audition 1944 1207/21 A. Senon.
4   CDCM 1FP26 Fonds J.M. Darthout.
5   Author interview with Camille Senon, March 2019.
6   Ibid.

A Path

1   ADHV 1517 W 424 Procès verbaux d'audition 1944 1207/22 P. Tarnaud.
2   Desourteaux, A., Hébras, R., *Oradour-sur-Glane: Notre village assassiné*, p.119.
3   Hébras, R., *Avant que ma voix ne s'éteigne*, p.74.
4   Full name Marie-Louise Vareille. Mathieu Borie had two younger sisters. Marie was
     the older of the two, born in August 1912. She had married Jean Hyvernaud in 1932,
     lived in Mazenty, south of Oradour and had children in school that day. Marie-Louise
     was born in April 1914. She married René Fernand Vareille in June 1939 and lived in
     Banèche, much nearer her mother's home, north of Oradour. All three Borie children
     were adopted as *pupilles de l'assistance publique*, therefore provided with state aid, when
     their father Léonard died in the early stages of the First World War.
5   CDCM 2A1P Massacre d'Oradour sur Glane, témoignage de Mme Perette Sauvet,
     résistante en Limousin. Copy of an article from a newspaper.
6   Ibid.

Part Three: Hellscape

Das Reich

1   ADHV 1517 W 424 Tribune militaire permanant Bordeaux testimony from J. Canou.
2   Journal de marche de la 2e SS PZ Division, SHD, microfilm n. 177, in Grénard, F., *Les
     maquisards.*
3   Hastings, M., *Das Reich: The March of the 2nd SS Panzer Division through France
     June 1944.*
4   Guingouin, G., *Quatre ans de lutte sur le sol limousin.*

Numb

1   ADHV 1517 W 424 Procès verbaux d'audition 1944 1207/18 L. Sage.
2   ADHV 1517 W 424 Procès verbaux d'audition 1944 1207/35 J. Guyonnet.
3   Author interview with Camille Senon, March 2019.
4   Here Camille is talking about the baby belonging to Olga Lacroix.
5   Author interview with Camille Senon, March 2019.
6   ADHV 1517 W 424 Procès verbaux d'audition 1944 1207/33 J. Courivaud.
7   CDCM 1FP16 Account in a letter written by Marguerite Villéger to journalist Serge
     Dobinet 1945.
8   ADHV 1517 W 424 Procès verbaux d'audition 1944 1207/40 A. Senamaud.

A Key with No Door

1   Author interview with André Desourteaux, March 2019.
2   ADHV 1517 W 424 Procès verbaux d'audition 1944 1207/36 R. Hyvernaud.
3   Ibid.
4   Author interview with André Desourteaux, March 2019.
5   CDCM 1FP26 Fonds J.M. Darthout.
6   ADHV 1517 W 424 Procès verbaux d'audition 1944 1207/40 A. Senamaud.

7   ADHV 1517 W 424 Procès verbaux d'audition 1944 1207/23 J. Hyvernaud.
8   Related only distantly to the Oradour Hyvernaud family.
9   As told to Sandra Gibouin at the Centre de la Mémoire in Oradour by Albert Hyvernaud.
10   Journal of 29 January 1953 quoted in Amouroux, H., *La grande histoire des Français sous l'occupation Vol 8. Joies et douleurs du peuple libéré 6 juin–1 Septembre 1944*, p.175.

Discoveries

1   ADHV 1517 W 424 Procès verbaux d'audition 1944 1207/1 A. Lévignac.
2   ADHV 1517 W 424 Procès verbaux d'audition 1944 1207/50 J. Darhout.
3   Apparently she was holding Machefer's youngest child but this detail is not confirmed. It was contained in the account of the discovery of Sarah Jakobowicz's body by her brother David, as recounted by Michel Jakobowicz.
4   Months later Sarah's body was relocated to a Jewish cemetery in Limoges during a ceremony in which Resistance fighters provided a guard of honour.

Monday and Tuesday

1   CDCM 1FP16 Account in a letter written by Marguerite Villéger to journalist Serge Dobinet 1945.
2   ADHV 1517 W 424 Procès verbaux d'audition 1944 1207/43 L. Devoyont, veuve Ledot.
3   This baby was Michel Jakobowicz, brother of Sarah who had been hiding at the home of Martial Machefer.

Destinies

1   CDCM 2FP 2 Fonds Marguerite Simon Letter from Hippolyte Redon to Amélie Simon, his sister, 21 July 1944.

Whispers

1   During this controversial period, *maquis* leaders meted out justice on informers and collaborators. Trials were summary and often insufficient. It lasted well into October 1944 when France's interim government regained some control.
2   ADHV 1517 W 424 Procès verbaux d'audition 1944 1207/9 J. Duquéroix.
3   For this reason, and for sensitivity, I have left out this witness' name.
4   Cattle dealer in Oradour.
5   ADHV 1517 W 424 Procès verbaux d'audition 1944 1207/47 A. Aymard.
6   ADHV 1517 W 424 Procès verbaux d'audition 1944 1207/63 M. Lavaud veuve Blanchon.
7   This interview is featured in *Oradour: Part One, Les Voix de la douleur, Part Two, Aujourd'hui la mémoire*, written by Marc Wilmart, directed by Michel Follin, FR3 Limousin-Poitou-Charente and the Conseil Général de la Haute-Vienne (1989).
8   This point on Albert Roumy was underlined by André Desourteaux during our conversations.

9   ADHV 1517 W 424 Procès verbaux d'audition 1944 1207/73 L. Couturier.
10 ADHV 1517 W 424 Procès verbaux d'audition 1944 1207/08 M. Barthélémy.
11 ADHV 1517 W 424 Procès verbaux d'audition 1944 1207/22 P. Tarnaud.
12 ADHV 1517 W 424 Procès verbaux d'audition October 1944 207/2 A. Renaud.
13 ADHV 1517 W 424 Procès verbaux d'audition 1944 1207/08 M. Barthélémy.
14 ADHV 1517 W 424 Procès verbaux d'audition 1944 1207/22 P. Tarnaud. This was second-hand information, provided by the garage owner Pierre Poutaraud before the massacre. Pierre Tarnaud lived in Le Theil.
15 *Croix de feu* was a right-wing veteran's movement of the inter-war years.
16 ADHV 1517 W 424 Procès verbaux d'audition 1944 1207/75 F. Verny.

Patry

1   ADHV 1517 W 424 Procès verbaux d'audition 1944 1207/78 G. Coudert.
2   ADHV 1517 W 424 Procès verbaux d'audition 1944 1207/79 E. Patry.

Filliol

1   Document published by La societe historique et archeologique du Perigord in its bulletin, No. 3 (2005) *Victimes du tortionnaire et assassin Filliol en Limousin (mai-juin 1944)* by Marc Parrotin.
2   ADHV 1517 W 424 Procès verbaux d'audition 1944 1207/81 Davoine, Camille, alias Decors.
3   Other eyewitness accounts confirm that this was Diekmann.

The Cathedral

1   Poitevin, P., *Dans l'enfer d'Oradour*, pp.97–100.
2   Several examples of this letter are held by the Centre de la Mémoire in Oradour.

The Same Question

1   Author interview with Robert Hébras, March 2019.
2   Author interview with Camille Senon, March 2019.
3   Beau, G., Gaubusseau, L., *R5 Les SS en Limousin, Périgord et Quercy*, pp.248–64.
4   In May 1947, aged 21, Camille was made a *pupille de l'assistance publique* due to the death of her father which helped them slightly. The following year she received some damages due to the destruction of the *Café du Chêne* as the surviving next of kin of Lucien Morlieras. This she shared with her mother.
5   Author interview with Camille Senon, March 2019.
6   Author interview with Robert Hébras, March 2019.
7   *Life* magazine, Vol. 34, No.8, 23 February 1953.
8   Ibid.

Smokescreen

1   CDCM 1 ETUD13 Tracts résistants relatifs au massacre à Oradour diffusés à Limoges en juin et juillet.
2   CDCM 2A23 'Oradour-sur-Glane, June 10th and 11th 1944, photo and documents, assembled by E. Munn PWD SHEAEF'.
3   Aymard interview with Felix Hugonnaud, *Commissaire de Police à la 17e Brigade de Police Judiciare à Limoges*, 5 August 1949.
4   These quotes, are translated from French, in turn translated from German and reported in Umbreit, H., 'Les Allemands face à la lutte armée', in *La Résistance et les Français: Lutte armée et maquis* (Besançon: Annales littéraires de l'Université de Franche-Comté, 1996), pp.207–8.
5   Grenard, F., *Une légende du maquis: Georges Guingouin, du mythe à l'histoire*, pp.251–3.
6   *L'echo du centre*, 5 December 1987 'Oradour: Barth avait fait perdre sa piste […] en restant lui-même'.
7   *L'echo du centre*, 10 May 1985 'Otto Kahn, est-il caché en Allemagne?'
8   *La Montagne*, 11 May 1985 'L'affaire Otto Kahn: L'ancien capitaine SS serait mort en 1977'.
9   *France d'abord*, January 1966 'Lammerding a franchi les bornes de l'impudence'.

Conclusion

1   Farmer, S., *Out of the Picture* in *France at War: Vichy and the Historians*, Fishman S. et al. (ed), pp.249–60.
2   Ibid.
3   Umbreit, H., 'Les Allemands face à la lutte armée' in *La Résistance et les Français: Lutte armée et maquis* (Besançon: Annales littéraires de l'Université de Franche-Comté, 1996), p.201.
4   This term, a gratuitous crime, was coined a number of times by my interviewees.
5   Umbreit, H., 'Les Allemands face à la lutte armée' in *La Résistance et les Français: Lutte armée et maquis* (Besançon: Annales littéraires de l'Université de Franche-Comté, 1996), p.201.

Select Bibliography

Archives

Archives Départmentaux de la Haute-Vienne (ADHV)
1517 W 424
1756 W 8
24 J 5
11 J 10
169 W 105, 185 W 1/44, 185 W 1/46, 185 W 1/58, 185 W 1/151
185 W 3/12–14, 185 W 3/15
186 W 1/130
187 W 92, 187 W 106, 187 W 116
188 W 10
646 W 260
893 W 124, 893 W 132
985 W 544, 985 W 633
986 W 141, 986 W 191, 986 W 258
986 W 461, 986 W 481, 986 W 633, 986 W 667
993 W 418–444, 993 W 177, 993 W 192, 993 W 572
995 W 123, 995 W 67
999 W
1081 W 238

Archives Départmentaux de la Dordogne (ADD)
14J 1–47
PRE 1–238, PRE1–231
1 W 1838
1 W 1833, 1 W 1834

Centre du documentation au Centre de la Mémoire d'Oradour-sur-Glane (CDCM)
1FP Pièces Isolés
1FP16, 1FP22, 1FP26, 1FP47, 1FP30, 1FP74, 1FP83,1FP111, 1FP128, 1FP13
2FP Fonds Marguerite Simon
8FP Fonds Jean Henry
11FP Fonds Jacqueline Pinède
14FP Fonds André Desourteaux
17FP Fonds Albert Mirablon
1A3, 2A1, 2A4, 2A5, 2A7, 2A11, 2A14, 2A18, 2A19, 2A20, 2A21, 2A22, 2A23
2A25, 2A29, 2A30, 2A31, 2A46
1ETUD12, 1ETUD13

Oradour-sur-Glane

ANACR Comité de l'Haute-Vienne, *Memorial de la Résistance et des victimes du nazisme en Haute-Vienne* (Limoges: ANACR, 1988)

Anon., *Le Martyre d'Oradour-sur-Glane* (Éditions Pierre Fanlac, 1944)

Bardet, J., *Cahiers de jeunesse de Denise Bardet* (Saint-Paul: Le Puy Fraud, 2002)

Baury, M., *Oradour-sur-Glane: Le récit d'un survivant* (Toulouse: Éditions Privat, 2018)

Baury, M., *Pourquoi Oradour-sur-Glane: Mystères et falsification autour d'un crime de guerre* (Rennes: Éditions Ouest-France, 2014)

Baury, M., Charron, P. and Jollivet, J., *Oradour-sur-Glane: Faits générateurs du massacre* (Paris: Éditions Jourdan, 2014)

Beau, G. and Gaubusseau, L., *R5 Les SS en Limousin, Périgord et Quercy* (Paris: Presses de la Cité, 1969)

Beck, P., *Oradour: Village of the Dead* (London: Leo Cooper, 1979)

Bélivier, M. and Sadry, B., *Oradour-sur-Glane: Regards et histoire* (Limoges: Association Les Enfants d'Oradour, Atélier Graphique, 2013)

Borie, M., and Borie, R., 'Oradour-sur-Glane: notre père, ce héros!' in *La Nouvelle Abeille* No. 1371 (12 July 2018)

Delage, F., *Oradour: Ville martyre* (Paris: Éditions Mellotée, 1944)

Desourteaux, A. and Hébras, R., *Oradour-sur-Glane: Notre village assassiné* (Nieul-les-Saintes: Les Productions du Pertuis, 1999)

Erkenbrecher, A., 'A Right to Irreconcilability?: Oradour-sur-Glane, German–French Relations and the Limits of Reconciliation after World War II' in Schwelling, B. (ed.), *Reconciliation, Civil Society, and the Politics of Memory: Transnational Initiatives in the 20th and 21st Century* Bielefeld: Transcript Verlag, 2012, pp. 167–200, from www.jstor.org/stable/j.ctv1xxswv.9

Farmer, S., *Martyred Village* (Berkeley: University of California Press, 1999)

Farmer, S., 'Oradour-sur-Glane: Memory in a Preserved Landscape' in *French Historical Studies*, 19(1) (1995), pp. 27–47, doi:10.2307/286898

Fischbach, B., *Oradour: L'extermination* (Strasbourg: Éditions Ronald Hirlé, 1994)

Fouché, J. (ed.), *Comprendre Oradour: Centre de la mémoire d'Oradour* (Limoges: Ed. Iti, 1999)

Fouché, J., *Oradour* (Saint-Paul: Éditions Lucien Souny, Le Puy Fraud, 2004)

Fouché, J., *Oradour, la politique et la justice* (Paris: Éditions Liana Levi, 2001)

Gibouin, S. (ed.), *Oradour: 70 ans après* (Limoges: Éditions Les Monédières, 2016)

Hastings, M., *Das Reich: The March of the 2nd SS Panzer Division through France June 1944* (London: Michael Joseph, 1981)

Hawes, D.B., *Oradour: The Final Verdict: New Edition*, (Bloomington: Authorhouse, 2007)

Hébras, R., *Avant que ma voix ne s'éteigne*, (Paris: Borderie, L. Elytel éditions, 2014)

Hébras, R., *Oradour-sur-Glane: Le drame heure par heure* (Honfleur: Les chemins de la Mémoire, 1992)

Hivernaud, A., *Petite histoire d'Oradour-sur-Glane* (Limoges, 1989)

Léger, Eva, 'Oradour-sur-Glane: On the emergence of a global site of memory in France' in *Culture & History Digital Journal*, 3(2) (2014), e019

Le Sommier, R., *Les Mystères d'Oradour* (Neuilly-sur-Seine: Michel Lafon, 2014)

Mackness, R., *Oradour: Massacre and Aftermath* (London: Corgi, 1988)

Mauriat, Jean-Jacques, 'Institutrices à Oradour: Brulées par les Boches 10.06.1944' in *D'onte ses: Publication du cercle généalogique historique et héraldique de la Marche et du Limousin*, No. 7 (2013)

Ménudier, H. 'Les massacres d'Oradour et du pont Lasveyras (1944)', *Allemagne d'aujourd'hui*, vol. 208, No. 2 (2014), pp. 147–69

Mouvement de Libération Nationale, *Les Huns à Oradour-sur-Glane* (Limoges: La Société PERFRAC, 1944)

Pauchou, G. and Masfrand, P., *Oradour-sur-Glane: Vision d'épouvante* (Limoges: Charles Lavauzelle, 1950)

Penaud, G., *La 'Das Reich' 2e SS Panzer Division* (Perigueux: La Lauze, 2005)

Perlier, G., *Camille Senon: Survivante du tramway d'Oradour-sur-Glane* (Limoges: Éditions Les Monédières, 2013)

Picaper, J., *Les Ombres d'Oradour* (Paris: L'Archipel, 2014)

Poitevin, P., *Dans l'enfer d'Oradour* (Limoges: Imprimerie Société des journaux et publications du centre, 1944)

Valade, A., *Oradour 10 Juin 1944: La page de catéchisme* (Neuvic-Entier: Éditions de la Veytizou, 1999)

Villégier, J., *De l'honneur et des larmes* (Panazol: Lavauzelle, 2013)

Wilmouth, P., *Des Mosellans dans l'enfer d'Oradour-sur-Glane* (Saint-Cyr-sur-Loire: Alan Sutton, 2010)

The Limousin Region

Farmer, S., 'Out of the Picture: Foreign Labor in Wartime France' in Fishman, S. (ed.) et al., *France at War: Vichy and the Historians* (Oxford: Berg, 2000)

Farmer, S., 'The Communist Resistance in the Haute-Vienn' in *French Historical Studies*, 14(1) (1985), pp.89–116

Fogg, S.L., *The Politics of Everyday Life in France: Foreigners, Undesirables and Strangers* (Cambridge: Cambridge University Press, 2009)

Grenard, F., *Une légende du maquis: Georges Guingouin, du mythe à l'histoire* (Paris: Vendémiare, 2018)

Guingouin, G., *Quatre ans de lutte sur le sol limousin* (Limoges: Éditions Lucien Souny, 1991)

Guingouin, G., Monediaire, G., *Georges Guingouin: Premier maquisard de France* (Limoges: Éditions Lucien Souny, 1983)

Jourdan, J. and Simon, P., 'L'Aquitaine, une terre de gauche?' in *Parlement(s), Revue d'histoire politique* (2005/3(HS 2)) (2005), pp.40–54

Plas, P., 'Les Espagnols dans les groupes de travailleurs étrangers, région de Limoges, l'internement sans barbelés' in *Oradour-sur-Glane, 70 ans après,* (Limoges: Éditions Les Monédières, 2016)

Plas, P. (ed.), *Genèse et développement de la Résistance en R5 1940–1943* (Limoges: Éditions Les Monédières, 2002)

Plas, P. (ed.), *Visages de la Résistance 1940–1944: Libération de Limoges* (Saint-Paul: Éditions Lucien Souny, 2005)

Plas, P. and Kiener, M., *Enfances juives* (Saint-Paul: Souny, 2006)

Poznanski, R., 'Rescue of the Jews and the Resistance in France: From History to Historiography', in *French Politics, Culture & Society,* 30(2) (2012), pp.8–32

Renault, G. (ed.), *La Résistance en Auvergne, Limousin, Beryy et Bourbonnais* (Geneva: Éditions Famot, 1975)

Rolland, D., 'Vichy et les réfugiés Espagnols', in *Vingtième Siècle. Revue d'histoire*, 11, (1986), pp.67–74

Vichy France

Alary, E. and Vergez-Chaignon, B., *Dictionnaire de la France sous l'Occupation* (Paris: Larousse, 2011)

Albertelli, S., Blanc, J. and Douzou, L., *La lutte clandestine en France: Une histoire de la Résistance 1940–1944* (Paris: Editions de Seuil, 2019)

Algan, A., *La France à l'envers* (Paris: Éditions Gallimard, 2020)

Amouroux, H., *La grande histoire des Français sous l'occupation, Vol 8. Joies et douleurs du peuple libéré 6 Juin–1 Septembre 1944* (Paris: Robert Laffont, 1988)

Atkin, N., *The French at War 1934–1944* (London: Pearson, 2001)

Atkin, N., *Pétain* (London: Longman, 1998)

Aziz, P., *Tu trahiras sans vergogne* (Paris: Fayard, 1970)

Baruch, M.O., *Le Régime de Vichy 1940–1944* (Paris: Éditions Tallandier, 2017)

Beau, G., and Gaubusseau, L., *R5 Les SS en Limousin, Périgord et Quercy* (Paris: Presses de la Cité, 1969)

Broch, L., *Ordinary Workers, Vichy and the Holocaust: French Railwaymen and the Second World War* (Cambridge: Cambridge University Press, 2016)

Chevet, E., 'Gendarmerie et maquis sous l'Occupation en France (1943–1944). Force est faiblesse', in *Guerres mondiales et conflits contemporains*, 242 (2011), pp.121–39

Cobb, M., *The Resistance: The French Fight Against the Nazis* (London: Simon & Schuster, 2009)

Cobb, R., *French and Germans, Germans and French* (New England: University Press of New England, 1983)

Diamond, H., *Fleeing Hitler: France 1940* (Oxford: Oxford University Press, 2007)

Diamond, H., *Women and the Second World War in France, 1939–1948: Choices and Constraints* (London: Routledge, 2015)

Douzou, L., 'La Résistance, une affaire d'hommes?' in *Cahiers de l'IHTP: Identités feminines et violences politiques*, 31 (1995)

Fishman, S., et al. (ed.), *France at War: Vichy and the Historians* (Oxford: Berg, 2000)

Foot, M.R.D., *Résistance: European Resistance to Nazism 1940–45* (London: Eyre Methuen, 1976)

Gildea, R., *Marianne in Chains: In Search of the German Occupation 1940–45* (London: Macmillan, 2002)

Gildea, R., 'Resistance, Reprisals and Community in Occupied France' in *Transactions of the Royal Historical Society*, Vol. 13 (2003), pp.163–85, from www.jstor.org/stable/3679250

Grénard, F., 'Les implication politiques du ravitaillement en France sous l'Occupation', in *Vingtième Siècle, Revue d'histoire*, 94 (2007), pp.199–215

Grénard, F., *Les Maquisards* (Paris: Vendemiare, 2019)

Halls, W.D., *Politics, Society and Christianity in Vichy France* (Oxford: Berg, 1995)

Jackson, J., *The Fall of France: The Nazi Invasion of 1940* (Oxford: Oxford University Press, 2003)

Jackson, J., *France: The Dark Years 1940–1944* (Oxford: Oxford University Press, 2003)

Jourdan, J. and Simon, P., 'L'Aquitaine, une terre de gauche?' in *Parlement(s), Revue d'histoire politique* (2005/3(HS 2)) (2005), pp.40–54

Kedward, H.R., *In Search of the Maquis: Rural Resistance in Southern France 1942–1944* (Oxford: Clarendon Press, 1993)

Kedward, H. R., *Occupied France: Collaboration and Resistance 1940–1944* (Oxford: Blackwell, 1985)

Kedward, H.R., 'Patriots and Patriotism in Vichy France', in *Transactions of the Royal Historical Society,* 32 (1982), pp.175–92

Kedward, H.R., *Resistance in Vichy France* (Oxford: Oxford University Press, 1978)

Kedward, H.R., 'Resiting French Resistance', in *Transactions of the Royal Historical Society* 9 (1999), pp.271–82

Laborie, P., *Le Chagrin et le venin: Occupation. Résistance. Idées reçues* (Paris: Éditions Bayard, 2011)

Laborie, P., *Les Français des années troubles: De la guerre d'Espagne à la Libération* (Paris: Desclée de Brouwer, 2001)

Marcot, F., 'Pour une sociologie de la Résistance: intentionnalité et fonctionnalité' in *Le Mouvement social,* 180 (1997), pp.21–41

Marcot, F. (ed.), *Dictionnaire Historique de la Résistance* (Paris: Robert Laffont, 2006)

Martres, E., 'Points de vue allemands sur Résistance et Maquis' in *La Résistance et les Français: Lutte armée et Maquis* (Besançon: Annales littéraires de l'Université de Franche-Comté, 1996)

Marrus, M., 'French Protestant Churches and the Persecution of the Jews in France' in Rittner, C., Smith, D. and Steinfeldt, I. (eds), *The Holocaust and the Christian World* (Jerusalem: Yad-Vashem, 2000), pp.88–91

Marrus, M. and Paxton, R., *Vichy France and the Jews* (New York: Basic Books, 1981)

Millington, C., *France in the Second World War* (London: Bloomsbury, 2020)

Ousby, I., *Occupation: The Ordeal of France 1940–1944* (London: John Murray, 1997)

Paxton, R., *Vichy France: Old Guard and New Order* (New York: Columbia University Press, 1982)

Pike, R., *Defying Vichy: Blood, Fear and French Resistance* (Stroud: The History Press, 2018)

Prost, A. (ed.), *La Résistance, une histoire sociale* (Paris: Les Éditions de l'Atélier, 1997)

Rousso, H., *Les Années Noires: vivre sous l'occupation* (Paris: Gallimard, 1992)

Rousso, H., *Le Syndrome de Vichy: 1944 à nos jours* (Paris: Éditions de Seuil, 1990)

Sainclivier, S., 'Les notables faces à la lutte armée', in *La Résistance et les Français: Lutte armée et Maquis* (Besançon: Annales littéraires de l'Université de Franche-Comté, 1996)

Semelin, J., *The Survival of the Jews in France 1940–1944* (London: Hurst and Company, 2018)

Sweets, J. F., *Choices in Vichy France: The French under Nazi Occupation* (Oxford: Oxford University Press, 1986)

Umbreit, H., 'Les Allemands face à la lutte armée', in *La Résistance et les Français: Lutte armée et Maquis* (Besançon: Annales littéraires de l'Université de Franche-Comté, 1996)

Valode, P. and Chauvy, G., *La Gestapo Française* (Paris: Acropole, 2018).

Veillon, D., and Sainclivier, J., 'Quelles différences sociales entre réseaux, mouvements et maquis?' in *Le Mouvement social,* 180 (1997), pp.43–54

Vinen, R., *The Unfree French: Life Under the Occupation* (London: Allen Lane, 2006)

Webster, P., *Pétain's Crime: The Full Story of French Collaboration in the Holocaust* (London: Macmillan, 1990)

Werth, L. (trans.) Ball, D., *Deposition 1940–1944: A Secret Diary of Life in Vichy France* (Oxford: Oxford University Press, 2018)

Wieviorka, O., *Histoire de la Résistance 1940–1945* (Paris: Perrin, 2013)

Websites

www.maitron.fr
www.geneanet.org
www.oradour.org
www.oradour.info
www.gallica.bnf.fr
www.francearchives.fr
www.museedelaresistanceenligne.org

Film

Oradour: Part One, *Les Voix de la douleur*, Part Two, *Aujourd'hui la mémoire*, written by Marc Wilmart, directed by Michel Follin, FR3 Limousin-Poitou-Charente and the Conseil Général de la Haute-Vienne (1989)

Une Vie avec Oradour, directed by Patrick Séraudi, France 3 Limousin, Pyramide (2011)

Oradour, Retour sur un Massacre, directed by Christophe Weber (2003)

Acknowledgements

Thank you to Robert Hébras, Camille Senon, Albert Valade and André Desourteaux for giving their time and fascinating insights during the preparation of this book. I was greatly helped by staff at the Centre de la Mémoire in Oradour-sur-Glane. Sandra Gibouin at the *Centre de documentation* has been an invaluable source of help and friendly encouragement, and read the text in English, offering key advice and corrections. I am also indebted to Babeth Robert at the centre for discussing the initial plan with me. I am equally grateful to Benoit Sadry, a superb guardian of Oradour's memory who discussed my proposed project with the Association des Familles des Martyrs d'Oradour-sur-Glane. Benoit cleared up countless queries for me and allowed me access to his extensive collection of photographs. At the Archives Départmentales de la Haute-Vienne, Thierry Duvall and the team were only too happy to dig out records for me despite an untimely refurbishment, so that I could approach research for this book using primary documentation and a fresh pair of eyes. I am also deeply appreciative of all of the relatives who allowed me to use images of family members. Jean Bardet provided me with key information and insights about his aunt Denise Bardet, and Hervé Machefer provided additional thoughts and facts about his father Martial Machefer. Michel Bielsa kindly put me right on a number of points about his father Millán Bielsa.

I could not have written this book without the advice of Professor Rod Kedward and Professor Hanna Diamond. Both are among the most esteemed experts in this period and both are extremely kind people. They were happy to review the early draft of the manuscript and offer detailed feedback. Thank you also to Doctor Chris Millington for reading and commenting on the manuscript, as well as Megan Ison who read the same early version. I look forward to reading her new research. At The History Press, particular thanks to Simon Wright and Alexandra Waite for their hard work, as well as Chrissy McMorris, Gareth Swain and Laura Perehinec for accepting the proposal.

In a way my Oradour research started way back in 1993 when my parents, Malcolm and Mary, first took me to visit so that I could photograph it (on black-and-white film no less) for my A-level French project. My mother passed away in 2001 and I only hope that she would have been proud of the book. Thank you to both of them, and to my brother Richard for his encouragement. Thank you also to the rest of my family in Worcester, Wales, Bath and beyond, as well as to those friends who have encouraged me and my writing over the last few years.

Lastly, the biggest thanks go to my wife Kate for her unending support during a very busy and difficult time for her. With my two boys, Joseph and Elliot, they have been enormously helpful and understanding, and I could not have done this without them.

Index

From the same author

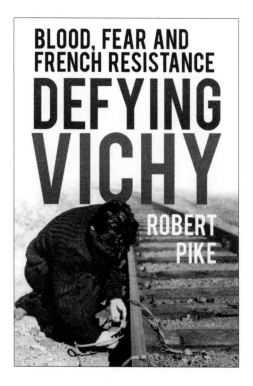

978 0 7509 8552 9

The History Press

The destination for history
www.thehistorypress.co.uk